The
Crisis
in Tax
Administration

The
Crisis
in Tax
Administration

Henry J. Aaron

Joel Slemrod

editors

BROOKINGS INSTITUTION PRESS
Washington, D.C.

Copyright © 2004
THE BROOKINGS INSTITUTION
1775 Massachusetts Avenue, N.W., Washington, D.C. 20036
www.brookings.edu

Library of Congress Cataloging-in-Publication data
The crisis in tax administration / Henry J. Aaron and Joel Slemrod, editors.
   p.   cm.
   Papers presented at a conference jointly sponsored by the Brookings
Institution and the Office of Tax Policy Research at the University of
Michigan Business School.
   Includes bibliographical references and index.
   ISBN 0-8157-0122-5 (cloth : alk. paper)
   ISBN 0-8157-0123-3 (pbk. : alk. paper)
   1. United States. Internal Revenue Service. 2. Tax administration and
procedure—United States. I. Aaron, Henry J. II. Slemrod, Joel. III. Title.
   HJ2361.C37 2004
   339.2'00973—dc22   2004000390

9 8 7 6 5 4 3 2 1

The paper used in this publication meets minimum requirements of the
American National Standard for Information Sciences—Permanence of Paper
for Printed Library Materials: ANSI Z39.48-1992.

Typeset in Adobe Garamond

Composition by R. Lynn Rivenbark
Macon, Georgia

Printed by R. R. Donnelley
Harrisonburg, Virginia

Contents

Preface

JUDGING BY MEDIA coverage, the U.S. public is gradually coming to recognize the grave fiscal challenge that this nation faces. The current federal budget deficit is projected to continue to grow over the next decade. The gap between revenue and outlay will widen still more as health care and pension costs to support retiring baby boomers drive up spending. To close those gaps, taxes are more likely to increase than to fall in the years ahead.

If the American public is to tolerate such increased burdens, it is in the vital national interest that the job of collecting taxes be done fairly and effectively. Despite this challenge, the resources of the nation's principal tax collection agency, the Internal Revenue Service, have been reduced, even as the complexity of the task of collecting taxes has increased. Major Senate hearings in 1997 on IRS operations reported numerous instances of abuse. Although nearly all of these allegations were found to be groundless, the hearings led to a fundamental reorganization of the agency in 1998.

As the contributors to this volume observe, good tax administration and good tax policy are integrally related, and this book comes at the start of a debate on how best to pay for the public services that the American public wants its government to provide. Against this background, the Brookings Institution and the Office of Tax Policy Research at the University of Michigan Business School convened a conference to examine the legal and economic challenges facing tax administrators here and abroad to make recommendations for improving the system. The conference was sponsored in collaboration with the American Tax Policy Institute and with the support of the ABA Section of Taxation and the Internal Revenue Service.

Henry Guttman, Robert McQuiston, Ronald Pearlman, Clarissa Potter, and Paul Sax, on behalf of ATPI, assisted in selecting authors and discussants for the conference. Mary Ceccanese at the Office of Tax Policy Research and Kathleen Elliott Yinug at Brookings handled conference arrangements. At the Brookings Institution Press, Holly Hammond edited the papers in this volume, and Carlotta Ribar and Enid Zafran provided proofreading and indexing services. Claude Goodwin designed the cover. Melissa Cox prepared summaries of the conference papers, which have been posted on the Office of Tax Policy Research and ATPI websites.

The
Crisis
in Tax
Administration

1

HENRY J. AARON
JOEL SLEMROD

Introduction

TELL SOMEONE YOU would like to discuss tax administration, and you are likely to see their eyes cross with anticipated boredom. Ask that same person what it was like to fill out last year's tax return or to respond to the last communication with the Internal Revenue Service, and you are likely to see fists clench and sense blood pressure rising. Tax administration is at once the dullest of topics and a government function that arouses powerful emotions.

The paradoxes do not end here. Complaining that taxes are too high and that the IRS is too intrusive is almost an American tradition. Yet most people pay their taxes. They do so for two reasons, despite the cost and complexity of complying with the tax law. On the positive side, many recognize, even if grudgingly, that paying taxes is a duty of citizenship rather than the outcome of a cost-benefit calculation. On the negative side, taxpayers know that the law requires payment, that evasion is a crime, and that willful failure to pay taxes is punishable by fines or imprisonment, even if the chances of being caught are remote. The practical questions for tax administration are how much to spend on enforcement to maintain the second of these motives for payment and how to organize administration to get the best results for each dollar spent. But the admittedly grudging willingness of many taxpayers to obey the law is critical to the operation of the income tax system. If most people stopped dutifully complying with the law, no feasible system of tax enforcement, short of police-state tactics, would suffice to maintain current levels of compliance.

Lately Congress has restricted spending on tax administration, forcing the Internal Revenue Service to curtail its enforcement activities. Between 1992 and 2001, when the number of individual returns increased from 114.7 million to

129.4 million and tax returns became increasingly complex because of new legal provisions, the proliferation of sophisticated new financial instruments, and the rapid increase of multinational business operations, the full-time-equivalent IRS work force fell from 115,205 to 95,511, and the number of field compliance personnel dropped from 29,730 to 21,421.[1] As a result, enforcement coverage steadily declined. For example, in-person examination of individuals fell from 5.8 per thousand returns in 1992 to 1.5 per thousand in 2001; correspondence examinations fell from 4.0 to 1.2 per thousand returns.[2] After lengthy congressional hearings, during which numerous witnesses alleged various forms of administrative abuse by the Internal Revenue Service (few of which were subsequently confirmed), Congress forced extensive reorganization on the nation's tax collection agency.

Tax legislation, globalization, financial innovation, and budgetary parsimony have combined to create something approximating a crisis in tax administration. Outgoing IRS Commissioner Charles O. Rossotti used exactly that word in his end-of-term report to the IRS Oversight Board, asserting that the "health of the federal tax administration system is on a serious long-term downtrend."[3] If the likelihood that evasion will be detected and punished falls too low, those induced by fear to comply will no longer do so. And, as evasion spreads, people who comply out of a sense of civic duty will come to feel like dupes and be tempted to flout the law. To examine this threat, the Brookings Institution in collaboration with the Office of Tax Policy Research at the University of Michigan commissioned ten original studies on tax administration. The papers were presented at a two-day conference sponsored by the Internal Revenue Service, in collaboration with the American Tax Policy Institute and with the support of the American Bar Association Section of Taxation. Each paper was reviewed by two discussants. Edited versions of the papers, gathered in this volume, examine various theories of tax administration, actual administrative practices (including recent modifications initiated in response to legislation), proposed modifications in that practice, and design of tax laws to facilitate compliance and enforcement. The authors and discussants include lawyers, economists, accountants, and officials from governments and international organizations.

The studies show clearly that tax administration has emerged from academic obscurity. Once a drab subject that held little interest for most serious scholars, tax administration has become a front-burner issue. The simple fact is that good theoretical concepts can easily founder on rocky administrative problems. The Senate hearings that led to reorganization of the Internal Revenue Service fur-

---

1. The work force statistics are taken from Rossotti (2002, p. 12) and refer to fiscal years. The return data are from IRS (2003, p. 235) and refer to calendar years.
2. Rossotti (2002, p. 15).
3. Rossotti (2002, pp. 12, 20).

ther fueled interest. In addition various proposals for fundamental tax reform raise profound issues for tax administration. In the case of tax policy, "good in theory, but bad in practice" means bad in theory, after all.

Tax shelters for corporations and wealthy individuals have recently become front-page news. Whether use of abusive tax shelters is increasing and, if so, what to do about it is indeed one of the most pressing issues in current tax administration policy. In practice, shelters are created by accountants and lawyers and are marketed aggressively. Current enforcement practice revolves around the "economic substance" doctrine, which allows the IRS to disregard transactions that lack nontax motivation or effect. But, as Joseph Bankman points out in chapter 2, there is no clear statement on how much economic substance is enough. A major goal of tax shelter authors is to invest the transaction with enough genuine economic purpose to pass review. Shelters are hard to detect on audit; even with improved reporting requirements, many shelters will go undetected. The government wins most, but not all, shelter cases it pursues, and there are no meaningful penalties for shelter use. Consequently the decision whether to use a tax shelter is a gamble that many find worth taking, even if their behavior may cross the (admittedly, often blurry) line between legal avoidance and tax evasion. Shelters directly reduce revenue, but the more serious problem is that awareness that shelters work undermines voluntary compliance. Some people justify shelters as a do-it-yourself way of converting the income tax to what many deem superior—a consumption tax. This argument is bogus, according to Bankman, because tax shelters do not lead to an accurate measure of a consumption tax base. Bankman explores various potential approaches to defining business transactions as prohibited tax shelters. While each has flaws, he argues that the war against shelters must continue, because the failure to wage it would threaten the capacity to collect taxes not only on capital income, but also—because of the capacity to transform labor income into capital income—on labor income as well.

The menu of challenges to tax administrators from international transactions is "prodigious," to quote David R. Tillinghast. Some of the problems result directly from the complexity of transactions involving many companies in various nations operating under different laws and accounting practices and with many currencies. Income is not defined identically in all nations. The largest single problem is the incapacity of the U.S. government to require information returns on various types of foreign-generated income or even to identify people who must file. Some problems arise from criminal transactions—Enron owned 186 entities chartered in the Cayman Islands. Tillinghast argues that a major objective in an increasingly globalized world should be to improve the voluntary exchange of data among governments. The IRS has recently moved to shut down a large tax avoidance ploy advertised by credit card companies—the use of debit cards issued to banks operating out of tax shelter countries that do not share information with the U.S. government. A continuing problem involves international transactions within commonly owned companies—the so-called transfer pricing problem. Such companies can set prices to allocate income to jurisdictions with relatively low tax rates. Tillinghast has high praise for advance-pricing agreements, in which the IRS and private companies agree in advance on the prices at which various transactions will subsequently be valued. Tilling-hast cautions that little simplification would likely result if the United States moved from taxing worldwide income to a territorial principle under which only income generated within the United States is subject to U.S. tax.

Small businesses receive favored treatment under the tax code, and some argue that such treatment may be justified, at least in part, as an offset to the regressive effect of other government regulations that particularly burden small businesses. But Joel Slemrod argues in chapter 4 that this argument ignores the relatively high rate of evasion by small businesses, a problem that justifies intensified audit-ing and other enforcement measures. Most small businesses report that they lose money. In part this result reflects genuine unprofitability. But it also reflects will-ful evasion, as careful audits show that small businesses have low rates of volun-tary compliance. This is consistent with evidence that shows that the small-business sector tends to expand when tax rates increase, because this increases the value of the greater tax avoidance and evasion opportunities in that sector. For the partnership and some corporation sectors, so-called pass-through entities, non-compliance benefits a highly affluent slice of the taxpayer population. Slemrod argues that application of optimal tax principles warrants intensified enforce-ment focus on pass-through entities owned by high-income individuals. Indeed the IRS recently announced a shift in focus toward that sector.[4]

One of the most important innovations in tax administration in recent years is the advent of software to assist individuals and professionals in computing their tax liabilities. Austan Goolsbee in chapter 5 examines whether such tax software has obviated the desirability of tax simplification. His unequivocal answer is no. Those who do not use tax software are precisely those for whom the losses from complexity are the greatest. Nor do those who use tax software do so in order to reduce tax complexity. Rather, use of tax software is a by-product of other characteristics that dispose the user to be computer-literate. According to Goolsbee, a much more promising road to simplification would be to convert the least complex tax form of all—the 1040EZ—to automatic, return-free electronic filing.

Over the past two decades, the earned income tax credit (EITC) has come to be the largest federal program of cash assistance to low earners. Unfortunately noncompliance with the rules of the EITC is widespread among those who claim this benefit. At the same time, many who are eligible for the benefit do not

4. IRS (2002, p. 3).

claim it. In chapter 6 Janet Holtzblatt and Janet McCubbin examine what to do about these and other problems confronting low-income filers. Many difficulties arise from complex and unstable marital and other living arrangements. Others arise from inconsistent definitions of such important terms as *dependent child* in federal programs. Certain "solutions" to the problem of administering the EITC—such as moving responsibility for refunding monies to an agency other than the IRS—would do little more than shift the problem's locus. Establishing a uniform definition of a dependent child would be of some help. A major challenge is to design rules that would improve compliance without raising obstacles to application that would reduce the proportion of eligible filers who receive the credit.

Marsha Blumenthal and Charles Christian report in chapter 7 that more than 70 million filers rely on tax preparers—2 million of whom file the one-page Form 1040EZ—to save time and effort and reduce uncertainty. Filers pay handsomely for this service, more than $10 billion, according to estimates by the authors. Unsurprisingly practitioners are used disproportionately by the poorly educated, the elderly, the self-employed, and those with complex returns. When Minnesota taxpayers were informed that they would be subject to an increased audit rate, the use of preparers increased slightly. Studies indicate that the use of preparers is associated with lower voluntary reporting of some types of income but an increased likelihood that filers will pay estimated taxes in the course of the year. The former result suggests that preparers may contribute to evasion. Although tax preparers are subject to IRS regulations and may be fined if they contribute to inaccurate tax reporting, it is unclear how vigorously these regulations are enforced. These considerations are of particular importance in the case of so-called tax shelters, in the design of which accountants and lawyers often play an active and initiating role. Filers who employ preparers are more likely than are unaided filers to use electronic filing, a practice the IRS is encouraging. However, the spread of electronic filing is lagging behind IRS goals.

Frank Cowell, in chapter 8, examines various economic theories of tax compliance and administration. The earliest models treat taxpayers as gamblers (TAG models) who weigh the potential monetary gain from successful evasion against the potential monetary loss if the evasion is detected and punished. The conclusions from TAG models are that people will evade whenever it pays to do so. Because it is a gamble, they will evade less if they are averse to the risk of being audited and punished. They will evade less if the audit rate or punishment increases. Surprisingly the models do not necessarily predict that evasion rises when the tax rate goes up. More detailed evidence about the nature and determinants of tax compliance in practice come from the now-defunct Taxpayer Compliance Measurement Program (TCMP), a system of extremely detailed audits—known informally as "the audits from hell." The IRS carried out these studies until 1988 to determine how best to allocate its limited enforcement resources. The TCMP revealed behavior that was not inconsistent with the TAG model but provided more detailed information as well. For example, compliance rates vary depending on the source of income, marital status, and age. Some recent research, including laboratory experiments, has cast doubt on the TAG model, suggesting that norms and framing influence compliance and shedding light on the contexts under which duty rather than calculation governs compliance behavior. Cowell suggests that improved theories should encompass taxpayer motivation and the way business conditions influence business compliance. They should also allow for the influence of norms and social interactions, factors that are excluded from TAG models, which treat each individual in isolation. Cowell emphasizes that choosing a model that accurately represents behavior is important to the extent that such models guide choices made by tax administrators.

In chapter 9 William G. Gale and Jeffrey Rohaly examine how specific proposals for tax simplification would affect the distribution of tax payments and the likelihood that individuals would rely on a tax preparer. They focus on three packages of reforms. Two would narrow or eliminate the alternative minimum tax, increase the standard deduction by alternative amounts, exclude proportions of interest and dividend income, and remove the distinction between capital gains and ordinary income. The third would replace the income tax with a value-added tax (VAT) for all but the highest-income filers, make other modifications, and add a wage subsidy and child credit. Shifts in tax payments among income classes differ among these three approaches, but middle-income filers pay more tax under all of them. Of the three packages Gale and Rohaly examine, the VAT plan raises taxes most for middle-income filers and lowers taxes most for upper-income filers. The authors also compute marginal tax rates under each package for different types of income. The income tax packages reduce the estimated use of tax preparers, but only marginally, while the VAT proposal would massively lower the use of preparers. The major contribution of the chapter is to show that the way simplification is achieved has important effects on how taxes are distributed and that a large reduction in the use of preparers (and hence of perceived complexity) is unlikely unless people are entirely excused from the need to file.

Like all other organizations, the Internal Revenue Service has limited resources to apply to the objectives it seeks to achieve. What should those objectives be? The answer, Alan H. Plumley and C. Eugene Steuerle assert in chapter 10, is not and should not be to raise as much revenue as possible. The IRS is also expected to raise the "right" amount of revenue from taxpayers, implement a vast array of social programs, quickly and accurately answer questions about the increasingly complicated Internal Revenue Code, and do all these things without being overly intrusive in taxpayer affairs. Plumley and Steuerle consider all the nonrevenue objectives as part of the service that the IRS provides. The IRS should not be required to perform many of these tasks, for a variety of reasons, including lack of adequate resources. Nonetheless the agency is seen as bearing responsibility for performing and monitoring them based on the costs and benefits. In particular Plumley and Steuerle argue that, although the IRS has pursued both revenue and service objectives over the past three decades, there have been remarkable shifts in emphasis over this period. They review this recent history and then offer a framework for identifying the proper balance between the revenue and service objectives that can be used to provide guidance for future resource allocation decisions.

All nations face similar challenges in collecting taxes. In chapter 11 Jeffrey Owens and Stuart Hamilton report on how other nations are coping with these problems and distill lessons for the United States. The first and most important lesson is that attempts at simplification without first simplifying underlying policies and legislation will yield few benefits. Several countries have learned this lesson and reformed their tax laws with an eye to simplification. Another lesson is that much complexity results from attempts to favor certain forms of income or certain economic activities, while preventing such concessions from unduly eroding the revenue base. Several countries recently moved to dual tax systems, under which capital income is taxed at a single proportional rate, while other income is taxed progressively. Owens and Hamilton note that analyses of the progressivity or regressivity of taxes are incomplete unless they encompass the whole tax system and extend to the expenditures that the revenues finance. Alone among member countries of the Organization for Economic Cooperation and Development, the United States imposes no value-added tax, partly because of concerns about regressivity. Some nations have simplified tax preparation for many taxpayers by tasking the government to compute liabilities. The United States is moving in this direction, but progress is slow. Small businesses challenge tax administration everywhere. One approach that merits consideration is to apply simple rules of thumb to small businesses and not attempt to measure income precisely. Harsh penalties, with a heightened risk of incarceration, might reduce the willingness to abet evasion through fraudulent shelters, but tax administration also needs to help those who wish to pay the correct amounts of tax by providing a better service to such taxpayers. Owens and Hamilton conclude by observing that if taxes are the price of civilization, as Justice Oliver Wendell Holmes famously said, the United States is spending less to make sure that taxes are paid than are most other OECD nations. While they do not judge the U.S. administrative system to be in crisis, they conclude that there is a lot of room for improvement, that simplified legislation is essential, and that providing adequate funding for the administration is a key to moving ahead.

The chapters in this volume address not only the crisis that now confronts the Internal Revenue Service but also the tensions that affect all tax administrations at all times. These tensions are nicely illustrated by the discussion of the

IRS in James Q. Wilson's study of bureaucracy. He compares the IRS favorably
to most other bureaucracies, noting that in tax administration the existence of
observable outputs, such as audits, and observable outcomes, such as taxes collected, simplifies the managerial problem. But, just one page later, Wilson again
cites the IRS in the context of the tendency of managers, by plan or inadver-
tence, to pay more attention to the more easily measured outcomes than to
those less easily observed or counted. He notes also that the IRS tends to judge
auditors solely on the basis of how much money they produce from each audit
and how many audits they conduct. "This can lead auditors to become so zeal-
ous in auditing that they annoy taxpayers who feel they are being treated
unfairly or hounded about minor errors."[5] Wilson's final reference to the IRS
nicely poses one of the key tensions facing the agency: "Members of Congress
may say they want an efficient Internal Revenue Service but in fact they want
one that is efficient only up to a point—the point at which voters begin complaining that they are being harassed."[6]

References

Rossotti, Charles O. 2002. "Report to the IRS Oversight Board: Assessment of the IRS
    and the Tax System" (September) (www.irsoversightboard.treas.gov/documents/
    commissioner_report.pdf) [July 23, 2003]).
U.S. Internal Revenue Service. 2002. "IRS Sets New Audit Priorities." Fact Sheet FS-
    2002-12 (September).
————. 2003. *Statistics of Income Bulletin* (Spring).
Wilson, James Q. 1989. *Bureaucracy: What Government Agencies Do and Why They Do It.*
    Basic Books.

5. Wilson (1989, p. 161).
6. Wilson (1989, p. 174).

2

JOSEPH BANKMAN

The Tax Shelter Battle

TAX SHELTERS—structured transactions with little or no independent business purpose—have always been part of the tax landscape. In recent years the tax shelter market has been composed of corporations and individuals with very high net worth. This chapter describes the modern tax shelter, discusses some of its effects, and evaluates government efforts to curb shelter use.

What Is a Shelter?

There is no agreed-upon definition of a tax shelter. There is certainly no definition that can be applied to any set of transactions to sift out shelters and only shelters. The following definition, while not mechanically applicable, encompasses nearly every transaction commonly described as a tax shelter.

A shelter is a transaction that (1) is marketed and tax-motivated, (2) succeeds under at least one literal reading of the governing statute or regulation, (3) misstates economic income, and (4) in so doing reduces the tax on capital, (5) in a manner inconsistent with any purposive or intentionalist reading of the statute or regulation.

Most of the recent wave of tax shelters involve the following additional characteristics: a promoter that is either a large accounting firm, an investment bank, or a "tax shelter boutique"; a corporate purchaser; an "accommodation party" that is not subject to tax; a transaction with little or no economic risk, in which a revenue stream is bifurcated for tax purposes into income and expense components, with the gain allocated to the accommodation party and the expense allocated to the corporate purchaser; financial reporting treatment that differs from tax treatment and that does not produce any noneconomic loss. In the past few years the tax shelter market has "gone retail," with products designed for individual taxpayers with as little as $10 million in capital gain to shelter.

One final shelter characteristic deserves mention. The tax law is strewn with provisions that, measured against the ideal of economic accrual of income, front-load recognition of income and back-load recognition of expense. Many of these provisions were adopted to fight against an earlier form of shelters or perceived taxpayer abuses. These provisions offer a fertile ground for the modern shelter. The accelerated taxable income is shifted to the accommodation party, leaving the shelter purchaser with the back-loaded deductions.

A few examples may prove helpful. In the so-called high-basis, low-value shelter, a domestic corporation was the taxpayer and shelter purchaser, and a foreign party was the accommodation party. The foreign party was not subject to U.S. tax and was located in a jurisdiction that did not tax gains from the sale of certain property. The foreign party transferred property that had fallen in value to the subsidiary of a domestic corporation, in exchange for the stock of that corporation. Assume, for example, that the property had a cost basis of 100x and a value of only 10x. The domestic corporation took the position that the transfer was a contribution to capital that qualified under the nonrecognition provisions of the corporate tax code, and that under those same provisions the corporation should assume the foreign party's 100x basis in the property. Both positions were (and are) consistent with a literal reading of the relevant statutes and regulations. The domestic corporation then resold the property and took a 90x tax loss. The foreign party was paid a disguised accommodation fee in the form of stock. If the value of the property were 10x, for example, the stock awarded the foreign party may have been 12x.

We can assume that the foreign party, located in a no-tax (or low-tax) jurisdiction, had property that had risen in value as well as property that had fallen in value. The shelter thus provided an asymmetrical treatment of gains and losses: Gains from the sale of property could be realized tax free, while property that had fallen in value could be contributed to a domestic corporation and yield tax savings.

Prospective purchasers knew that the shelter was likely to be challenged by the Internal Revenue Service if uncovered on audit, that a court was apt to agree with the government's position, and that the government was likely to adopt rules to combat the shelter. They assumed, however, that the shelter was apt to escape detection, that if detected they could settle with the government on favorable terms, and that any rules adopted would be prospective in application.

In fact it was not until years after shelters were first marketed that the government announced its opposition to them. No cases involving shelters have yet been litigated, suggesting that the majority of purchasers won their bet on the "audit lottery" and escaped detection and that those caught on audit settled on favorable terms.

Corporate-owned life insurance (COLI) shelters were built on the favorable treatment of life insurance. An insurance policy purchased for, say, $20,000 might pay out $100,000 on the death of the insured. The difference between the cost and the payout reflects interest or other investment return earned on the insurance policy between purchase and death. As the policy comes closer to payout, and investment return accumulates, the present value of the policy increases. Insurers generally allow the holder of the policy to borrow out some or all of the policy value. A primary attraction of whole life insurance is that the investment return—the $80,000 in this example—is not subject to tax.[1] In the COLI shelter, simply stated, the taxpayer borrows $100 million at 11 percent from an insurance company and uses the proceeds to purchase life insurance on its employees, with itself as the beneficiary and a predicted return (if the employees live to life expectancy) of 10.5 percent. In the first year the value of the policies increases by $10.5 million. The taxpayer borrows out this increase, adds $500 thousand million of his or her own funds, and pays the insurer $11 million on the loan used to purchase the policies. This is repeated almost every year of the contract.[2] On a pretax basis the taxpayer loses money each year and borrows out virtually all the equity in the insurance policies. The attraction of the shelter is that the interest paid is (according to shelter promoters) deductible, while the appreciation of the policy, which provides the basis for most of the interest payment, is tax-free. In this example the taxpayer has an out-of-pocket cost of $500 thousand but receives an $11 million tax deduction.

The COLI shelters have produced huge tax deductions for a hundred or so taxpayers. For example, the supermarket chain Winn-Dixie purchased life insurance policies on 36,000 employees with itself as the beneficiary, under a plan that contemplated a before-tax cost (over sixty years) of approximately $700 million and an after-tax savings of about $2.7 billion.[3] The government denied benefits in COLI shelters and won a number of victories in early litigation[4] but then settled the remaining cases on terms thought favorable to the taxpayers.[5]

1. 26 U.S.C. (Internal Revenue Code, hereafter I.R.C.), sec. 101.

2. To avoid running afoul of an existing rule on point, the premiums were not borrowed for four of the first seven years of the shelter.

3. See *Winn-Dixie Stores, Inc.* v. *Commissioner,* 113 T.C. 254 (1999), aff'd 254 F.3d 1313 (11th Cir. 2001).

4. See, for example, *Winn-Dixie* v. *Commissioner; American Electric Power* v. *United States,* 136 F. Supp. 2d 762 (S.D. Ohio 2001).

5. The settlement allowed taxpayers to retain 20 percent of the claimed interest deductions (IRS, 2002). The motives for settlement are discussed briefly in *Winn-Dixie,* infra.

The Market for Tax Shelters

Tax shelters—sometimes referred to as tax products or structured tax prod-ucts—are developed and marketed by investment banks, small tax shelter shops (or boutiques), and large accounting firms. A large shelter promoter may pay scores of accountants or lawyers to develop shelters and an even larger group to sell them. A shelter can cost $1 million to develop and market—a sum that can be recovered in a single sale. There is a competitive market in shelter promotion and little effective intellectual protection. A promoter often offers its own ver-sion of a shelter developed by a competitor. At any given time a large shelter pro-moter offers clients a selection of tax products.[6]

For obvious reasons, shelter promoters do not reveal shelter sales; purchasers are equally reticent. It is impossible, therefore, to come up with any verified fig-ures on shelter use. Some years ago this author estimated that shelters might cost the government as much as $10 billion a year—a figure that was picked up by the Clinton Treasury Department and attacked by some in and out of the shel-ter industry.[7] Since that time a number of generic shelters, each producing tax losses in the billions of dollars, have been uncovered on audit. Recently the IRS announced that voluntary disclosures under its tax amnesty provisions had yielded over $30 billion in shelter-related deductions and that it was pursuing leads on newly discovered shelters.[8] Estimates vary widely as to the tax losses produced by shelters that have escaped detection. Economists who have looked at the issue have found indirect evidence of substantial shelter activity.[9]

The Problem of Tax Shelters

Shelters impose considerable certain costs in the form of accounting and legal fees, fees paid to promoters, and so on. Shelters also impose less easily monetized costs. They redistribute the tax burden, lowering the rate on purchasers and requiring higher rates on everyone else. This raises an obvious fairness problem; it may create inefficiencies as well, as the marginal cost of replacing funds exceeds the cost of raising funds in the no-shelter world.

6. The market for tax shelters is described more fully in Bankman (1999a, p. 1,775).

7. See Janet Novack, "The Hustling of X-Rated Shelters," *Forbes Magazine,* December 14, 1998, p. 198; Kies (1999, p. 1,463); Bankman (1999b, p. 1,813).

8. Rossotti (2002).

9. A recent study by the economist Mihir Desai found that the gap between book and tax income grew from next to nothing in the early 1990s to $288 billion in 1998; most of the gap remains after allowing for increased depreciation and stock options and other non-shelter-related causes. Desai concludes that part of that enormous gap is most reasonably explained by shelters (Desai 2002). See also Manzon and Plesko (2002).

Perhaps most significantly, shelters threaten to undermine tax compliance. The high-basis, low-value shelter described above takes a plausible, if wooden, literal interpretation of a governing statute. Many other shelters interpret statutes in a much more aggressive and implausible manner. These shelters are often extremely complex. The complexity may be a necessary element of the shelter, but it also serves as a screen against governmental detection and public scrutiny. Shelters have nonetheless begun to attract attention in the general media. The knowledge that the largest companies and wealthiest individuals are using shelters to reduce taxes is likely to infuriate many taxpayers. These taxpayers may view the complexity of the deals as a sign of guilt or at least have no sympathy for the technical (and in many cases implausible) legal arguments upon which the shelter is based. The significant role in shelter promotion played by large accounting firms, still tarnished by their part in recent accounting scandals, is likely to further anger taxpayers. The danger is that some of these taxpayers may respond by reducing their own tax payments, not through tax shelters but by crude measures such as overstated deductions, understated income, and nonfiling. The IRS and Justice Department now find themselves hard pressed to pursue current noncompliance. The government would be incapable of responding to any widespread tax revolt. Wages compose by far the single largest source of tax revenue, and a decline in compliance from this revenue source would have a dramatic effect on government programs and the economy.

The Relationship between Tax Shelters and an Ideal Tax

The current tax law is inconsistent in its treatment of investment (and labor). Taxes inevitably affect investment choices. The goal of current anti–tax shelter legislation is to prevent purely tax-driven transactions. Transactions that are only partially motivated by tax considerations are accepted as impossible to prevent, consistent with legislative intent, or both. Stopping tax shelters under current law thus requires measuring and policing the amount of tax motivation underlying a given transaction—a difficult enterprise, discussed in detail below.

The inconsistencies under current law pose another problem for those who wish to shut down tax shelters. Congress and the IRS have tried to shore up current law with thousands of stopgap measures; as noted earlier, some of those measures were poorly worded or not thought out and have become the basis for more recent shelters.

An ideal income or consumption tax would remove the basis for current shelters and make it easier to address the shelters that do appear. Less ambitious reforms would also help—rationalizing the treatment between corporate and noncorporate investment, debt and equity, and so on.

While reform would undoubtedly reduce the severity of the shelter problem, is it important to keep in mind that tax shelters will exist even under a nearly ideal tax system. Individual statutes and regulations will never be drafted perfectly, to reflect the desires of the drafters in all relevant situations. So long as rules are vulnerable to differing interpretations, advisers can be expected to come up with interpretations that reduce taxes and to sell those interpretations to their clients.

Shelters reduce the tax on corporations and on capital more generally. Shelters are sometimes defended as a second-best means of achieving corporate integration or, at the limit, a cash-flow tax. The difficulties with this argument are enumerated above: Shelters pose certain efficiency costs and harder-to-measure fairness and compliance costs. A more sophisticated version of this argument is that shelters make the transition to an integrated corporate tax or cash-flow tax possible. Shelters, it is argued, drain the revenue from the corporate or capital tax base. Once that occurs, the transition to a more sensible and rule-bound system of integration or cash-flow tax is easy, because it does not require any revenue sacrifice. Most policymakers would not find this an attractive path to travel. The costs are certain, while the payoff for even those who favor a cash-flow or integrated tax is uncertain.

The Costs and Benefits of Shelter Investments

The shelter market is complex, and the government's response to shelters has been multifaceted. One way to evaluate the current state of affairs is to look at a representative shelter through the eyes of a prospective purchaser. Consider the following self-evident statement: An economically motivated taxpayer will purchase a shelter if and only if benefits outweigh costs. This can be written formulaically as $B > C$, where B = net benefit promised by the promoter, and C = potential costs. B is simply the taxes saved, which we can state as t. We can define C to include the more easily monetized costs as

$$fc + d^* \, l(t + p),$$

where fc are fixed costs, d is the odds the shelter will be detected, l is the odds the shelter will lose in court, and p is the expected penalty levied on a shelter that is detected and loses in court. This model is obviously simplistic; it assumes that purchasers are risk-neutral and that cases are litigated without cost or settle without litigation for their expected value, and it ignores the bad (or good!) publicity that might come from being branded as a shelter purchaser. (These and other assumptions are relaxed later in the chapter.)

The first term in the cost equation, fc, or fixed costs, consists primarily of transaction costs, promoter fees, and the harder to monetize internal cost of labor that the transaction absorbs. Transaction costs and promoter fees increase absolutely but fall relatively with the size of the shelter. For individuals with only $10 million or so to shelter, these costs might amount to one-quarter or more of the tax savings.[10] More typical corporate shelters involve tax savings in the tens or hundreds of millions of dollars and transaction costs and promoter fees of 10 to 20 percent of tax savings.[11] An assumption that fixed costs amount to 15 percent of the tax benefit for an average-size shelter is probably reasonable.

Improved IRS Detection

Fixed costs, as estimated above, can reduce the benefit of a shelter to only 85 percent of the taxes saved. If the shelter escapes detection, the rest of the cost equation drops out: There will be no required return of tax savings, no penalty, no bad publicity, and so on. In the past it was common knowledge that virtually any shelter had a good—some would say likely—chance of escaping detection on audit. This was true even though Treasury Department regulations require reporting and listing from shelter promoters and purchasers, most purchasers are subject to continuing audits, and most shelters produce a disparity between book and tax income that must be disclosed on Schedule M. The reasons shelters usually escaped detection were many, including that Schedule M adjustments are often a netting of many unrelated items, so finding a shelter in a Schedule M for a Fortune 100 company is not easy work.

Temporary Treasury regulations, amended as recently as October 2002, are aimed at improving shelter disclosure.[12] Under the regulations, promoters must report and maintain client information for transactions that have been "listed" by the Treasury as shelters; a like disclosure requirement befalls purchasers of those transactions. The same disclosure and list-keeping requirement applies to certain nonlisted transactions. These include transactions that produce or are reasonably expected to produce a loss in excess of $10 million in a single year or $20 million altogether, or, for certain publicly traded companies, transactions

10. For example, materials sent to investors to accompany the KPMG foreign leveraged investment strategy (also known as the basis-shift shelter) offered a tax savings of $2.4 million for a fixed after-tax cost of about $500,000. (Materials available from this author at jbankman@stanford.edu.)

11. For example, the so-called contingent installment sale shelter purchased by AlliedSignal from Merrill Lynch required the taxpayer to incur estimated fixed costs of approximately $12 million in return for an artificial tax loss of approximately $300 million which would reduce taxes paid (or produce a tax refund) of approximately $140 million. *ASA Investerings Partnership* v. *Commissioner*, T.C. Memo 1998-305.

12. Treasury Regulations, sec. 1.6011-4T, sec. 301.6112-1T.

that produce a difference in tax and financial reporting of more than $10 million.[13] Certain exceptions to disclosure, such as for transactions for which there is "no reasonable basis" for denial of tax benefits, have been eliminated. The 2002 amendments to the temporary regulations greatly increase their impact. Of particular importance is the elimination of the exceptions to disclosure. Under prior regulations taxpayers routinely took the position that there was "no reasonable basis" for denial of benefits to any shelter and, pursuant to the regulation, did not disclose anything but listed shelters. Of course the regulations cannot be completely effective in ferreting out shelters. Some shelters are not reportable under the regulations: The shelter may produce a loss not covered by the regulations, or the loss may fall below the threshold requirements. The government may have difficulty isolating shelters from other transactions that are reported. The regulations are not now backed by any significant penalties, although the IRS has stated that it will not waive certain penalties for nondisclosed shelters, and that nonwaiver may be seen as a penalty in itself.

The IRS has taken steps that, in conjunction with reporting regulations, have significantly increased its ability to detect shelters. These steps include training at the field level aimed at shelter detection, use of the government's general subpoena power, and most notably a (presumed) one-time-only amnesty provision. There is a fair amount of redundancy in the government's disclosure arsenal. If the IRS finds a marketed shelter, it can follow a paper trail to those who purchased that same shelter from the same promoter. Disclosure by one taxpayer (or discovery of the shelter on audit) may, as a practical matter, serve as disclosure for all taxpayers who purchase a given shelter.

These changes have made it much more likely (and, as an absolute matter, likely) that a given shelter will be detected on audit or through disclosure. An optimistic but perhaps not unrealistic assumption is that the IRS has an 85 percent chance of detecting any given shelter.

What Happens to Detected Shelters? Are Shelters Illegal?

The issue raised by shelters comes up frequently in the modern state: A subject of regulation engages in behavior that (at least from the subject's point of view) complies with the literal language of a statute but (from the government's view) is inconsistent with legislative intent or purpose. In most fields the issue is fought in a (somewhat) straightforward manner, as a battle of interpretive modes. The private citizen cites the statute and relies on interpretive theories that support a literalist or plain-language meaning; the government relies on

13. The $10 million and $20 million thresholds apply to corporate taxpayers; the threshold is lower for individuals. Certain differences in tax and financial reporting, such as those caused by depreciation, are excluded for purposes of determining whether the $10 million threshold is exceeded. See, generally, Nijenhuis, Chung, and Kulikov (2002).

more intentionalist interpretive theories. In tax, intentionalist and purposive arguments have been pretty much absorbed into common law doctrines, which in turn have been absorbed into the economic substance doctrine. In brief, the economic substance doctrine allows the IRS to disregard transactions that lack nontax motivation or effect.

The doctrine, which I have written about at length elsewhere, is problematic.[14] First, as is perhaps obvious, the amount of nontax motivation or effect the doctrine requires is unspecified. Will a dollar of before-tax profit qualify? A before-tax profit equal to the rate on a non-tax-favored investment? A before-tax profit equal to the rate on a tax-favored investment?

Second, as the last question demonstrates, a requirement that a transaction earn a positive return on a before-tax basis rests uneasily with the fact that tax advantages and disadvantages are embedded in asset prices. To make sense, the doctrine must be interpreted to exclude tax-motivated transactions that offer a low or nonexistent before-tax return but that are consistent with legislative intent or purpose. Consider, for example, an investment that qualifies for the low-income housing credit or, more generally, property subject to favorable depreciation rules. It may be that the before-tax return is negative but that the transaction cannot be attacked under the economic substance doctrine. The tax benefits were intended to drive demand up and return down. The transaction is consistent with legislative intent, so the doctrine simply cannot apply here.

Consider now a harder issue. Suppose that, in a particular area, Congress draws a bright line and specifies that on one side of that line an interest deduction is unavailable. The line is intended to stop a set of tax-motivated transactions. At the time the legislation is enacted, Congress knows that the line it draws will only imperfectly catch a set of transactions it wishes to prevent. A line drawn in a different place, however, is thought too draconian. Some years later a shelter is marketed. The shelter does not cross the line Congress has drawn. However, the shelter produces a result that the present Congress cannot live with, and it seems likely that, had the previous Congress known of the shelter, it would have drawn the bright line in a different place.

This roughly corresponds to the set of affairs that led to corporate-owned life insurance shelters. Congress had adopted a number of bright-line rules that precluded individuals from engaging in the shelter and other rules that limited the use of the shelter by both individuals and corporations. The taxpayer in the COLI cases argued that the legislature, after weighing the issue, decided to establish a clear-cut rule and that the COLI transactions complied with that rule. The government argued that, while Congress established an outer boundary beyond which the interest deduction would be lost, Congress did not intend to bless any transaction that did not cross that boundary. Instead Congress

14. Bankman (2001).

assumed that such transactions would continue as before to be subject to attack under the economic substance doctrine. I think the second argument is the better one, and courts have agreed.[15] For our purposes, however, the important point is that the economic substance doctrine does not eliminate the vexing problem of determining legislative intent or purpose. The corporate-owned life insurance cases may have been litigated under the economic substance doctrine, but that litigation entailed arguments over legislative intent or purpose.

Finally the economic substance doctrine does not specify what constitutes the transaction that must have a nontax motivation. Suppose, to illustrate this point, a taxpayer obtains needed capital by a financing method that effectively makes the repayment of principal, rather than just interest, deductible. Is it the method of financing that must have a nontax business purpose or effect? Or is it enough that the monies obtained are used in the normal course of business?[16]

It is tempting to think that these and other problems might be eliminated by tweaking the doctrine or by substituting another judge-made doctrine in its place, such as step transaction, sham transaction, or substance over form. A moment's reflection, however, reveals that all these doctrines suffer from many of the same problems and some additional problems, to boot. Suppose, instead, that we eliminate the use of this and other broad-based doctrines altogether and attack shelters on different, more narrowly focused grounds. There is much to recommend this approach, which is favored by such diverse commentators and policymakers as Lee Sheppard and some members of the Bush administration. One can imagine denying the benefits of almost every shelter on grounds narrower than economic substance, and in fact in some cases the government has made such narrower arguments. As noted earlier, many modern shelters have a nontaxable accommodation party; for tax purposes only a revenue stream is split into component parts of income and expense, and the income is allocated to the accommodation party, leaving the expense with the shelter purchaser. The revenue stream is often split for tax purposes using a partnership, with income allocated in one year to the accommodation party and expense allocated in a later year to the shelter purchaser.

The government almost invariably attacks these transactions under the economic substance doctrine, and the courts usually view these doctrines through the prism of economic substance. But the government has also argued that these transactions are invalid because, on the specific facts of the case, the partnership was a sham. The only "true" investor was the domestic corporation, which must recognize both the early gain and later loss produced by the transaction. In at least one leading shelter case, *ASA Investerings Partnership* v. *Com-*

15. See, for example, *Winn-Dixie* v. *Commissioner.*

16. The scope-of-the-transaction issue is not confined to financing transactions. It arises whenever a tax-structured transaction is tied to a transaction motivated by nontax considerations.

missioner, a court held for the government and based its decision on the lack of partnership.[17]

Unfortunately many doctrines that seem much narrower raise many of the same issues as the economic substance doctrine. For example, the determination in *ASA Investerings* that no partnership existed required the court to look into the parties' subjective motivation and the ex ante and ex post possibilities of profit and to implicitly measure motivation and result against some norm.

In addition we do not want to overturn the form of the transaction chosen by private parties in run-of-the-mill business deals, so we need a metarule that tells us when to apply the narrower doctrines that substitute in place of the economic substance doctrine. We can see the necessity of this in the doctrine used by the court in *ASA Investerings.* The distinction between an equity investor or partner (the form chosen by the parties in that case) and a lender is elusive, and clearly in most cases the government will not challenge the parties' characterization. What is it, then, in a predictive sense, that will tell us when a partnership will be found to be a sham? It is the presence of factors that are either part of the economic substance doctrine or are associated with its use.

All that said, it might be wiser to rely more on arguments that are more narrowly focused. We might supplement this approach with a more straightforward form of nonliteral statutory interpretation. This will not solve our fundamental problem, however. We will have reintroduced some portion of the economic substance doctrine through the back door (because the narrower doctrines overlap with the economic substance doctrine or because we need a metarule to explain when we use the narrower doctrines). More generally we will be stuck with the irreducible ambiguity of nonliteral statutory interpretation.

Should we go further and ditch the whole nonliteralist project? The answer is no, for three reasons, two minor and one overwhelming. First, and least important, the costs of ambiguity entailed in applying the economic substance doctrine to tax-related transactions fall disproportionately on promoters and others who plan to approach (and in many cases step over) whatever line the tax law draws. The sad truth, known to economists, is that, all else equal, tax planning is a deadweight loss to the system. Reducing the payoff to aggressive tax planning is hardly a social evil. Second, it is not impossible to apply the tax law in a manner consistent with underlying purpose and intent. Indeed many of the same lawyers who argue for literal interpretation in the shelter context argue for purposive interpretation in cases in which the literal language disadvantages their clients. To be sure there are close questions, but literal interpretation raises close questions as well. The third and most important reason to retain the doctrine is this: Without the doctrine, a wide array of somewhat narrow doctrines,

17. *ASA Investerings Partnership* v. *Commissioner,* T.C. Memo 1998-305.

and willingness to engage in nonliteral interpretation, we cannot raise significant revenue from capital, and possibly not from labor either.

This seems like an overstatement, but it is not. The tax law is enormously complex, and it has been cobbled together over the years by tens of thousands of legislators, legislative aides, and administrators. Some of these drafters were wordsmiths, others were not. Some sections were sensibly worded for the time in which they were drafted but must be reinterpreted in light of more recent developments. The short of it is that our tax law is riddled with what literal interpretation would reveal to be legal tax shelters, which for purposes of exposition I will refer to as loopholes.

Making the law loophole-free is like retrofitting all the buildings in California to make them earthquake-proof. There are not the resources in the world to do it. Or perhaps a better analogy is to land mines: It is prohibitive or unfeasible to remove all the mines buried in a field, and removing most of them is not enough. All it takes is a few loopholes to siphon off most tax revenues. The simple high-basis, low-value shelter mentioned earlier illustrates this point. In this shelter a foreign person transfers high-basis, low-value property to a domestic company in a transaction that otherwise qualifies as a contribution to capital. The U.S. company sells the asset and takes a loss. If we are stuck with a literal translation of the tax law, the transaction works. The supply of high-basis, low-value assets is infinite—it can be created through offshore straddles. The shelter can be used at low transaction costs (which come down with high volume) to reduce corporate income to near zero.

Those who favor a literal approach to the tax law note that a shelter such as this one will be discovered by the government and closed by legislation. That is true, but by then shelter promoters will have discovered another existing flaw and will be exploiting that. If, as is currently the case, legislation has only prospective effect, then at any given time we can expect a state of affairs under which we raise no significant money from capital.

It is sometimes said that the government, as a matter of principle, ought to stand by the literal language of its rules. The remedy for a badly written rule is a government that takes more care in drafting rules. The difficulty with this argument is that we are already stuck with a law full of badly written rules, and under the best of circumstances at least some badly worded rules will be written in the future. If we wish to adhere to this principle, we must as a practical matter give up taxing capital.

An objection to the dilemma just posed may be phrased as follows: It is asserted that literal interpretation would reduce the tax on capital to near zero. Suppose, though, we put the government and courts in the hands of those who believe in that mode of interpretation. We might expect, as a practical matter, that the tax on capital would not fall so dramatically. That is true: Those who favor literal interpretation would not take the tax on capital to zero. But that is only because, at some point, as a result of political outcry or the need to maintain government services or both, the principle of literal interpretation would be dropped.

Of course the view of the economic substance doctrine and the need for nonliteral methods of interpretation set forth above is (alas!) not that important. What counts is what the parties think who must enforce that doctrine: the courts and the executive branch.

The modern shelter wars started off marvelously—at least from the perspective of the government litigator. The doctrine was upheld in a spate of tax shelter cases (all involving the same shelter) litigated in Tax Court, and upheld, albeit by a two-to-one decision, as the first case was appealed to the Third Circuit.[18] Since then, things have gone somewhat downhill, with a number of significant taxpayer victories, including appellate court decisions that overturned decisions, previously noted, that went in favor of the government.[19] It is difficult to draw from this still small sample any definite ratio of wins and losses; some cases in which the doctrine was invoked did not involve paradigmatic tax shelters,[20] some tax shelter cases were decided on other grounds,[21] and decisions in favor of the taxpayer often were based on narrow application, rather than rejection, of the doctrine.[22] Moreover we cannot transform judicial decisions into ex ante predictions without a theory of which cases get litigated. We are now seeing the litigation outcome of yesterday's tax shelters; more recent tax shelters may be designed to take advantage of the twists and turns of today's decisions and fare better in tomorrow's courts. On the other hand, Enron-related scandals may have a spillover effect in the shelter area and make the judiciary more skeptical of highly structured transactions designed to produce noneconomic losses. All that said, one might reasonably conclude that in the Tax Court the government is winning decisively. In the district and circuit courts, the government's edge is slight, if any. Taxpayers can chose the forum in which to litigate and, not surprisingly, the forum of choice is now the district

18. *ACM Partnership* v. *Commissioner,* 73 T.C.M. 2189 (1997), aff'd 157 F.3d 231 (3d Cir. 1998); *Winn-Dixie Stores* v. *Commissioner,* 113 T.C. 254 (1999), aff'd 254 F.3d 1313 (11th Cir. 2001); *Saba Partnership* v. *Commissioner,* 78 T.C.M. 684 (1999); *Compaq Computer Corp.* v. *Commissioner,* 113 T.C. 214 (1999); *ASA Investerings Partnership* v. *Commissioner,* 76 T.C.M. 325 (1998), aff'd 201 F.3d 305 (D.C. Cir. 2000).

19. *Boca Investerings Partnership* v. *U.S.,* 167 F. Supp. 2d 298 (D.D.C. 2001); *IES Industries, Inc.* v. *Commissioner,* 253 F.3d 350 (8th Cir. 2001); *Compaq Computer Corp.* v. *Commissioner,* 277 F.3d 778 (5th Cir. 2001); *UPS, Inc.* v. *Commissioner,* 254 F.3d 1014 (11th Cir. 2001). But see *Boca Investerings Partnership* v. *U.S.,* Opinion 01-5429 (D.C. Cir. 2003), reversing district court opinion.

20. *UPS* v. *Commissioner,* for example, involved an attempt to move corporate income offshore and did not involve a marketed tax product.

21. See, for example, *ASA Investerings* v. *Commissioner.* Decided on the grounds that the transaction, which to work for the taxpayer required an allocation of partnership gains and losses, did not involve a true partnership.

22. See, for example, *Boca Investerings* v. *U.S.* (existence of nontax profit motive).

court. Most observers now believe that a taxpayer with a shelter of "average" aggressiveness has a reasonable chance of winning in court.

In the future, shelter purchasers may have even greater success in court. The form of literal interpretation upon which shelters are predicated is more popular among young lawyers than among older lawyers and much more popular among conservatives than liberals.[23] Judges appointed by the Republican Bush administration are likely to be more receptive to the literalist arguments of shelter purchasers than the judges they replace.

Penalties, Litigation Costs, and Government Strategy

An obvious weakness of the cost-benefit model I have drawn is that it provides a simplistic view of administrative behavior and motivations. This may be seen by looking at the question of litigation strategy. Suppose the IRS adopted a policy of litigating to the hilt every shelter case it felt it was likely to win or every shelter case in which it felt it had the better argument. The presence of litigation costs would then enter into the taxpayer's cost-benefit calculus. It is possible that the ex ante expected litigation costs would be so great as to make shelter purchases unattractive.

Of course the downsides to this strategy are obvious. The government would face litigation costs as well. Tax shelter litigation already threatens to swamp the government's legal staff; it may well be that private industry is more capable of reacting to increased litigation than the government. Litigation—particularly with a relatively untrained or junior staff—is risky. A few taxpayer victories would make shelters more attractive and perhaps would more than offset any increase in expected litigation costs. Finally, it might be considered unjust for the government to use litigation in this matter and that, as a normative matter, the government ought to settle cases for their expected value.

In fact it is difficult to summarize current government litigation strategy, in part because there are too few data points, in part because the strategy may be based on facts (for example, weaknesses in the factual record) that are not publicly disclosed, and in part because that strategy may be changing. As noted earlier, the government has offered to settle corporate-owned insurance cases on terms thought favorable to the taxpayers. The COLI cases are the largest single shelter cases thus far brought and the only shelter cases in which the government has an unbroken string of victories. Most of the remaining litigants have already agreed to the settlement.[24] The government has over the years offered reasonable settlement terms on most other shelter cases. On the other

23. See Bankman (2001).
24. See, generally, Sheppard (2002).

hand the government's settlement offer to taxpayers who purchased the so-called basis-shift shelters is thought to be much less generous and has thus far attracted virtually no takers.[25] No basis-shift cases are yet in the trial stage, however, and it seems likely that most of these cases will settle before trial, either because of a new settlement offer or government victories in early litigation. In general the record thus far does not show the government using litigation as a significant weapon; a taxpayer can reasonably expect to settle a shelter case for its expected value.

Some of the same factors that lead the government to settle cases also lead it to drop penalties. Literal interpretivism gives taxpayers a reasonable chance of winning most shelter cases. Insisting upon penalties in a case in which the taxpayer may be proven right in court may seem unjust. A court that rules in favor of the government on the merits of a shelter might nonetheless find the issue too close to sustain penalties. Penalties increase the odds of litigation and raise the costs described above. Perhaps, for these reasons, the government has generally waived penalties for taxpayers who settle cases. Penalties might still play an important role in the cost-benefit calculation if they were high enough. In fact the highest penalty thought to apply to a typical shelter is 20 percent.[26]

The government could affect the cost-benefit calculus in a quite different manner by deciding to accept, rather than challenge, the tax treatment claimed through a particular tax product or shelter. The government might agree with a literal interpretation of a given rule; it might also feel that, as a normative matter, any interpretation that is more likely than not to be upheld in court ought to be accepted in whole and not just settled for an expected value. While this response is not typical, it has occurred and must be factored into an ex ante calculus.[27]

Finally the government might push for strong substantive or penalty-related legislation that would affect the cost-benefit calculus for future purchasers. In fact the Treasury Department in the Bush administration has opposed most legislation thus far proposed, including legislation drawn up by members of its own party.[28]

Where does all this leave the prospective shelter purchaser? If a shelter leaves the taxpayer with 85 percent of the tax benefit net of fixed costs, and there is an

25. Sheppard (2002).

26. See Bankman (1999a, pp. 1,791–92).

27. See Rev. Rule 2002-31, I.R.B. 2002-22. Issuers of contingent convertible debt may deduct interest at the rate applicable to issuers of noncontingent convertible debt. This effectively ignores the value of the option embedded in the debt and overstates interest deductions.

28. In a confirmation hearing in August 2002, Assistant Secretary of the Treasury Pamela Olson stated that she did not support the proposal offered by Republican Representative Thomas to codify the standard version of the economic substance doctrine. The Treasury has not offered legislation on its own and has not supported legislation primarily associated with Democratic representatives.

85 percent chance of detection, then, focusing only on easily monetized costs, a shelter offers a positive return so long as it has any chance of winning in court. In fact shelters can and do win in court. Litigation costs and penalties reduce the expected return but can generally be avoided through settlement. The possibility that a shelter will be detected on audit but not challenged by the IRS (in which case it will be thought of ex post as merely a tax-structured transaction) increases the expected return. Of course the parameters of the various cost factors will change over time, and the above estimates are just that. Some shelters will be more likely than others to escape audit or government challenge if uncovered on audit, or succeed in court. Shelters that share any of these three characteristics are apt to be attractive purchases.

Hard-to-Quantify Shelter Costs

If the financial cost-benefit calculus of shelters looks so good, why is everyone not doing them? Part of the answer, of course, is that lots of taxpayers are. Other taxpayers eschew shelters because they are risk-averse, because of nonfinancial costs (such as bad publicity), or because the shelters are inconsistent with their norms or the norms of their organization. The rest of the answer lies with the uncertainty created by the wave of corporate governance scandals, perhaps most closely associated with Enron.

The forces that led (in part) to the Enron fiasco bear striking parallels to the dynamics we see in the tax shelter market. What might be referred to as the corporate governance side of the Enron bankruptcy[29] had its origin in off-balance partnerships that were controlled by Enron but had a small smattering of outside investors.[30] The presence of those investors was said by Arthur Andersen—which helped structure the partnerships—to make the partnerships independent. In fact the entire purpose of the partnerships was to enable related-party transactions and hide Enron debt—in short, to allow the company to present a false income and balance sheet to investors. The use of partnerships for this purpose was inconsistent with the standard of accurate financial reporting but was not specifically prevented by any rule and was consistent with accounting practices. Structuring off-balance partnerships was part of the way in which Andersen and other national and regional accounting firms raised profits above the steady but unspectacular returns realized from providing auditing services.

---

29. Obviously, bad business decisions that led to economic loss played the largest role in Enron's decline. Enron relied on off-balance-sheet partnerships in part to hide that loss and, absent the scandal surrounding the partnerships, that loss would have greatly reduced the company's value.

30. See, for example, William C. Powers Jr., "Report of Investigation by the Special Investigation Committee of the Board of Directors of Enron Corp.," February 12, 2001. Available from jbankman@stanford.edu.

Of course, once the partnership was structured, with the assumed smattering of outside investors lending the partnerships a thin veneer of respectability, Enron promptly cut back on the number of those investors, who in any event were hard to come by. The exposure of the partnerships—and the deceit inherent in their use—contributed to the collapse of the company.

Tax shelters are also designed by accounting firms (and other intermediaries) to hide income. The legal opinions that accompany the shelters assume real business—that is, nontax—motives. The shelters are inconsistent with any standard of accurate measure of income but are not prohibited by any rule and in some cases are consistent with a narrow reading of a statute or regulation. Structuring tax shelters is a way in which accounting firms increase profits above the returns made from auditing. Once the shelters are structured, with the assumed business purpose of making the transactions appear respectable, the taxpayer often drops even the pretense of having anything but tax motives. A surprising fact in the early shelters is that taxpayers did not even create a paper record of business purpose.

The similarities between off-balance-sheet partnerships and tax shelters have not gone unnoticed by corporate America. Many companies have put off shelter purchases they would have made in the past. The Enron scandal has resurrected shelter legislation and, perhaps most important, has encouraged a new group of reporters to look into the issue.

Will the Enron debacle have a sufficient long-term effect so as to reduce the shelter problem to manageable proportions? The answer is probably not. The two phenomena may be similar in many respects but differ enormously in their victims. False financial statements impose losses on investors. Investors who hold stock directly (rather than through pension plans) feel the loss keenly. The loss is still more concentrated on those employees who find themselves without work. Moreover the loss, if not its cause, is visible to the public at large. The victims constitute a lobbying force that is formidable, though in fact somewhat unnecessarily so. Media attention has made the justice of their cause plain to the electorate at large and, one suspects, to all but the most hardened legislator. Of course, here as elsewhere, one can criticize the steps taken by our political system as both too mild and too draconian.

Shelter losses may well be of the same magnitude as losses suffered because of misleading financial statements. But the losses are not concentrated among easily identifiable victims: They are felt by borrowers, who must pay more because the government must borrow more; by taxpayers, who must sooner or later cough up more money to make up the loss; and by those who benefit from government services that, in the wake of the revenue shortfall, must be cut. The wave of public indignation necessary to move legislation or regulation on this issue has been absent. More likely, memories of Enron will fade, and the shelter market will come back strong.

The Political Economy of the Shelter War

It might be useful to close with a brief examination of the political economy of the shelter battle. What forces are arrayed on either side, and what motivates those forces? The easiest way to provide the big picture here is to contrast the fight over tax shelters with the fight over environmental policy. In each field, private parties who are disfavored by regulation make arguments against regulation. Those arguments are directed at the regulatory agency and at members of the executive and legislative branches that control that agency. This of course is quite proper, and it is also proper for those arguments to be based, to the extent possible, on something other than the loss that is to be suffered by the private party and its stakeholders. Accounting firms that sell shelters point out that antishelter legislation is imperfect and may affect a wide array of business transactions. Energy producers argue that the costs of environmentally clean energy will be borne by consumers, and that these costs may be large enough to reduce economic growth.

In the environmental field, private lobbying is offset by groups such as the Natural Resources Defense Council and the Sierra Club. In the shelter arena, however, there is no organized opposition.[31] The shelter battle, as it were, is fought on one side by a handful of academics, practicing lawyers, and journalists. The latter, in particular, can be quite effective. Janet Novack at *Forbes* has done a tremendous job ferreting out the shelter market and explaining that market to her readers; David Cay Johnston of the *New York Times* won a Pulitzer Prize, in part for his work in this area. Still, not many are taking up the challenge, and most of those who do cannot afford or do not wish to do it full time. This group is further hobbled by the complex nature of the problem; it is difficult to explain the dynamics of the shelter in a way that can be understood by a legislator, let alone by a constituent. That is one reason why there are no publicly funded groups that play a role in this battle.

What of the professions? One cannot expect representatives of the Big Four accounting firms to play a disinterested role; they are leading sellers of shelters. Smaller national and even regional accounting firms have the same conflict. Lawyers have somewhat more freedom, and some members of the private bar have done yeoman's duty in this area. However, the lawyers most in the thick of things are also conflicted. Those of us in academia who write on the issue frequently get calls from members of the bar who are willing to give the outlines of an argument, or a shelter, but who feel that they cannot take a public stand on the matter for fear of alienating clients.

---

31. The closest analog is perhaps the Citizens for Tax Justice. That organization has been influential and active across a number of issues. It has not played (and perhaps due to resource constraints could not have played) a major role in the tax shelter debate.

The imbalance here poses a bit of a dilemma for any administration wishing to make high-level appointments. Many, if not most, top lawyers and accountants have worked, directly or indirectly, for shelter promoters or taxpayers who bought shelters and needed them defended. Of course experience with industry will in some cases make one a better regulator—better in the sense that one knows when to accept the industry position as correct and in the sense that one knows how to battle industry when its position is incorrect. Moreover most appointees to high office will have previously served in government as well as in private practice. Political conviction may in some (perhaps most) cases outweigh prior experience. While in private practice, Les Samuels gave a favorable opinion on the contingent installment sales shelter, but that did not stop him, in his stint as assistant secretary of the treasury for tax policy, from vigorously pursuing shelters.

All that said, it is only natural for someone who has spent a substantial portion of his or her professional life working for one set of clients to identify with those clients. Consider, for example, the lawyer who works with an investment bank to design tax products and sees that her client, which intended to stay close to but on one side of a line, has, in the government's view, crossed that line. The government of course looks at the matter through the lenses of an imperfect and fuzzy doctrine such as economic substance. The lawyer sees the problems caused by the application of that doctrine to her client and feels her client's pain. It may be harder for the lawyer to imagine the more diffuse pain felt by borrowers, who must pay slightly higher interest, because the government must borrow more money, because her client has helped deplete the government's coffers by exploiting an unintended loophole.

Imagine a world in which a form of "tax farming" was allowed: Private firms could discover and litigate tax shelter cases and receive a share of the proceeds. The best and brightest young lawyers and accountants might go to these firms; a partner in an established tax farming firm might earn $2 million a year. Would a partner who came from one of these firms and went into high government office have a different perspective than a partner who had spent years representing the shelter promoters? It is a little like asking whether a lawyer who has spent years filing environmental suits against manufacturers is likely to have a different perspective from the lawyer who, on behalf of those manufacturers, has defended the suits.

Conclusion

Tax shelters siphon off resources from more productive ventures, redistribute the tax burden, and threaten to undermine compliance. The IRS has greatly improved its ability to detect shelters, but gains in that area may be offset by an increasing reliance on literal statutory jurisprudence. Significant gains in the shelter battle will require some combination of structural tax reform, higher penalties, or a retreat from literalist jurisprudence.

COMMENT BY
David Cay Johnston

In his chapter Joseph Bankman talks about a moral component to taxes. If you are going to talk about tax shelters, and about taxes in this country, you cannot lose sight of that moral component. You can have a police state on any issue regulating people's lives, or you can come up with regulatory mechanisms that are self-enforcing and reward good behavior. We are not doing that in this area, and Bankman's chapter addresses that.

Think about the morality of the system that we have now, where we take poor people—many of whom are poor because they were not endowed with a lot of brains—and we say to them, "You have to prove with all these records that this child was in your home. And by the way, your child's report card may not be enough," in order to get a tiny benefit from society. And then we have a regulation that says you can steal $3,499,999 a year from the U.S. government, and you do not have to tell about it, which is what a recently promulgated regulation from Treasury does in the tax shelter field. What is wrong with that picture? Did any of you go to Sunday School or Hebrew School? It is morally bankrupt to be doing that. It is an outrage.

In a world in which you can legally buy an ounce of pharmaceutically pure cocaine, if you are a dentist, for $40, and then illegally cut it and sell it for $10,000, we have shown, after twenty years of law enforcement, that you cannot stop it with law enforcement. That is not the way to get at it. In a world in which somebody can dream up a tax shelter (I have asked several lawyers how much time and money they think it takes to dream one up, and the most expensive was $100,000) and can make millions of dollars in fees off that shelter, I do not think a law enforcement approach is necessarily what is going to work. The incentives are too high, particularly when your risk of being put in a cage is zero. You have a mathematical calculus that says, "Go ahead and do it." So what are other ways to get at this problem?

We need to look at the issue of tolerance. For all the talk of law and order in America, it is astonishing how tolerant Washington is about lawbreaking when it comes to taxes. You can steal $3,499,999 a year under the policies of this government, and you do not have to tell anybody about it. One of the ways to deal with this liberal attitude toward lawbreakers is to put public disclosure to work. The cheapest disinfectant ever invented is the public spotlight. We should be talking about making corporate tax returns public. Not many people would read them, but we should think about the cost of it. What would we give up, in terms of people's competitive advantage?

We already have a lot of shareholder disclosure. Maybe we need some limited tax disclosure. Maybe we need to have a matrix in the footnotes of the financial statements of corporations—where I spend a great deal of my time—that asks for "income as reported to you" and "income as reported to Uncle Sam," "taxes as reported to you" and "taxes as reported to Uncle Sam." "Every item contributing 10 percent or more, here it is." That could effectively shut down morally indefensible tax shelters.

The cable television industry has never reported a profit and keeps generating higher and higher stock prices. They have trained all their investors to pay attention to cash flow, so they do not have any profits. Despite the possibility that Wall Street may change the way it measures companies, maybe we should think about making shareholder accounting the same as taxpayer accounting. Then, over the 100-year, 50-year, 15-year, or 2-year life of a corporation, we should get some semblance of reality. If we want to use the tax code to encourage investments in physical capital or human capital, we could make those explicit items.

Years ago there was a picture in *Fortune* magazine of the chief tax officer of Chrysler standing next to the company's tax return for that year. It was chest-high. Of course *Fortune* was saying, "Oh, the terrible regulatory burden of complying with the federal tax code." I looked at the picture and said, "They probably made more money off that pile of paper than building Plymouths."

When I interviewed John Trani, the head of Stanley Works, about their plan to go to Bermuda, he confirmed that there was no one thing he could do to raise his company's shareholder value, increase his bonuses, or make his company healthier, than to get rid of taxes. There was nothing else in the same league. There were lots of little things he could do to make the company more efficient, but that would be a lot of hard work over a long period of time, entailing a lot of thought and risk. Instead he said, "Hey, we can just stop paying taxes. We'll get a mail drop in Bermuda."

Bankman's point that the moral component is important should permeate how we treat the professions. We hold accountants to a different standard than we do lawyers, and not by accident. The accounting profession is in the forefront of tax shelters, not the legal profession.

I asked the head of PricewaterhouseCoopers at a lunch one day, "What if we eliminated all your consulting businesses and said you could only be in the accounting business?" He said, "We couldn't survive. We couldn't make enough money." I said, "Excuse me, I went to the Chicago School of Economics. That can't be true. Prices would rise to justify the need for that service, particularly since government mandates it." "We wouldn't want to be in that business," was his answer. That is the real truth of the matter.

We need to think about the way the regulatory scheme encourages misconduct, allowing firms to both sell tax shelters and then pass on the buyer's books. That is a system that, by its very nature, is corrupt.

We will never solve this problem. For a period in my life I covered police red squads, particularly the Los Angeles squad. They had officers undercover all over the world—Moscow, Havana. Chief Daryl Gates assigned at least one officer (one I was able to prove, although I knew there were many others) to sleep with a woman to get information out of her. People's homes and cars were burglarized; mine were burglarized. Nobody was arrested, no crimes found, it was just a political spying operation. Finally the city council acted, the courts acted, and I remember one of the leading activists turned to me and said, "Well, finally, we've solved that problem." And I said, "No, we haven't. The police need to have a spying operation to keep us protected. All we have done is remove some of the excesses. The issue goes on the back burner. If we're going to live in a free society, the problem will be here 10,000 years from now."

The problem of cheating on taxes will never go away. The issue is do we encourage it or do we discourage it? Do we do have a system that enforces compliance efficiently and effectively? Self-policing mechanisms work better than a police state. You have to have enough cops to do the job, but you do not need one for each tax return if the design of the system encourages honest tax returns.

IRS Commissioner Charles O. Rossotti has produced a report that Congress requires for the oversight board, and it lists all the people they are letting off who are known tax cheats. Eighty percent of people with offshore accounts, whom they have already identified, will be let go. They are not going to collect from them. Imagine what would happen if you picked up the paper tomorrow morning and read, "The FBI says we have to let 80 percent of the bank robbers go because we lack funds to pursue them."

Ronald Reagan said, "The most important idea in the history of the world is the United States of America." Why do we not treat stealing from the United States through tax cheating the same as selling drugs? The same as cheating people in the stock market? The same as cheating people in their employment? Stealing is wrong. If we do not think about it in those terms, then people are going to do what they should not do. Our tax enforcement system needs to be designed to minimize cheating. It should follow the algebra.

COMMENT BY

David A. Weisbach

I agree with almost everything Joseph Bankman says. He has been the leading researcher in uncovering the extent of the tax shelter market and its details. Due in part to this research, tax shelters have become one of the most important business tax issues over the past several years. In his chapter Bankman summarizes and updates much of his prior work. His comments on the market for tax shelters, the incentives on the various parties, and the social context in which this takes place are particularly worth noting.

I would like to further explore two aspects of his discussion. First is the effects of tax shelters. Bankman largely focuses on the compliance effects, arguing that sheltering by some taxpayers reduces compliance by others. I would like to analyze more closely the efficiency effects of shelters and attempts to limit shelters, because I think they are far from obvious. Second, Bankman discusses the use of the economic substance doctrine and other vague overlays to our system of rules, arguing that they are inevitable. I would like to explore why such a system, one of rules with a vague overlay of standards, is desirable.

Begin with efficiency. To add some context, consider the facts of the *Knetsch* case, a Supreme Court decision from 1960.[1] The taxpayer in that case borrowed $4 million from a life insurance company at a 3.5 percent interest rate. He then invested this money, with the same company, in deferred annuity bonds that offered only a 2.5 percent return. He thereby arranged to earn about $100,000 per year, at a cost of about $140,000 per year. The catch was that interest on the borrowing was immediately deductible, but earnings on the annuity were deferred. Tax rates at the time were more than 90 percent, which meant that even though the deal was a money loser absent taxes, it was extremely profitable once taxes were taken into account. The transaction recalls the quote attributed to Michael Graetz that a tax shelter is a deal done by very smart people that, absent tax considerations, would be very stupid. The Supreme Court disallowed the interest deductions.

What is interesting about the case is not the perhaps unsurprising Supreme Court decision but the fact that it is hard to identify the efficiency losses from the transaction. The reason the Supreme Court disallowed the tax benefits was that nothing happened. Money merely went around in a circle. But if nothing happened, no resources were misallocated. There may be some wasted transactions costs, but if the Supreme Court had not stepped in, these would quickly have been bid down to a low amount. In a perfect shelter, like the shelter in *Knetsch*, there are no apparent efficiency losses!

Most people respond that there are efficiency losses because there is a reduction in tax receipts as a result of the shelter. The efficiency loss from *Knetsch*-type transactions would, under this argument, be the deadweight loss from replacing the lost revenue via some other source. But this cannot be right and, in fact, may significantly overstate the problem. There are not one but two sources we can

---

1. *Knetsch v. United States*, 364 U.S. 361 (1960).

use to replace the lost revenue. We can, as noted, use some other replacement source that has a low cost of funds, but we can also attempt to limit the shelter directly and raise revenue that way. We should choose whichever is cheaper. Therefore, the deadweight loss from replacing the lost revenue via another source is a cap on the size of the deadweight loss from shelters, but the loss could easily be much less. To understand the effects of shelters, we need to look directly at the efficiency effects of trying to shut them down. That is, we must compute a marginal cost of funds for decisions like *Knetsch* and the economic substance doctrine.

The way that I propose to think about attacks on shelters is as expansions of the tax base. The story might be something like the following. The tax base cannot be perfectly specified, perhaps because the economy is complex, and there are limits to our ability to describe the tax base to cover all possible situations that might occur in such an economy. Given this imperfect specification, there will be gaps—transactions that are not taxed. Some of these gaps can be viewed as shelters (such as the transaction in *Knetsch*), some perhaps might be intentional (such as subsidies for behaving in socially desirable ways), and some might be viewed as inevitable gaps that we simply choose to tolerate (such as the failure to tax imputed rent).

Suppose we decide to address a given shelter. We can do so through vague doctrines such as the economic substance or business purpose doctrines or through a change in the rules that normally govern the tax base. In *Knetsch* both were done. The Supreme Court disallowed the deductions based on a vague interpretive doctrine, and Congress also changed the tax rules on a going-forward basis to deny deductions from this sort of transaction. I will discuss the trade-off between these approaches below. For purposes here, it does not matter which is chosen. No matter which route is taken, however, I will assume that the tax base remains imperfectly specified, and that other shelters or tax avoidance opportunities remain.

Suppose we deny the tax benefits of a *Knetsch*-type transaction. Think of it as a marginal increase in the strength of our response to tax shelters. The particular transaction in *Knetsch* will immediately disappear—absent taxes, the transaction loses money with certainty, so nobody will do it once the tax benefits are removed. If the transaction were consumption or savings, we might be concerned by this high elasticity, but in this case the transaction is solely a product of the tax system, and its disappearance does not, in and of itself, cause efficiency losses.

While we need not worry about the disappearance of the *Knetsch* transaction, we can isolate two effects that do matter. The first is that some people who previously sheltered income will decide that the increased cost of sheltering (their first-choice shelter has been eliminated, so their next choice must be more expensive) is not worth it. On the margin, those who shift away from sheltering are not worse off. Prior to the change in tax rules, they were indifferent between sheltering an additional dollar and paying an additional dollar in tax (perhaps because the cost of the shelter was a dollar). After the tax law change, they now pay that dollar to the government, rather than as a tax shelter expense. While the taxpayer is indifferent, society is better off, because the dollar that previously went toward unproductive tax sheltering is now raised in taxes.

The second effect is that some individuals will choose to continue sheltering. These inframarginal individuals will shift to a more expensive shelter, but the additional cost will be worth the tax savings. These individuals are worse off because of the tax law change—they now pay more to shelter income—but society is not better off, because they continue to shelter. I have previously called this effect on inframarginal taxpayers the distortionary effect.[2] The idea is that the shelters that remain become worse when we increase the strength of our attacks on shelters. For example, taxpayers might engage in *Knetsch*-type transactions but not have the money go in an instantaneous circle. They might, for example, inject some otherwise undesirable risk into the transaction.

The overall effect of addressing shelters is the sum of these two effects. We raise a dollar from the marginal taxpayer at the efficiency cost imposed on the inframarginal taxpayers. One way to think about it is that increasing attacks on shelters reduces sheltering but makes those that remain worse.

The analysis has not yet mentioned administrative and compliance costs, because these are not traditionally considered part of efficiency. Nevertheless they are central to analyzing shelters. Suppose we considered efficiency without administrative costs. The logic given above would argue for the strongest possible attack on shelters. The reason why is that, as we increase the strength of the attack on shelters, there are fewer and fewer inframarginal taxpayers. At the extreme, a single taxpayer would be left sheltering. The marginal cost of funds would correspondingly decrease. Administrative and compliance costs are what keep us from getting to this position. As attacks on shelters get stronger, the tax system becomes more complex or more vague, and administrative costs go up. We cannot indefinitely increase the attacks on shelters, because the administrative and compliance costs get too high. We want to set the strength of antishelter rules so that, on the margin, the combined efficiency and administrative costs are equal to the costs of other funds.[3]

Bankman points to some additional effects of shelters that must be considered. He focuses in particular on the compliance effects. His argument is that we should think of shelters as having a multiplier effect. Allowing shelters by some taxpayers reduces compliance by others, and reducing shelters by some taxpayers

---

2. See Weisbach (2002).

3. Note the parallel between the logic here and the more general case of expansion of the tax base when there are administrative costs. See Yitzhaki (1979).

correspondingly increases compliance by others. There might be many reasons for this. One could argue that this effect occurs because of norms about paying tax. Alternatively one could argue that allowing a broad market in shelters reduces their costs—there are economies of scale in creating shelters. Whatever the mechanism, Bankman is right that some effect of this sort seems likely. One way to think of this is that paying taxes has something akin to a positive externality—it causes others to pay more as well. If we take this externality into account, we would want to increase our attacks on shelters beyond that considered in the above analysis.

Given this analysis, let me venture some empirical hunches. I would guess that significantly stronger attacks on shelters are efficient. For example, we could greatly increase the strength of the business purpose doctrine, requiring maybe an overwhelmingly dominant business purpose for entire transactions and each and every step in a transaction. The intuition behind this idea is that we need to compare the inframarginal effect (the shelters that remain becoming worse) with the marginal effect (the reduction in shelters). I think that with a strong attack on shelters, there would be few inframarginal taxpayers. Most would give up. The reason is the sense, only anecdotal but I think shared among many tax practitioners, that taxpayers have a low tolerance for actually changing their real business operations to shelter taxes. They are willing to engage in "nothing" transactions but not transactions that impose real costs on their business. There also might be a strong compliance effect—reduction in sheltering by some might reduce sheltering by others.

Note that this is somewhat contrary to Bankman's analysis of the incentives on taxpayers to engage in shelters. He shows that, absent high rates of detection and high chances of the taxpayer losing, it makes sense to engage in tax shelters. Indeed, absent penalties that are orders of magnitude greater than those found in current law, rational taxpayers should engage in far more sheltering than we see under present law. It is not easy to explain why we do not see more sheltering, but the sense I get from practitioners is that businesses are happy to purchase shelters if nothing real has to change, but that they are reluctant to rearrange their real businesses to shelter income. Bankman similarly argues that there must be hard-to-quantify shelter costs, such as fallout from Enron and similar corporate scandals. My view is that the hidden costs of shelters to businesses go up quickly as more business purpose and more economic substance are required, which means that the economic substance and business purpose doctrine have real power.

A proposal of this sort would increase administrative and compliance costs, because it would make the law much more uncertain. The most difficult issue would be the treatment of tax provisions whose purpose is to change behavior. Many of these would be easy. Explicit subsidies could be identified and exempted from the rule. For example, taxpayers could be allowed to buy low-income housing, subject to the low-income housing tax credit, even if doing so made no sense absent taxes. But in many cases the issue would be tricky, because the tax law contains a subtle blend of ordinary rules and either subsidies or provisions designed to minimize the impact of the rules. For example, we would have to determine whether the rules providing nontaxation of gain on certain corporate mergers or acquisitions are designed to encourage behavior, and whether and when taxpayers should be allowed to structure into these rules without a business purpose. I do not think most of these issues are insurmountable and, once some baselines were established, the law would be relatively clear. If the proposal would increase administrative costs too much, it might not be worth the benefits, but my intuition is that the increase in administrative costs would not be that high. Taxpayers know when a transaction has a real and substantial business purpose and when it does not, which means that the basic information to apply such a proposal is already at hand.

Now to turn to the second question: Why are vague doctrines like the economic substance doctrine desirable? The short answer, as articulated by Stanley Surrey years ago, is that vague standards "save the tax system from the far greater proliferation of detail that would be necessary if the tax avoider could succeed merely by bringing his scheme within the literal language of substantive provisions written to govern the everyday world."[4] That is, even though standards are vague and uncertain, it is cheaper to use standards than to respond to the problem of shelters through ever more detailed rules.

More specifically we can think of the problem as concerning the mix of rules and standards in the tax system. We can think of rules as laws that are promulgated before individuals act. They are the everyday tax law: If you earn $x, you owe $y in tax; if you sell property, you pay tax on the gain, and so on. The advantage of rules is that they are relatively cheap to promulgate and for individuals to learn. Although there are a large number of them, and their interactions are complex, in essence one need only look them up. Standards are laws that are given detailed content only after individuals act. "Drive safely" is a standard, because the exact meaning is given content only after you have been pulled over and given a ticket. The economic substance and business purpose doctrines are standards; we have a vague sense of what they mean but do not know exactly how they apply to any given case until there is a final determination by a court.

The question is why a detailed system of rules, such as the tax system, should have an overlay of standards. The reason, as Surrey indicated, is complexity. Suppose we are promulgating a system of rules to govern some area of the law. It is most likely desirable to write rules covering everyday situations;

4. Surrey (1969).

the promulgation costs would be worth the benefit of clear rules. The promulgation costs might no longer be worth the benefit, however, for highly unusual situations. There are thousands or millions of transactions that could potentially happen in the future. Anticipating all these transactions and promulgating rules to govern them would be extremely costly and the benefit small, because many will never occur, and others will occur only rarely. Because they are so unusual, if the law does not treat these transactions properly, there is likely to be only a small cost to pay.

While this strategy might be appropriate for some areas of the law, it does not work in the tax system. If a rare transaction is mistaxed, taxpayers have an incentive to find it and exploit it. It will cease to be rare as the tax benefits are understood. *Knetsch* is probably like this; nobody anticipated borrowing to buy an annuity. The rules for borrowing and the rules for annuities probably seemed, at the time, perfectly sensible. The rare transaction of combining the two was terribly mistaxed, but when discovered, could have become common.

We want to respond to this problem of unanticipated transactions in the cheapest way possible. One way is to spend more resources developing rules that are more precise and that govern a greater number of potential transactions. This approach is likely to be expensive. It is hard to anticipate all future transactions and to draft rules accordingly. In addition, at some point the strategy becomes self-defeating. As more and more rules are promulgated, there are more interactions among the rules (with interactions rising more than proportionately with the number of rules). These interactions will inevitably lead to mistaxed transactions, and the process reiterates.

Standards, however, allow one to deal with unanticipated transactions only as they arise, because one only needs to determine exactly how the law should treat a given transaction after the fact. Thus, if there are 1,000 possible future transactions and only five occur, we only need to invest resources to determine how to treat the five that actually do occur, if we use standards. If we use rules, we would have to anticipate all 1,000, because getting any of them wrong would create a tax shelter opportunity. With rules, rare mistaxed transactions become common as they are exploited. With standards, rare transactions stay that way. This means that standards are likely to be much cheaper than rules in responding to the problem of tax planning. Thus a system of rules to govern everyday transactions, with an overlay of standards to prevent the mistaxation inherent in this system of rules from being exploited, is not only inevitable but also desirable.

Bankman, in this volume as well in as in prior work, has criticized the economic substance doctrine and similar doctrines for being incoherent, although he agrees that they are inevitable. I think each of his arguments is sound, but the core of the criticism misses the mark. He attempts to articulate the doctrines much as if they were rules and then criticizes this articulation. There is nothing wrong with his articulation of the rules and of the logical dilemmas they create.

The virtue of vague standards, however, lies in the very fact that they are not given content except when applied to particular facts. They may not be capable of rational articulation ex ante, but this is not a flaw; it is their key feature.

References

Bankman, Joseph. 1999a. "Bankman Examines the New Market in Corporate Tax Shelters." *Tax Notes* 83: 1775–95.

———. 1999b. "Bankman Asks Kies to Back Up His Assertions with Facts." *Tax Notes* 83: 1813.

———. 2001. "The Business Purpose Doctrine and the Sociology of Tax." *S.M.U. Law Review* 54 (1) 149–57.

Desai, Mihir A. 2002. "The Corporate Profit Base, Tax Sheltering Activity, and the Changing Nature of Employee Compensation." Working Paper 8866. Cambridge, Mass.: National Bureau of Economic Research (March).

Kies, Kenneth. 1999. "A Critical Look at the Administration's 'Corporate Tax Shelter' Proposals." *Tax Notes* 83: 1463–85.

Manzon, Gil, and George Plesko. 2002. "The Relation between Financial and Tax Reporting Measures of Income." *Tax Law Review* 55 (2): 175–214 .

Nijenhuis, Rika, David Chung, and Maxim Kulikov. 2002. "The New Disclosure and Listing Requirements for Tax Shelters." *Tax Notes* 97: 943–58.

Rossotti, Charles O. 2002. "Report to the IRS Oversight Board. Assessment of the IRS and the Tax System." *Tax Notes Today* 2002: 186–17.

Sheppard, L. 2002. "Where Are We Going with Tax Shelter Settlements?" *Tax Notes* 97: 417–21.

Surrey, Stanley S. 1969. "Complexity and the Internal Revenue Code: The Problem of the Management of Tax Detail." *Journal of Law and Contemporary Problems* 34 (4): 673–710.

Weisbach, David. 2002. "An Economic Analysis of Anti-Tax Avoidance Doctrines." *American Law and Economics Review* 4 (1): 88–115.

U.S. Internal Revenue Service. 2002. Bulletin 2002-43. Government Printing Office.

Yitzhaki, Shlomo. 1979. "A Note on Optimal Taxation and Administrative Costs." *American Economic Review* 69 (3): 475–80.

3

DAVID R. TILLINGHAST

Issues of International Tax Enforcement

T HE NUMBER OF challenges facing the Internal Revenue Service in administering and enforcing compliance with the international provisions of the
U.S. tax law is indeed prodigious, and there is no feasible way of commenting
on them all. The range of compliance issues stretches from dealing with money
laundering through simple nonreporting by U.S. citizens living overseas to enormously complicated audits of multinational groups. Criminal types are not, of
course, cooperative, nonreporters are hard to find, and the multinationals, even
when compliant or relatively so, present a daunting range of issues of both legal
and factual complexity.

There is considerable scope for simplifying the international aspects of the
tax law, and this would clearly make the IRS's job easier. Some of the fixes are
probably politically impossible, however, and others are simply unlikely to
engage Congress's attention.

Limitations on the IRS's ability to obtain information from overseas presents
a major problem. This is being addressed at least marginally through expansion
of the network of tax treaties and exchange of information agreements, but how
successful this program will be remains to be seen. The war on terrorism has
coincidentally expanded the IRS's legal basis for demanding information in
criminal cases, but these measures are probably not helpful in the broad range
of civil enforcement.

The author wishes to thank his colleagues William Garofalo and David Balaban for their helpful assistance in the preparation of this chapter.

Clearly the IRS is understaffed in the international area, as in other areas. This is an endemic condition not readily remedied. Even with an increase in funding, the IRS would require a long time to build the capability that it needs in this area.

Limited Access to Information

Certainly the largest single source of difficulty in administering the international aspects of the U.S. tax law is that a large part of the information the IRS needs is not directly available to it, by reason of jurisdictional limitations. There are many facets to this problem.

Lack of Withholding or Information Returns

In a broad range of cases the IRS cannot require foreign persons to withhold U.S. tax or to provide it with information. It has had considerable success (at immense effort) in inducing foreign financial institutions to "volunteer" to act as withholding agents with respect to U.S.-source investment income. Moreover, it considers any foreign person making payments of U.S.-source income to be a statutory withholding agent. It has no practical way to enforce this obligation, however, and few foreign persons (who are not engaged in business in the United States) comply. If the payment is something other than U.S.-source income subject to U.S. withholding tax, the IRS has no basis for requiring compliance. Among other things, this makes it impossible in a broad range of cases to run the kind of computer matching programs that the IRS uses in a domestic context.

Identifying Persons outside the United States Required to File Returns

Several categories of persons located outside the United States may be required to file U.S. tax returns and to pay tax. These include U.S. citizens resident abroad, who are subject to U.S. tax on their worldwide income; foreign persons who are deemed to be fully taxable U.S. residents, often only because they have "green cards" entitling them to permanent residence; and foreign entities or individuals deriving income effectively connected with a U.S. trade or business.[1]

It is at least relatively difficult for the IRS to identify these persons. For example, it is my understanding that the IRS does not systematically cross-check green cards or passports against filed returns to find persons outside the United

1. Treasury Regulations, sec. 1.6012-1(a) and (b).

States who are not filing. The principal tool it has available is to threaten to penalize those who fail to comply. A full range of civil and criminal penalties apply to U.S. citizens or residents who fail to file returns. An Internal Revenue Code (IRC) provision requires foreign persons to file an information return disclosing the fact that they have relied upon an applicable tax treaty to exempt them from tax for which they would otherwise have been liable under the IRC (for example, a green-card holder who claims the benefit of a treaty "tie-breaker" residence provision or a business that might not have a permanent establishment in the United States, even though it would be considered engaged in trade or business here).[2] The penalty for failure to comply with this rule is modest, however, and although numerous filings are in fact made, compliance is surely less than 100 percent.

A more draconian penalty denies foreign persons who fail to file a required return any deductions in computing income subject to U.S. tax.[3] In many cases, obviously, the impact of this is devastating: Imposing the U.S. tax on gross income produces a liability well in excess of profit, in the case of most types of business income (and in some cases, as where there are losses, investment income as well). The IRS has attempted to mitigate the severity of this rule by permitting foreign persons to avoid penalty by filing protective returns, returns that report no taxable income but alert the IRS to the possibility that an issue of taxability exists. Tax advisers differ on the merits of making such a filing, and many foreign taxpayers simply refuse to do it, on the simple ground that they do not want to be "in the IRS computer." There is no statistical evidence, but anecdotal evidence suggests that the IRS pays little if any attention to these filings.

Foreign Law Limitations on Disclosure

Of critical importance in this context are the restrictions imposed under foreign law on the disclosure of information that the IRS requires. The specter of bank secrecy laws looms large, and other restrictions apply in many countries. In many cases, therefore, even if the IRS has someone to whom it can issue a summons, necessary information is unavailable.

The Need to Work with Foreign Tax Authorities

Many of the international issues facing the IRS can be appropriately resolved only with the cooperation of its foreign counterparts. Examples include obtain-

---

2. Internal Revenue Code of 1986 (hereafter I.R.C.), sec. 6114.
3. I.R.C., secs. 874(a), 882(c).

ing information under the exchange-of-information provisions of tax treaties, the conclusion of bilateral advance-pricing agreements, and implementing the mutual agreement procedure provided for in most tax treaties. As might be expected, the help that the IRS gets tends to be spotty. In some countries the administration is not very responsive. Even in countries that have relatively efficient administrations, getting results may not be easy.

Exchange of Information

A U.S. income tax treaty typically grants the IRS the right to request its foreign counterpart to provide information that is either in its possession or obtainable by it when the information is needed to enable the IRS to enforce the U.S. tax law. (The IRS, of course, undertakes a reciprocal obligation.) Under these treaty provisions, a number of countries engage in what are called automatic information exchanges. These typically consist of information concerning investment income items paid to U.S. persons, derived from the foreign country's withholding tax records. Given the vast number of transactions involved, this can be accomplished only by furnishing computerized data. The IRS has experienced some difficulties here, since its computer systems have turned out to be incompatible with those (largely European) systems that generate the data. It is in the process of ironing this out. The process would work far better if taxpayers were assigned universally applicable identification numbers, but this concept has so far fallen on deaf ears.

Beyond automatic information exchanges, the IRS can request a foreign tax authority to provide information relevant to a specific audit. In practice this can be done only in a limited number of cases. While many countries, like the United States, try to comply with this obligation in good faith, available resources are limited, and taxpayers typically resist these efforts forcefully.

In some rare instances treaty partners offer what are known as spontaneous exchanges of information. These occur when the tax administration, in the course of an examination, uncovers facts that suggest that a U.S. tax issue is present. For example, it might be discovered that a transaction that has been characterized one way in the foreign country has been characterized in a different way in the United States. This of course does not always mean that the characterization is not correct under U.S. law, but the foreign administrator may want to check.

Exchange-of-Information Agreements

In recent years the United States has, in theory at least, expanded its ability to secure information from the governments of countries with which the United

States does not have tax treaties, notably several tax haven countries, by concluding a number of executive agreements calling for the exchange of information necessary for the administration of the tax laws. The Organization for Economic Cooperation and Development (OECD) has promulgated a model information exchange agreement similar to the tax information exchange agreements negotiated by the United States. Many of the countries that have signed these agreements are tax haven countries, through which the IRS suspects large money laundering and other illegal transactions are conducted. Agreements with the United States have been signed by Antigua and Barbuda, the Bahamas, the British Virgin Islands, the Cayman Islands, Guernsey, and the Netherlands Antilles, with more agreements on the way. Most of the agreements do not go into effect, however, until 2004 at the earliest.

There are both legal and practical impediments to the use of these agreements, and it is too early to tell how successfully the IRS can overcome these. Typically the IRS must provide the identity of the taxpayer under investigation and reasonable grounds for believing that the information requested is obtainable and relevant to a tax inquiry. The IRS also must establish that it has exhausted all means available to obtain the information in its own territory. (As discussed below, however, if the IRS already knows that a U.S. citizen or resident has a tax haven bank account, it can demand the information directly from the taxpayer and have the taxpayer incarcerated for contempt by court order if the records are not provided.)

Thus the tax haven exchange-of-information agreements may not yield much information. The tax havens have to provide information only when the United States already knows who the taxpayer is and has a pretty good idea of what the taxpayer is up to. There is no equivalent of a John Doe summons, by means of which the United States could engage in a fishing expedition for tax evaders it has not identified. Furthermore the agreements give the tax haven countries plenty of questions to raise if they are reluctant to hand over information in any particular case. Despite these limitations, there is little question that the tax haven agreements are a big step forward and will prove useful to the IRS. If nothing else, the information exchange agreements may scare some taxpayers away from these tax havens.

There may be a number of reasons why a country would sign such an agreement. A major factor inducing some to do so is the unfair tax competition initiative of the Committee on Fiscal Affairs of the OECD, which in effect blacklists countries that maintain secrecy laws or otherwise impede efforts to seek out tax evaders. To date, most tax havens have agreed to comply with the OECD initiative at some point in the future. Only seven holdouts remain at this juncture (Andorra, Liechtenstein, Liberia, Monaco, the Marshall Islands, Nauru, and Vanuatu). The OECD program does not require action to be taken until

December 31, 2005, however, and it is quite possible that some tax havens may yet back out if they perceive that the ultimate OECD sanctions will not be severe. Furthermore the OECD must also clean its own house, particularly dealing with restrictive disclosure rules in Switzerland and Luxembourg.

Advance-Pricing Agreements

In an effort to ease the enormous administrative burden of policing cross-border transfer pricing, the IRS has created the advance-pricing agreement (APA) procedure.[4] This program seeks to reduce the IRS's audit and litigation load by inducing taxpayers to reach agreement with the IRS in advance on transfer prices to be used in its dealings with related persons. (Some agreements cover past years as well.) While concluding an advance-pricing agreement is hardly effortless, it requires a commitment of resources far smaller than those consumed in transfer-pricing audits and litigation, which can be gargantuan. Most observers would say that the APA program has been a great success. In both 2000 and 2001 approximately sixty APAs and twenty renewals of APAs were concluded. While this is surely a small percentage of the total number of transfer-pricing cases out there, these APAs typically involved large corporations and immense revenues. Moreover the APA staff has a reputation for being among the smartest and most effective in the IRS; it seems unlikely that the IRS is giving away anything by settling these cases in advance.

The IRS will enter into a unilateral agreement—that is, an agreement between the IRS and the taxpayer alone—but in most cases the taxpayer is interested in reaching agreement not only with the IRS but also with one or more foreign countries, to assure consistency and avoid economic double taxation. A large number of the leading trade partners of the United States have embraced the advance-pricing agreement concept, but obviously bringing another government (or governments) into the picture complicates the process considerably. Here again, results vary. In addition to differences in administrative efficiency, some countries find it more difficult than others to reach acceptable compromises when their transfer-pricing ideas differ from U.S. transfer-pricing concepts.

Mutual-Agreement Procedure

United States income tax treaties typically contain a provision directing the so-called competent authorities (the IRS and its foreign counterparts) to consult together to attempt to resolve disputes or difficulties arising in the application

---

4. See Rev. Proc. 96-53, 1996-2 C.B. 375 (describing the APA procedure).

or interpretation of the treaty. The principal use of this authority is to resolve particular differences on a case-by-case basis at the request of taxpayers seeking relief from economic double taxation—for example, cases in which the two countries have made inconsistent transfer-pricing determinations. In addition the competent authorities are authorized to consult each other to resolve in a more general way any difficulties that arise in the application of the treaty. Here the IRS acts in the atypical role of assisting taxpayers to avoid improper taxation, double taxation, or both, rather than enforcing compliance with U.S. law. It is, however, a function that is important in avoiding tax impediments to foreign investment and trade, and the IRS appropriately devotes substantial resources to it.

These activities obviously involve the IRS in extensive dealings with foreign tax authorities. While the IRS has made substantial progress in speeding the resolution of disputes falling under the mutual-agreement procedure, cases often drag on for years and some are never resolved. One practitioner cited a proceeding that had been pending for more than ten years, and taxpayers sometimes simply give up and withdraw their application for assistance.

It is clear that the IRS is not the principal cause of this problem. While it obviously has its own inefficiencies, most practitioners would lay principal blame for inadequacies in the process on foreign governments, some of which are notoriously unresponsive and inflexible in their approach to solving the double-taxation problems presented.

Complexity

The law relating to the taxation of international income is indeed complex. The reasons for this are many.

The Code

In the first place the international provisions of the Internal Revenue Code itself are complex, in many aspects needlessly so.

Foreign Law and Treaties

In administering the law, the Internal Revenue Service unavoidably has to apply not only the IRC but also the many income tax treaties that the United States has signed (which are standardized to a large extent but always different in some respects). Moreover it is frequently necessary to understand applicable foreign law in order to apply U.S. law, for example in the determination of the foreign tax credit.

Proliferation of Entities

The nature of international business and investment transactions assures an almost infinite proliferation of foreign entities. Not every U.S. corporation may have the 186 Cayman affiliates that Enron is said to have created, but this is only a question of degree. It is commonplace to form separate subsidiaries or joint ventures to operate in individual foreign countries and often to house distinct business functions in the same country. Different ventures may involve different partners or participants, and each of these must be kept separate. In recent years many multinationals have acquired other multinational groups, often producing redundant groups of entities in many countries. Even passing the cases in which proliferation is intended to obfuscate, therefore, the number of entities that may be relevant to an international tax examination may be huge.

Entity Tiering

A related complication that the IRS faces is the phenomenon of tiering—that is, creating structures in which a directly held foreign entity in turn owns another or others, which may in turn own another or others, and so forth. The foreign tax credit rules follow corporate chains down as many as six tiers, and some structures may go deeper than that. This may require the IRS to undertake the arduous task of poring though each of the tiered entities in order to find out what it needs to know about a lower-tier entity. To take a simple example, special U.S. tax consequences flow if a U.S. person is a shareholder (even a portfolio investor) in a foreign corporation that is a passive foreign investment corporation, or PFIC. But the U.S. investor may invest directly in a corporation that is not itself a PFIC but owns an interest in a lower-tier corporation that is a PFIC. In this case the rules require a "look-through" to apply the PFIC tax regime to the U.S. shareholder.[5] This is not necessarily different from what happens domestically, but the work gets harder when the tiers of corporations cross national boundaries or consist of different types of entities created under foreign law, and information may not be readily available from all the entities involved, even if they are ultimately U.S.-owned.

Foreign Currency

Measurement of income derived abroad is complicated by the fact that most of it is derived in foreign currency. In the simplest case, the foreign currency amounts must merely be translated into U.S. currency. In other cases, however,

5. I.R.C., sec. 1297(c).

gain or loss is recognized on changes in foreign currency values, and this introduces complex issues of measurement. For example, a foreign branch of a U.S. taxpayer or foreign partnership in which the taxpayer is a partner may do business and keep its books in a foreign currency. By the time that entity makes a distribution to the U.S. person, the value of the foreign currency may have changed, and that may require adjustments in the dollar amounts recorded. Similar issues arise in computing foreign tax credits.

Hybrids and Tax Arbitrage

In this day and age, however, undoubtedly the biggest single source of complexity arises out of inconsistencies in the characterization in the United States and the characterization in a foreign country of particular entities and particular financial instruments and the tax arbitrage transactions that taxpayers structure to gain advantage from these inconsistencies. The so-called check-the-box regulations issued in 1997 give U.S. taxpayers broad latitude to treat a foreign business entity as either a corporation (a separate taxable entity) or a pass-through entity (branch or partnership, depending on whether there are one or more interest holders).[6] In addition a large number of financial transactions are treated inconsistently in the United States and in foreign countries. These include leveraged leases, equity-flavored debt, lease in–lease out transactions, repos, and many more. The number of variations is truly mind-boggling, and instruments keep changing all the time. From personal experience, I can say that it is difficult enough for a practitioner well supported by staff to keep up with what is going on, and it certainly is harder for the IRS.

Coping with Complexity

The U.S. law governing the taxation of the foreign income of U.S. persons is needlessly complex. I commented on this subject twelve years ago (as others had before me), but (to no one's surprise) virtually nothing has changed.[7] A large part of this complexity is generically unavoidable, as it arises out of the circumstances in which foreign income is earned. Other parts, however, are not. To take a simple example, we now have a number of regimes designed to tax through currently to U.S. shareholders income derived by foreign corporations in which they are shareholders—controlled foreign corporation provisions, foreign personal holding company provisions, passive foreign investment corpora-

6. Treasury Regulations, sec. 301.7701-2-3.
7. See Tillinghast (1990).

tion provisions, and foreign investment company provisions.[8] These could certainly be rationalized into a more integrated, single regime, and within the provisions there are literally dozens, if not hundreds, of complicating rules that could be eliminated.

It is popular these days to push for a territorial system, in which foreign income is exempt. While this primarily raises a policy issue, often it is advertised as a simplification measure. That claim should be taken with a large grain of salt. While an exemption system would indeed do away with some of the more complex international provisions (such as, for example, the supercomplex regime of separate foreign tax credit limitation "baskets"), any system that is likely to be adopted would retain many complicated provisions. For example, as in the systems used by European countries, while business income would be exempt, presumably nonbusiness, passive income would not. It would therefore be necessary, first of all, to sort income into (and attribute expenses to) each category, to trace through entity tiers, and to operate a foreign tax credit system with respect to the passive side. This is not so simple. And the pressure on transfer-pricing enforcement would intensify.

Inconsistent Entity and Income Characterization

Major complexity arises simply because the U.S. tax law characterizes entities and income items differently from the way they are characterized under the laws of other countries. As indicated above, the adoption by the United States of the so-called check-the-box regulations exploded the number of cases in which entities are inconsistently characterized, and this has greatly expanded the scope for taxpayers to structure often highly complicated tax arbitrage transactions.

It would greatly simplify the IRS's job if those inconsistencies could be removed. The check-the-box rules replaced a set of rules that made the corporate or noncorporate status of an entity depend upon whether it exhibited or failed to exhibit four corporate characteristics. A return to that system would be anathema to the private sector, and so, for both political and technical reasons, it will not likely occur. That may be for the best; determining how a foreign entity should be characterized under those rules required extensive fiddling with foreign law and imposed an enormous burden on the IRS, both in ruling on technical issues and in auditing.

The only obvious alternative would be to adopt a rule that treats a foreign entity as a corporation for U.S. tax purposes if it is treated as a taxable entity in its home jurisdiction. This would, to an extent at least, restrict the tax arbitrage transactions that are now so prevalent. Any such proposal raises a number of

8. See I.R.C., secs. 951-959, 551-558, 1291-98, and 1246-1247.

issues, however. It is a major policy question whether foreign law should govern U.S. tax consequences and whether eliminating those transactions broadly is desirable. Again, the private sector certainly would forcefully resist.

It seems more likely that continuing IRS efforts to block the use of abusive tax shelters (several foreign tax arbitrage transactions are already "listed transactions" for purposes of the tax shelter rules) may shrink back the use of the more exotic transactions, leaving the IRS to focus on commonly used and better understood transactions.

Smaller Steps

If broad-scale simplification seems unlikely, more modest steps could be taken to ease the IRS's international administrative burden. A huge portion of that burden arises from the IRS's need to police cross-border transfer pricing in multinational groups. Transfer-pricing compliance is consistently listed by the multinationals as their biggest international headache, and the IRS necessarily devotes extensive resources to this area. As discussed above, the advance-pricing agreement program has already gone a long way toward easing this burden. It will undoubtedly continue and be expanded.

Other proposals for diminishing the effort that the IRS must make to deal with transfer-pricing issues include the idea that the IRS could create "safe harbors," wherein taxpayers whose pricing fell within a predetermined range would not be subject to readjustment. For example, the IRS could announce that it would seek no adjustment in the price charged by a foreign manufacturer to its U.S. distributor if the profits of the U.S. subsidiary met a stated target. Depending upon how industry-specific it wanted to be, the IRS could state this target in terms of markup, profit split, minimum return on assets (probably not desirable), or other criteria.

Another approach to simplifying international administration is to minimize inconsistencies between the United States and foreign tax treatment of the same items of income and expense. Widespread substantive harmonization is not in the cards, of course, but reduction in the often arbitrary or unreasonable positions taken by foreign tax administrations would help. A taxpayer, caught between an IRS determination on one side and an inconsistent determination by a foreign country that is simply unreasonable, is likely to resist the IRS just to avoid double taxation.

The committee on fiscal affairs of the OECD attempts to bring harmony to international tax issues. Its model income tax convention has long since become the reference point for negotiation of bilateral income tax treaties between developed countries. In its outreach program the committee is seeking to engage nonmember countries—largely developing countries—in a dialogue designed to explore how differences among tax systems can be minimized. A wide gulf exists between capital exporting countries (mainly in North America and Europe) and capital importing countries (mainly developing countries but also some developed countries, such as Australia and New Zealand) concerning the extent to which business income should be taxed at the source. This has been exacerbated by the advent of e-commerce, which in many cases radically reduces the need for a physical presence in the market served. This is a major source of double taxation and complexity at the moment, and a resolution, though no doubt elusive, needs to be pursued.

The IRS can, and to some extent does, use its authority to consult with its treaty partners with respect to tax issues between the two countries. In recent years India has been rather aggressive in asserting the right to tax American (and other) companies providing software and e-commerce services to Indian customers. This provoked a high-level effort by the IRS to reach an accommodation, not only to resolve individual cases but also to reach agreement on general approaches to the issues. (The OECD and the International Fiscal Association also assisted by sponsoring a conference in Mumbai on e-commerce issues.) This effort resulted in the settlement of several cases, and there has been at least some moderation of the approach taken by the Indian authorities. But an overall resolution of different policy views is still required.

A final way to attempt to improve administration of international tax law is to expand the network of U.S. tax treaties. Apart from the role of treaties in authorizing the exchange of information, negotiation of a treaty affords an opportunity to remove sources of substantive law conflict, which avoids the need to consult to avoid double taxation in individual cases.

Strategies for Obtaining Information

In light of its limited ability to access foreign information, what strategies can the IRS follow in an attempt to administer the international provisions of the Internal Revenue Code? The IRS basically has four potential sources of information: It can procure information from U.S. taxpayers relevant to computing their tax or the tax of a related person. It can procure such information from U.S. third parties. It can procure information from foreign governments under treaties or exchange-of-information agreements. It can procure information from foreign persons, including financial institutions, not necessarily related to the taxpayer but involved in his or her affairs.

Procuring Information from U.S. Taxpayers

U.S. taxpayers are required to file a number of information returns relating to their foreign activities. Taxpayers must disclose access to any foreign bank account by checking a box on schedule B of Form 1040 (for individuals) and filing a foreign bank account report (FBAR).[9] U.S. taxpayers must annually report transactions with related foreign persons on Forms 5471 and 5472. They must report the formation, recapitalization, or liquidation of any foreign corporation in which they are a substantial shareholder (or, in the case of individuals, a director).[10] Similarly taxpayers must report the formation or ownership of, or any distribution received from, or any contribution to, a foreign trust.[11] U.S. partners owning 10 percent of a foreign partnership with over 50 percent U.S. ownership also must file reporting forms.[12] An annual filing is required with respect to any controlled foreign corporation.[13] Moreover, special information returns are required to be filed by U.S. corporations that are foreign-controlled.[14] In addition to these tax forms are filing requirements for monetary transactions, including currency transactions over $10,000 and international transportation of financial instruments or currency over $10,000.[15] In short, there exist a plethora of required reporting forms, many bearing severe penalties for noncompliance.

These forms do not prevent tax evasion. In reports filed with Congress in connection with its consideration of the Patriot Act, the IRS estimated that perhaps 10 percent of taxpayers with foreign bank accounts (177,000 out of a total of possibly 2 million) checked the box and filed the required FBAR forms. The IRS estimated similar filing percentages for abusive foreign trusts. Certainly most taxpayers engaged in tax evasion do not file forms disclosing their evasion. Possibly a few tax evaders file because they believe that the IRS never checks the forms. All these filings prove useful if a taxpayer is under examination, and sometimes the filings are used as a source for investigations. But clearly the IRS cannot examine even a small portion of the millions of these forms filed every year. And, as previously stated, most tax evaders are not going to file these forms anyway. Ultimately taxpayer filings assist the IRS in auditing relatively compliant taxpayers but usually are of little value in detecting tax evasion.

In addition, of course, the IRS can issue a summons to a U.S. taxpayer requiring the taxpayer to furnish information that exists outside the United States.[16] This is frequently done. In cases where the foreign records are protected by bank secrecy laws, courts have forced taxpayers to consent to the release of the documents, under threat of contempt of court.[17] Several Internal

9. 31 U.S.C. 5314 and Code of Federal Regulations 31, sec. 103.24.
10. I.R.C., sec. 6046.
11. I.R.C., sec. 6048.
12. I.R.C., sec. 6038.
13. I.R.C., sec. 6038.
14. I.R.C., sec. 6038A.
15. 31 U.S.C. 5313 and 5316.
16. I.R.C., sec. 7602.
17. See *John Doe* v. *United States*, 487 U.S. 201 (1988); Internal Revenue Manual, secs. 42.2.1, 25.5.4.4, and 34.12.3.10.

Revenue Code provisions add to the effectiveness of IRS demands for foreign documents. One provision bars taxpayers that fail to comply with IRS demands for foreign-based documents from using the foreign documents in court at any later time.[18] The Tax Court has also barred any testimony based upon foreign documents not produced in response to any IRS demand.[19] A second provision requires any foreign shareholder of 25 percent or more in a U.S. company to appoint the U.S. company as its agent for service of process. The IRS can then demand records from the foreign shareholder through the U.S. company. If the shareholder fails to comply, the IRS has broad discretion to adjust the value of any transaction between the foreign shareholder and the U.S. company. The taxpayer can reverse the IRS adjustments only by introducing clear and convincing evidence that the adjustment is incorrect.[20] These IRC provisions give the IRS a great deal of power to obtain foreign documentation in the possession of the taxpayer (or the taxpayer's foreign shareholder).

Procuring Information by Third-Party Summons

The IRS also has considerable powers to require third parties to produce information about other taxpayers by issuing summonses. As long as the third party is within the jurisdiction of U.S. courts, the IRS generally can obtain any needed information within the third party's possession (subject to privilege rules and other limitations). Problems arise, however, if the IRS tries to summons third parties outside the jurisdiction of the U.S. courts.

In one well-known case involving the Bank of Nova Scotia, a grand jury issued a subpoena to the Canadian bank's Miami branch, demanding information located in the bank's Cayman and Bahamian branches.[21] Cayman and Bahamian bank secrecy laws prohibited disclosure of the information by the bank. The Eleventh Circuit Court applied a balancing test, weighing the interests of the United States in obtaining the information against the interests of the Caribbean countries in maintaining bank secrecy. Not surprisingly the court found that the bank secrecy laws had to give way to the subpoenas and upheld a $1.8 million contempt-of-court penalty against the bank for failing to turn over the information in a timely fashion.

The Bank of Nova Scotia case and similar cases are generally viewed as allowing the IRS and other government agencies to force third parties to reveal information covered by foreign bank secrecy law, if the agencies have legitimate law enforcement reasons for demanding the information. Of course, if the U.S. courts have no jurisdiction over the third party, then penalties for contempt are an empty

18. I.R.C., sec. 982.
19. *Flying Tigers Oil Co.* v. *Commissioner*, 92 T.C. 1261 (1989).
20. I.R.C., sec. 6038A.
21. In re *Grand Jury Proceedings the Bank of Nova Scotia*, 740 F.2d 817 (11th Cir. 1984).

threat. Many banks and other firms structure themselves so that the entities located in tax havens are not branches but rather subsidiaries with no direct contact with the United States. In these instances, U.S. jurisdiction over the tax haven subsidiaries and information they possess is much more problematic.

In many cases information concerning foreign transactions and entities will not be in the hands of U.S. persons. A central purpose for using tax haven jurisdictions for tax evasion is to have the funds located outside the reach of U.S. law enforcement. Taxpayers attempting to hide funds offshore are potentially vulnerable to detection, however, at two points: when they move the funds out of the United States and when they bring the money back to use it.

The IRS has made several attempts to uncover tax evasion at these two points, because movement of the funds into and out of the United States usually involves third parties subject to U.S. jurisdiction. But the problem for the IRS is simply that the huge volume of international financial traffic makes identifying the movement of tax evasion funds like finding a small needle in a large haystack. The General Accounting Office has estimated (as of 2000) that there are 290 million electronic payments totaling $2.74 trillion made in the United States every business day.[22]

The IRS has made some sporadic efforts to issue summonses to banks relating to wire transfers to tax haven jurisdictions.[23] The investigations of the persons making these wire transfers consume a great deal of IRS manpower but are perceived as reasonably successful in detecting some cases of tax evasion. These investigations obviously involve only a small percentage of the total wire transfers to tax havens made in any given year.

For many years, travel magazines, the Internet, and seminars have brazenly touted tax haven debit cards as a method for tax evaders to have their offshore funds secretly available for any purpose. The debit card charges are paid out of the taxpayer's secret tax haven bank account, and no paperwork exists in the United States to reveal the taxpayer's finances to the IRS. The IRS undertook a striking initiative beginning in 2000 when, in an effort to detect unreported income, it issued summonses to American credit card companies, demanding the identities of United States persons with signature authority over debit cards issued by tax haven banks.[24]

In many cases the credit card companies do not know the identities of the cardholders; the companies merely have the account numbers. In these situations the IRS has taken the debit card numbers to various vendors and

---

22. See GAO (2002).

23. See, for example, in re *Tax Liabilities: John Does,* 1991 U.S. Dist. Lexis 9704 (N.D. Ca. 1991) (court approved a summons on wire transfers through Bank of America).

24. See *In the Matter of the Tax Liabilities of John Does,* 86 A.F.T.R. 2d 6727, 2000 U.S. Dist. Lexis 17841 (S.D. Fla. 2000) (court approval for John Doe summons for MasterCard and American Express records) and various IRS and Department of Justice press releases.

demanded that they reveal the identity of the customers using the cards. For example, an airline must know the identity of its passengers when they fly and can match the card number to the identity of the passenger using that card. The IRS has indicated that it has already begun over 900 investigations based on leads from the credit card summonses and eventually expects to uncover hundreds of thousands of U.S. persons with tax haven debit cards. Presumably people with these cards also have tax haven bank accounts linked to the cards and are not paying tax on funds deposited in or income earned by those accounts.

It is not clear exactly what the IRS will do if it uncovers such extensive tax evasion. Senate Finance Committee Chairman Max Baucus recently noted that "These cases are very labor intensive, requiring hundreds of IRS staff hours to complete just one examination. More alarming, however, is the fact that there are thousands of cases waiting to be investigated and a potential avalanche expected when complete disclosure of account information is made by credit card companies."[25] Typically the IRS prosecutes well under a thousand people every year for tax crimes. The IRS clearly lacks the resources to prosecute even a significant portion of the people with tax haven debit cards. Even if it knows the taxpayer's identity, it still has difficulty obtaining accurate information concerning the amount of the taxpayer's income or even proof that the owner of the tax haven debit card also has a tax haven bank account. No one in the United States, other than the taxpayer, has the bank statements. It is possible that the exchange-of-information agreements referred to above will assist in this context.

Having tracked down tax evaders in an innovative way, perhaps it is time for the IRS to also use the data innovatively. Traditionally the IRS investigates taxpayers one at a time. In the past when a corporate tax issue mushroomed, the IRS used a settlement initiative to offer taxpayers a standard settlement that would resolve many cases with as little investigation as possible. Examples include the initiative offered to resolve the thousands of pending cases dealing with the amortization of intangibles in the early 1990s, the initiative designed to resolve many of the employee-versus-independent-contractor withholding cases in the late 1990s and since, and the tax shelter disclosure initiative, in which the IRS forgave penalties on companies making late disclosures of their tax shelter investments. In each of these initiatives the IRS gave taxpayers "deals" in which penalties and even some tax were forgiven, but it resolved large numbers of pending cases.

If the credit card summonses produce an avalanche of cases that the IRS cannot resolve one by one, it might consider a one-time offer waiving criminal prosecution to those who report all back taxes, agree to some limited civil penalties, and then pay up. IRS enforcement statistics suggest that these hundreds of thousands of taxpayers have a thousand-to-one chance of avoiding criminal

25. Baucus (2002).

prosecution anyway, just because the IRS lacks the resources to investigate and prosecute all these cases individually. Even the threat of possible criminal prosecution and imposition of civil penalties may deter many of these taxpayers from voluntarily cooperating with the IRS. The IRS historically has refused to offer amnesties, although its comprehensive settlement programs have had a similar result. The IRS may regret failing to take advantage of this opportunity to bring many taxpayers into compliance. A theme of this chapter is that the United States has effectively innovated in several instances but needs to further extend these innovations to keep up with a more complex financial world, in an era of diminishing resources for tax law enforcement. This may be another instance in which innovation is needed to solve big problems without sufficient resources.

Now that tax evaders are aware that their use of tax haven credit cards may be disclosed to the IRS, they are likely to use other means to repatriate funds. These other methods might include, for example, the use of wire transfers from a tax haven to a dummy entity in a non-tax-haven jurisdiction and then a payment to the taxpayer or his business or to his credit card company. Perhaps taxpayers will otherwise disguise repatriations in various foreign-to-foreign transfers that the IRS can unravel only with great difficulty. These more complex evasion schemes will prove difficult to detect without international cooperation.

Procuring Information from Foreign Governments

As discussed above, treaties enable the IRS to procure information needed in audit or enforcement proceedings from foreign governments. In addition, information may be available under exchange-of-information agreements. These procedures are cumbersome and, in the case of exchange-of-information agreements, virtually untested. In fact most tax haven exchange-of-information agreements do not even come into force until 2004 or later. The IRS can do relatively little to improve the exchange-of-information process, because the improvement required is at the other end of the pipeline. The IRS has, however, long carried on a training function, in which it dispatches experienced IRS personnel to work with foreign tax administrations to improve their competence. Such efforts are not normally directed at the exchange-of-information process as such, but increasing efficiency in foreign tax administration assists the performance of that function as well as others, including the competent authority jurisdiction discussed above.

Procuring Information from Foreign Third Parties

The IRS is normally in no position to require a foreign person to furnish information to it. One recent commentary has suggested that it can, nevertheless, make any foreign person that wants to do business in or with the United States agree to supply information when requested.[26] Two examples used to illustrate this possibility are the so-called qualified intermediary rules recently adopted with respect to withholding on U.S.-source investment income and the Patriot Act adopted in the fight against terrorism.

Obviously a large number of foreign persons invest in securities in the United States. Some of the returns they receive—principally dividends—are subject to U.S. withholding tax. However, the withholding tax is normally reduced when the recipient of the dividend is a resident of a country with which the United States has an income tax treaty. There has always been a tension between the IRS's goal of assurance that the reduced rate of tax will not be claimed by someone who is not entitled to it under the treaty and the goal of most foreign investors to remain anonymous, at least to the IRS.

For many years the applicable regulations allowed a withholding agent (that is, a person making payment of a dividend) to assume that the recipient was entitled to the reduced rate of a treaty if the address to which the dividend was paid was in that country. Particularly considering that most foreigners invest in the United States through banks or other financial intermediaries, this rule was something of a joke. When the IRS proposed to require more effective identification, it created an uproar. Consideration was given initially to requiring a certification by the tax administration of the treaty country that the recipient of the payment paid tax there as a resident. Not surprisingly this foundered on a number of grounds, not the least of which was that foreign governments were not prepared to accept the administrative burden this implied. The private sector also objected to the idea, on the ground that the loss of anonymity would deter portfolio investment in the United States. In the end, despite all the intervening twists and turns, a compromise was worked out.

Under this system, a foreign financial institution may enter into an agreement with the IRS to become what is known as a qualified intermediary (QI). U.S. information reporting rules normally require that the so-called beneficial owner of each payment of U.S.-source income be identified and reported to the IRS. The compromise made available by the QI rules works as follows.[27]

First, a financial institution that becomes a QI enters into an agreement with the IRS, under which the QI agrees to obtain detailed information about each of its account holders investing in U.S. securities. However, QIs are permitted to rely on existing local laws and internal procedures for obtaining account holder information (so-called know-your-customer rules) to pass on to U.S. custodians, rather than collecting IRS forms from each account holder. Compliance with this requirement is monitored through biannual audits by

26. See Michaels and O'Donnell (2002).
27. See Treasury Regulations, sec. 1.1441-1 et seq.

independent accounting firms, the results of which must be made available to the IRS.

Second, instead of providing account-holder-specific information to U.S. custodians making payments to the QI for the benefit of its direct foreign account holders, a QI can provide aggregated (or pooled) data about these account holders. Besides the obvious confidentiality concerns that this rule alleviates, it also significantly reduces the sheer amount of paper that U.S. custodians must review in performing their compliance functions. Financial institutions that are not QIs must provide account-holder-specific information, or payments to their account holders are subject to U.S. withholding tax.

Third, a U.S. custodian's compliance with U.S. information reporting rules with respect to payments to a QI's direct foreign account holders can be accomplished by providing the IRS with aggregated payment data rather than recipient-specific information. For example, a U.S. custodian can use one form to report the payment to a QI of $1 million in dividends subject to a 15 percent withholding rate. Absent the QI rules, the U.S. custodian would have to report the identity of each ultimate recipient of a portion of that dividend payment and the amount that they each received.

Last, the QI rules do not modify U.S. information reporting principles applicable to U.S. account holders. A QI that complies with the first requirement—obtaining information from account holders—must provide account-holder-specific information about U.S. account holders to U.S. custodians who, as part of their information reporting functions, report this detailed recipient-specific information to the IRS.

While implementing the QI provisions of the withholding regulations required a gargantuan effort by the IRS (as well as by the financial institutions) and was delayed several times, they can be regarded as a real success story, since over 3,800 institutions from a large number of countries have signed up.

Congress enacted the Patriot Act in October of 2001 in response to the terrorist attacks on September 11.[28] The act aimed to expand the ability of the United States to fight terrorism and money laundering but also increased the IRS's ability to gather information and take action outside the United States. The act expands the extraterritorial jurisdictional reach of U.S. courts. It also imposes new requirements on various third parties to monitor their customers and transactions.

The Patriot Act expands the reach of U.S. courts in several instances. For example, any foreign bank with an interbank account in the United States may have that account frozen to the extent that the United States is attempting to freeze the assets of one of the foreign bank's customers. These provisions increase the ability of the United States to obtain data or even collect assets from foreign

28. The U.S.A. Patriot Act of 2001, Pub. L. 107-56.

banks and financial institutions. Effectively the act requires foreign institutions to submit to U.S. laws as a price of engaging in certain transactions with U.S. businesses.

The Patriot Act also extends know-your-customer and reporting rules to additional industries and expands the requirements of those rules for those already covered. For example, foreign correspondent accounts have long been an issue for U.S. law enforcement. These accounts allowed foreign banks to combine the activities of multiple foreign customers in one account, without revealing individual customer identities to the U.S. bank handling the account in the United States. Under the Patriot Act, foreign correspondent accounts not only are subject to increased due diligence and know-your-customer requirements, but the non-U.S. banks must also appoint their U.S. bank correspondent as an agent for service of process as a condition of maintaining such an account. As a result non-U.S. persons who could previously transact business through these accounts with a high degree of confidentiality are now subject to increased scrutiny.

There is no question that, while the Patriot Act was solely the result of the terrorist attacks of September 2001, it arms the IRS with considerably expanded authority to make foreign investigations in other cases. This may prove useful in its efforts to combat money laundering and similar criminal activity.

The issue is whether a similar approach can be taken to solve a broader range of information-gathering issues. The matter should, it is submitted, be approached with caution. The Patriot Act is brand new and essentially untested. It applies only to a limited range of cases. The willingness of foreign financial institutions to volunteer to act under QI provisions of the withholding regulations is attributable to their huge financial interest in acting for their clients in the U.S. capital markets and investors' need to avail themselves of the services of the leading institutions. In other contexts, if the IRS were to impose requirements on persons doing business in or with the United States, one could expect at least a substantial number of players in the financial markets to structure their affairs so that the person or entity that has the information the IRS needs has no contact whatsoever with the United States, even if somewhere in the organization there is an affiliate that does business in or with the United States.

COMMENT BY
James R. Hines Jr.

It is a pleasure to read David Tillinghast's whirlwind tour of issues facing the Internal Revenue Service in enforcing compliance with U.S. tax laws in the international context. The chapter is insightful and lively, so much so that its main message—the vastness of the challenge facing the IRS—seems not as distressing as it might otherwise. The IRS has responded to the needs of international tax enforcement in several sensible ways, and while aggressive taxpayers and their agents nevertheless have access to avoidance methods of varying degrees of effectiveness, the system is not crumbling, it is merely under strain.

Perfect enforcement of international tax provisions is of course impossible, as is perfect enforcement of domestic tax provisions. Tillinghast's chapter considers three ways in which international tax enforcement faces even greater challenges than those facing domestic tax enforcement: the added difficulty of obtaining taxpayer information, the need to work with foreign tax authorities, and the greater complexity of the underlying tax laws.

Information

The foreign information problems are obviously severe, because the IRS has little ability to demand information from reluctant foreign sources that are unconnected to the United States. Information is a commodity that is available when someone perceives it to be in his or her interest to provide it, and it is generally unavailable otherwise. This leaves three options for the IRS, each with its own limitations. The first option is to work with foreign governments to exert leverage over foreign-located financial intermediaries and others possessing information that might help U.S. tax authorities. The second is to threaten uncooperative foreign entities with penalties that would apply if they were ever to have business connections to the United States. And the third is to increase the penalties for U.S. taxpayers taking advantage of the absence of foreign-provided information by underreporting income or in other ways being noncompliant. None of these responses is likely to solve the problem by itself, and all entail other costs in burdening and thereby discouraging legitimate business activity and in straining relations with other countries.

Tillinghast's chapter notes that some important steps have been taken to obtain information using all three methods. One gets the sense both that much more needs to be done and that what has already been done has come at considerable cost. These are of course not quite consistent, and they raise the possibility that the payoff from additional pressure on foreign governments, or more severe penalties for noncompliance, might not be worth the cost, at least in the absence of innovative new methods of using the information thereby obtained.

Intergovernmental Cooperation

Working with foreign tax authorities poses problems but also creates some opportunities for creative tax enforcement. Foreign tax concepts of income and expense can differ markedly from each other, and from those used by the United States, both in theory and in practice. (Foreign tax practices are, in the language of travelogues, truly lands of contrasts.) This creates inconsistencies with American definitions, thereby reducing the ability of the IRS to use without modification the information available from foreign tax authorities. Taxpayers and others worry, perhaps excessively, about the prospect of double (or at least more than single) taxation in such situations, and fret that intergovernmental cooperation might be insufficient to rectify double taxation in all instances. A much greater danger, it seems, is that the inability to rely on foreign governments to obtain and process appropriate taxpayer information produces governmental responses (such as arbitrary transfer-pricing rules or stiff penalties for small violations) that impede the normal functioning of international commerce, introducing distortions and discouraging foreign investment.

One of the benefits of working with foreign tax authorities is the possibility of combining the information they have available with the information available to U.S. tax authorities. There are situations in which requiring taxpayers to submit information in different forms, and according to different concepts, might enable the IRS to identify anomalous tax entries with greater precision than is possible using only the information available on U.S. tax forms. Furthermore the incentives that taxpayers have to avoid the sum of worldwide tax obligations, not just the U.S. portion, imply that it is not infrequently in the interest of taxpayers to engage in transactions that reduce foreign taxes at the expense of American taxes.

Complexity

No one disputes that the rules governing international transactions are excessively complex. Many people advocate reforms directed at simplification, but alas these proposals differ greatly, and the most likely reform outcome might be to adopt parts of each, thereby retaining the current level of complexity in the guise of reform. It is important to be wary of simplification claims, because it is so tempting to compare actual, flawed tax systems to idealized alternatives. Even the pure versions of suggested reforms are likely to be exceedingly complex in the international arena. For example, I share David Tillinghast's skepticism that the currently trendy alternative of territorial taxation, if adopted, would be likely to reduce complexity once Congress finishes refining it and all the knotty details are addressed.

Embracing simplification requires letting go of some other cherished goals. The U.S. rules governing the taxation of foreign income include thousands of provisions designed to encourage and discourage behavior of various types (foreign investment, exports, repatriations, use of debt finance, exploitation of technology, and so forth), all of them adding complexity to the system and thereby contributing to the difficulty of enforcement. Even the provisions designed individually to make enforcement more effective have the perverse effect, when taken as a collective, of contributing to the difficulty of enforcement by making the system more complex. Complexity makes a taxpayer's situation more opaque to tax authorities and everyone else, thereby making it harder to identify noncompliance and reducing the likelihood that the legal system will be willing to impose penalties for noncompliance that is plausibly, at least in part, a consequence of the complexity.

Does it follow that it is hopeless to seek simplification in the international tax arena? I think not, and I think that simplification is urgently needed. But in order to achieve simplification it is necessary to relax at least some other objectives, particularly those designed to prevent or punish all conceivable behaviors that are thought to be undesirable. Effective simplification requires a bit more choosiness than the United States has previously exhibited in selecting tax laws and regulations. Such choosiness will be easier to adopt once we are clearer about the goals that we seek to achieve in taxing international income.

National Interest

The bottom line from the standpoint of the United States is how to construct and enforce a tax system that advances the goals of the United States and the world. The international provisions of the tax system exist to raise revenue in an efficient and equitable manner, doing so in part by defending the domestic tax base from various forms of international arbitrage. These provisions are useless unless they can be effectively enforced—which they largely have been, due to the unstinting efforts of the IRS. It is up to Congress, however, to show greater sensitivity to the position in which they put tax authorities, and taxpayers, by devoting more attention to the ramifications of the rules they enact. Everyone benefits from a smoothly functioning tax system, and the fact that the IRS is mostly able to hold the system together in the international arena is, by itself, cold comfort to one who cares about the economy performing at a high level of efficiency. The United States needs to clearly define its goals in taxing international transactions and adopt less complex and more easily enforceable laws and regulations in order to pursue them most effectively.

COMMENT BY
Stephen E. Shay

The topic of tax administration in an international context receives little attention in the United States, and David Tillinghast makes a valuable contribution to the subject. He addresses three challenges that the Internal Revenue Service faces in the area of international tax administration and enforcement. The first challenge is the IRS's limited ability to obtain information from overseas. As examples, he points to the inability of the IRS in many circumstances to require foreign persons to provide information, to identify persons outside the United States who may be required to file returns, and to surmount foreign law limitations on disclosure of information. The second challenge is the IRS's need to interact with other tax authorities, with respect to exchange of information, advance-pricing agreements, and mutual-agreement procedures. The chapter's final topic is the complexity of the substantive law issues. I take up these subjects in reverse order. I preface my comments with a brief review of the economic and legal context in which current U.S. international tax administration and enforcement efforts take place.

Background

In the past quarter century, the U.S. economy has become significantly more open to international trade and cross-border activity. Total trade (measured as imports plus exports) increased from 16 percent of gross domestic product (GDP) in 1975 to 26 percent in 2000.[1] Liberalized economic rules, including virtual elimination of currency controls and reductions in barriers to trade in goods and services, have been accompanied by technological developments in computing and telecommunications that have dramatically reduced transactions costs of cross-border economic activity.[2] The challenges to tax administration identified in chapter 3 have been significantly exacerbated by these economic and technological developments.

Notwithstanding numerous statutory refinements and extensions, the basic framework of U.S. international tax rules has remained substantially unchanged during the same twenty-five-year period. The United States taxes the worldwide income of U.S. citizens, resident aliens, corporations and trusts, and estates. Generally the United States allows a taxpayer to elect to credit foreign income taxes up to the U.S. tax on foreign-source income in the same foreign tax credit limitation category. Most active foreign business income earned by U.S.-owned foreign corporations is not taxed until distributed as a dividend (this is referred to as deferral). Foreign persons that carry on a U.S. trade or business are taxed on their net income effectively connected with that trade or business. (If resident in a treaty country, the foreign person's income must be attributable to a so-called permanent establishment in the United States.) Foreign persons earning U.S.-

---

1. Council of Economic Advisers (2001, table B-1, pp. 274–75).
2. See generally, Gordon and Hines (2002); Avi-Yonah (1997).

source income not connected with a U.S. trade or business are taxed on U.S.-source interest, dividends, royalties, and other fixed or determinable, annual, or periodical (FDAP) income at a rate of 30 percent (or lower treaty rate) on the gross amount of the income.

The preceding rules require administration and enforcement of laws that tax foreign income of U.S. persons and U.S. income of foreign persons. In other words, the scope of tax administration is international. The need for international administration and enforcement capability, however, is not a function of the specific contours of the U.S. income tax rules. Virtually all income tax systems tax nonresident persons on locally sourced income, and even territorial systems need to assure that their residents do not treat taxable domestic income as exempt foreign income. Although the current pattern of U.S. international tax rules may make administration somewhat more difficult than in other countries, the international tax administration and enforcement challenges the IRS faces have increased most dramatically as a consequence of the increased integration of the U.S. economy with the global economy.

Complexity

Tillinghast identifies several sources of complexity. The Internal Revenue Code's international provisions are complex, in many respects needlessly so. In addition, international tax issues often require application of income tax treaties and, sometimes, knowledge of other countries' laws. Tillinghast also cites entity proliferation, taxpayer structures using tiers of entities, and transactions in foreign currencies as sources of complexity. He identifies as the single biggest source of complexity, however, inconsistent characterizations between the United States and foreign tax laws and the resulting opportunities for tax arbitrage.

When it comes to solutions to complexity, Tillinghast is not optimistic. He observes that solving complexities arising from inconsistent entity characterizations, for example by limiting foreign corporate status to entities that are taxable in their residence country, is politically impractical. He considers more realistic smaller steps to address complexity, such as transfer-pricing safe harbors, reaching international agreement on income classification issues, and expanding the network of U.S. treaties. He cautions against crediting claims that a territorial system is a simplification panacea, but he does observe that there is low-hanging fruit to be harvested for simplification by eliminating dozens or hundreds of complicating rules.

I agree with Tillinghast that it would be possible to eliminate numerous tax law provisions in the international area; however, this will not materially affect the IRS's burdens in administering international rules. I concur with the observation in Jeffrey Owens and Stuart Hamilton's chapter in this volume that tax law simplification cannot be meaningfully separated from policy simplification. In the context of the U.S. constitutional system of shared legislative responsibility between the executive and legislative branches (generally requiring agreement of the two major political parties), pursuit of tax law simplification independently of policy changes that reduce underlying complexity is not the highest and best use of scarce political capital for tax law changes.

Turning to potential policy simplifications, I agree with Tillinghast that the simplification potential of a territorial system is easily overstated, and I have made similar observations in testimony before the House Ways and Means Committee.[3] Nonetheless, from a complexity perspective, a territorial system compares favorably with worldwide taxation with a limited foreign tax credit and deferral.

Sources of International Tax Law Complexity

The principal sources of tax law complexity are tax policy decisions intended to achieve policy goals other than simplification. Moreover, since there is little consensus regarding what policies should guide international tax rules, the resulting provisions tend to be haphazard in effect.

The simplest system for taxing international income would be to tax all income in exactly the same way and to allow a deduction, not a credit, for foreign income taxes. Under this regime, it would not be necessary to define foreign income nor to identify creditable foreign taxes. Allowing only a deduction for foreign taxes, however, would discourage foreign investment and would be inconsistent with U.S. treaty obligations.

Once a decision is made to mitigate double taxation by using an exemption system or, as the United States has since the first quarter of the last century, by using a foreign tax credit system subject to a limitation to the U.S. tax on foreign income, it becomes necessary to define foreign income and to allocate expenses between domestic and foreign income. Each further refinement in the taxation of foreign income adds to complexity.

The current U.S. system of worldwide taxation with a limited foreign tax credit and deferral offers significant elections to taxpayers and exceeds the complexities of even a realistic territorial system.[4] Unlike in a territorial system, it makes a significant difference under the U.S. system of deferral whether you conduct low-taxed foreign operations through a branch of a domestic corporation or through a foreign corporate subsidiary. If foreign losses are conducted

---

3. Statement of Stephen E. Shay before House Committee on Ways and Means, hearing on the World Trade Organization's extraterritorial income decision, February 27, 2002.

4. As every tax administrator knows, each additional election increases tax law complexity, and all elections are made against the fisc.

through a branch, foreign losses may offset U.S. income. If foreign business operations are conducted through a foreign corporation, most foreign business income is deferred from current U.S. tax until income is repatriated. As a result of a foreign tax credit for corporate-level income taxes combined with deferral, complicated rules are required to associate the foreign taxes with multiple years of earnings. In order to avoid a "repatriation tax," a taxpayer must engage in complicated foreign tax credit limitation averaging.

For all its faults as a method of taxing foreign income, and the complexity of actually implementing a territorial system (which normally does not exempt all foreign income and often includes a controlled foreign corporation antideferral regime), a territorial system at least mitigates the effects of electing to use a foreign corporate entity. Moreover, under a territorial system, exempt foreign income may be redeployed to its best use without extensive expatriation planning. If one favors reduced taxation of active foreign business activity, there is little question that from a complexity perspective a principled territorial system could be superior to our current system.

Unmentioned by the author is another alternative to current law that also would decrease the weight placed on electing the foreign corporate form—expansion of current taxation of U.S.-owned foreign corporate income. As Cliff Fleming, Robert Peroni, and I have argued, expanding current taxation of foreign income would have substantial simplification benefits, while avoiding the incentive under an exemption system to locate investment in low-tax countries.[5] Irrespective of one's views regarding taxation of foreign income (and acknowledging that the devil is in the details), a credible argument can be made that one of the most significant simplifications we can make is to move away from elective deferral of U.S. taxation of foreign business income.

The consequences for complexity of giving important substantive effect to the use of a foreign corporation, whether or not it pays a meaningful corporate tax in the United States or a foreign country, have long been a part of U.S. international tax law. The increased flexibility of the check-the-box entity classification rules adds to the complexity, but in my judgment it is not as important a component of the problem as the underlying substantive rules that accord excessive significance to legal forms, independent of economic or even tax substance. So why is there a problem now if we have tolerated it for so long? To paraphrase the 1992 campaign mantra: It's the (open) economy, stupid. What was tolerable in the economy of the 1960s, with fixed exchange rates and a small international sector, is subject to greater stress today.

What are the prospects for international tax law reform that achieves structural simplification? Not great.

5. Peroni, Fleming, and Shay (1999).

One Reason for International Tax Law Complexity

Why has the trend of U.S. tax policy in the 1990s been toward substantially increased tax law complexity, from the benchmark of the 1986 Tax Reform Act? There are numerous reasons, but one deserving mention is the low level of U.S. public discourse on tax policy issues. I note two examples.

During the 2001 legislative consideration of the present administration's trillion-dollar tax cut legislation, there was no acknowledgment or discussion of the interaction of the tax cut and the alternative minimum tax (AMT), including the future effects on middle-income taxpayers. The political agenda of the tax cutters outweighed reasoned and transparent tax policy. The failure to address the AMT issue will result in enormous complexity for greatly increasing numbers of taxpayers.

This is a bipartisan disease. The Clinton administration undertook a disingenuous effort to perpetuate an inefficient export subsidy, using a strained and highly questionable legal interpretation that has failed. In addition to adopting a new version of the subsidy costing U.S. taxpayers $4 billion a year, the Extraterritorial Income Exclusion Act of 2000 leaves the United States exposed to countervailing duties of an equal amount. Although it is unlikely that these penalties will actually be imposed, it is naïve to think that the United States will not have to give up something to the Europeans of approximately the same magnitude. This is yet another of many instances in which special-interest politics, in this case catering to the largest U.S. multinational businesses, appears to have foreclosed a full analysis of whether this tax subsidy was sound policy.[6]

Joseph Bankman's chapter in this volume discusses the political economy of tax shelters and observes, correctly, that there has been no organized opposition to tax shelters outside of a handful of academics, journalists, and practicing lawyers. A similar analysis can be applied to the international provisions of the Internal Revenue Code, which involve significant revenue. The provisions are technically complex and comprehensible only with an anthropological understanding of the history, and sometimes the policies, underlying the provisions. The directly interested parties are almost exclusively large multinational companies. Worse than in the case of tax shelters, the only opposition to international tax expenditures favoring U.S. companies come from an even smaller handful of academics and journalists. I am pessimistic regarding the prospects for international tax law reform that would achieve structural simplification.

6. A 2000 report on the Foreign Sales Corporation (FSC) by the Congressional Research Service observes that, under traditional economic analysis, the FSC by definition reduces U.S. economic welfare (as opposed to the welfare of the firms benefited by the subsidy and their shareholders) because at least some portion of the benefit is presumed to be passed on to foreign consumers in the form of lower prices.

Interaction with Foreign Tax Authorities

I do not share Tillinghast's level of concern regarding the current state of inter-actions with foreign tax authorities. In my experience, which admittedly is under current law, sophisticated taxpayers generally manage to use self-help measures to avoid double taxation and to avoid the need to resort to competent authority. Competent authority and advance-pricing agreements are only safety valves for the everyday operation of domestic tax rules and treaties. They are not intended to be and should not be relied on as primary tax law administration mechanisms. The international tax law must be capable of implementation with minimum possible governmental intervention—but it must be capable of gov-ernment audit.

Ability of the IRS to Obtain Information

Tillinghast's discussion of the mechanisms available to obtain information is a useful review of this area. The mechanisms for obtaining information using compulsory means or the assistance of foreign governments are time- and resource-intensive. Nonetheless it is important that they be employed and that successes be publicized. In the international arena, success in obtaining infor-mation can have a high deterrence effect, particularly after a long period of inac-tivity. The basis-shifting transaction described in Joseph Bankman's chapter illustrates that international tax avoidance is widely available. The credit card summonses described in Tillinghast's chapter suggest that offshore evasion, not just avoidance, has reached Main Street.[7] The charge card and other enforce-ment initiatives are important and should be encouraged.

Like Tillinghast, I would single out the new withholding rules as one of the most significant and successful international tax administration initiatives since the expansion of information reporting in the early 1980s—with certain caveats. The principal objective of the change in rules is to police relief from U.S.-source tax; the rules generally are designed to frustrate but not catch U.S.-resident evaders. The new qualified intermediary rules affirmatively maintain the confidentiality of foreign investors and thereby prevent disclosure of their identity to their home government. Nonetheless an IRS official recently stated that revenues from withholding taxes had increased as a result of the adoption

7. Indeed former IRS commissioner Donald Alexander appears to have been surprised at the middle-class tastes of the offshore credit card users. When it was disclosed that some of them shopped at the Gap, he is quoted as saying, "I thought it would have been a little more upscale, like Tiffany's, the Ritz Carlton, things like that. This is not exactly top-of-the-line, one might say." (Hamilton 2002, pp. 1291–92).

of these rules. This is in welcome contrast to the widespread disregard and abuse of these rules a decade ago.

Resource Allocation

Tillinghast notes in passing that understaffing in the international area is an "endemic condition" not easily remedied. International tax administration challenges are made more difficult to address when other tax administration projects, such as IRS restructuring and tax systems modernization, claim higher priority and substantial managerial and budget resources.

Alan Plumley and Eugene Steuerle's chapter in this volume sets out a framework for identifying the tax administration's goals: It should seek to allocate resources so as to collect the right amount of tax from each taxpayer at the least cost (including inconvenience) to the people. In allocating resources, the tax administration starts from the three taxpayer obligations—filing, reporting the correct amount of income, and payment of tax—in order to identify three phases of tax administration: prefiling (to help tax payers understand their obligations), filing (processing returns, payments, and refunds), and postfiling (mostly enforcement).[8] It might be useful to consider international administration issues using the same framework.

Tillinghast suggests that the IRS does relatively little to address foreign taxpayers at the prefiling stage. Clearly more work could be done, perhaps in conjunction with the Immigration and Naturalization Service, to advise nontourist foreign visitors of their U.S. tax obligations. The allocation of resources to enforcement of international issues in the postfiling stage for large and midsized business taxpayers has been blurred (at least to the outsider) by the IRS reorganization along broad industry lines. While I agree with the theory that international issues should not be pigeonholed, I am concerned that the expertise of the former international examiner corps will be diluted—which the IRS can ill afford, when matched against the taxpayers' resources. It is my anecdotal impression that the role of international enforcement in the protection of the domestic tax base is underappreciated. If this is correct, there could be disproportionate understaffing in the international area. Until there has been more audit experience under the new organization, however, it is too soon to make a judgment in this regard. The place of international tax administration in IRS resource allocation is a worthwhile subject for future study and analysis.

8. Plumley and Steuerle report that the IRS estimate of the gross tax gap for 1992 breaks down to 8 percent for nonfiling, 78 percent for underreporting, and 14 percent for untimely payment of amounts shown on tax returns. It would be interesting to know what this distribution would be for international taxpayers.

The Revenue Rule

Tillinghast clearly had to limit his discussion of topics in a large area, but perhaps some mention should be made of the current reluctance of countries to assist other countries in tax collection. This is not a major issue as a matter of revenue, because in fact the IRS can, in most cases, effect collection when it has achieved a final assessment. The collection issue is more important as a matter of deterrence. A multilateral agreement to assist collection would have a salutary effect for a relatively small investment of IRS resources.

References

Avi-Yonah, Reuven S. 1997. "International Taxation of Electronic Commerce." *Tax Law Review* 52 (3): 507–56.

Baucus, Max. 2002. "Letter to the Office of Management and Budget." *Tax Notes Today.* 179-19.

Congressional Research Service. 2000. "The Foreign Sales Corporation (FSC) Tax Benefit for Exporting and the WTO." December 4. Washington.

Council of Economic Advisers. 2001. *Economic Report of the President.* H. Doc. 107-2, 107 Cong. 1 sess. Government Printing Office.

Gordon, Roger H., and James R. Hines Jr. 2002. "International Taxation." Working Paper 8854. Cambridge, Mass.: National Bureau of Economic Research (March).

Hamilton, Amy. 2002. "Profile of Offshore Bank Customers Emerges in Latest IRS Filings." *Tax Notes* 96 (10): 1291–92.

Michaels, Marnin J., and Thomas A. O'Donnell. 2002. "The Death of Information Exchange Agreements?" *Journal of International Tax* 13 (8): 8.

Peroni, Robert J., J. Clifton Fleming, and Stephen E. Shay. 1999. "Getting Serious about Curtailing Deferral of U.S. Tax on Foreign Income." *SMU Law Review* 52 (455): 512–15.

Tillinghast, David. 1990. "International Tax Simplification." *American Journal of Tax Policy* 8 (2): 187–247.

U.S. General Accounting Office. 2002. "Money Laundering: Extent of Money Laundering through Credit Cards Is Unknown." Report 02-670.

4

JOEL SLEMROD

Small Business and
the Tax System

THE U.S. TAX code contains many provisions that seem to grant preferential treatment to the income earned by small businesses, the most obvious example of which is the graduation of the corporation income tax schedule. Why these preferences exist may be explained—but not justified—by the political power and influence of small business, although it is not clear that this power and influence exceeds that of big business.[1]

What economic arguments could justify these apparent preferences? One set of usually vague arguments holds that small businesses are the engine of growth, or that most of the new jobs in the economy are created by small business.[2] Neither of these arguments is a compelling justification for preferential tax treatment, unless some kind of positive externality or spillover is generated specifically

David Lenter and Hui Shan provided outstanding research assistance.

1. Whatever the reality, it is clear that most Americans do not believe that small business has too much power and influence. According to a Harris poll of 1,021 adults conducted by phone on February 13–19, 2002, 87 percent of Americans said they believed small business had too little power and influence in Washington, while only 5 percent said it had too much power (Taylor 2002). This is in sharp contrast to views about big business. According to the same poll, 87 percent of people think that big business has too much power and influence, while only 5 percent say it has too little power. This is the mirror image of the poll results about small business.

2. For example, William Dunkelberg (2001), chief economist of the National Federation of Independent Business, testified before the House Small Business Committee on October 10, 2001, that "Small business is the major job generator for the economy. Tax cuts that infused money into the small business sector would certainly make it possible for small business to retain more employees and to support the hiring of new employees."

by small businesses.[3] For example, if small-business owners were particularly innovative, and innovations spurred further innovations, then the beginning of a case on externality grounds for some kind of subsidy emerges. However, if such externalities exist, they are probably connected with the act of innovation, research, or entrepreneurship rather than all small-business operations per se, so they are better addressed with more targeted incentives. A related line of argument is that market failures plaguing the small-business sector—such as constraints on obtaining financing because intangible assets of entrepreneurs are not good collateral—can be addressed or offset by preferential tax policy.

A distinct defense of tax preferences for small business is that they appropriately offset the inordinate costs that government itself imposes on small businesses by requiring compliance with myriad regulations including, and maybe particularly, the tax system itself. The argument is that tax preferences are needed to maintain a level playing field in the face of the steeply regressive compliance costs that the tax system imposes on small business.

In this chapter I assess the argument that explicit tax preferences for small businesses offset the compliance cost burden imposed by the tax system. I first conclude that the compliance costs are indeed highly regressive, so that the cost as a fraction of size is larger for small businesses. I expand this notion by examining the effective enforcement of the tax burden on small businesses, noting that small-business noncompliance rates are higher than those of most other sources of income.[4] For at least one class of small business, the average compliance cost burden is of approximately the same order of magnitude as the average amount of tax not paid due to noncompliance. The aggregate response of self-employment activity when tax rates change suggests that this sector has a lower effective tax rate, but that could be offset by relatively high compliance costs that are not affected by tax rates.

---

3. That small business is an important and critical sector of the economy is not in dispute, only whether it should receive preferential policy treatment.

4. Although the focus of this chapter is the U.S. federal income tax system, the issues related to the taxation of small business are endemic to all countries and all kinds of taxes. Small business tax noncompliance is a serious problem throughout the world, and regressive compliance costs (for those businesses within the tax net) are also widely observed. Tax policies often adjust to the realities of administering and enforcing taxes on this sector. For example, it is common under value-added taxes for small businesses to be outside the tax net due to an exemption level based on annual sales. Proposals for a national retail sales tax in the United States often feature small-business exemptions. This issue is especially important in developing countries, where constraints on tax administrative capacity mean that small businesses are often out of the tax net either explicitly or de facto, and presumptive methods of tax are widespread. There is a large potential economic cost of a system in which tax obligations arise only for businesses above a certain size. As Kagan (1989, p. 93, italics added) says, "There is an unavoidable tension between desire for the higher income that can be produced by business growth and the desire to keep one's income invisible to tax authorities. Generally speaking, to retain invisibility an entrepreneur must *sacrifice opportunities for substantial growth.*"

I close by addressing whether the IRS should devote more (or fewer) resources to noncompliance by small-business owners. I propose a framework for analyzing this and related questions that is based on calculating the marginal social cost of funds of alternative tax policy changes. Given that noncompliance rates are higher in the small-business sector than in almost any other and, for the partnership and small-corporation subsectors, this noncompliance on average benefits a highly affluent slice of the taxpayer population, I tentatively conclude that an intensified enforcement focus on pass-through entities owned by high-income individuals is probably warranted. The key piece of missing information is the marginal deterrent effect of the intensified enforcement.

Background

Before addressing these issues, I present some background about the small-business sector and the tax laws that may afford preferential treatment to income generated in that sector.

What Is Small Business?

There is neither a universally accepted nor a conceptually clear-cut dividing line that distinguishes businesses that are small from those that are not. The IRS itself has implicitly adopted a definition by virtue of its recent reorganization into four operating divisions, each of which focuses on a particular group of taxpayers. Its Small Business and Self-Employed Operating Division (SB/SE) covers approximately 40 million taxpayers, including about 6.2 million small partnerships and corporations, 19.3 million partially or fully self-employed individuals, 13 million individual filers with supplemental income or business expenses,[5] and 1.2 million non-small-business taxpayers who are considered specialty tax filers.[6] (Another IRS unit, the Large and Mid-Sized Business Operating Division [LMSB], covers corporations and partnerships with assets of more than $10 million.)[7]

There is certainly a lot of heterogeneity among the small-business sector defined in this way. The tax issues that apply to a cash-only day-care provider are

5. Supplemental income earners are wage earners who file a Form 1040 with a Schedule E for rental, royalty, or other supplemental income. Wage earners with business expenses file a Form 1040 with a Form 2106 attached.

6. Specialty tax filers include international filers and filers of fiduciary, excise, and estate tax returns.

7. There is, to be sure, substantial year-to-year migration across categories such as these. For example, Ashby (2000) reports that, according to IRS data, about 2.2 million individuals who filed for tax year 1995 as pure wage earners filed for tax year 1996 as sole proprietors, and 1.7 million individuals who filed as sole proprietors for tax year 1995 filed as pure wage earners in tax year 1996.

undoubtedly different from those that apply to a corporation with $5 million of assets. With respect to enforcement, what is key about small business is that there is neither an independent source of information about income (as there is for wages and salaries) nor pervasive audit coverage (as there is for the largest companies that are part of the IRS Coordinated Industry Case program).[8] With respect to compliance costs, small businesses cannot leverage the economies of scale in dealing with the tax compliance process.

Facts about Small Business

Because there is no standard definition of small business, there is no standard way to summarize the sector's size and economic importance. One can, though, get a sense of it by looking at table 4-1. It shows that, of over 125 million individual tax returns, about 18 million filed either Schedule C or C-EZ, reporting nonfarm sole proprietorship activity, and over 2 million filed Schedule F reporting farm sole proprietorship activity. About three-quarters of those with nonfarm sole proprietorship income show net income, but nearly two-thirds of those with farm sole proprietorship income report a deficit. In addition nearly 2 million individual returns report some partnership income or deficit on Schedule E, with about two-thirds reporting net income. Over 80 percent of partnerships report assets of less than $1 million.

About 2.7 million individuals report income (or a loss) from subchapter S corporations, of which approximately two-thirds show net income. This reflects extraordinary growth of S corporation filings since 1985. In 1985 there were 736,900 Form 1102S filings, compared to 2,887,100 filed in 2000, reflecting growth of 292 percent over that period. In stark contrast, there were 2,161,700 Form 1120 filings (for subchapter C corporations) in 2000, compared to 2,432,300 in 1985, an 11 percent decline in filings.[9]

Table 4-1 also reports a breakdown of all corporations by whether assets exceeded $1 million. It shows that, although most corporate income is earned by large corporations, most corporations are small. About 90 percent of corporations report assets of less than $1 million, but over 93 percent of the net income less deficit is received by the corporations with assets that exceed $1 million.

Who Owns Small Businesses?

Whether small businesses tend to be owned by people with small incomes or by relatively affluent people is critical for understanding the distributional impli-

---

8. Note that this is not entirely a conceptual distinction, as it depends on IRS audit policy.

9. Filings slightly exceed the number of individual returns reporting that form of income, because an individual might have an interest in more than one partnership or more than one Subchapter S corporation.

Table 4-1. *Summary Data on Small Businesses*

Type of business	Number of returns	Total receipts[a] ($)	Income, deficit, net income ($)
Nonfarm sole proprietorships			
Net income	13,307,842	875,098,239	245,230,626
Deficit	4,596,889	145,859,044	30,515,328
Total	17,904,731	1,020,957,283	214,715,298
Farm sole proprietorships			
Net income	725,782	na	9,201,162
Deficit	1,320,526	na	15,444,078
Total	2,046,308	na	−6,242,916
Partnerships			
Net income	1,225,916	1,313,821,059	348,467,958
Deficit	711,003	441,151,354	120,029,853
Total	1,936,919	1,754,972,413	228,438,105
Small (assets < $1 million)	1,589,400	na	na
Not small (assets > $1 million)	347,500	na	na
S corporations			
Net income	1,766,274	1,778,923,022	240,561,633
Deficit	959,501	1,521,945,740	46,805,222
Total	2,725,775	3,300,868,762	193,756,411
All corporations[b]			
Small (assets < $1 million)	4,445,912	2,449,913,506	61,046,898
Not small (assets > $1 million)	489,991	16,442,472,187	867,908,628

Source: IRS, *Statistics of Income Bulletins: Sole Proprietorship Returns, 2000,* Summer 2002; *Individual Income Tax Returns, 1999,* Fall 2001; *Partnership Returns, 1999,* Fall 2001; *S Corporation Returns, 1999,* Spring 2002; *Corporation Income Tax Returns, 1999,* Summer 2002; *Selected Historical and Other Data,* Summer 2002.

a. Total receipts for nonfarm sole proprietorships include income from sales and operations and other business income; total receipts for partnerships include business receipts, ordinary income from other partnerships and fiduciaries, farm net profit, net gain (noncapital assets), and other income (net); total receipts for S corporations include business receipts, interest on state and local government obligations, net gain (noncapital assets), and other receipts.

b. Refers to all corporations, including but not limited to Subchapter C and S corporations.

cations of tax policy directed toward small business. It is also critical for assessing the impact of a change in IRS policy toward this sector.

Two data sources shed light on this issue. The first is evidence from individual tax returns, collected in tables 4-2, 4-3, and 4-4. Table 4-2 shows, by adjusted gross income group, who reports income or loss, and how much, for sole proprietorship (Schedule C) income, income from partnerships or Subchapter S corporations (from Schedule E), and farm income reported on

Table 4-2. *Individual Income Tax Returns, by Group and Size of Adjusted Gross Income, 1999*

| | Total, all groups | | Business or profession | | | |
| | | | Net income | | Net loss | |
Adjusted gross income	Number of returns	Total adjusted gross income ($)	Number of returns	Amount ($)	Number of returns	Amount ($)
No adjusted gross income	1,066,171	–53,860,647	123,848	1,550,759	282,235	5,462,350
$1 to $5,000	13,349,971	35,429,722	983,615	2,663,392	121,301	550,543
$5,000 to $10,000	12,979,714	97,360,406	1,481,327	9,104,450	170,113	892,511
$10,000 to $15,000	12,275,717	153,523,887	1,073,852	9,251,058	221,709	1,084,785
$15,000 to $20,000	11,783,174	205,107,333	953,205	9,580,941	246,274	1,259,884
$20,000 to $25,000	9,967,211	223,695,901	832,462	8,836,658	227,305	916,416
$25,000 to $30,000	8,392,769	229,838,965	704,960	7,671,192	235,476	1,167,074
$30,000 to $40,000	13,288,379	461,841,650	1,258,347	15,066,903	469,016	2,127,062
$40,000 to $50,000	9,870,199	441,506,289	1,057,761	13,717,571	436,247	1,770,966
$50,000 to $75,000	16,755,560	1,023,707,214	1,999,763	32,436,066	803,683	3,145,842
$75,000 to $100,000	7,811,626	671,217,536	1,024,184	23,719,898	438,809	1,849,472
$100,000 to $200,000	7,104,712	934,766,661	1,189,897	46,122,061	346,412	2,119,652
$200,000 to $500,000	1,876,561	542,447,737	382,818	34,907,443	113,048	1,199,692
$500,000 to $1 million	348,256	235,700,884	64,174	9,152,882	20,879	535,537
$1 million or more	205,124	653,184,370	35,104	9,964,964	14,301	1,250,383
All returns	127,075,145	5,855,467,909	13,165,318	233,746,237	4,146,807	25,332,170

Source: IRS, *Statistics of Income Bulletin,* Fall 2001, Publication 1136 (rev. 11-2001).

Schedule F. Tables 4-3 and 4-4 restate these data for the number of returns and income, respectively, as a fraction of the income group's total returns and total adjusted gross income.

These tables reveal some interesting patterns. First, consider sole proprietorships. Having sole proprietorship income is about twice as likely for individuals with adjusted gross income (AGI) over $100,000 as it is for those with adjusted gross income below $100,000; about 18 percent of the higher-income group has this kind of income, compared to about 9 percent of the lower-income group. However, sole proprietorship income as a fraction of AGI is highest among those with positive AGI less than $10,000, and it is also relatively high in the $100,000 to $500,000 AGI groups. It is lowest of all among those with AGI greater than $1,000,000.

The story for partnership and Subchapter S corporation income is strikingly different. This type of income is rare for low-income taxpayers; less than 2 percent of those with AGI less than $20,000 have a gain or loss. Its prevalence increases sharply among higher-income taxpayers. The prevalence of this source of income approaches 10 percent for those with AGI between $75,000

| Partnership or S corporation | | | | Farm | | | |
| Net income | | Net loss | | Net income | | Net loss | |
Number of returns	Amount ($)	Number of returns	Amount ($)	Number of returns	Amount ($)	Number of returns	Amount ($)
40,171	1,334,865	161,838	18,604,337	21,107	293,577	93,057	2,830,896
73,147	239,889	62,597	543,814	57,487	141,932	29,432	216,356
105,867	507,038	65,402	771,427	50,064	290,750	56,883	489,518
103,407	669,213	62,090	758,162	63,481	388,078	74,458	519,339
113,829	1,000,851	80,701	773,402	54,159	396,639	96,332	862,034
125,824	1,150,129	70,157	646,479	49,721	430,118	92,794	787,278
126,286	1,449,377	74,637	595,178	47,681	397,656	69,746	652,760
261,516	2,727,605	142,074	1,297,347	71,853	947,019	158,017	1,494,488
290,509	3,693,857	145,266	1,229,034	58,747	634,265	122,098	901,391
632,201	9,384,983	353,336	2,720,548	126,617	1,783,382	272,008	2,220,894
500,282	10,091,548	264,739	2,211,195	57,899	1,180,685	108,769	995,970
931,467	34,996,585	363,787	5,059,164	49,275	1,443,705	97,568	1,431,236
580,146	56,347,561	188,720	5,754,731	13,265	515,917	34,183	981,091
162,614	38,924,100	48,539	3,174,866	2,397	168,831	9,215	425,239
107,512	107,240,229	37,957	14,546,182	2,028	188,607	5,965	635,588
4,154,776	269,757,830	2,121,841	58,685,867	725,782	9,201,162	1,320,526	15,444,078

and $100,000, is nearly 20 percent for those with AGI between $100,000 and $200,000, and is 40 percent, 60 percent, and 70 percent, respectively, for those with AGI between $200,000 and $500,000, between $500,000 and $1,000,000, and over $1,000,000. For those with AGI over $200,000, net income from partnerships and S corporations comprises over 10 percent of overall AGI from all sources. Of the aggregate net income less deficit of $211 billion, over 60 percent of it, or $128.4 billion, was reported by taxpayers with AGI in excess of $500,000, although they make up less than 0.5 percent of taxpayers and receive about 15 percent of overall AGI. I suspect that a similar skewing of ownership also applies to relatively small, closely held C corporations, although the tax return data do not shed light on this. The portfolio data from the Survey of Consumer Finances, discussed below, are consistent with this hypothesis.

What is perhaps most striking about farm sole proprietorships is the ubiquity of reported losses. Of those taxpayers that report this activity, almost twice as many report a deficit as report net income. This phenomenon occurs for all AGI classes, except for those with positive AGI less than $5,000, and is most

Table 4-3. *Income Tax Returns, by Group and Size of Adjusted Gross Income, 1999*

Adjusted gross income	Total number of returns ($)	Business or profession (percent of total returns)			Partnership and S corporation (percent of total returns)			Farm (percent of total returns)		
		Gain	*Loss*	*Either*	*Gain*	*Loss*	*Either*	*Gain*	*Loss*	*Either*
No adjusted gross income	1,066,171	11.62	26.47	38.09	3.77	15.18	18.95	1.98	8.73	10.71
$1 to $5,000	13,349,971	7.37	0.91	8.28	0.55	0.47	1.02	0.43	0.22	0.65
$5,000 to $10,000	12,979,714	11.41	1.31	12.72	0.82	0.50	1.32	0.39	0.44	0.82
$10,000 to $15,000	12,275,717	8.75	1.81	10.55	0.84	0.51	1.35	0.52	0.61	1.12
$15,000 to $20,000	11,783,174	8.09	2.09	10.18	0.97	0.68	1.65	0.46	0.82	1.28
$20,000 to $25,000	9,967,211	8.35	2.28	10.63	1.26	0.70	1.97	0.50	0.93	1.43
$25,000 to $30,000	8,392,769	8.40	2.81	11.21	1.50	0.89	2.39	0.57	0.83	1.40
$30,000 to $40,000	13,288,379	9.47	3.53	13.00	1.97	1.07	3.04	0.54	1.19	1.73
$40,000 to $50,000	9,870,199	10.72	4.42	15.14	2.94	1.47	4.42	0.60	1.24	1.83
$50,000 to $75,000	16,755,560	11.93	4.80	16.73	3.77	2.11	5.88	0.76	1.62	2.38
$75,000 to $100,000	7,811,626	13.11	5.62	18.73	6.40	3.39	9.79	0.74	1.39	2.13
$100,000 to $200,000	7,104,712	16.75	4.88	21.62	13.11	5.12	18.23	0.69	1.37	2.07
$200,000 to $500,000	1,876,561	20.40	6.02	26.42	30.92	10.06	40.97	0.71	1.82	2.53
$500,000 to $1 million	348,256	18.43	6.00	24.42	46.69	13.94	60.63	0.69	2.65	3.33
$1 million or more	205,124	17.11	6.97	24.09	52.41	18.50	70.92	0.99	2.91	3.90
All returns	127,075,145	10.36	3.26	13.62	3.27	1.67	4.94	0.57	1.04	1.61

Source: IRS, *Statistics of Income Bulletin*, Fall 2001, Publication 1136 (rev. 11-2001).

Table 4-4. *Adjusted Gross Income, by Group and Size of Adjusted Gross Income, 1999*

Adjusted gross income	Total adjusted gross income (less deficit) ($)	Business or profession (percent of total returns)			Partnership and S corporation (percent of total returns)			Farm (percent of total returns)		
		Gain	Loss	Either	Gain	Loss	Either	Gain	Loss	Either
No adjusted gross income	−53,860,647	−2.88	10.14	7.26	−2.48	34.54	32.06	−0.55	5.26	4.71
$1 to $5,000	35,429,722	7.52	−1.55	5.96	0.68	−1.53	−0.86	0.40	−0.61	−0.21
$5,000 to $10,000	97,360,406	9.35	−0.92	8.43	0.52	−0.79	−0.27	0.30	−0.50	−0.20
$10,000 to $15,000	153,523,887	6.03	−0.71	5.32	0.44	−0.49	−0.06	0.25	−0.34	−0.09
$15,000 to $20,000	205,107,333	4.67	−0.61	4.06	0.49	−0.38	0.11	0.19	−0.42	−0.23
$20,000 to $25,000	223,695,901	3.95	−0.41	3.54	0.51	−0.29	0.23	0.19	−0.35	−0.16
$25,000 to $30,000	229,838,965	3.34	−0.51	2.83	0.63	−0.26	0.37	0.17	−0.28	−0.11
$30,000 to $40,000	461,841,650	3.26	−0.46	2.80	0.59	−0.28	0.31	0.21	−0.32	−0.12
$40,000 to $50,000	441,506,289	3.11	−0.40	2.71	0.84	−0.28	0.56	0.14	−0.20	−0.06
$50,000 to $75,000	1,023,707,214	3.17	−0.31	2.86	0.92	−0.27	0.65	0.17	−0.22	−0.04
$75,000 to $100,000	671,217,536	3.53	−0.28	3.26	1.50	−0.33	1.17	0.18	−0.15	0.03
$100,000 to $200,000	934,766,661	4.93	−0.23	4.71	3.74	−0.54	3.20	0.15	−0.15	0.00
$200,000 to $500,000	542,447,737	6.44	−0.22	6.21	10.39	−1.06	9.33	0.10	−0.18	−0.09
$500,000 to $1 million	235,700,884	3.88	−0.23	3.66	16.51	−1.35	15.17	0.07	−0.18	−0.11
$1 million or more	653,184,370	1.53	−0.19	1.33	16.42	−2.23	14.19	0.03	−0.10	−0.07
All returns	5,855,467,909	3.99	−0.43	3.56	4.61	−1.00	3.60	0.16	−0.26	−0.11

Source: IRS, *Statistics of Income Bulletin*, Fall 2001, Publication 1136 (rev. 11-2001).

striking among those that report negative overall AGI and those with reported AGI over $200,000.

Note that these data refer to reported, preaudit information. If, as we document later, there is substantial noncompliance, this will tend to skew the portrait of who receives this type of income; recipients are on average more affluent than tables 4-2, 4-3, and 4-4 suggest.

Another informative data source is the Survey of Consumer Finances. Christopher Carroll shows, based on the 1995 Survey of Consumer Finances, that 74.3 percent of households in the top 1 percent of net worth have privately held businesses, compared to 12.8 percent for the other 99 percent. For the top 1 percent, these privately held businesses comprised 41.4 percent of net worth, compared to 14.8 percent for the other 99 percent.[10] Gentry and Hubbard, based on the 1989 Survey of Consumer Finances, find that 56.3 percent of those in the top percentile of income own one or more active businesses with a total market value of at least $5,000, compared to 8.7 percent of the overall population.[11]

In summary, although nonfarm sole proprietorship income is fairly evenly distributed across the population, income from partnerships and S corporations—and probably small, closely held C corporations—is highly concentrated among the affluent. This will become important later when I discuss what is appropriate enforcement strategy regarding this type of business income.

Income Tax Preferences for Small Business

This chapter is not primarily about the tax code itself but rather about the impact of how the code is administered and enforced. Nevertheless it bears noting that the tax code has aspects that appear to grant small business preferential treatment, both explicitly and implicitly, and other aspects that appear to be prejudicial against small business, in this case usually implicitly.[12] The most obvious explicit small-business preference is that a business organized as a traditional corporation (a C corporation under the Internal Revenue Code) is subject to a 15 percent tax on its first $50,000 of taxable income, a 25 percent rate on its next $25,000, and a marginal rate of at least 34 percent on taxable income over $75,000. Several other preferential features apply only to small businesses. IRC section 179 permits small businesses to expense immediately certain capital expenditures that under the normal rules would be amortized. IRC section 1044 allows investors (subject to certain dollar limitations) to defer tax on gain

10. Carroll (2000). The figures for the "other 99 percent" refer to an average over 1962 to 1995.
11. Gentry and Hubbard (forthcoming).
12. By an implicit preference (or penalty) I mean one for which the tax code makes no mention of a size-of-business qualifying standard but which applies to activities that naturally tend to be undertaken more by small or large businesses. For example, a preference that is unavailable to C corporations (of any size) will tend to disfavor very large businesses.

realized from the sale of publicly traded securities to the extent that the proceeds from the sale are invested within 60 days in a qualified, specialized small-business investment company. Section 1202 allows taxpayers to exclude half the gain realized from the sale of stock of certain small business corporations held for more than five years, and section 1244 provides that taxpayers generally may convert a capital loss on stock to ordinary loss, if the stock is in certain small-business companies.[13]

Some tax accounting rules favor businesses not organized as C corporations, and so favor small businesses to the extent that larger companies tend to be organized as sole proprietorships, partnerships, and limited liability companies. In particular, C corporations generally are required to follow the accrual method of accounting, but partnerships, sole proprietorships, and S corporations typically may use the cash method; in using the cash method, a business may be able to accelerate or defer revenues and expenses near the end of a calendar year in a way that reduces overall tax liability.

Small businesses also can be harmed by certain tax rules. For example, the reorganization provisions of the Internal Revenue Code, which allow taxpayers to enter into certain mergers or sales without recognizing taxable gain, are available only to C corporations, not to businesses organized in other forms. Second, the passive activity loss and at-risk rules, which limit the availability of certain deductible losses, are not applicable to most large C corporations. Finally, the qualified retirement plans for self-employed taxpayers are subject to more onerous restrictions than those that apply to corporate employees. For example, a loan between a qualified plan of an unincorporated entity and a self-employed individual is a prohibited transaction subject to penalty taxes. As of 2002 the tax law limited full deductibility of health insurance costs for sole proprietorships only.[14] Some argue that the progressive nature of the tax system that puts severe limits on loss offsets is particularly harsh on the volatile income streams that often characterize entrepreneurial activities.[15]

No one has attempted to quantify the aspects of the tax law that favor or disfavor small businesses, much less businesses of other sizes. More attention has gone into quantifying the costs of compliance and the rate of compliance of business.

13. Note that this is not meant to be an exhaustive list of small-business preferences.

14. As of 2003 full deductibility is granted to sole proprietorships. See Mastromarco and Burton (2002) for a listing of de jure and de facto aspects of the tax law that discriminate in favor of large businesses.

15. On a historical note, Charles Babbage (1851), now remembered for his invention of the "difference machine" to carry out mathematical calculations (a precursor of the modern computer) argued against small business tax preferences using the benefit principle of taxation. He argued that it cost the government more to protect small than large capitalists, for a vendor of apples on the street corner needed the police to prevent theft of stock, whereas a great merchant house such as Barings was able to shift its capital around the globe and so avoid risk (quoted in Daunton, 2001, p. 151).

Compliance Costs

It is widely believed that the burden of government regulation, defined to include but not restricted to tax, is regressive with respect to firm size, in the sense of being larger in proportion to size for smaller companies compared to larger companies. The idea is simply that a firm must spend resources to determine whether a regulation or tax provision applies to it and, in the case of regulations, whether it is in compliance and what actions must be taken to be in compliance. These information-gathering costs are fixed regardless of firm size, and larger firms can spread this fixed cost over more units of output, sales, or assets. In part this problem is handled by the outsourcing of tax compliance matters. Indeed, as Cornelia Ashby reports, according to the IRS, between 80 and 88 percent of small businesses rely on tax practitioners to prepare their returns.[16] In some instances Congress and regulatory agencies have exempted small firms through "tiering" of the laws and rules.[17]

Nevertheless, a report by the Small Business Administration Office of Advocacy calculates that the overall regulatory burden to small firms (where the cutoff between small and nonsmall is 500 employees) was approximately 50 percent more for each employee than the cost to large firms. The report concludes that "this inequitable cost allocation gives large firms a competitive advantage, a result at odds with the national interest in maintaining a viable, dynamic, and progressive role for small businesses in the American economy."[18]

Hard quantitative evidence about the income tax compliance costs incurred by businesses in the United States is not abundant; it comes almost entirely from survey-based studies.[19] These studies suggest that, on average, self-employed taxpayers spend nearly three times as much of their own time on tax compliance as other taxpayers (60 hours, as opposed to 22 hours[20]) and are almost twice as likely to use professional assistance to prepare their taxes.[21]

Analysis of the largest U.S. companies reveals that over half of these costs are personnel costs within the firm.[22] Moreover they show that larger firms incur greater compliance costs, and there are clear economies of scale, so that compliance costs as a proportion of firm size decrease as a firm's asset size increases. The

16. Ashby (2000).

17. See Brown, Hamilton, and Medoff (1990, p. 84).

18. SBA (1995, p. 5).

19. Most estimates come from four survey-based studies: Slemrod and Blumenthal (1996), Slemrod (1997), a study commissioned by the Internal Revenue Service and carried out by Arthur D. Little in 1985 (ADL 1988), and Slemrod and Venkatesh (2002). Others such as Payne (1993) and Hall (1995) have reinterpreted and reevaluated data from the Arthur D. Little study.

20. In the 1989 survey, the average time spent on taxes by taxpayers that were homemakers, employed, or retired was about 27 hours.

21. See Slemrod and Sorum (1984); Blumenthal and Slemrod (1992).

22. See Slemrod and Blumenthal (1996); Slemrod (1997).

regressivity of compliance costs is corroborated in studies of intermediate-sized companies, defined as companies with assets of greater than $5 million but that are not large enough to rank among largest 1,500 companies. A survey-based analysis of this sector concludes that the asset elasticity of total compliance costs was 0.60—that is, a company with 1 percent more in assets on average has only 0.60 percent higher compliance costs.[23] The 0.60 elasticity implies, for example, that a company with 5 times the assets of another will have about 2.5 times the compliance costs, so that the cost-to-assets ratio is just half as much. When other characteristics of companies are held constant, the estimated asset elasticity falls, but only to 0.467, suggesting that some—but not most—of the association of size with costs is due not to size per se but rather to the type of characteristics that larger firms tend to have, such as operating in foreign countries and being publicly owned.

All these studies are based on questionnaires mailed to companies. The low response rate of the survey questionnaires—between 10 and 40 percent—raises concern about respondent bias. However, the direction of the bias is not clear. It is conceivable that on average the respondents are irate taxpayers who consider tax compliance to be onerous, in which case the results would overstate the true costs of compliance.[24] On the other hand, it has been suggested that taxpayers who find tax forms particularly objectionable are more likely not to respond to complicated questionnaires.[25] Such behavior would understate the true compliance cost. Furthermore the incremental cost of tax compliance—the cost that is incurred by the company solely because it needs to comply with the income tax—is difficult to measure. This is particularly true of smaller firms, because those firms often do not have separate accounting departments. These caveats aside, the consensus is that the compliance costs incurred by businesses are indeed regressive; as a fraction of any of number of size indicators, the costs are lower for larger companies.

The regressivity of compliance costs is apparently a universal phenomenon. As a proportion of turnover, small companies in Australia and New Zealand generally have greater total compliance costs than larger firms.[26] One careful study of the United Kingdom reveals that businesses' compliance costs for the corporate tax (and for other taxes studied) are strongly regressive: Small businesses (up to £100,000 of taxable turnover) had compliance costs equal to 0.79 percent of taxable turnover, while compliance costs for medium-sized (£100,000 to £1 million) and large (over £1 million) businesses were 0.15 and 0.04 percent, respectively, of taxable turnover. A study of the Netherlands also found that compliance costs

---

23. See Slemrod and Venkatesh (2002).
24. Tait (1988, p. 352).
25. Sandford (1995).
26. See Sandford and Hasseldine (1992); Pope (1995); Goodwin (1995).

per employee and as a proportion of turnover decreased significantly as firm size increased.[27]

The vastly different survey populations, as well as the divergent tax law and processes across countries, not to mention nonuniform survey methodologies, make it impossible to draw many clear generalizations about the level and nature of the cost to businesses of complying with income tax laws. It is, though, universally concluded that compliance costs are regressive with respect to any of several measures of firm size.

Note that these survey-based estimates of compliance costs do not distinguish between involuntary costs that must be expended to comply with the law and discretionary costs that are incurred to avoid or evade taxes. Mills, Erickson, and Maydew show, for large companies, that greater compliance costs are associated with a lower effective tax rate, other things equal, suggesting that at least some of these costs represent tax planning and the like.[28] More generally the resource cost of tax collection refers to the social rather than the private cost of collection. Businesses and many individuals can deduct the monetary costs of compliance in computing taxable income, so their private cost is less than the social cost. In addition employers earn interest on withheld employee taxes, because they need not remit tax to the IRS immediately.

One of the most trenchant criticisms of the use of survey-based methods to estimate compliance costs owes to Ian Wallschutzky. For each of twelve small businesses in Australia, he conducted an initial interview and subsequent quarterly interviews and also had the business managers complete monthly diaries of their time spent on compliance activities. Based on this study he concludes that survey-based studies probably overstate the costs and problems of complying with taxes. Perhaps his most telling conclusion, however, is that "measuring any aspect of compliance in small businesses is likely to be fraught with danger," due to uncertainty about what exactly constitutes a compliance activity and the difficulty of locating one person who is aware of all the company's compliance activities.[29] This is an important caveat to all quantitative estimates of tax compliance costs and probably applies most to small businesses.

Compliance and Noncompliance

A principal objective of this chapter is to place the well-established regressivity of compliance costs into the context of an assessment of the regressivity or pro-

---

27. See Allers (1995).
28. Mills, Erickson, and Maydew (1998).
29. Wallschutzky (1995, p. 295).

gressivity of the compliance behavior of businesses. If, for example, small businesses are much more noncompliant than other businesses, then it might be true that the tax system (other than the explicit aspects of the law) actually favors small business. In other words, their greater noncompliance on average may offset their regressive compliance cost burden.

Before addressing this question quantitatively, it is worthwhile to step back and consider the nature of tax evasion. A large economics literature now exists on the subject, dating from the seminal paper by Allingham and Sandmo, which models an individual's choice regarding tax evasion as a choice under uncertainty—a gamble—in which there is a trade-off between a gain if the evasion is undetected and a loss if the evasion is detected and penalized.[30] Taxpayers are neither honest nor dishonest but merely rational calculators of what is in their best interest. The determining factors in this model are the probability of detection and punishment, the penalty structure, and the risk aversion of the potentially evading taxpayer.[31] A budding literature in political science and sociology (with some economists contributing) stresses that evasion involves more than a cost-benefit calculation and reflects the taxpayer's sense of duty, perception of the fairness of the tax system, and trust in government and the political system more broadly.[32]

Nearly all the theoretical and empirical literature on tax evasion focuses on evasion by individuals.[33] In this context it is natural to assume that risk aversion of the individual places a natural barrier on the amount of evasion that is optimal. In the context of a large, publicly held firm, this assumption is unsatisfactory, as presumably the shareholders hold diversified portfolios, implying that the firm should behave as if it is risk-neutral, even if its shareholders are not.[34] This alternative is not, however, relevant to closely held small businesses, whose owners' wealth is generally not well diversified. For these situations it is clear that the tax situation of the company and the tax situation of the owners are intimately related and must be analyzed simultaneously.

Small business noncompliance is an endemic problem in tax systems that rely on remittance of taxes by business (perhaps through withholding of labor income taxes) and information returns provided by business—that is, most

---

30. Allingham and Sandmo (1972).

31. The economics literature on tax administration, evasion, and enforcement is surveyed in Andreoni, Erard, and Feinstein (1998) and in Slemrod and Yitzhaki (2002).

32. These new perspectives on tax evasion are critically reviewed in Slemrod (2002).

33. An interesting exception is Andreoni (1992), who treats some business tax evasion as a last-resort loan from the IRS, and the IRS as a "loan shark." See the discussion below of Rice (1992), who finds some evidence that is consistent with this notion.

34. In large corporations another issue arises: Those who make decisions about tax compliance are not the shareholders but rather agents of the shareholders. See Crocker and Slemrod (2003) for a positive and normative treatment of corporate tax evasion within a principal-agent framework.

modern tax systems. It is difficult for the tax agency to obtain corroborating information,[35] and it is probably not cost-efficient for them to audit small businesses extensively. Moreover there are inherent and tricky interpretation issues, such as pertain to the use of business resources for private consumption.

TCMP Evidence

Certainly the most comprehensive, and probably the most accurate, data on tax compliance for any country at any time were collected by the IRS through its Taxpayer Compliance Measurement Program. The TCMP consisted of intensive examinations of a sample of tax returns filed for tax years 1973, 1976, 1979, 1982, 1985, and 1988. By comparing these examined returns with the original returns as filed, supplemented by other evidence, the IRS estimated the total amount of underreported income and overstated subtractions in each of these years (and projected estimates for out years) and estimated the total loss of tax revenue due to various forms of noncompliance.

To be sure, the TCMP-based estimates of noncompliance are not precise. The potential inaccuracy is perhaps best illustrated by the fact that the estimates recognize that TCMP examinations do not detect all underreported income, and so the IRS tax gap model augments the TCMP data with estimates from other studies of underreported income not detected by the TCMP. The IRS study makes use of a multiplier of 3.28, on the assumption that for every dollar of income undetected by TCMP examiners without the aid of information report documents, another $2.28 went undetected.[36] A separate procedure is used for estimating underreported informal supplier income.

The TCMP studies for the most part paint a stark and clear contrast between the relatively low income tax compliance rates of small business and the much higher compliance rates associated with other sources of income, particularly wages and salaries.[37] Table 4-5 summarizes the conclusions of two IRS TCMP studies. The IRS estimates that in 1987 the percentage of wages and salaries that was voluntarily reported (the voluntary reporting percentage, or VRP) was 99.5 percent for income from wages and salaries and 94.6 percent for interest and dividends.[38] In stark contrast, this ratio was just 42.1 percent for partnership and S corporation income, only 13.1 percent for informal suppliers, and

35. This is especially problematic for cash businesses, as stressed in Bankman and Karlinsky (2002).

36. IRS (1996).

37. There is a long history to the suspicion that small businesses have relatively high rates of noncompliance. A study done in 1870 by the British Board of Inland Revenue claims that 40 percent of assessments of unincorporated business were undertaxed, and in 1893 the chairman assumed there was, in effect, a 20 percent reduction in the income tax from trade and professions (Daunton 2001, p. 197).

38. IRS (1988a, 1988b). Estimates refer to filers only.

Table 4-5. *Taxpayer Compliance, by Underreporting Gap Component, 1987 and 1988*

	Tax year 1987		Tax year 1988	
Underreporting gap component	VRP (percent)[a]	Gap ($ billions)[b]	NMP (percent)[c]	Gap ($ billions)
Nonbusiness income		15.7		15.7
Wages and salaries	99.5	1.4	0.9	2.7
Interest income	94.6	3.2	2.3	1.1
Dividends	d	d	7.8	1.3
State income tax refunds	95.2	0.1	0.8	<0.05
Alimony income	71.0	0.2	13.3	0.1
Pensions and annuities	98.4	0.1	4.0	1.4
Unemployment compensation	89.1	0.3	6.9	0.1
Social Security benefits	96.7	d	4.2	0.1
Capital gains	88.3	6.7	7.2	3.2
Income from sales of business property	e	e	28.0	0.6
Other income	e	3.6	24.7	5.1
Business income		32.6		31.3
Nonfarm proprietor income	50.9[f]	16.6	32.3	14.4
Informal supplier income	13.1[f]	7.7	81.4	10.8
Farm income	e	1.9	32.2	1.7
Rents and royalties	e	3.1	17.2	2.0
Partnership and S corporation income	42.1[f]	3.2	7.5	2.4
Offsets to income		6.1		7.2
Adjustments	106.3	0.5	2.0	0.2
Deductions	104.4	3.5	4.4	4.3
Exemptions	104.2	2.0	4.5	2.7
Tax credits	e	0.9	40.2	4.1

Source: IRS (1988a), tables I-1 and I-2; IRS (1996), table 7.

a. Voluntary reporting percentage: the ratio of the total amount of income or other related items that are voluntarily reported to the corresponding correct amount.

b. Gross tax gap estimate.

c. Net misreporting percentage: the ratio of the net misreported amount in the taxpayer's favor to the sum of the absolute values of what should have been reported. For income items, the NMP value corresponds approximately to 100 minus the VRP. For offsets, the NMP corresponds approximately to the VRP minus 100.

d. Item is combined with the item above.

e. Not reported.

f. Figure was not reported in IRS (1988a) but was calculated by the author from other information reported there.

50.9 percent for other (that is, not informal) nonfarm proprietor income.[39] In sum, for these last sources of income, less than half of true taxable income was reported to the IRS.

The most recent IRS study is based on the 1985 and 1988 TCMP and a 1988 TCMP survey of nonfilers.[40] The results are summarized in the second column of table 4-5. It estimates that in 1988 the net misreporting percentage[41] (NMP, approximately equal to 100 minus the voluntary reporting percentages discussed above) of wages and salaries was 0.9 percent; the estimated NMP was 2.3 percent and 7.8 percent for interest income and dividends, respectively.[42] In contrast the NMP for informal supplier income was 81.4 percent, for nonfarm proprietor income was 32.3 percent, and for partnership and small business corporation income it was just 7.5 percent. The NMP of 81.4 percent for informal supplier income is not inconsistent with the earlier VRP estimate of 13.1 percent. But the later estimates for nonfarm proprietor income and partnership and small business income suggest much lower noncompliance rates than the 1988 report does. These and other differences are ascribed by the IRS to "major changes in the methods used," but the precise reasons for the huge changes in the estimated noncompliance rates for these categories of income are not entirely clear.

Table 4-6 estimates the rate of compliance in 1982, 1985, and 1988, not by source of income but by categories of taxpayers based on IRS examination classes.[43] (Classification of returns for audit examination purposes is based on the largest source of income on the return and certain other characteristics.) In 1988 the voluntary compliance level (VCL, similar to the VRP discussed above) for business returns was 79.9 percent, compared to 94.5 percent for nonbusiness returns.[44] Among business returns, the lowest VCL of 63.9 percent was for those

39. According to IRS (1988a, 1988b), informal suppliers include roadside or sidewalk vendors, moonlighting craftsmen or mechanics, unlicensed providers of child and elderly care services, and similar operators with informal business styles. These voluntary reporting percentages (VRPs) are calculated from table I-2 of IRS (1988a, 1988b). The components of the ratios are reported there, but the ratios themselves are not reported because "they would be distorted by the combination of positive and negative amounts of income."

40. IRS (1996).

41. The net misreporting percentage is defined as the ratio of the net misreported amount (NMA) in the taxpayer's favor to the sum of what should have been reported, expressed in percentage terms. For an income item, the NMA is defined as the sum of all amounts underreported minus the sum of all amounts overreported on the item. For an offset item (such as deductions or credits), the NMA is defined as the sum of all amounts overstated minus the sum of all amounts understated on the item.

42. Table A3 of IRS (1996), from which these numbers are taken, lists a high and a low estimate, which are always quite close. The text uses the high numbers.

43. This is taken from Christian (1994).

44. The voluntary compliance level is defined as the ratio of the total tax liability reported to the sum of the total tax liability reported and the tax increase recommended after examination, times 100.

Table 4-6. *Voluntary Compliance Levels, by Examination Class, 1982, 1985, 1988*[a]

Examination class	1982	1985	1988
Nonbusiness	93.6	93.1	94.5
TPI < $25,000 (1040A type)[b]	93.1	92.4	87.6
TPI < $25,000	89.8	85.6	85.9
$25,000 ≤ TPI < $50,000	94.6	92.8	94.4
$50,000 ≤ TPI < $100,000	94.6	94.7	95.7
TPI ≥ $100,000	93.7	95.3	96.6
Business	75.7	76.7	79.9
Schedule C			
TGR < $25,000[c]	65.6	60.8	63.9
$25,000 ≤ TGR < $100,000	74.7	71.0	76.5
TGR ≥ $100,000	77.8	81.8	83.7
Schedule F			
TGR < $100,000	75.2	75.1	76.6
TGR ≥ $100,000	81.7	82.3	82.5
Total	92.2	91.5	92.7

Source: Christian (1994).

a. Voluntary compliance level is defined as the ratio of the total tax liability reported to the sum of the total tax liability reported and the tax increase recommended after examination, times 100.

b. TPI is total positive income (income from positive sources only).

c. TGR is total gross receipts.

Schedule C filers with total gross receipts less than $25,000. The VCL is generally higher for businesses with higher reported receipts.[45] In addition, business activities traditionally associated with cash income have lower than average VCLs (for example, transportation and retail trade, with VCLs in 1988 equal to 68.9 and 67.8 percent, respectively), and activities with relatively little cash income (for example, real estate and wholesale trade, with 1988 VCLs of 84.4 and 82.8, respectively) have higher VCLs.[46] Over 30 percent of the unreported tax detected in the 1988 TCMP examinations of individuals came from sole proprietors, which composed only 5.5 percent of the returns filed.[47]

45. As Christian (1992a) notes, one reason for the apparent increase in compliance after 1985 might be the reduction in the incentive to incorporate due to the Tax Reform Act of 1986. If fewer of the larger, and historically more compliant, proprietorships incorporated (thus remaining sole proprietors), an increase in the VCL would be observed. This is consistent with the finding of Morton (1992) that the VCL of small corporations (that is, with assets less than $10 million or no balance sheet) declined over this same period.

46. More details are presented in Christian (1992a).

47. This is based on Christian (1992b).

Of particular relevance here, Eric Rice examines data from the special 1980 TCMP study of corporations with assets between $1 million and $10 million.[48] He draws three relevant conclusions from his econometric analyses of these data. First, compliance is positively related to being publicly traded and in a highly regulated industry, so that characteristics that assure public disclosure of information also tend to encourage better tax compliance. Second, firm profitability exerts two opposing effects. Managers of corporations whose profit performance falls short of its industry norm may resort to noncompliance as a means of shaving costs. In contrast, high-profit companies may take advantage of their greater ability to underreport income without being audited. Finally Rice finds that the reporting gap grows with value added as a measure of firm size. However, because of the estimated elasticity of between one-third and one-half, the ratio of noncompliance to value-added declines with firm size. These results suggest that noncompliance is a regressive phenomenon in the same way that compliance costs are: It is larger in proportion to firm size for smaller companies.

Carolyn Morton examines both the 1980 and 1987 special TCMP studies of small corporations.[49] Several of her conclusions are relevant. First, the voluntary compliance level is lower for younger firms; in the 1987 study the VCL was 50.9 percent for firms less than three years old, 55.1 percent for firms between three and nineteen years old, and 75.5 for companies at least nineteen years old. Second, the VCL was systematically lower in services (VCL of 48.0) and retail trade (VCL of 55.5) compared to manufacturing (VCL of 74.4). Finally, within the class of small corporations with balance sheets, the voluntary compliance rate rises monotonically by asset class, as the econometric analysis of Rice, discussed above, corroborates. The VCL in 1988 for corporations with less than $50,000 of assets was just 26.8 percent, and the VCL rises continuously by asset class until it reaches 77.0 percent for corporations with assets between $5 million and $10 million; it was 61.1 percent overall for this sector.

Analyses of the Policy Determinants of Evasion

For policy purposes the extent of evasion is not as interesting as how it responds to policy. Pinning this down is, however, quite challenging because of the difficulty of measuring evasion itself and such crucial aspects of the policy environment as the perceived probability of detection of a given act of evasion. Early analyses of cross-sectional data from the TCMP focused on the effect of the tax rate on evasion and produced mixed results.[50] Analysis of state-level time-series cross-sectional data holds more promise for ascertaining the impact of changing

48. Rice (1992).
49. Morton (1992).
50. Compare Clotfelter (1983a); Feinstein (1991).

enforcement policies, but it has been plagued by the absence of a direct measure of noncompliance.[51]

One unambiguous finding is that, across line items on the individual income tax return, noncompliance rates are related to proxies for the traceability, deniability, and ambiguity of the items, which are in turn related to the probability that evasion will be detected and punished.[52] Moreover there is evidence of a "substitution effect" across line items, such that greater noncompliance on one item lowers the attractiveness of noncompliance on others, because the latter jeopardizes the expected return to the former by increasing the probability of detection.

Analysis of both cross-section and time-series historical data is subject to severe difficulties of measuring the parameters of the environment and of knowing the source of any variation in these parameters. Controlled experiments can avoid all these problems but, for cost and other implementation reasons, are rare. One recent exception is reported by Slemrod, Blumenthal, and Christian, in which the State of Minnesota Department of Revenue conducted a randomized controlled experiment with respect to four aspects of the tax compliance environment: the threat of an audit, the provision of special return preparation information services, moral appeals, and a redesigned tax form.[53] They find that, for low- and middle-income taxpayers, a threat of certain audit[54] produced a small but statistically significant increase in reported income, which was larger for those with greater opportunities to evade.[55] However, for high-income taxpayers, the audit threat was associated with, on average, a lower income report. The authors speculate that sophisticated, high-income taxpayers view an audit as a negotiation and treat taxable income reported on the tax form as the opening (low) bid in a negotiation which does not necessarily result in the determination and penalization of all noncompliance. Based on the same experiment, Blumenthal, Christian, and Slemrod find no evidence that either of two written appeals to taxpayers' consciences had a significant effect on aggregate compliance.[56]

Indirect Analyses of Evasion

Because even the extensive TCMP studies are subject to a number of methodological challenges, some researchers have pursued more indirect ways to shed

51. Dubin, Graetz, and Wilde (1990).
52. Klepper and Nagin (1989).
53. Slemrod, Blumenthal, and Christian (2001).
54. The audit threat was delivered by letter in January following the tax year.
55. The approach is a difference-in-difference analysis; that is, the increase in reported income over the previous year of the treatment group is compared to the increase in reported income of the control group.
56. Blumenthal, Christian, and Slemrod (2001).

light on the magnitude and nature of evasion. One such approach was pioneered by Pissarides and Weber, who estimate tax noncompliance of the self-employed in the United Kingdom without relying on inferences from operational or special audit programs.[57] They estimate food expenditure equations conditional on household characteristics and recorded incomes, allowing for differences between the self-employed and other households. Making the (reasonable) assumption that self-employed people have the same preferences regarding food as others, and the (stronger) assumption that the noncompliance rate among employees is negligible, differences in the estimated relationship between reported income and food expenditures may be attributed to under-reporting of income by the self-employed. In other words, if one finds that the self-employed spend a higher fraction of their reported income on food, Pissarides and Weber assume that it is because they have underreported their income and not because they eat more than others. After adjustment for the statistical implications of differing variances of self-employment incomes, Pissarides and Weber estimate that self-employed people in the United Kingdom on average underreported their income by about one-third.[58]

Slemrod and Feldman recently carried out a related exercise for the United States.[59] Using individual tax return data and charitable contributions rather than food expenditures, they investigate whether the relationship between contributions and income depends on the source of income. Their preliminary results indicate that noncompliance ratios depend upon the source of income and that positive reported Schedule E income is associated with the most noncompliance.

In sum, there is substantial evidence that the extent of evasion among small business is high compared to such income sources as wages, salaries, interest, and dividends. Several but not all the TCMP-based studies suggest that noncompliance is as high as one-third to one-half of true income. Other methods provide evidence that is consistent with these higher estimates. What is much more unclear is how responsive noncompliance is to changes in enforcement policy, such as more extensive auditing.

Audit Coverage Facts and Trends

One determinant of the extent of tax noncompliance is the perceived probability that attempted evasion will be detected and punished. While perceptions themselves cannot be accurately measured, the IRS makes available much information on actual audit coverage that presumably will influence taxpayer per-

57. Pissarides and Weber (1989).

58. In a follow-up study of the United Kingdom, Baker (1993) also estimated underreporting of income.

59. Slemrod and Feldman (2002).

ceptions. Table 4-7 presents information on returns filed in calendar year 2000. It lists, for various classes of tax returns, the total number of returns filed, the number examined, and the ratio of returns examined to returns filed. The classification of returns as Schedule C or Schedule F for audit examination purposes is based on the largest source of income on the return and certain other characteristics. Therefore some returns with business activity are reflected in the nonbusiness category.

According to table 4-7, the coverage ratio is more than three times higher for what the IRS classifies as business returns versus nonbusiness returns, 1.55 percent versus 0.51 percent. Interestingly, among the business return groups, the coverage ratio is highest for the group with the lowest total gross receipts. The coverage ratio was 2.72 percent for business returns with total gross receipts less than $25,000, compared to only 1.20 percent for those with total gross receipts greater than $100,000. This pattern does not, though, characterize the farm sole proprietorships.

Among C corporations, the coverage ratio rises monotonically with size, from 0.25 percent for corporations with assets under $250,000 to 32.09 percent for corporations with assets of $250,000,000 or more. The 1,500 or so largest companies that are in the Coordinated Industry Case program are for the most part subject to annual—even continual—audit. For the purposes of this chapter, what is important to note is that, if the standard for being a small business is having assets less than $1,000,000, then the coverage ratio is just 0.37 percent; if it is having $5,000,000 or less in assets, the coverage ratio is only 0.53 percent. Either of these two figures is less than the coverage ratio for individual income tax returns as a whole.

The coverage ratio for both partnership returns and S corporation returns is comparable to the smallest examination class among C corporations. It is 0.25 percent for partnerships and 0.43 percent for S corporations. There is evidence that the coverage ratio is higher for the largest pass-through entities. In 2001 the coverage ratio for partnerships with assets over $10 million was 2.7 percent (1,298 out of 47,815), while the coverage ratio for S corporations with assets over $10 million was 13.8 percent (2,825 out of 20,547).[60]

The Relationships between Compliance and Compliance Costs

Up to this point I have examined compliance costs (caused partly by tax complexity) and noncompliance (motivated in part by self-seeking taxpayers) as

60. I thank Richard Teed and Sally Warner of the IRS for making the information on the coverage ratios of large pass-through entities available to me.

Table 4-7. *Tax Returns Filed and Examined, by Type and Size of Return, Fiscal Year 2001*

Type and size of return	Returns filed in calendar year 2000	Returns examined Total	Returns examined Percent covered
Individual income tax returns, total	127,097,400	731,756	0.58
Nonbusiness returns	118,478,400	598,379	0.51
Forms 1040A with TPI[a]			
under $25,000	41,716,800	357,954	0.86
All other returns by size of TPI			
Under $25,000	13,948,800	55,624	0.40
$25,000 to $50,000	30,108,900	67,109	0.22
$50,000 to $100,000	23,377,600	53,433	0.23
$100,000 or more	9,326,300	64,259	0.69
Business returns	8,619,000	133,377	1.55
Schedule C returns by size of TGR[b]			
Under $25,000	2,553,300	69,332	2.72
$25,000 to $100,000	3,399,400	34,650	1.02
$100,000 or more	2,012,200	24,080	1.20
Schedule F returns by size of TGR			
Under $100,000	382,100	2,104	0.55
$100,000 or more	272,000	3,211	1.18
Corporation income tax returns, except Form 1120S, total	2,453,000	23,268	0.95
Returns other than Form 1120F			
No balance sheet returns	294,600	1,935	0.66
Balance sheet returns by size of total assets			
Under $250,000	1,432,500	3,576	0.25
$250,000 to $1,000,000	424,200	3,314	0.78
$1,000,000 to $5,000,000	191,700	3,912	2.04
$5,000,000 to $10,000,000	29,900	1,595	5.33
$10,000,000 to $50,000,000	31,800	3,071	9.66
$50,000,000 to $100,000,000	7,900	973	12.32
$100,000,000 to $250,000,000	7,800	1,369	17.55
$250,000,000 or more	10,300	3,305	32.09
Form 1120F returns	22,300	218	0.98
Nontaxable returns			
Partnership returns, Form 1065	2,066,800	5,070	0.25
S corporation returns, Form 1120S	2,887,100	12,437	0.43

Source: IRS Data Book (www.irs.gov/pub/irs-soi/01db10ex.xls).
a. Total positive income.
b. Total gross receipts.

separate phenomena. In what follows I examine the connections between the two issues.

Does Complexity Cause Noncompliance?

Compliance costs and noncompliance may be intimately related if tax complexity generates noncompliance.[61] There are many possible links. One is that complexity overwhelms the resources of taxpayers and causes inadvertent noncompliance, or plain old mistakes. Another is that complexity overwhelms the resources of the IRS and thus provides opportunities for some taxpayers to take advantage of the complicated rules and limited IRS enforcement. Conceivably frustration about the complexity of the tax system could increase noncompliance as well.[62]

Indeed, in a survey of small businesses done by the General Accounting Office and reported in Ashby, complexity was the most commonly mentioned reason why small businesses might have trouble complying.[63] Small businesses can encounter complex tax issues but do not always have the resources that they need to understand and deal with those issues. The same survey revealed that many small businesses were either unaware of IRS outreach services or were aware and did not use them. But if unfamiliarity with the law is the issue, one would expect to find mistakes that are symmetric around zero—about the same number and extent of tax overstatements as there are understatements. That is certainly not consistent with the evidence from the TCMP and other studies.

Comparing the Size of Compliance Costs and Tax Evasion

It is possible to compare the magnitudes of compliance costs and noncompliance, but only in a rough, back-of-the-envelope way. The survey results reported in Slemrod and Venkatesh show that the average compliance costs for a company with assets in the $5 million to $10 million range are about $35,000 per year.[64] If a company with assets of $7.5 million (the midpoint of this range) earns a certainty-equivalent of 4 percent rate of return, its earnings would be $300,000 per year. If the company were a C corporation, then the graduated rate schedule would imply a tax liability of $100,250 on a taxable income of

---

61. There also may be interaction between nontax regulatory burdens and tax compliance. Kagan (1989, p. 101) has suggested that regulation-avoiding entrepreneurs, hoping to remain "invisible" to regulatory enforcement officials, also may be reluctant to file a return with the IRS (even though the IRS is not likely to contact state or local regulatory authorities).

62. The interactions among complexity, compliance costs, and tax evasion are explored at length in Slemrod (1989).

63. Ashby (2000).

64. Slemrod and Venkatesh (2002). There are no reliable estimates for smaller companies.

$300,000; if it were a partnership or S corporation, the incremental tax liability would depend on the marginal tax rate of the partners or owners, but a $100,000 incremental tax liability is not unrealistic. Recall that Morton reports the noncompliance rate of corporations of this size to be 39 percent.[65] Applying the 39 percent noncompliance rate to a tax liability of about $100,000 implies that the average corporation is evading $39,000 in taxes. Considering the deductibility of the average $35,000 of compliance costs, the cost of compliance and the noncompliance magnitudes approximately offset one another.

Several caveats apply to this exercise. The numbers chosen are in some cases arbitrary and in all cases are subject to error. Also, the amount of noncompliance probably overstates the private gain to the business, because it does not net out the costs of undertaking the evasion, including the exposure to uncertain penalties. On the compliance cost side, one would want to differentiate voluntary from involuntary compliance costs. That is, some compliance costs are imposed on firms in an effort to administer the law and monitor and enforce compliance and reduce evasion, but other costs are incurred by firms in order to reduce tax liability. Recall that Mills, Erickson, and Maydew present evidence that, all things being equal, firms that incur higher compliance costs have lower effective average tax rates, suggesting that some of these costs earn a return to the firm; this return is not considered in the calculation above.[66]

Finally it is important to keep in mind that the figures presented above are all averages. Within any size category of business, there is undoubtedly much variation in the compliance costs incurred and in the amount of evasion attempted. This fact is especially important in the discussion of fairness and efficiency that follows.

The Net Effect of Taxes on Small Business Viability: Aggregate Evidence

The previous exercise compares the implicit tax preferences and penalties afforded to small business through the enforcement and administration of the tax system. Because it does not address at all the explicit preferences or penalties that are summarized above, it cannot offer an answer to whether the tax system overall favors or penalizes small business. An alternative approach is to look at the relationship between aggregate measures of the level and mix of taxes and the performance of the small-business sector. Most of the research that has examined the relationship between economy-wide summary measures of taxation and self-employment rates concludes that higher tax rates are associated with higher self-employment rates.[67] This is consistent with the idea that, because self-employment facilitates evasion,

65. Morton (1992).
66. Mills, Erickson, and Maydew (1998).
67. See, in particular, Long (1982), Blau (1987), and Parker (1996). Note, though, that Fairlie and Meyer (2000) find no significant relationship between tax rates and self-employment.

self-employment becomes more attractive when the level of taxes is higher. More-over an intriguing recent study that examines microdata from the Panel Study of Income Dynamics offers evidence that the higher an individual's expected mar-ginal tax rate, the higher the probability of entry into self-employment, although an increase in the average self-employment tax rate has the opposite effect. The author rationalizes this result by noting that differential tax treatment also affects the incentive to evade or avoid taxation: "If some entrepreneurs are actually cre-ative tax-evaders, then reducing their marginal tax rates could encourage them to close their 'businesses.'"[68]

Although the research on the aggregate impact of taxes on the self-employed sector does not speak with one voice, the broad conclusions are as follows: When the overall level of taxes rises, the small-business sector attracts resources. However, when taxes specifically levied on small business go up, holding con-stant other taxes, this causes a contraction of small-business activity. This evi-dence is consistent with a world in which small business is relatively tax-favored compared to other activities.

The fact that the small-business sector seems to attract resources when the level of taxes rises suggests that, considering the noncompliance opportunities and explicit tax preferences, its effective tax rate is lower than that of other sec-tors. But this is not the end of the story, because compliance costs are, for the most part, unrelated to the rate of tax. Thus it is possible that the regressive nature of compliance costs implies that, overall, the tax system discourages small business, even though the relative tax burden that is related to tax rates favors small business. Alas, the available evidence cannot resolve this question.

The Economics of Taxing Small Business

Why does it matter whether the tax system favors or penalizes small businesses? First, the tax system might cause an inefficient allocation of resources, by induc-ing people to organize and operate their businesses in ways that, while tax-efficient, may be inefficient from society's perspective. Second, the tax system may generate a capricious or systematically inequitable assignment of tax burden among the nation's citizens. Separating out the efficiency issue from the equity or fairness issue is especially tricky in this context, given the dictum that it is people, and not businesses, that bear taxes. This implies that one must always try to trace the distribution of tax burden back to individuals, considering their multiple roles as business owners, employees, consumers, and so on. It also means that it is neither adequate nor meaningful to say, for example, that a pol-icy is "unfair to small business."

68. Bruce (2002, p. 8).

To be sure, the fairness and efficiency issues are intimately connected. To see this, consider an example having to do with house painting. Assume, for the sake of argument, that an inordinately high fraction of the income received by housepainters is not reported to the IRS. If there is completely free entry into house painting, the ultimate effect of undetected evasion is to lower the relative price of getting one's house painted but not to raise the return to being a house-painter. This is so because the effectively tax-free nature of the business attracts entrants until house painting offers an after-tax reward that is no higher than other, less effectively tax-free, occupations do. Thus, the easy answer to the question of who gains from tax evasion—those who get away with it—may not be the end of the story.[69] (By the way, the same reasoning applies to identifying the ultimate incidence of compliance costs. If they are particularly high in one sector, then this does not necessarily imply that, in equilibrium, businesses in that sector earn a lower after-tax and after-compliance-cost rate of return.)

At first blush this situation is not horizontally inequitable, as housepainters end up no better off than others. It does, though, create an inefficiently large allocation of resources to house painting. But this conclusion about inefficiency is too facile and may be wrong. Whether there is an inefficient excess of house-painters depends on the technology of tax-evasion detection. If there is something inherent about house painting, or any sector, that makes its income more difficult to monitor, then it may be better policy to accept a glut of house-painters than to devote the enforcement resources needed to eliminate the effective tax preference due to facilitated evasion.

What if, on the other hand, evasion is relatively easy in all small businesses, regardless of the line of business, so that the tax system on net provides an incentive for a business, regardless of what goods or services it produces, to be small? What implications does this have for real activity? This depends on whether firms need to change their real operations to take advantage of the tax noncompliance opportunities available to small business. If not, then a business might expend some legal costs to look small for tax enforcement purposes but need not sacrifice much in terms of economies of scale. If so, the economic cost of a small-business preference is the sacrifice of economies of scale. If, considering the compliance costs as well as the noncompliance environment, there were a net tax penalty to small business, the economic cost would be the sacrifice of the organizational and other advantages that attend small business.

In reality there is undoubtedly wide variation in both the willingness and ability of business owners to evade that is unrelated to the size of the company or the sector it is in. In this case there will be horizontal inequity on the dimension of honesty or aggressiveness. This is because the pretax profitability of the sector will be determined by the average honesty or aggressiveness of business

69. These issues are discussed in more detail in Kesselman (1989) and Martinez-Vazquez (1996).

competitors, and the after-tax return will be lower for those who are relative compliers with the tax law. This suggests that inherently honest (or unaggressive) business owners should avoid sectors that facilitate evasion.[70]

Small Business and Tax Enforcement Policy

One important policy question is whether the tax system favors or penalizes small business more than it should, given the technology of tax collection and any externalities or market failures that apply to small business. This question is, alas, beyond the scope of this chapter, because quantifying any externalities or market failures is highly speculative and would take the chapter far beyond its focus on tax enforcement.

The importance of the technology of tax collection to this question, though, deserves comment. Because for small business there is no independent source of information about income (as there is for wages and salaries), it is inevitable that the cost of enforcement will be relatively high. This suggests that, other things equal, the appropriate level of audit coverage is lower than otherwise; this may look like undue favoring of the sector, but it may in fact be warranted by the technological realities of tax collection. Furthermore, because small businesses cannot leverage economies of scale, even at a lower level of audit coverage it is probably appropriate that compliance costs be somewhat regressive; this may look like undue penalization of small business, but again it may be warranted by the technological realities. An optimal policy should, in theory, weigh all these factors. Even if it turns out that on average the compliance cost burden of small business approximately equals the sector's tax saving from noncompliance, this is not a sign that all is well—efficient and fair—with the taxation of small business. It is a relevant input into the policy discussion but is not a desideratum in and of itself.

Economic reasoning can provide a framework for considering these issues in policy formulation. For some issues it is easier to identify inappropriate principles for guiding IRS resource allocation decisions than it is to state the appropriate principle in an operationally helpful way. For example, consider the principle for deciding how big an overall enforcement budget the IRS should receive. The right rule is not to set the marginal revenue raised equal to the marginal cost of raising the revenue. Following this rule would maximize revenue collected net of

---

70. This is different from arguing that untrustworthy people prosper in a milieu of trusting "suckers." For a theory and evidence on that proposition, see Slemrod and Katuscak (2002). An examination of the 1990 World Values Survey data for the United States reveals that there is no significant difference between small-business owners and other people with regard to their responses to whether tax cheating is acceptable or whether lying in one's own interest is acceptable. Further details are available from this author.

the cost of raising the revenue, but it is inappropriate because, while the costs of new auditors and computers represent a social opportunity cost, the marginal revenue raised is not a benefit to society but rather a transfer from private hands to public hands.[71] Such transfers might very well have a social benefit, but that benefit is not measured by the dollars raised.

One can, however, state the appropriate rule for tax policy design in a general form. It applies to all tax policy instruments, including both standard tax policy tools, such as tax rates, and tax enforcement tools, such as audit rates. The rule is that the ratio of marginal social cost per dollar of revenue raised, adjusted for the distributional implications of raising revenue with that instrument, should be equal for each instrument used.[72] The social cost in the numerator of this expression includes the direct utility loss to taxpayers when their tax burden (including penalties) is raised, plus any additional burden due to marginal compliance costs. The denominator of this term recognizes that taxpayer responses to tax policy (including substitution away from taxed activities, avoidance, and evasion) may erode the revenue gain (and make the revenue gain less than the utility cost to the taxpayer), as will the marginal administrative cost of raising revenue through any given tax instrument. The adjustment for distributional implications allows for the possibility of introducing the policy guideline that, other things equal, relieving a burden on a lower-income taxpayer may have a higher social value than relieving a burden on a higher-income taxpayer.

One key assumption that underlies this rule is that the objective of tax policy is to maximize the well-being of citizen-taxpayers, where taxpayers may be weighted differently depending on their level of well-being but not weighted differently depending on whether they are evaders. This means that an increased effective tax burden on evaders directly reduces social welfare and is desirable largely because of the revenue generated.

The information needed to assess whether IRS policy follows this rule is, to be sure, hard to come by. The IRS calculates the additional revenue directly generated by its enforcement activities (per return and per hour devoted to the enforcement effort) for different categories of taxpayers. This is, though, an average calculation (additional revenue divided by resources devoted) rather than the marginal calculation called for by the rule stated above.[73] But the much larger problem with using these figures for policy purposes is that they refer only to direct collection revenue and completely ignore the revenues collected through the deterrent effect of increasing the probability that evasion will be

---

71. This argument is developed in Slemrod and Yitzhaki (1996).

72. This rule is derived and discussed in Slemrod and Yitzhaki (1987) and generalized in Mayshar (1991).

73. For operational purposes, assuming that the ratio between average and marginal collections per resource dollar is the same across audit categories might be a reasonable approximation to the truth.

detected. In other words, when enforcement activities are expanded, revenues presumably increase even from people who are not audited but who now view the cost-benefit calculation of evasion to be less favorable than before. The deterrence consequences of increased enforcement on evasion could easily dwarf the direct revenue consequences, and there is no reason to believe that the deterrent effects will be proportional to the direct (average) revenue estimates published by the IRS.

The rule requires that, other things equal, resources should be directed to those enforcement activities that produce a higher revenue bang per administrative cost buck.[74] This rule also implies that, other things equal, enforcement should be directed at noncompliance undertaken by higher-income taxpayers.[75] Tables 4-2, 4-3, and 4-4 suggest that, among the small-business category, this is much more likely to characterize the owners of partnerships and S corporations, and probably small C corporations, than it is to characterize sole proprietorships. Nevertheless, overall distributional considerations make enforcement of evasion among high-income taxpayers a more attractive option than otherwise.

The framework that underlies the marginal cost of funds rule also clearly implies that, if compliance costs (or administrative costs) can be reduced without other ramifications, this is worth doing. In reality it is difficult to identify policies that are pure simplifications—that is, without other implications. The search for the right balance is important, to be sure. The United States is not alone among OECD (Organization for Economic Cooperation and Development) countries in undertaking steps to reduce the administrative and compliance costs related to small business.[76] For example, Australia recently introduced a measure that allows small businesses to determine their income and expenditure on a cash basis and provides for assets costing below a certain amount to be written off immediately.[77] But the latter policy also establishes a lower cost of capital for small-business investments that, absent some externality or market failure argument, is inefficient. Such a policy must trade off this inefficiency against the reduction in compliance costs.

Should the IRS devote more (or fewer) resources to noncompliance by small business owners? Here is what we know. We know that noncompliance rates are higher in this sector than almost any other and, for the partnership and small corporation subsectors, this noncompliance on average benefits a highly affluent

74. It is much trickier to establish a similar guideline with respect to the level of monetary penalty to be assessed to evasion, because the fine itself does not represent a real resource cost, as do hiring more auditors or buying more computers.

75. This conclusion follows only if the social cost of a given burden is judged to be higher the lower is the taxpayer's level of well-being.

76. See Chen, Lee, and Mintz (2002).

77. If simplification is in fact the goal of such a policy, then immediate expensing of a fraction of capital costs may provide simplification without providing a lower cost of capital.

slice of the taxpayer population. For policy purposes, though, the key factor is not the extent of evasion but the potential marginal effectiveness of policy in reducing the extent of evasion, and a key element of that is the deterrent effect, about which we know little.[78] Thus a key piece of information is missing and is likely never to be known with great certainty. Based on what we do know, however, my sense is that an intensified enforcement focus on pass-through entities owned by high-income individuals is probably warranted.

There is some evidence that the IRS has recently concluded that this sector does indeed merit more enforcement attention. A new IRS initiative begun in 2002 matched information obtained from taxpayers who reported income on Schedule E from partnerships against what had been reported separately to the IRS on the entity's Schedule K-1.[79] More generally in September 2002 the IRS said that in the future it would devote more of its attention to wealthy taxpayers suspected of hiding income from their businesses, partnerships, and investments. In an interview reported by David Cay Johnston, outgoing IRS commissioner Charles O. Rossotti said that much of the new IRS emphasis will shift to "people with large incomes who are in control of what is reported to the government, including business owners."[80]

Much of what we think we know about income tax compliance in the United States comes from the Taxpayer Compliance Measurement Program, which will soon be fifteen years out of date. Although the IRS has since 1988 undertaken multiple research initiatives to inform its activities, the central importance of a comprehensive random sampling of the taxpayer (and potential taxpayer) population can hardly be overstated. Information about compliance can both help the IRS identify the characteristics of taxpayers who have difficulty understanding and meeting their tax responsibilities and better direct its enforcement resources to those classes of taxpayers that willfully evade the tax laws. As Ashby argues, the absence of up-to-date information on voluntary compliance could hinder small business efforts more than others, because this population has a greater potential for noncompliance.[81] Over the long term, it is important that the IRS both carefully formulate the objectives that guide resource allocation and also acquire the information to implement such guidelines. The new IRS initiative of National Research Program (NRP) examinations that began in the fall of 2002 holds promise for providing this kind of information. The IRS stresses, however, that the NRP will be different from the TCMP, and in par-

78. I like the analogy to oil reserves, where what matters for exploration policy is not the extent of reserves, but rather the extent of economically recoverable reserves.

79. The matching program was halted as of August 2002 because of complaints about errors in the mismatch notices. See Tom Herman, "IRS to Modify Matching Plans after Tax Advisers Find Flaws," *Wall Street Journal*, October 10, 2002, p. D-2.

80. David Cay Johnston, "Hunting Tax Cheats, I.R.S. Vows to Focus More Effort on the Rich," *New York Times*, September 13, 2002, p. A1.

81. Ashby (2000).

ticular will be less intrusive and time-intensive for taxpayers.[82] Where the NRP lies on the trade-off between intrusiveness and time cost on the one hand and the provision of essential information on the other hand remains to be seen.

COMMENT BY
William M. Gentry

Joel Slemrod starts with what appears to be a straightforward question: Does the tax code have an inherent bias, either for or against, small businesses? The analysis is one of positive economics—asking how the system actually works—rather than normative analysis of the optimal policy toward small businesses. Even with the positive focus, the question is far harder than it might first appear. As might be expected in a chapter written for a volume on tax administration, Slemrod quickly moves from the statutory differences in the treatment of small business to two critical compliance-related issues for small business. First, tax compliance often has a fixed cost component without offsetting diseconomies of scale, so that smaller firms inherently have a higher average compliance cost. Second, a common perception is that small-business owners engage in more tax evasion or tax avoidance than larger firms or wage earners.

The chapter's back-of-the-envelope calculation gives an illusion of "rough justice" between these competing concerns: The high fixed compliance cost imposed on small firms is roughly offset by their higher rate of noncompliance. However, as noted by Slemrod, this crude calculation carries several important caveats. In the end, despite Slemrod's careful marshaling of the available evidence (much of which comes from his seminal work on compliance costs and evasion), the easier conclusion to draw is that currently available data are too crude to provide a reliable answer to whether the tax system favors or penalizes small business.

My comments center on two issues. First, I discuss statutory differences that might affect small and large businesses differently—either as a matter of statutory incidence or economic incidence. Second, I have several points about interpreting compliance costs, measuring evasion, and comparing these two different costs as a net measure of whether the tax system favors small businesses.

Statutory Differences and Economic Incidence

While the primary goal of the Slemrod chapter is not to catalogue potential differences in how particular tax code sections apply to businesses of different sizes,

82. IRS (2002).

I find it instructive to consider some of the statutory differences that might be relevant, as a way of defining the scope of the problem. My first reading of the chapter led me to think about the tax treatment of business income across organizational forms and across firms of different sizes. My first instinct was to assume that small businesses would not be subject to the corporate tax, but that the equity-financed returns to large firms would be subject to double taxation—a corporate-level tax and an investor-level tax on dividends (or capital gains). Interestingly Slemrod cites the graduation of corporate tax rates as an explicit preference for small businesses, even though this point only applies within the group of firms that organize as C corporations.

Another issue is that many of the tax differences for small and large firms are not centered on the taxation of business income. Instead, as discussed by Mastromarco and Burton, many of the tax concerns of small business deal with employee compensation.[1] For example, some organizational forms favored by small business (S corporations, for example) face restrictions on using tax-favored forms of compensation, such as certain types of fringe benefits. Moreover, even without de jure differences in tax rules, the high fixed costs of administering certain types of compensation create a de facto tax-related disadvantage for small businesses.

Given these concerns, two issues need to be emphasized. First, in considering the taxation of small businesses, it is important to keep in mind the taxation of the entire value added of the enterprise—both the capital income earned by the owner and the labor income of the owner and the employees. Second, the tax bias for or against small businesses must be measured compared to something else; in making this comparison, it is natural to compare small firms with large firms (especially large C corporations), keeping in mind the taxation of both capital and labor income.

A concrete example may help illustrate the various statutory tax issues facing a small business that competes with larger businesses and how these statutory differences relate to the economic incidence of the tax differences.[2] Compare a self-employed dentist, who owns a small practice that employs a small staff, with a large (corporate) dental practice that has many locations with a large staff of dentists, hygienists, and office staff.

One hallmark issue for the small business is distinguishing the capital income from the labor income of the owner. For tax purposes, this means that, if capital income is taxed differently than labor income (for example, labor income is

---

1. Mastromarco and Burton (2002).

2. The economic incidence of the tax difference measures who bears the burden of the tax after allowing for behavioral changes and price changes due to the tax; for example, Slemrod mentions that if housepainters can avoid taxes, then their pretax wage will fall as more people become housepainters so that, in equilibrium, housepainters do not reap any special return to being able to avoid taxes.

subject to both payroll and income tax), then the small business could face a different tax burden than the large business does. Furthermore the self-employed dentist may well tie up a substantial amount of household savings in his or her small business. If this dentist faces financing constraints, then he or she may forgo opportunities to take advantage of tax-favored forms of saving, such as retirement accounts.[3] In contrast the corporate dental practice may raise funds from investors who are taking advantage of such tax-advantaged forms of saving.

The large dental practice may be able to compensate its staff with several types of tax-advantaged fringe benefits that the self-employed dentist either is prohibited from using or would find uneconomical due to the high fixed cost of establishing such plans. These differences in labor taxation may provide an advantage for the large dental practice. To the extent that the small practice compensates staff with less tax-advantaged forms of compensation, the self-employed dentist may have a higher cost of hiring workers, because attracting workers requires paying the same after-tax value as the corporate dental practice. From the government's perspective, the staff of the self-employed dentist reports more taxable wages than the staff of the corporate practice and incurs a higher tax liability on their labor income. Thus labor income generated in small firms may face a higher tax burden than does the labor income generated in larger firms.[4]

Another tax issue that can burden small businesses more than large corporations is the possibility that successful ventures face higher tax rates than unsuccessful ventures. For a sole proprietor, the asymmetric taxation of successful and unsuccessful ventures arises from the graduated tax rates under the personal tax system, as well as limitations on the offset of losses for capital invested in the project. Thus, if the self-employed dentist chooses a poor location or turns out to be a poor manager of the practice, he or she will have low income (and face a low tax rate) and may have to wait to take deductions for the capital invested in the practice (and these deductions may be taken at relatively low tax rates); in contrast, if the self-employed dentist creates a successful practice, he or she will land in a relatively high tax bracket. The asymmetry in the tax system can raise the expected tax liability of a potential entrepreneur and discourage entry into entrepreneurship. Gentry and Hubbard find that the asymmetries associated with

3. For evidence on the lack of diversification of the portfolios, see Gentry and Hubbard (forthcoming). For a discussion of the use of tax-advantaged retirement savings plans by the self-employed, see Power and Rider (2002), who find that contributions to these plans by the self-employed are quite sensitive to their tax rates.

4. Note that I have implicitly assumed that the employee does not bear the tax imposed by the self-employed dentist not offering a tax-advantaged compensation package. The employee is indifferent to being on the staff of either type of practice. The self-employed dentist may bear a large part of the burden in the form of higher compensation expense. One can make other incidence assumptions about who bears this tax, but, under most of the alternatives, the government raises more revenue if fewer workers get tax-advantaged forms of compensation.

graduated personal income tax rates deter entry into self-employment and business ownership.[5] Loss offset rules and the graduated corporate tax rate structure could create similar disincentives for corporate investment; however, for large corporations, it seems more reasonable to assume that gains and losses are taxed symmetrically, because the firm pools many investments (for example, a location of a specific dental practice).

If the large dental practice organizes as a C corporation, then it faces potential double taxation of equity-financed investment. While the single-dentist practice could organize as a C corporation, it is unlikely that it would, unless the owner perceived a tax advantage, because other organizational forms (an S corporation, for example) offer the advantages of incorporation without double taxation. Whether the double taxation of corporate income creates a higher tax burden than alternative organizational forms depends on the tax rates for both corporations and investors. However, empirical studies on organizational form suggest that double taxation of corporate income discourages firms from organizing as C corporations, implying that large firms bear a higher tax burden than smaller firms that are more likely to opt out of being C corporations.[6]

My goal in mentioning these broad examples of tax differences is not to provide a detailed analysis of whether the overall tax code either explicitly (de jure) or implicitly (de facto) provides a bias for or against small firms. Instead the examples illustrate the broad concepts that affect the relative taxation of small and large firms (abstracting from the administrative concerns of compliance costs and noncompliance, which I discuss below). Ultimately the direction of any bias for or against small firms is an empirical issue. More importantly a mere reading of the statutes cannot determine the economic consequences of any bias based on firm size. The economic consequences and economic incidence depend on the behavioral responses to the tax code.

For example, in the dental practice example, dentists choose between self-employment and being on the staff of a larger practice based on the after-tax returns of the choices. Potential dentists will make occupational choices depending on the after-tax return of being a dentist, which in equilibrium does not depend on the organizational form at the margin. In equilibrium one would expect the marginal self-employed dentist to have the same after-tax return as the marginal dentist in a large practice (after adjusting for any risk premium associated with the choice). These are the typical predictions of considering the economic incidence of tax policy differences: The quantities of different activi-

---

5. Gentry and Hubbard (2000).

6. See, for example, Goolsbee (2002) and the references therein. In contrast, as argued by Cullen and Gordon (2002), the option to incorporate for a successful business may mean that tax planning can mitigate the burden of having a successful business and of the corporate tax; in part, they argue that the firm may need to incorporate as several different businesses to gain the full advantage of the lower tax rates on small corporations.

ties will adjust so the after-tax returns are the same across the sectors for the marginal decisionmaker. Thus the tax system may distort the organizational form of the practice of dentistry but might have a relatively minor impact on the overall level of dental services provided in the economy.[7]

These simple predictions about economic incidence mask one critical aspect of self-employment and entrepreneurship: Not all entrepreneurs are identical. Entrepreneurs differ in their talent for running a business. For example, some dentists have more skill in managing employees and organizing an office, while others may have less aptitude for such tasks or prefer to avoid the risks associated with being self-employed. The former group is more likely to be self-employed, regardless of the tax treatment, relative to the latter group. These "inframarginal" dentists bear the burden of a higher tax on self-employment or reap the benefit of a lower tax on self-employment, because the tax treatment of self-employment affects the return to their particular skill.[8] Such heterogeneity in skills and preferences could play an important role in who benefits from any bias for or against small firms.

Do Compliance Costs Offset Rates of Noncompliance?

Before considering the logic of comparing the economies of scale in tax compliance with the potential heterogeneity in noncompliance by firm size, it is useful to make several observations about the measurement of compliance costs and noncompliance. One can think of the total cost of the tax system to a taxpayer as the sum of the tax liability plus the compliance cost associated with filing the tax return. The first caveat for this definition is that tax liability is a measure of the statutory tax incidence, rather than the economic incidence of the tax. An activity that has a low tax liability (relative to other activities) may attract entrants such that the pretax return to the activity falls. A second caveat is in trying to

7. I have chosen an example in which the tax distortion mainly falls on organizational form rather than the amount of output produced, since the good can be produced by both small and large firms. A distortion along this margin can still have economic efficiency consequences, either by affecting the overall cost of producing the good (that is, it might be more cheaply produced in the more heavily taxed organizational form) or by affecting the mix of goods when the organizational form of the provider matters (for example, suppose patients have preferences over the comfort afforded by the small office of the self-employed dentist or the potential convenience provided by a larger practice). In general, for some goods, changing the firm size may have consequences for the amount of the good produced. For a general equilibrium analysis of tax distortions when corporate and noncorporate firms produce the same good, see Gravelle and Kotlikoff (1989).

8. If all potential dentists are equivalent along all dimensions of talent and preferences toward risk, then all potential dentists will be the marginal dentist, and thus these effects on the inframarginal dentists would be trivial. However, in the case of entry into self-employment, it seems reasonable to assume that tastes and preferences are an important part of the decision (see, for example, Hamilton 2000).

infer the importance of compliance costs by comparing them to the statutory tax liability.

As an example of how this measure can be problematic, consider a firm that includes in its cost of compliance for the income tax the costs associated with the withholding of employee income taxes. The statutory incidence of the employee income taxes is on the worker, so that these compliance costs should not be correlated with the tax liability of the firm; instead these compliance costs are one of the fundamental reasons why voluntary compliance on individual wage income is relatively high. A third caveat, as mentioned in the chapter, is that some reported compliance costs are actually the costs associated with tax planning activities designed to reduce taxes. These are resource costs from the perspective of the firm, but one would not want to imply that these costs are imposed by the tax system, because tax planning is a voluntary activity.

The chapter documents the well-established result that the cost function for tax compliance appears to have both a fixed component and a variable component, which depend on the number of transactions undertaken by the firm. The overall compliance cost structure appears to have increasing returns to scale, so that larger firms have a cost advantage. One would expect that such a cost structure would increase the minimum efficient scale of firms in an industry, which would increase the average size of firms and lead to the exit of some smaller firms. For the dentist above, the added cost of tax compliance for the marginal self-employed dentist may be the straw that breaks the camel's back and pushes the marginal dentist into the larger firm. The economic distortion from this change in behavior is similar to the distortion from having a higher tax liability on smaller firms.

On the measurement of evasion, the standard claim is that smaller businesses are less compliant with the statutory tax code, with a systematic downward bias in tax payments, compared to larger firms. While the fixed cost of compliance has an inherent intuitive appeal, the theoretical prediction of the relationship between firm size and tax evasion is less clear. The empirical evidence cited in chapter 4 suggests that the standard claim is true. However, in measuring tax evasion, three cautions are in order. First, as noted in the chapter, in considering policy tools to combat evasion (such as audits), one should measure both the direct effect of the audit (that is, the revenue collected directly by the audit) and the deterrent effects. Second, I would emphasize that much of the evasion may not be detected in the audit. For example, the self-employed dentist may buy his or her children's school supplies at the office and take them home for the children to use; it is unlikely that an audit would uncover such behavior. Of course the dentist who works as a corporate employee make take office supplies home, as well, but this behavior carries the risk of being caught by the boss. This example is the evasion version of the "hidden consumption" problem for taxing the self-employed, in which the self-employed deduct the cost of consumption goods they would have to purchase with after-tax dollars if they worked as an employee.

Third, the discussion in the chapter limits the hidden consumption problem to issues of evasion; however, in many cases, the hidden consumption problem takes the form of legally deducting business expenses that might not be deductible for an employee. For example, the travel expenses associated with a dental conference in an exotic location are tax-deductible for the self-employed dentist but might not be deductible (or the deduction may be limited) for the dentist at a large firm. The trip may inherently have a consumption element that is not measured by the tax system.[9] This consumption element does not fit nicely into the label "evasion." However, as with some of the compliance issues, the economic incidence of the perquisite may differ from the statutory incidence.

In comparing the compliance costs for small firms with the potential non-compliance of these firms (or any statutory differences across firm size), it is important to note that the compliance costs are a deadweight loss from the tax system, whereas changes in tax payments are transfers from one set of taxpayers to another. That is, the cost of complying with the tax system is an economic cost above and beyond the cost (from the perspective of the taxpayer) of the tax liability. If legislation reduces compliance costs without changing tax liabilities, then the taxpayer who benefits from the low cost is better off, but no one else is affected. In contrast, if legislation is passed that favors small firms over large firms by reducing the tax liabilities of the smaller firms, then the government must either raise taxes in other areas or cut the level of government services. The same point is true for tax evasion: When someone evades taxes, he or she benefits at the expense of other taxpayers. Therefore, unlike compliance costs that are a deadweight loss, tax preferences and tax evasion create transfers across groups of taxpayers. This transfer nature of tax evasion is why Slemrod points out that the optimal government policy toward tax evasion is not necessarily to compare the marginal audit cost with the marginal revenue collected from the audit (even if the deterrence effects on revenue are included).

One underpinning for this dictum that the government should not merely compare the marginal audit cost with the marginal revenue generated is that the social welfare function does not weight people based on whether they are tax evaders. Moving away from this assumption allows for audit rules that consider the punitive aspects of the process. After all, why should society care equally about honest and dishonest people? The desire to distinguish between honest

9. Of course, at some level, these hidden consumption items are a discussion about the relative propensities of different organizational forms to indulge in certain behaviors. One could imagine a large dental practice that pays the travel expenses for its dentists to attend the conference. For more on this issue, see Clotfelter (1983b).

and dishonest people is what breaks the equivalence of evasion, and taking advantage of an explicit tax preference for a behavior in terms of both behaviors results in a transfer from all taxpayers to a specific taxpayer.

The heterogeneity in honesty among taxpayers also raises an important cautionary note for making aggregate comparisons of compliance costs and noncompliance. The small-business owner who may bear the biggest tax cost may be the meticulously honest entrepreneur. This person may incur the highest compliance cost and also pay the highest tax burden.[10] In contrast some forms of noncompliance may actually lead to lower compliance costs and lower tax payments.[11] At a minimum one wonders whether high compliance costs, complexity, and high perceived rates of noncompliance contribute to social attitudes toward the income tax.

Conclusion

Like beauty pageant contestants whose one wish is for world peace, public finance scholars might wish for a simple, fair tax system with full voluntary compliance. It turns out that these goals are easier wished for than accomplished. Small-business taxation is just one of the most prominent areas of the tax system in which compliance costs and the opportunities for both tax avoidance and tax evasion are substantial. Of course the positive correlation between opportunities for tax planning and compliance cost is to be expected: Where planning and evasion opportunities exist, tax authorities must spend more time writing rules and regulations.

While reading statutes and analyzing tax payments can provide some information on the relative tax treatment of small and large firms, Slemrod's chapter suggests that these issues merely scratch the surface of whether the tax system favors or disfavors small businesses. A complete understanding of the issue requires understanding compliance costs and rates of noncompliance (to which I would also add legal tax avoidance) as well as the economic incidence of both de jure and de facto differences in tax situations of large and small firms; unfortunately, as documented in the chapter, data on such issues are scarce. Nonetheless the chapter provides a comprehensive overview of what we know about

10. My implicit assumption is that compliance costs increase with following the law. This assumption may be wrong if compliance costs are really driven by a desire to understand all the details of the tax system in order to best game the system—by which I mean to use all available tax planning opportunities to legally avoid paying taxes.

11. Even for tax evasion (as opposed to tax avoidance), it is difficult to know the relationship between compliance (or, more accurately, noncompliance) costs and the amount of evasion. For example, is it expensive to fabricate additional receipts in order to overstate deductions? Is it cheap or expensive to underreport receipts?

these critical issues and provides many helpful insights on what remains to be learned.

COMMENT BY
Morton A. Harris

As Joel Slemrod states, there are many definitions of small business, which various government agencies and the private sector use for a variety of purposes. Typically, one of four general measures is used to define a small business: size of capital, size of assets, number of employees, or amount of revenue. As noted by Slemrod, the IRS uses an asset size below $5 million, and the Small Business Administration (SBA) uses fewer than 500 employees as the basis for their definitions of small business. It should also be noted that over 99 percent of all businesses are small under any of the definitions. Slemrod observes that small-business taxpayers include a wide variety of types, sizes, and levels of economic success, ranging from the small, low-income, "mom and pop" business to the large, successful, privately owned business. Most of these relatively successful and larger companies are considered small businesses under either the IRS or SBA definitions, because they have less than $5 million in assets and fewer than 500 employees, albeit their revenues and profits may be quite large. Included in the characterization of small business are many so-called family businesses (a term that also has several definitions).[1]

This author agrees with Slemrod's observations that the smaller segment of the small-business community has the greatest need for simplicity and stability in the tax laws. Although the more successful (not necessarily larger) small businesses are also in need of simplicity and stability, they are better able to cope with complexity and change of the tax laws, because they can better afford the professional advisors needed to effectively deal with the problem.

Supplementing Slemrod's observations about the size and the diverse character of small business, it may be useful to compare the vast number of small businesses (most of which are privately owned) with large businesses, many of which are publicly traded. There are estimated to be over 25 million privately owned businesses in the country, approximately 10 million of which are part-time operations (the weekend musician, "moonlighters," and so on).[2] By comparison, I estimate that there are fewer than 30,000 publicly owned companies: 2,800 traded on the New York Stock Exchange (NYSE), 800 on the American

1. See Internal Revenue Service Statistics of Income data showing the size of business measured by assets and by gross receipts (IRS 1996, pp. 51–58).
2. IRS (1999).

Exchange (AMEX), 4,000 on NASDAQ, 8,400 traded over the counter (by Pink Sheets, Bulletin Board, and so forth), with the rest being traded so rarely they are not listed.[3] It can therefore be seen that privately owned businesses represent over 99 percent of all businesses in the country. Almost all these businesses are relatively small, there being no more than 115,000 businesses (both public and private) with more than 100 employees and no more than 17,000 with more than 500 employees.[4]

In disagreement with Slemrod's references to "vague arguments" about the economic importance of small business, it appears to be generally recognized (based on published economic data) that small businesses employ over 55 percent of all working Americans, generate approximately 55 percent of GDP, and have consistently in recent years been responsible for over 75 percent of all net new jobs, as well as being responsible for 30 percent of U.S. exports. Small business has increasingly been recognized as the most dynamic and vibrant segment of the country's economic system (including producing the most innovations).[5] In fact many say that America's small businesses are the country's best hope to maintain a successful private enterprise system.[6]

Congressional recognition of small business was formalized in 1950, when both houses of Congress established standing committees on small business. In 1953 the Small Business Administration was created as an independent agency, based on the recognition that small business has special needs, a unique philosophy, and different capabilities. In 1976 an independent Office of Advocacy within the SBA was created and charged with the responsibility of promoting the causes of small enterprises in Congress and the executive branch. Since that time Congress has consistently encouraged federal agencies to be sensitive to the special needs of small business.

During the 1980s small business became popular in Washington. In 1981 Congress authorized, and President Reagan convened, the first President's White House Conference on Small Business. Another White House conference was held in 1986, with the most recent in 1995. The major purpose of the White House conferences was to create a forum for small-business owners to communicate with each other and determine their needs and concerns, with a view toward the executive, Congress, and regulatory agencies enacting, repealing, or amending legislation and regulations to meet those needs.

However, Congress's outward love affair with small business does not often translate into attention to its practical needs and interests. These needs are often

---

3. See www.nyse.com; www.amex.com; www.nasdaq.com; www. pinksheets.com; www. otcbb.com.

4. SBA (2000).

5. SBA (1996a).

6. See Erik Calhonius, "Blood and Money," *Newsweek,* Winter 1990, p. 82; Francois de Visscher and Mauritis Bruel, "The Adolescent of American Family Business," *FBN Newsletter* 9, May 1994.

overlooked when major legislation is being crafted, especially when it involves complex tax and employee benefit matters. In addition, during the past twenty years (1981–2002), there has been a flood of tax and employee benefit legislation (twenty-four major revenue acts involving changes to 13,042 Internal Revenue Code sections and subsections). Unfortunately most of this legislation contains significant additional complexities (and often additional compliance requirements) that are particularly onerous to small businesses and their owners.[7]

In analyzing the reasons for the inconsistency between Washington's small-business rhetoric and actual legislation, one is drawn to the conclusion that small businesses are much less effective (in contrast with large businesses) in influencing the outcome of tax legislation. Large businesses have full-time, sophisticated lobbyists monitoring and focusing on specific provisions during the legislative process, whereas most small businesses and the dozens of small-business organizations are not sophisticated enough in tax matters to effectively influence meaningful tax legislation. Although a number of small-business organizations actively monitor tax legislation, only a few have the expertise in the areas of tax or employee benefits to be effective (examples are the National Federation of Independent Business; the Small Business Council of America, which has the expertise and does focus on tax and employee benefit issues; and National Small Business United). Further, the broad diversity of interests among small businesses (resulting from differences in size, level of economic success, and type of business) often results in agendas that are unfocused and sometimes contradictory.

One reason for the frequent changes in tax and employee benefit legislation and related regulations, which (as Slemrod acknowledges) negatively affect small businesses, is the notion held by many in Washington that small businesses can, to a greater degree than large businesses, manipulate the tax and employee benefit laws to avoid paying their fair share of taxes or avoid providing appropriate levels of benefits to their employees. Recent events (like the scandals at Enron, WorldCom, and Tyco) have resulted in some reassessment of this notion. This author's opinion is that much of the reason for the high frequency of tax legislation (and the frequency of legislation in general) is the basic nature of our political environment which, reflecting the public's clamor (if not demand) for both action and fairness from our legislators, has created enormous pressure on the men and women in Congress to actively promote change in our laws, especially in the tax and employee areas. This political pressure to be active, aided by the ability to produce large quantities of legislation (thanks to dozens of highly specialized staff), has brought about enormous and ongoing change and complexity in our tax laws.[8]

7. Apolinsky (2002).
8. For an interesting analysis of the reasons for the proliferation of laws at all levels of our legal system, see Younger (1980).

I agree with Slemrod's conclusion that the continuous changes and growing complexity of our tax laws have had a disproportionately negative impact on small businesses compared to larger businesses. This is because most small businesses have no internal specialized staff to help them comply with, let alone understand, the constantly changing rules.[9]

Congress has, however, adopted some tax legislation designed to encourage small businesses, the most significant being subchapter S, added to the Internal Revenue Code in 1958. The rules of subchapter S were partially a response to earlier proposals (which continue to this day) to eliminate the taxation of corporations entirely, on the theory that "double taxation" is inherently unfair. Critics of the system (pointing to subchapter K of the IRC and its taxation of partners) argue that a tax at the corporate level, in addition to a tax on shareholders, amounts to a penalty for conducting business in corporate form. These are the same arguments made in support of President Bush's current legislative proposal to eliminate the individual's tax on dividends from certain C corporations, albeit this does nothing directly to benefit the corporation. Although Congress has not eliminated taxation at the corporate level (in fact for some it increased the corporate tax in 1986, with the elimination of the general utilities doctrine), significant changes were made in the taxation of small-business corporations electing under subchapter S, which, for the most part, provides for a single tax at the shareholder level.[10] Recent legislation has further simplified and expanded the usefulness of subchapter S.[11]

Particularly Troublesome Tax Laws

As recognized by Slemrod throughout his chapter, small businesses are particularly vulnerable to complexity and change. The cost to a small-business owner in time spent dealing with complex and constantly changing tax laws, as well as the direct costs that must be paid to outside professional help, is greater for the smallest of small businesses.

Qualified Retirement Plans

During the past twenty years, the pension laws have been especially burdensome to small businesses, due in large part to the constant changes in the laws in the 1980s, especially those requiring plan amendments to be made on an almost biannual basis—specifically, the Tax Equity and Fiscal Responsibility Act of

9. See Brown, Hamilton, and Medoff (1990, pp. 85–85).
10. Subchapter S Revision Act of 1982, P.L. 97-354, 97 Cong. 2 sess.
11. See Small Business Job Protection Act of 1996, 104 Cong. 2 sess.

1982 (TEFRA), the Deficit Reduction Act of 1984 (DEFRA), the Retirement Equity Act of 1984 (REA), and the Tax Reform Act of 1986 (TRA-86). Although TRA-86 postponed the requirement to actually amend the plans until several years after enactment, its 1,700 pages of pension legislation created immediate compliance problems for many small businesses, because the plans had to operate from the effective date of the law, beginning in 1987, as if the plans had in fact been amended to comply with the 1986 act. In addition, IRS regulations issued between the effective date and the final date for amendment resulted in some plans having to be amended more than once. During this period the number of qualified retirement plans sponsored by small businesses declined substantially (over 100,000 plans terminated between 1986 and 1988) from an already low level of small-business plan sponsorship (less than 25 percent of small businesses with twenty-five or fewer employees sponsor any form of retirement plan). Now plans are required to conform to the so-called GUST amendments, which resulted from tax legislation during the late 1990s, as well as the Economic Growth and Tax Relief Reconciliation Act of 2001 (EGTRRA) amendments.[12]

Although we have not yet fully experienced the effect of recent pension simplification and the creation of an improved SIMPLE plan (Savings Incentive Match Plan for Employees, designed especially for small businesses) contained in the Small Business Job Protection Act of 1996, or the more recent improvements and simplification to the pension laws contained in EGTRRA, these improvements should be attractive to many small businesses and encourage more small businesses to adopt plans. The SEP–IRA plans (Self-Employed Plan–Individual Retirement Account), which do little to promote long-term employment, have not been popular with most small-business owners, except the smallest businesses.

Gift and Estate Taxes

Gift and estate tax laws can be burdensome to large, privately owned businesses and their owners, and the proposed repeal of these laws has been strongly supported by many family business owners. Estate tax relief was one of the top ten issues at the 1995 White House Conference on Small Business.[13] This of course is both a policy and a revenue issue, as well as a simplification issue.

The gift and estate tax provisions of EGTRRA were fully 25 percent of the act and, although designed to reduce and eliminate the transfer tax burden (which it currently has done for individuals with less than $1 million in net

12. GUST refers to changes in six acts: the Uruguay Round Agreement Act, the Uniform Services Employment and Reemployment Act, the Small Business Job Protection Act, the Tax Reform Act of 1997, the IRS Restructuring and Reform Act of 1998, and the Community Renewal Act of 2000.
13. See SBA (1996b, pp. 25, 47).

worth), it has created even more complexity for many affluent business owners and their advisors. In summary, the new law provides for a nine-year phase-in of rate reductions and increased exemptions, a four-year phased-in elimination of state credits, and the full repeal of the estate tax (but not the gift tax) law in 2010, followed by a "sunset" of the law in 2011 which would reinstate the prior law. Prior law in 2011 would then provide a $1 million exemption, which was due to be phased in by 2006. During the only year of full repeal in 2010, there would be a modified carry-over basis (rather than step-up basis) and a separate gift tax (splitting the current unified gift and estate tax system) with a $1 million gift tax exemption.

Working with the new rules will be complex and will necessitate significant (and more frequent) attention to planning (and greater costs) during the phase-in period (2002–2009) to keep up with the changes in exemption amounts, rate reductions, and the possibility of the old law being restored. This additional cost, however, should affect only the most successful of small-business owners which, as Slemrod recognizes, have adequate wealth to deal with the additional complexity and the costs.

Employee or Independent Contractor

An area especially burdensome to small businesses is determining whether a worker is an employee or an independent contractor. Small businesses have actively sought more workable criteria for making this determination, and the issue was the number-one concern (out of almost 300 topics) at the most recent White House Conference on Small Business. Some relief was given in this area in the Small Business Job Protection Act of 1996.

Paperwork Reduction

"Unnecessary paperwork" is one of the prime issues of the National Federation of Independent Business (NFIB), the largest of the small-business trade associations. Confirming Slemrod's observations, the typical small business simply does not have staff to deal with extensive paperwork. Therefore the owner, who needs to spend most of his or her time managing and operating the business, is distracted from doing so by governmental paperwork. It is this author's opinion that most small-business owners make a sincere effort to keep up with required record-keeping and government filings, but in many cases the volume is overwhelming and destructive to the operations of the business—a significant factor in the relatively high level of noncompliance among this group.

There are certainly other issues of concern to small-business owners—payroll tax relief, higher expense deductions for capital investment, reduction in the capital gains tax, and liberalization of the home office deduction—but the four areas discussed give us sufficient insight to evaluate the impact of the tax system on the small-business community.

Income Tax Laws Designed to Benefit Small Business

Congress has from time to time passed legislation specifically designed to benefit small businesses. Much of this legislation has been in response to requests from small-business organizations and to issues raised in the White House conferences on small business.

Choice of Business Entity

Prior to June 30, 2001, individuals were taxed at graduated tax rates, ranging from 15 percent (taxable income of joint filers up to $40,100) to 21.8 percent (taxable income of joint filers of $100,000). The marginal tax rates at upper-income levels are further increased by phase-outs of personal exemptions and itemized deductions.

The income tax rates for individuals were significantly changed by EGTRRA, beginning after June 30, 2001, to create a new 10 percent rate for income up to $12,000 for joint filers and a reduction of other rates. But this was not a simplification, because the rate changes are to be phased in over a six-year period. The 15 percent rate on taxable income up to $45,300 (for joint filers) remains the same; however, the prior tax rates of 28, 31, 36, and 39.6 percent are reduced each year from 2002 through 2006, when the rates will be 25, 28, 33, and 35 percent.

The regular C corporation rates (which were not changed) are taxed as separate entities at rates of 15 percent on taxable income up to $50,000, 25 percent on taxable income between $50,000 and $75,000, and 34 percent on taxable income from $75,000 to $10,000,000. The graduated rates below 34 percent are phased out by a 5 percent surtax on taxable income between $100,000 and $335,000, thus in effect creating a "bubble" bracket of 39 percent. Taxable income over $10,000,000 is taxed at 35 percent. I disagree with Slemrod's reference to these graduated corporate rates as a small-business preference, because the rates apply (and are of benefit) to all C corporations of any size, and these graduated rates are consistent with the overall philosophy of our graduated tax system, being no more a preference for small business than are the graduated rates applicable to all individuals.

Owners of businesses may choose to conduct their activities either through pass-through entities—sole proprietorships, partnerships, limited liability companies, and S corporations—which results in one level of tax at the individual tax rate of the owner(s), or as a C corporation, taxed at separate corporate rates.

Relief For Small-Business Investors

Directed tax relief for small business is provided in section 1202 of the Internal Revenue Code, added by OBRA-93 (the Omnibus Budget Reconciliation Act of 1993), which provides rules for certain "qualified small-business stock." A noncorporate taxpayer who holds qualified small-business stock for more than five years may exclude from income 50 percent of any gain on the sale or exchange of the stock. To qualify for this benefit, the net assets of the business on the date of issuance of the stock cannot exceed $50 million. The business must be in the active conduct of a qualified trade or business other than the performance of services in the fields of health, law, engineering, architecture, accounting, or any other businesses where the principal asset is the reputation or skill of one or more of its employees. Also excluded from the benefit of this provision is stock in banking, insurance, leasing, financing, investing, or similar businesses. This targeted preference may provide some encouragement to invest in certain small businesses, but it does nothing to improve the successful operations of the business.

Losses on Small-Business Corporation Stock

Section 1244 of the IRC provides that individual shareholders can treat up to $50,000 ($100,000 on a joint return) of losses on certain small-business stock as an ordinary loss. A corporation is a small-business corporation, for this purpose, if capital does not exceed $1 million at the time of issuance of the stock and certain record-keeping formalities are followed. This provision gives no benefit to small business that affects the operational success of the business.

Tax-Exempt Financing

State and local governments may issue qualified small-issue bonds to provide tax-exempt financing for capital expenditures for certain manufacturing businesses and first-time farmers. No more than $1 million of qualified small-issue bond financing of a single facility may be outstanding at any one time.

Expensing of Capital Investment

A small business may, in lieu of depreciation, elect under Internal Revenue Code section 179 to expense and deduct up to $24,000 of the cost of qualifying property placed in service during the taxable year. This amount is phased out for businesses that place in service more than $200,000 in qualifying property during a taxable year. The $24,000 annual limit will be increased in

2003.[14] This preference is ongoing and is a significant benefit to the operations of a small business. The administration's current tax proposals would increase the annual deduction limit to $75,000 and the current eligibility limit from $200,000 to $375,000.

Accounting Methods

Special statutory rules allow small businesses to use accounting methods that are unavailable to larger taxpayers. Some of these rules were designed to alleviate the tax accounting burdens of small businesses, and others were designed as a tax incentive for small businesses. The general rule is that a taxpayer must use the accrual method of accounting for federal income tax purposes if the taxpayer's gross receipts exceed $5 million. However, individuals, partnerships, S corporations, and qualified personal service corporations (PSCs) are exempt from this requirement. Therefore many small business entities are exempt from the mandated use of the accrual method of accounting (and therefore may use the cash method) either because the entity is not a C corporation, or it is a C corporation but has annual gross receipts of less than $5 million, or it is a qualified personal service corporation.

Conclusion

I agree with Slemrod's acknowledgment that a number of questions remain to be answered before we can say with confidence whether the tax system favors or penalizes small business. Slemrod concludes that the effective tax rates for small businesses are lower than for other classes of business taxpayers, but that the highly regressive nature of compliance costs may, on balance, result in an overall negative impact on small businesses, especially the smallest ones. He then states that the more difficult question is whether a tax favor or penalty toward small business is justified, either to offset greater noncompliance or to reflect the higher cost to the IRS of raising revenue from this sector. I would suggest, as an additional reason for favoring small business, the desirability of creating a level playing field, as Slemrod also notes.

Slemrod asks whether the IRS should devote more of its limited resources to small-business tax enforcement, concluding that it should do so where higher-income individual taxpayers are likely to be owners. He concludes that owners of S corporations, partnerships, and C corporations within the small-business community would likely be taxpayers at the high end of the income spectrum.

14. SBA (1996a).

This is probably a good observation, and I would merely add that it would also be beneficial to include high-income sole proprietors, who have the same, if not greater, control over tax compliance considerations.

Slemrod states that, other things being equal, resources should be directed to those enforcement activities that produce a higher revenue bang per administrative buck. This sounds like good policy. Other factors that influence the allocation of enforcement resources should also be considered—for example, specific industry groups, such as nightclubs.

Finally I generally agree with Slemrod's several recommendations on enforcement policy and with his observation that more effective enforcement will be a deterrent to others. This should produce additional revenue by improving the level of compliance.

Slemrod's chapter examines special provisions in the Internal Revenue Code that favor small business and then proceeds to give reasons to justify these favorable provisions. He concludes, however, that only one such reason (to offset highly regressive compliance costs) may be justified. I agree with his conclusion that special provisions for small business are appropriate but disagree that there is only one reason for doing so. An additional reason is the value of promoting small business to encourage the continued success of the private enterprise system. In addition to likely significant economic benefits to the country (based on recognized economic data), I suggest that the broader political and social benefits (generalized and unprovable as they are) are also important. Our federal tax system creates a nightmare of complexity for small business which, coupled with constant changes, has led to (and in my opinion is mostly responsible for) a high level of noncompliance among this sector of taxpayers. Increased and targeted auditing and enforcement efforts are certainly warranted to ensure that our voluntary tax system continues to be just that; however, there can never be enough enforcement funds or IRS agents to overcome a wholesale disregard for tax laws. The simplification and stability of these laws would go a long way toward allowing small-business taxpayers to feel good enough about paying their fair share of taxes to do so at a high level of compliance.

In addition to Slemrod's suggestion for further study, I recommend that we expand our insight into the causes of noncompliance beyond the simple observation that people will cheat if they can or if the economic burdens of compliance are too great. Further studies should determine whether the complex nature of the tax system and its constant changes encourage noncompliance and to what degree, especially by those who cannot, within reasonable levels of effort and expense, conform with it. As Alvin Toffler noted in *Future Shock*, human beings simply do not have the mental or psychological capacity to deal with rapid change beyond a certain point and will, after attempting to deal with change for a time, become frustrated and simply turn away.

From a purely pragmatic standpoint, the laws created to level the playing field for big and small businesses are probably effective to some limited degree; however, these laws would be more effective if there were legislative and regulatory progress toward less complexity and reporting requirements and more stability in the laws.

Slemrod suggests (but does not conclude) that our tax laws are, on balance, a negative force on small business. To me it appears clearly so.

References

Allers, Maarten. 1995. "Tax Compliance Costs in the Netherlands." In *Tax Compliance Costs: Measurement and Policy*, edited by Cedric Sandford, 173–95. Bath, U.K.: Fiscal Publications.

Allingham, Michael G., and Agnar Sandmo. 1972. "Income Tax Evasion: A Theoretical Analysis." *Journal of Public Economics* 1 (November): 323–38.

Andreoni, James. 1992. "IRS as Loan Shark: Tax Compliance with Borrowing Constraints." *Journal of Public Economics* 49 (October): 35–46.

Andreoni, James, Brian Erard, and Jonathan Feinstein. 1998. "Tax Compliance." *Journal of Economic Literature* 36 (June): 818–60.

Apolinsky, H. 2002. "Need for Fundamental Tax Reform." Washington: Americans for Fair Taxation.

Arthur D. Little. 1988. *Development of Methodology for Estimating the Taxpayer Paperwork Burden.* Report to the Department of the Treasury, Internal Revenue Service (June).

Ashby, Cornelia M. 2000. *IRS' Efforts to Serve Small Business Taxpayers.* Testimony of the General Accounting Office before the Senate Committee on Small Business. GAO/T-GGD-00-138.

Babbage, Charles. 1851. *Thoughts on the Principles of Taxation with Reference to a Property Tax and Its Exceptions.* 2d ed. London: John Murray.

Baker, Paul. 1993. "Taxpayer Compliance of the Self-Employed: Estimates from Household Spending Data." Working Paper 93/14. London: Institute for Fiscal Studies.

Bankman, Joseph, and Stewart Karlinsky. 2002. "Developing a Theory of Cash Businesses Tax Evasion Behavior and the Role of Their Tax Preparers." In *Fifth International Conference on Tax Administration: Current Issues and Future Developments*, by M. Walpole and R. Fisher. Sydney: Timebase.

Blau, David M. 1987. "A Time-Series Analysis of Self-Employment in the United States." *Journal of Political Economy* 95 (June): 445–67.

Blumenthal, Marsha, and Joel Slemrod. 1992. "The Compliance Cost of the U.S. Individual Income Tax System: A Second Look after Tax Reform." *National Tax Journal* 45 (June): 185–202.

Blumenthal, Marsha, Charles Christian, and Joel Slemrod. 2001. "Do Normative Appeals Affect Tax Compliance? Evidence from a Controlled Experiment in Minnesota." *National Tax Journal* 54 (March): 125–38.

Brown, Charles, James Hamilton, and James Medoff. 1990. *Employers Large and Small.* Harvard University Press.

Bruce, Donald. 2002. "Effects of the United States Tax System on Transitions into Self-Employment." *Labour Economics* 7 (September): 545–74.

Carroll, Christopher. 2000. "Portfolios of the Rich." Working Paper 7826. Cambridge, Mass.: National Bureau of Economic Research (August).

Chen, Duanjie, Frank C. Lee, and Jack Mintz. 2002. "Taxation, SMEs, and Entrepreneurship." Working Paper 2002/9. Paris: OECD.

Christian, Charles W. 1992a. "The Deterrent Effects of Audits on Noncompliance by Sole Proprietors." Research Conference, Department of the Treasury, Internal Revenue Service. Document 7302, number 64956T. Government Printing Office.

———. 1992b. "Compliance of Sole Proprietors: Findings from the 1988 TCMP Phase III, Cycle 10." *IRS Research Bulletin.* Publication 1500 (12/92). Government Printing Office.

———. 1994. "Voluntary Compliance with the Individual Income Tax: Results from the 1988 TCMP Study." *IRS Research Bulletin.* Publication 1500 (9/94): 35–42. Government Printing Office.

Clotfelter, Charles T. 1983a. "Tax Evasion and Tax Rates: An Analysis of Individual Returns." *Review of Economics and Statistics* 65 (August): 363–73.

———. 1983b. "Tax-Induced Distortions and the Business-Pleasure Borderline: The Case of Travel and Entertainment." *American Economic Review* 73 (December): 1053–65.

Crocker, Keith, and Joel Slemrod. 2003. "Optimal Policy Regarding Corporate Fraud: The Case of Tax Evasion." University of Michigan Business School.

Cullen, Julie B., and Roger Gordon. 2002. "Taxes and Entrepreneurial Activity: Theory and Evidence from the U.S." Working Paper 9015. Cambridge, Mass.: National Bureau of Economic Research.

Daunton, Martin. 2001. *Trusting Leviathan: The Politics of Taxation in Britain, 1799–1914.* Cambridge University Press.

Dubin, Jeffrey A., Michael J. Graetz, and Louis L. Wilde. 1990. "The Effect of Audit Rates on the Federal Individual Income Tax, 1977–86." *National Tax Journal* 43 (December): 395–409.

Dunkelberg, William. 2001. "Role Small Businesses Can Play in Jump-Starting the Economy." Testimony prepared for House Small Business Committee (www.house.gov/smbiz/hearings/107th/2001/011010/dunkelberg.html [July 14, 2003]).

Fairlie, Robert W., and Bruce D. Meyer. 2000. "Trends in Self-Employment among Black Men, During the Twentieth Century." *Journal of Human Resources* 35 (4): 643–69.

Feinstein, Jonathan S. 1991. "An Econometric Analysis of Income Tax Evasion and Its Detection." *RAND Journal of Economics* 22 (Spring): 14–35.

Gentry, William M., and R. Glenn Hubbard. 2000. "Tax Policy and Entrepreneurial Entry." *American Economic Review* 90 (May): 283–87.

———. Forthcoming. "Entrepreneurship and Household Saving." In *Advances and Economic Analysis and Policy.* Berkeley: Berkeley Electronic Press.

Goodwin, Michael. 1995. "The Compliance Costs of the United Kingdom Tax System." In *Tax Compliance Costs: Measurement and Policy,* edited by Cedric Sandford. Bath, U.K.: Fiscal Publications.

Goolsbee, Austan. 2002. "The Impact and Inefficiency of the Corporate Income Tax: Evidence from State Organizational Form Data." Working Paper 9141. Cambridge, Mass.: National Bureau of Economic Research.

Gravelle, Jane G., and Laurence J. Kotlikoff. 1989. "The Incidence and Efficiency Costs of Corporate Taxation When Corporate and Noncorporate Firms Produce the Same Good." *Journal of Political Economy* 97 (August): 749–80.

Hall, Arthur. 1995. "Compliance Costs of Alternative Tax Systems." Tax Foundation Special Report. Washington (June).

Hamilton, Barton H. 2000. "Does Entrepreneurship Pay? An Empirical Analysis of the Returns to Self-Employment." *Journal of Political Economy* 108 (June): 604–31.

Kagan, Robert A. 1989. "On the Visibility of Income Tax Law Violations." In *Taxpayer Compliance*, Vol. 2 of *Social Science Perspectives*, edited by Jeffrey A. Roth and John T. Scholz, 76–125. University of Pennsylvania Press.

Kesselman, Jonathan R. 1989. "Income Tax Evasion: An Intersectoral Analysis." *Journal of Public Economics* 38 (March): 137–82.

Klepper, Steven, and Daniel Nagin. 1989. "The Anatomy of Tax Evasion." *Journal of Law, Economics, and Organization* 5 (Spring): 1–24.

Long, James E. 1982. "Income Taxation and the Allocation of Market Labor." *Journal of Labor Research* 3 (Summer): 259–76.

Martinez-Vazquez, Jorge. 1996. "Who Benefits from Tax Evasion: The Incidence of Tax Evasion." *Public Economics Review* 1 (December): 105–35.

Mastromarco, Dan R., and David R. Burton. 2002. *The Internal Revenue Code: Unequal Treatment between Large and Small Firms.* Washington: The Prosperity Institute (www.nsbaonline.org).

Mayshar, Joram. 1991. "Taxation with Costly Administration." *Scandinavian Journal of Economics* 93 (1): 75–88.

Mills, Lillian, Merle Erickson, and Edward Maydew. 1998. "Investments in Tax Planning." *Journal of the American Taxation Association* 20 (1): 1–20.

Morton, Carolyn M. 1992. "Trends in the Compliance of Small Corporations." *IRS Research Bulletin.* Publication 1500 (12/92). Government Printing Office.

Parker, Simon C. 1996. "A Time Series Model of Self-Employment under Uncertainty." *Economica* 63 (August): 459–75.

Payne, James L. 1993. *Costly Returns: The Burdens of the U.S. Tax System.* San Francisco: ICS Press.

Pissarides, Christopher A., and Guillermo Weber. 1989. "An Expenditure-Based Estimate of Britain's Black Economy." *Journal of Public Economics* 39 (June): 17–32.

Pope, Jeff. 1995. "The Compliance Costs of Major Taxes in Australia." In *Tax Compliance Costs: Measurement and Policy*, edited by Cedric Sandford, 101–25. Bath, U.K.: Fiscal Publications.

Power, Laura, and Mark Rider. 2002. "The Effect of Tax-Based Savings Incentives on the Self- Employed." *Journal of Public Economics* 85 (July): 33–52.

Rice, Eric. 1992. "The Corporate Tax Gap: Evidence on Tax Compliance by Small Corporations." In *Why People Pay Taxes*, edited by Joel Slemrod, 125–61. University of Michigan Press.

Sandford, Cedric T. 1995. *Tax Compliance Costs: Measurement and Policy.* Bath, U.K.: Fiscal Publications.

Sandford, Cedric, and John Hasseldine. 1992. *The Compliance Costs of Business Taxes in New Zealand.* Wellington: Institute of Policy Studies, Victoria University.

Slemrod, Joel. 1989. "Complexity, Compliance Costs, and Tax Evasion." In *Taxpayer Compliance,* Vol. 2 of *Social Science Perspectives,* edited by Jeffrey A. Roth and John T. Scholz, 156–81. University of Pennsylvania Press.

———. 1997. *Measuring Taxpayer Burden and Attitudes for Large Corporations: 1996 and 1992 Survey Results.* Working Paper 97-1. Report to the Coordinated Examination Program, Internal Revenue Service. University of Michigan Business School (March).

———. 2002. "Trust in Public Finance." Working Paper 9187. Cambridge, Mass.: National Bureau of Economic Research (September).

Slemrod, Joel, and Marsha Blumenthal. 1996. "The Income Tax Compliance Cost of Big Business." *Public Finance Quarterly* 24 (October): 411–38.

Slemrod, Joel, Marsha Blumenthal, and Charles Christian. 2001. "Taxpayer Response to an Increased Probability of Audit: Evidence from a Controlled Experiment in Minnesota." *Journal of Public Economics* 79 (March): 455–83.

Slemrod, Joel, and Naomi Feldman. 2002. "Estimating Tax Evasion with Evidence from Tax Returns." University of Michigan Business School.

Slemrod, Joel, and Peter Katuscak. 2002. "Do Trust and Trustworthiness Pay Off?" Working Paper 9200. Cambridge, Mass.: National Bureau of Economic Research (September).

Slemrod, Joel, and Nikki Sorum. 1984. "The Compliance Cost of the U.S. Individual Income Tax System." *National Tax Journal* 37 (December): 461–74.

Slemrod, Joel, and Varsha Venkatesh. 2002. *The Income Tax Compliance Costs of Large and Mid-Sized Businesses.* Report to the Large and Mid-Size Business Division, Internal Revenue Service. University of Michigan Business School (September).

Slemrod, Joel, and Shlomo Yitzhaki. 1987. "The Optimal Size of a Tax Collection Agency." *Scandinavian Journal of Economics* 89 (September): 183–92.

———. 1996. "The Cost of Taxation and the Marginal Efficiency Costs of Funds." *International Monetary Fund Staff Papers* 43 (1): 172–98.

———. 2002. "Tax Avoidance, Evasion, and Administration." In *Handbook of Public Economics,* vol. 3, edited by Alan Auerbach and Martin Feldstein, 1425-70. Amsterdam: North-Holland.

Tait, Alan A. 1988. *Value Added Tax: International Practice and Problems.* Washington: International Monetary Fund.

Taylor, Humphrey. 2002. "Large Majorities Believe Big Companies, PACs, Media and Lobbyists Have Too Much Power and Influence in Washington." Harris Poll 17, April 10, 2002. Rochester, N.Y.: Harris Interactive (www.harrisinteractive.com/harris_poll/index.asp?PID=294 [July 14, 2003]).

U.S. Internal Revenue Service. 1988a. *Income Tax Compliance Research; Gross Tax Gap Estimates and Projections for 1973-1992.* IRS Publication 7285 (March).

———. 1988b. *Income Tax Compliance Research: Supporting Appendices to Publication 7285.* IRS Publication 1415 (July).

———. 1996. *Federal Tax Compliance Research: Individual Income Tax Estimates for 1985, 1988, and 1992.* IRS Publication 1415 (rev. 4-96).

————. 1999. "Tax Returns Filed in 1999."

————. 2002. "IRS Sets New Audit Priorities." Fact Sheet FS-2002-12 (September).

U.S. Small Business Administration. 1995. Office of the Chief Counsel for Advocacy. *The Changing Burden of Regulation, Paperwork, and Tax Compliance on Small Business: A Report to Congress* (www.sba.gov/advo/laws/archive/law.brd.html [July 14, 2003]).

————. 1996a. "The Facts about Small Business, 1996" (October).

————. 1996b. "First Annual Report on Implementation of the Recommendations of the 1995 White House Conference on Small Business." (September).

————. 2000. "The State of the Small Business: A Report to the President."

Wallschutzky, Ian. 1995. "Costs of Compliance for Small Business: Results from Twelve Case Studies in Australia." In *Tax Compliance Costs: Measurement and Policy,* edited by Cedric Sandford, 275–98. Bath, U.K.: Fiscal Publications.

Younger, I. 1980. "Socrates, Law, and the Congress of the United States." Charles Evans Hughes Memorial Lecture, New York County Lawyers' Association (May).

5

AUSTAN GOOLSBEE

The TurboTax Revolution: Can Technology Solve Tax Complexity?

A FUNDAMENTAL TRADE-OFF in the tax code surrounds the issues of complexity and the costs of compliance. Over the past two decades, policymakers facing strict rules about budget expenditures have increasingly turned to the tax code to promote various types of behaviors or give money back to particular constituencies (see, for example, the overview of tax policy in the 1990s by Eugene Steuerle[1]). Doing so, however, necessarily involves adding layers of complexity to the system that are both costly and that tend to increase people's opposition to the system.

Academics typically think of these compliance costs as additional deadweight loss from raising revenue. As such, they are important for various positive and normative theories about the size of government.[2] If, however, a new technology arrived on the scene that could reduce the cost of complying with the tax code, it could potentially eliminate the dilemma faced by the policymakers, at least in the short run. Policymakers might be able to target the behaviors they want without worrying about the problems raised by added complexity. I refer to this idea as a technological solution to the policymakers' complexity dilemma. The technological solution is not as far-fetched as it might sound. Indeed some have argued that information technology in general and tax planning software in particular may be just such a solution.[3]

1. Steuerle (2002).
2. See, for instance, Becker (1983); Becker and Mulligan (2003).
3. Orszag (2002) and Burman (2002), for example, discuss the potential of tax software to allow for more complexity without the typical costs.

This chapter considers the economic issues associated with the rise of tax planning software by using data on more than 60,000 households, which includes information on whether they use such software. Specifically the chapter deals with three issues: whether the use of these programs is widespread or is restricted to a narrow class of people, whether consumers are actually using these programs to reduce complexity, and whether the gain from expanding the use of tax software, such as the recent Bush administration free-filing initiative, would be as large as pursuing other technology-based solutions, such as return-free filing of 1040EZ forms.

The data essentially answer all three in the negative. First, use of tax planning programs is quite small, concentrated among highly educated people (as well as people with high incomes), and is unlikely to be widespread for many years to come. As a result, the people who would be hurt by increasing the complexity of the tax code are the ones not using the software—precisely the people for whom complexity is the most costly: those with little education, few resources, who frequently do not speak English.

Second, though, and more important, the data do not provide any evidence that people adopt tax software in order to reduce the complexity of their tax compliance (as opposed to, say, getting the services they might get from an accountant but at a cheaper price). Regression analysis of people's decisions to use the software shows that, holding other things equal, a host of factors that should make the tax situation more complicated—operating a business from home, having children under six years old, having a complex state income tax, and the like—do not make people more likely to adopt. Instead the decision seems to be driven primarily by the computer- and Internet-savvy of the taxpayer. People use the programs when the costs of learning how are low, not when the benefits from improved simplicity are high.

The chapter then makes the point that switching some or all of the 1040EZ returns to automatic, return-free electronic filing would have a bigger impact on the complexity of the tax system in the near term and would be geared toward people for whom complexity is most difficult. Even if this could be done only for childless single people and married couples with one working spouse, to reduce administrative problems, it could still eliminate compliance costs for as many as 18 million taxpayers, which are on the order of $1 billion to $2 billion per year in time savings alone, or up to $2 billion in expense if they are using paid tax preparers.[4]

---

4. Discussion based on nationally representative Forrester data and U.S. Census and IRS data.

The Tax Assistance Industry

It is not surprising that, for something as complicated as filling out a tax return, there would be a booming business in assisting people who do not know much about the process. The traditional form of help has been the accountant. H&R Block and Jackson Hewitt are the best-known national brand names, but there are thousands of accountants throughout the country that do similar work.

In recent years there has been a fairly significant rise in the number of individuals using tax management software to help them fill out their returns rather than turning to an accountant. The market leader is Intuit's TurboTax, but there are several others, including Kiplinger's TaxCut, owned by H&R Block, and many other small players. According to Michael Mahoney and the data cited by Intuit, TurboTax has approximately 70 percent of the market.[5]

Basically these programs allow the taxpayer to enter information into a computer program, which asks questions about possible deductions, sources of income, and so on, and at the end it prints out a tax return and tells the payer how much is owed or due as a refund. For people who use financial planning software such as Microsoft Money or Intuit's Quicken, it is possible to load data directly into the software without having to type it in. Similarly, some financial firms, such as Fidelity, have deals with Intuit that allow users to download information on capital gains distributions and realizations and interest income directly.

In general these types of programs are not geared toward the truly complex tax returns of people at the top of the income distribution, and their help with advice on things like bequest management and estate taxation is limited. They are instead geared toward almost everyone else paying the personal income tax—and certainly not just itemizers.

The cost of these programs is small compared with the cost of a typical accountant. In 2001, for example, TurboTax for the web cost between seven and ten dollars for a 1040EZ form and fifteen to twenty dollars for a standard 1040. TurboTax in a box costs a bit more (about thirty dollars for the basic package). Completing a state income tax form involves another small charge.

It is important to note at the outset that tax management software is not the same thing as filing electronically. Electronic filing refers only to the method of delivery to the IRS. While there is much overlap between the two groups, if there is to be a technological solution to the complexity problem, it will rest with tax planning software, not with electronic filing. The main advantages of

5. Michael Mahoney, "Online Tax Filing Firms in Battle of Goliath vs. Goliath," *E-Commerce Times*, March 12, 2001 (www.ecommercetimes.com/perl/story/8092.html); "Another Record Tax Year for TurboTax," press release, April 18, 2002 (www.intuit.com/company/press_releases/2002/04-18.html [January 2003]).

electronic filing include knowing right away if the return has been received and accepted and receiving a refund in a substantially shorter amount of time. There are many brick-and-mortar accountants—H&R Block, for example—where a taxpayer can file electronically even if they have not used a computer program themselves. The filing is done by H&R Block and to the taxpayer is no different from going to an accountant in the presoftware days, except that one can get a refund quicker. This is electronic filing with no reduction in complexity.

On the other side, at the conclusion of a tax management software program, taxpayers receive a copy of their tax return and then they can decide to mail it in as in a conventional filing or to file electronically. If they mail it in, they benefit from reduced complexity by using the program but not by filing electronically. The software is the key.

Data Sources and Basic Results

To examine the impact of tax planning software, I rely on data from the Technographics program of Forrester Inc., a leading market research firm. The Technographics 2001 benchmark sample includes detailed microdata from more than 90,000 people across the United States. The fieldwork was done by NFO Worldgroup, using a mail survey to a subset of its ongoing survey panel. The data are meant to be nationally representative and, in addition to extensive demographic and economic information about the individuals, the respondents answered questions about how they manage their finances, including whether they use "tax planning software (like TurboTax)."[6] For those with access to a personal computer at home, the respondents answered information such as how frequently they use the computer, whether they have ever bought online, whether this is their first computer, and so on.

From this information I construct a profile of the users of tax management software and seek to explain who uses it and why. This is the only systematic source of microlevel information about the use of such programs in existence. It allows me to match people's demographics to their tax situations in a way that would be impossible using tax return data, even if one could get individual-level information, because returns do not include much demographic information.

Because it will be the basis of the results, however, it is important to know whether the data are truly nationally representative regarding this type of software. Looking at the data as of January 2001, some 9.9 percent of households reported having used tax planning software, an increase of 13 percent from the

---

6. This is the same data source used in Goolsbee (2000). It is described in more detail in Yonish and others (2001).

level in 2000 (8.8 percent), corresponding to between 10 million and 11 million households. Intuit claims that TurboTax users totaled 7.6 million in 2001.[7] Given the 70 percent market share, this would imply an overall market of 10.9 million, so the Forrester data appear to match the national numbers fairly well.

Who Uses Tax Software?

The first step in evaluating the role of tax planning software is to understand how many people are using it and who they are. Using just the aggregate number (about 10 percent of households), it is quite clear that, without a dramatic increase in adoption over the next several years, policymakers' technological solution will have to wait. At current growth rates, it could take decades. Further, because about one-third of U.S. households have no access to a computer, even with rapid growth among computer users, it may take a long time for software usage to become comprehensive. In the near term, in all likelihood, the most that could be hoped for would be for penetration rates to rise as high as other related activities, such as using financial planning software or buying products online. In 2001, 22.3 percent of households reported using financial planning software, and 46.9 percent reported having bought online. These percentages are significantly larger than the numbers for tax planning software, but they are still not at all comprehensive.

The limited use of tax software means that making the Internal Revenue Code more complex while relying on the software to simplify it could make the costs of compliance worse for the 90 percent of households who do not use the software. It is highly relevant, then, who the users and nonusers are. The work on tagging and heterogeneity of Akerlof and Kopczuk has shown that an optimal tax system might allow certain groups to avoid taxes so long as the social welfare function says those groups should receive more weight.[8] The problem with applying that argument here is that it potentially gives a special reduction in complexity to highly skilled people (computer software users). The people suffering from the higher complexity might well be people unprepared to deal with it—households with less education and lower incomes.

To gauge the relevance of this point in reality, table 5-1 presents the demographic and economic characteristics of users compared to nonusers in 2001. It is clear that the two differ quite a lot. In particular the tax software users have average incomes almost 40 percent higher than nonusers, are substantially more likely to have assets such as retirement accounts and brokerage accounts, and

---

7. "Another Record Tax Season." See "Intuit Reports Third-Quarter Fiscal 2001 Results," press release, May 22, 2001, Mountain View, Calif.

8. Akerlof (1978); Kopczuk (2001).

Table 5-1. *Demographic Characteristics of Tax Planning Software Users, 2001*
Percent, except as indicated

Demographic characteristics	Tax software users	Tax software nonusers
Income (thousands of dollars)	78.3	56.8
Age (years)	46.8	49.9
White	0.92	0.89
Single	0.21	0.32
High school or less	0.15	0.39
College	0.61	0.48
Postgraduate	0.24	0.14
Republican	0.45	0.37
Democrat	0.28	0.37
Unaffiliated, other	0.27	0.26
Have mutual funds	0.42	0.26
Have retirement account	0.70	0.45
Have brokerage account	0.46	0.26

Source: Author's calculations, based on IRS data.

have a great deal more education. The share of software users with a high school degree or less, for example, is only 15.4 percent, versus almost 40 percent for nonusers. The software users also tend to be slightly younger and are slightly more likely to be white, Republican, and to have children, but these are much smaller differences than the income, asset, and education differences.

Though a separate issue from the prevalence of tax software, it is worth considering the ways that software usage may differ from the use of paid tax preparers. There is no information in the Forrester data on the subject, but I can compare it to the zip code data from the Internal Revenue Service which (among other things) provides average adjusted gross income (AGI) and share of returns prepared by a paid preparer.[9] The files are released by state. For simplicity I use information from the top seven states, together accounting for about 40 percent of the U.S. population.[10] There are more than 17,000 zip codes included in those data. I restrict the sample to zip codes with at least ten respondents in the Forrester data and then rank them by average AGI.

The share of returns signed by a paid tax preparer is 55.8 percent, and the share of respondents in the Forrester data reporting that they use tax software is about 13.0 percent. Among the zip codes with average AGI in the bottom quartile (with average AGI less than $36,000), almost 56.7 percent of returns are

9. IRS (2003a).
10. These are California, Texas, New York, Florida, Illinois, Pennsylvania, and Ohio.

signed by a paid tax preparer, but only 9.8 percent of Forrester respondents report using tax software. Among zip codes in the highest quartile (with average AGI greater than $59,700), the share of returns signed by a paid tax preparer is actually a slight bit lower, at 55.7 percent, while the share using tax software is much higher than before, at 15.1 percent. So the use of these programs does not appear to be closely tied to an overall demand for tax assistance.

Is Tax Software about Simplification?

Most of the discussion about tax software has taken for granted that people adopt it because it substantially simplifies tax filing, as opposed to merely providing the same services as an accountant provides but at a lower price. I question whether this is, in fact, the case. Essentially taxes complicate people's lives in three ways: They induce people to engage in complicated transactions that they would not otherwise engage in, they necessitate extra record-keeping, and they are complicated to compute and file. Software has no effect on the first, almost no effect on the second, and a large effect on the third, but the third is the least important of the three.

Without being able actually to observe why people use the software, it is important to look for indirect evidence. If a main attraction of these programs is to make things simpler, we would expect to see that, holding other things equal, people with more complex tax filing situations should be more likely to use them. We are essentially asking about the demand curve for tax software. This regression will not estimate the demand for tax planning in general, because the data do not include information about paid tax preparers. It will estimate the demand for the software, given the current existence of substitutes. If accountants did not exist, people might all switch to tax software, and its benefits might be great. Given that accountants do exist, though, we want to know whether complexity is leading people to use software. If complexity leads people to switch to accountants, the answer will be no. If the only thing tax software can do is reduce minor complexity and, once you get past that, an accountant takes over, it is hard to see a large welfare gain for the consumer.

There are two alternative explanations for what drives tax software adoption, other than the desire to reduce complexity. One is that the adoption decision is driven, or at least correlated, with various demographic factors, such as more education, greater wealth, and so on. The second is that tax software is simply a complement to computer usage and particularly to certain types of computer usage, such as keeping family budgets on computer.

I examine the individual-level decision to use tax planning software by doing regression analyses on the Forrester data. Given the nature of the survey respondents, it is probably most appropriate to do this regression only among people who actually do have the choice of using such software, which means people with personal computers. People without computers will answer no to the question rather automatically. More interesting is examining why the people who actually could adopt choose not to.[11] Restricting the sample to people with a home personal computer reduces the sample to just over 60,000 respondents. I also present results including people without home computers, to be sure that selection is not a problem. The results are similar. Table 5-2 lays out several regressions where the dependent variable is the individual {0,1} decision of whether to use tax planning software.

Column 1 presents a basic linear probability specification. Factors that are correlated with more complex returns (to test whether a desire to reduce complexity drives the software adoption decision) include the number of lines on the state income tax form, whether the person's state has an income tax at all, dummies for the number of children under six years old in the household (which make it more likely to have day-care expenses), whether they run a business from home either full or part-time, and whether they have bought or sold a house in the past year. These coefficients are listed in the first rows of the specification.

Variables to control for the independent influence of demographics and other factors include gender, race, education, family size, and market-size dummies, as well as dummies for the types of assets the respondent has (such as full-service brokerage accounts, discount brokerage accounts, mutual funds invested indirectly and in banks, and retirement accounts) as well as a cubic function of their age and income.

Variables to control for either an attraction to new technology or the complementarities between tax software and other computer software include dummies for the frequency of computer usage, whether an individual has ever bought something online, whether this is the first personal computer the household has owned, whether the respondent uses a computer at work, owns a cellular phone or a PalmPilot or other personal digital assistant (PDA), and whether the respondent uses Microsoft Money, Intuit's Quicken, or another type of financial planning software. In the full sample regression, I drop some of the computer variables but add a variable for whether the individual has access to a personal computer at home.

The results in table 5-2 are not supportive of the view that tax management software is driven by a desire to reduce complexity. Taxpayers do not appear to be any more likely to use it if their tax status becomes more complicated. The number of lines on the state income tax form has the wrong sign—more entries

11. The regression with only computer users will have a selection bias if, as an example, people are more likely to buy computers if they want to do their taxes using the software. I do not view this as especially problematic. Including the entire sample, on the other hand, will then make the results influenced by the factors that drive the adoption of personal computers. Goolsbee and Klenow (2002) cover that topic in some detail.

Table 5-2. *Regression Analysis of Taxpayer's Use of Tax Management Software*[a]

	1, OLS	2, PROBIT	3, OLS	4, OLS	5, OLS
Number of lines on state income tax	−0.0003 (0.0001)	−0.0003 (0.0001)	−0.0002 (0.0001)	−0.0004 (0.0001)	−0.0004 (0.0001)
No state income tax	−0.0021 (0.0046)	−0.0028 (0.0043)	−0.0026 (0.0035)	−0.0063 (0.0060)	−0.0061 (0.0060)
Single	−0.0130 (0.0034)	−0.0129 (0.0031)	−0.0112 (0.0024)	−0.0092 (0.0043)	−0.0095 (0.0043)
One child under 6 years	−0.0048 (0.0049)	−0.0034 (0.0044)	−0.0048 (0.0038)	−0.0080 (0.0064)	−0.0081 (0.0064)
Two or more children under 6 years	−0.0051 (0.0081)	−0.0037 (0.0070)	−0.0057 (0.0063)	−0.0107 (0.0104)	−0.0110 (0.0104)
Home-based business	0.0041 (0.0035)	0.0045 (0.0031)	0.0077 (0.0028)	0.0037 (0.0045)	0.0037 (0.0045)
Male	0.0123 (0.0026)	0.0111 (0.0024)	0.0090 (0.0020)	0.0158 (0.0035)	0.0158 (0.0035)
Bought home in past year	−0.0082 (0.0060)	−0.0061 (0.0055)	−0.0055 (0.0047)	−0.0102 (0.0080)	−0.0103 (0.0080)
Sold home in past year	0.0126 (0.0074)	0.0082 (0.0065)	0.0125 (0.0058)	0.0104 (0.0092)	0.0107 (0.0092)
Have a home computer			−0.0304 (0.0027)		
Use Microsoft Money	0.0943 (0.0044)	0.0724 (0.0035)	0.1072 (0.0038)	0.0974 (0.0054)	0.0972 (0.0054)
Use Intuit Quicken	0.1660 (0.0034)	0.1106 (0.0027)	0.1842 (0.0029)	0.1676 (0.0042)	0.1676 (0.0042)
Use other financial program	0.1132 (0.0070)	0.0770 (0.0053)	0.1204 (0.0058)	0.1101 (0.0087)	0.1104 (0.0087)
Use cellular phone	0.0023 (0.0029)	0.0037 (0.0028)	0.0056 (0.0022)	0.0070 (0.0038)	0.0071 (0.0038)
Use Palm Pilot, other PDA	0.0351 (0.0050)	0.0183 (0.0044)	0.0373 (0.0040)	0.0329 (0.0061)	0.0328 (0.0061)
White	−0.0077 (0.0048)	−0.0075 (0.0048)	0.0003 (0.0033)	−0.0129 (0.0064)	−0.0128 (0.0064)
Use computer 4 to 6 times a week	−0.0102 (0.0034)	−0.0089 (0.0030)		−0.0119 (0.0043)	−0.0118 (0.0043)
Use computer 2 to 3 times a week	−0.0145 (0.0044)	−0.0136 (0.0039)		−0.0139 (0.0058)	−0.0140 (0.0058)
Use computer 1 time a week	−0.0194 (0.0069)	−0.0203 (0.0062)		−0.0265 (0.0097)	−0.0266 (0.0097)
Use computer 2 to 3 times a month	−0.0265 (0.0079)	−0.0350 (0.0069)		−0.0473 (0.0121)	−0.0475 (0.0122)
Use computer 1 time a month	−0.0170 (0.0126)	−0.0190 (0.0125)		−0.0386 (0.0227)	−0.0378 (0.0227)
Use computer less than 1 time a month	−0.0265 (0.0072)	−0.0458 (0.0064)		−0.0608 (0.0156)	−0.0603 (0.0156)
Bought online	0.0408 (0.0030)	0.0443 (0.0027)		0.0426 (0.0039)	0.0426 (0.0039)
This is not first PC	0.0368 (0.0030)	0.0489 (0.0031)		0.0434 (0.0041)	0.0433 (0.0041)
Use computer at work	0.0100 (0.0033)	0.0162 (0.0033)	0.0163 (0.0025)	0.0083 (0.0044)	0.0084 (0.0044)

(continued)

Table 5-2. *Regression Analysis of Taxpayer's Use of Tax Management Software (Continued)*[a]

	1, OLS	2, PROBIT	3, OLS	4, OLS	5, OLS
Full-service online broker	−0.0009 (0.0041)	0.0000 (0.0035)	0.0013 (0.0033)	−0.0036 (0.0052)	−0.0035 (0.0052)
Full-service broker, not online	−0.0016 (0.0038)	−0.0012 (0.0033)	0.0007 (0.0030)	−0.0027 (0.0048)	−0.0028 (0.0048)
Discount online broker	0.0669 (0.0048)	0.0365 (0.0037)	0.0751 (0.0040)	0.0663 (0.0058)	0.0663 (0.0058)
Discount broker, not online	0.0054 (0.0083)	0.0050 (0.0069)	0.0040 (0.0065)	0.0002 (0.0104)	0.0001 (0.0104)
Mutual fund, purchase direct	0.0165 (0.0031)	0.0124 (0.0027)	0.0145 (0.0025)	0.0120 (0.0039)	0.0120 (0.0039)
Mutual fund, purchase through bank	−0.0095 (0.0055)	−0.0080 (0.0049)	−0.0105 (0.0042)	−0.0040 (0.0070)	−0.0039 (0.0070)
Retirement account, online	0.0497 (0.0034)	0.0359 (0.0029)	0.0466 (0.0027)	0.0512 (0.0042)	0.0512 (0.0042)
Retirement account, not online	0.0166 (0.0032)	0.0134 (0.0029)	0.0150 (0.0026)	0.0145 (0.0041)	0.0146 (0.0041)
Have no investments	0.0084 (0.0040)	−0.0046 (0.0041)	0.0098 (0.0030)	0.0092 (0.0055)	0.0092 (0.0055)
< High school	−0.0283 (0.0073)	−0.0329 (0.0063)	−0.0286 (0.0048)	−0.0364 (0.0103)	−0.0368 (0.0103)
High school diploma	−0.0301 (0.0046)	−0.0271 (0.0038)	−0.0348 (0.0035)	−0.0336 (0.0059)	−0.0339 (0.0059)
Some college	−0.0224 (0.0043)	−0.0150 (0.0036)	−0.0252 (0.0034)	−0.0254 (0.0054)	−0.0257 (0.0054)
College graduate	0.0057 (0.0040)	0.0058 (0.0034)	0.0042 (0.0032)	0.0029 (0.0049)	0.0029 (0.0049)
Applied for mortgage this year				0.0068 (0.0070)	0.0069 (0.0070)
Democrat				−0.0092 (0.0044)	−0.0092 (0.0044)
Republican				−0.0031 (0.0042)	−0.0031 (0.0042)
Income	Cubic	Cubic	Cubic	Cubic	34 dummies
Age	Cubic	Cubic	Cubic	9 dummies	9 dummies
Dummies	Market size, family size	Market size, family size	Market size, family size	Market size, family size, assets value, hours of leisure, year of comp.	Market size, family size, assets value, hours of leisure, year of comp.
N	61,724	61,724	84,493	42,170	42,170
R^2	0.12	—	0.13	0.11	0.11

Source: Author's calculations, based on Forrester data.

a. The dependent variable is a {0,1} of whether the individual reports using tax planning software. Standard errors are in parentheses. Columns 1, 3, 4, and 5 are linear probability models. Column 2 gives the marginal effects from a PROBIT. Column 3 includes all people. The other columns include only people with a home personal computer.

make one less likely to use tax software, although the coefficient is quite small (the mean of the dependent variable is 0.099). Not having a state income tax has an extremely small coefficient that is not significant. Having child-care-age children also has no significant effect on the likelihood of using a tax program, and the point estimate is negative. There is similarly no significant effect of buying or selling a house nor of operating a business from home.

Many of the demographic variables do matter—college graduates and people with graduate education are much more likely to use the software (controlling for everything else). Men are more likely, as are young people, though the age coefficients are not reported in the table to conserve space. Race plays little role, as does the ownership of most types of financial accounts.

Clearly the strongest determinant of tax planning software use is the individual's use of computers and especially financial planning software. By far the biggest coefficients as well as the most significant are on the usage of Microsoft Money, Intuit's Quicken, and other financial planning software. Use of one of these products doubles or even triples the probability that the respondent uses a tax planning program. Because the market leader by far is Intuit's TurboTax, the fact that Intuit's Quicken has the largest coefficient is not surprising, because it is presumably the easiest one from which to integrate information into the tax program. Of course, combined advertising or something of that nature might be a factor.

Essentially all other measures of computer usage show up significantly and with the correct sign. Compared to people who report using their computers every day, for example, less frequent usage is correlated with a lower likelihood of using tax software. Usage is greater for respondents who own a PalmPilot or other PDA, those for whom their current PC is not their first, and people who use a computer at work. Interestingly, even the controls for the types of financial accounts point to the computer usage explanation, in that the largest coefficients are on ownership of discount brokerage and retirement accounts for which there is online access. The same accounts without online access have small or insignificant effects on tax software adoption.

Column 2 repeats the same specification but in a probit model rather than the linear probability model. The estimated marginal effects are close to the linear model in almost every respect, so this does not seem to be a particularly troubling issue.

Column 3 expands the sample to include all survey respondents (including non–computer users) and adds a variable to the regression of whether the individual has a computer at home. Doing this regression necessitates dropping the computer usage–related variables, such as frequency of use, having bought online, and so on, since these are not asked of the non–computer users. The results are similar to those in the sample of just computer users. All the tax variables have the same insignificant or perverse signs or both, with the exception of home-based business, which still has a small coefficient (having a home-based business raises the probability of using TurboTax by 0.007—less than one-quarter of a standard deviation) but now is significant. It is still rather clearly the computer and technology-related factors that are the primary determinants of the decision to use the software.

Column 4 returns to the base specification in column 1 but includes further information, including dummies for the total value of assets, for hours of leisure each week, and for the year the respondent's latest computer was purchased; a full set of age dummies and income dummies rather than the cubic functions; a dummy for whether the individual applied for a mortgage in the past year; and dummies for whether the respondent is affiliated with Republicans or Democrats (unaffiliated or other is the omitted category). Several of these other variables include missing observations, so the number in the sample falls from 61,724 to 42,170, but the results are highly similar. It is still the case that tax complexity variables are not correlated with a higher likelihood of using tax software, but the use of computers and other software is.

The bottom line is that people seem to adopt tax planning software not when their taxes are complex but rather when the costs of learning how to use the program or to integrate it into financial planning that they already do are particularly low. Examining how the programs work, perhaps this is not too surprising. They make filling out the forms more convenient, but they do not really make it much simpler to qualify for various deductions or anything like that. Indeed research done by the Internal Revenue Service indicates that, holding everything else equal, people who use tax software end up spending more time doing their taxes than comparable people not using the programs.[12] At the least, it is hard to see how these programs make filing a tax return any simpler than they have been for many years with an accountant.

The main reason for adoption may be that software can provide services similar to a paid tax preparer but at lower cost. The reason this distinction matters for estimating the value of the software is that, if the software is merely doing something that already exists but at a slightly lower price, the consumer welfare gain is rather seriously bounded above by the change in the price from the first alternative—a small number—rather than the typical entire-area-under-the-demand-curve calculation one would do for a completely new good. In short, no one can have a high valuation (that is, dramatically higher than the price they have to pay) for the tax planning services offered by the software because, if they did, they could have hired an accountant to do the same thing at prices only slightly higher than what the software costs.

12. IRS (2002a).

Alternative Technological Approaches to Simplification

The recent decision of the Bush administration to make free electronic filing available to people is a move in the direction of trying to accelerate the expansion of tax planning software. An alternative approach to simplification would have greater benefit to taxpayers in the near term and might be a better place to devote resources. Ironically this benefit comes from converting the least complex tax form of all—the 1040EZ—to automatic, return-free electronic filing, even just for some fraction of such filers.

As of 2001 the data suggest that something like 11 million households prepared tax returns using tax planning software. As of 2000, though, around 22 million 1040EZ returns were filed.[13] Clearly the EZ forms are not as complicated as other forms, but it is equally evident that eliminating EZ filings would affect more people than increasing the use of the tax software can.

Economists and other tax analysts—people who typically have a great deal of education themselves—are not used to thinking of the 1040EZ form as being complicated and, indeed, frequently say there is not much objection to the compliance costs with such a form.[14] The irony is that the people who find the EZ form simple are exactly the ones who cannot use it. For the typical person filling out a 1040EZ, the process is not always trivial. As an example, note that, although the form is only thirteen lines long, the instruction booklet on the Internet is some thirty-two pages. It involves several worksheets and a fair amount of gathering and computing numbers and then adding and subtracting.

Although there is no information from the IRS on the educational backgrounds of people using EZ forms, in the Forrester data, among people with household incomes less than $50,000 that hold no brokerage or mutual fund accounts (something approximating the requirements of the EZ form), close to 60 percent have a high school diploma or less. The work of Bernheim and others has emphasized that retirement savings tend to be inadequate among people without education and have argued for a program of financial literacy.[15] This may be analogous to the situation with taxes. Basic computational tasks, which are obviously vital for filling out tax returns, are not trivial to many people. Perhaps that is one reason why as many as half those filing the easiest forms hire a paid tax preparer, typically at a cost of $100 to $200.[16]

The IRS's own time disclosure estimate suggests that it would take someone three hours and forty-three minutes to fill out the 1040EZ form, and such num-

---

13. Of course some people using tax planning software are using it to fill out EZ forms, so the groups are not exclusive (IRS 2002b).

14. See, for example, Sperling (2002).

15. Bernheim and Scholz (1993).

16. See Berube and others (2002).

bers are typically thought to be underestimates.[17] In the aggregate, people are spending more than 80 million hours filling out the easiest form the IRS has— time worth something like $1 billion to $2 billion at average wage rates. The odd thing about the entire enterprise is that, for many if not most of these tax- payers, all the information they fill out on their 1040EZ is already reported to the IRS directly. So why not just have employers pay the money directly and skip the 1040EZ form altogether? Even if employers simply filled out 1040EZs for their employees and distributed them instead of W-2s, complexity would be greatly reduced. The employees would just have to sign them and send them in.

Clearly, enacting complete return-free status would entail some additional costs to the IRS, but would they really total $1 billion to $2 billion a year? As a comparison, the IRS indicates that the entire IRS budget for processing, admin- istration, and management (covering all taxpayers) was $3.6 billion in 2001.[18] These would be the simplest types of reforms imaginable. If attempting to con- nect married payers across employers is too complex or too costly a task, con- sider applying the return-free option only for single people. The Forrester data suggest that about 45 percent of people with household incomes of less than $50,000 and no brokerage or mutual fund accounts are single. This is close to 10 million people. Only one-third of married households have both spouses working, leaving some 7.5 million more people potentially covered by this most simple case.[19] Of these single and married people with one earner, 70 percent do not have children. Restricting reforms to just the childless, to avoid any com- plications arising from the Earned Income Tax Credit, would still leave more than 12 million potential beneficiaries of the program.

This revision to the tax system would be concentrated at the low end of the income distribution. Even the restricted program (childless single people and married couples with only one working spouse) could reduce the time spent on 1040EZ forms by more than 50 million hours, or up to $1 billion worth of time each year. If these people were going to pay tax preparers at a cost of $150, the reform would save the 12.25 million taxpayers almost $2 billion in accountant costs.

Conclusion

This chapter has considered the promise and problems associated with relying on electronic tax software as a solution to the complexity problem of the tax

---

17. IRS (2001). Slemrod and Sorum (1984), Blumenthal and Slemrod (1992), and Arthur D. Little (1988) have considered the true compliance burdens of tax filing and preparation.

18. IRS (2003b).

19. Gale and Holtzblatt (1997) look in detail at the issues involved in converting to a return-free system.

code. There are two basic difficulties with relying on the technological solution. The first is that, in the near term, only a small number of people use such software, and those who do are highly educated and have high incomes. The people who do not use the software tend to be precisely the people for whom the losses from complexity are the greatest.

The second difficulty is that regression analysis of the individual decision about whether to use such software suggests that people are not using it because it makes filling out their tax returns less complicated. Many individual factors associated with more complexity—such as having a complex state income tax (or a state income tax at all), running a business from home, having children under six, and the like—do not increase the likelihood that taxpayers use tax management software. Instead the determinants seem to be computer-related factors, such as how long the taxpayers have had access to the Internet, whether they have ever bought things online, whether they use a computer for family budgeting or paying bills, and whether they have brokerage accounts with online access. In other words, people use tax management software when the costs—either price or learning costs—are low, not when the simplification benefits are high.

An alternative approach that could reduce complexity for 10 million to 15 million Americans, although it might not do much to eliminate the complexity trade-offs in policymaking, would be to eliminate many or even all 1040EZ filings and replace them with automatic return-free filing through the employer. In the near term the distributional considerations and the limited spread of tax planning software suggest that that reform would have a bigger impact.

Perhaps it is also worth considering the deeper issue of whether a purely technological solution to complexity is the right approach. In the extreme such solutions have the potential to make the tax system a black box: At the end of the year, a machine tells you to pay some amount. If people do not understand the incentives embodied in the system, they will not respond to them. On the one hand this makes the system efficient and nondistortionary: People will not do things just because of the tax rules. On the other hand the ability to influence behavior was exactly the policymakers' point in creating the complex tax system to begin with. In the long run that purpose would be lost.

COMMENT BY

Gerald H. Goldberg

It is hard to quarrel with the conclusion that proprietary software such as Turbo-Tax has not solved the complexity problem of the tax code. (By using the term *solve,* I assume that Austan Goolsbee's focus is on enabling taxpayers to easily and successfully use the code, as opposed to actually reducing the complexity of the law. Clearly, reducing the complexity of the law is the responsibility of lawmakers and is probably beyond the scope of any technology solution.) But the use of technology for tax purposes is in its infancy. Both taxpayers and software manufacturers are still learning its potential. Moreover, maneuvering through the tax code is only part of the tax burden. Many taxpayers have less difficulty filing correctly than dealing with the tax agency after they have filed. If we regard compliance complexity as more than a filing matter, then I would argue that examples abound of how technology is assisting taxpayers in dealing with their tax obligation.

On a pragmatic level, I also agree with Goolsbee's proposal that one way to reduce tax filing complexity for millions of taxpayers is to institute some method of return-free filing. Indeed some tax agencies already are pursuing this return-free strategy to improve compliance and ease the burden of tax filing.

At the broader, public policy level, Goolsbee's concluding question about whether a purely technological solution to complexity is the right approach certainly is intriguing. But, because he did not develop that concept beyond raising the question, my comments address the main topic that tax preparation software has not solved the complexity problem of the tax code.

While software has not solved complexity, it is a major step in the right direction. First, there is a direct relationship between the complexity of a taxpayer's return and the use of software. This relationship is, however, nonlinear.[1] Up to a certain level of complexity, the use of software rises. But at some level of complexity taxpayers use professional tax preparers. Many taxpayers with complex returns have no need for general-use tax software because they find an advantage in professional tax planning. Many highly paid executives, who would be expected to have complex returns, are provided with professional tax planning advice and tax preparation as a job perk. Large CPA firms routinely prepare the returns of key executives of their clients.

Second, most professional tax practitioners use tax software. Intuit, for example, which manufactures TurboTax, also makes software for professional tax preparers. If the professional's use of software were factored into the numbers, you would probably see a linear relationship between complexity and use of tax software. Taxpayer use of paid preparers to complete their returns continues to slowly rise. In California professional tax practitioners prepared 54 percent of all returns in 1984 and 64 percent of all returns in 1999.[2] (While H&R Block sells a software package, TaxCut, to compete with Intuit's Turbo-Tax, Block is also the nation's largest tax preparer. Because profits are clearly

1. Unpublished data.
2. Unpublished data.

larger in their stores than in software sales, it is not difficult to imagine the mixed feelings the company must have about their software development division.) The fact that tax practitioners, rather than taxpayers, are using software does not mean that technology is not diminishing complexity. However, the additional ease for tax professionals in preparing returns may not be transparent to taxpayers, because it may not be reflected in reduced costs to prepare a return.

But, if taxpayers with complex taxes are not preparing their own returns, then, you might ask, who is buying software such as TurboTax? My guess is that the purchasers are primarily computer-literate taxpayers who, previously having filled out their own paper returns, have recently experienced a modest increase in the complexity of their filing experience. This modest increase may or may not be connected with increased code complexity. I suspect that many taxpayers turned to software with the recent stock market boom. Taxpayers' stock transactions, for example, became too numerous to handle without computerized assistance. (One manufacturer touts the ease with which you can import your 1099 investment information from participating employers and financial institutions.) Tax software advertising has also increased markedly in the past several years. Moreover, e-filing coupled with tax software holds out the promise of a faster refund. In California we have seen a continual decline in the filing of paper returns. This trend of moving from paper to software, even if not from paid preparer to self-prepared, indicates that software may be helping to reduce complexity.

Goolsbee bemoans the fact that the people who do not use the software tend to be just the people for whom the losses from complexity are the greatest. If by losses from complexity he means failing to take credits and deductions, I would question his basis for that finding. I agree with him that taxpayers who do not use tax software are less likely to be highly educated and to have high incomes, but these are the people who also tend to have the simplest returns. They tend to be people who cannot itemize their deductions. Many of these people go to professional tax preparers because they are afraid or unable to complete even the simplest return, whether it is on paper or through software. For example, 41 percent of Californians who file California's simplest form, the Form 5402EZ, were identified as using a tax preparer, although evidence suggests that many do so to obtain fast refunds from refund anticipation loans.[3]

For taxpayers who truly want to understand the code and not merely navigate through it, numerous software tools are available. They range from sophisticated tax research tools provided by Bureau of National Affairs Tax Management, Commerce Clearing House (CCH), and others, to website offerings from the Internal Revenue Service and many states. CCH will soon be offering a

3. Franchise Tax Board statistics for 2001 tax returns, filed in calendar year 2002. Unpublished data.

"clickable" software product that will link the Internal Revenue Code provisions with the California Revenue and Taxation Code, California regulations, and an explanatory text in the CCH *California State Tax Reporter*. These tools are not, with the exception of the government websites, designed for use by the average taxpayer, but they clearly demonstrate technology's power to unlock the tax code. It would seem only a matter of time before more sophisticated tax software is designed for the general public.

A related issue, which is beyond the scope of Goolsbee's chapter, is the proper role of the public sector versus the private sector in tax software development. Does government have a responsibility to develop and deploy technology that helps taxpayers navigate through the filing experience, or should this be the exclusive province of the private sector? Can a hybrid government–private sector approach, now in evidence for 2003 with the IRS and the Free File Alliance, made up of several companies, offer a model that meets taxpayer expectations? It is noteworthy that these expectations focus not only on no-cost filing options but also on options that do not require the disclosure of confidential financial and tax information to private sector companies. The resolution of this issue of responsibility could significantly shape not only how taxpayers comply with tax laws but also the basic relationship between tax agencies and taxpayers.

At the state level, according to the Federation of Tax Administrators, more than twenty-five state revenue departments now provide web-enabled, free tax filing options that allow taxpayers to file their returns directly. Complexity is addressed in several different ways. Some states enable direct filing only for those taxpayers filing simple returns. Others may provide only simple "data entry" electronic forms without much guidance, assuming that taxpayers will navigate through the complexity of instructions to correctly file. The technology environment is constantly evolving to provide the opportunity for new direct filing models.

Compliance complexity is about more than being able to successfully navigate the tax form and getting all the proper deductions and credits. For many taxpayers, paying their taxes is a much larger issue than figuring how much they owe. These taxpayers need help in arranging installment payments, removing liens, stopping garnishments, and so forth. Technology is helping to improve the ability of taxpayers to cope with this type of complexity.

In California the Franchise Tax Board (FTB) has deployed on its website a capability for taxpayers to set up their own installment agreement, provided that the amount owed is less than $10,000. With a click of the mouse, taxpayers can set both the amount of each monthly payment and the term of the agreement. Obviously there are limits, but the arrangement is freeing up taxpayers to arrange their finances for their own convenience. Allowing taxpayers more control over their finances has proven to benefit both the taxpayers and the state.

Other technology applications are not directly controlled by the taxpayer but nonetheless help taxpayers solve the complexity problem. Currently available technologies such as secure e-mail, automated lien release, refund status inquiry, and so forth, are taxpayer-friendly and reduce the taxpayer's perception of complexity. One of the more amusing uses of technology is the FTB's e-mail reminders to nonfilers that they have a filing requirement. This application came about largely at the request of some chronic nonfilers who simply forget to file their taxes on time.

Goolsbee suggests that one approach to simplification is to provide for automatic, return-free filing. The FTB, in a pilot project, has already offered a version of such a service to some chronic nonfilers. This possibility has raised some alarm among manufacturers of tax software, who see it as a threat to their market share. The latest FTB pilot project used data collected in the normal course of business to prepare returns for 28,000 taxpayers who historically had only wage and interest income or who had previously filed a tax return with the IRS but not with FTB. Using the data already provided to the government, FTB mailed the completed return to taxpayers who, under penalty of perjury, had to validate that the information on the return included income from all sources. Taxpayers who received these returns reacted favorably to them. Expanding the concept of return-free filing is well within the future capabilities of many tax agencies. It is certain that, given the discomfort some have expressed about the amount of personal data gathered and shared among government agencies, we need to tread carefully before this type of service is expanded. Clearly we want to consider the broader societal impacts, and whether returns prepared by tax agencies could hint of Big Brother.

In sum, technology, and particularly tax planning and filing software, is not a panacea for tax complexity, but it presents a great opportunity for making the tax system less overwhelming for many, if not most, taxpayers. While some people, for a variety of reasons, will never use commercially available software, technology may still be easing the complexity of their tax experience. Additionally, in the future, tax software will undoubtedly entice some taxpayers who currently use professional tax preparers to start preparing their own returns, and this trend will probably increase as young, technology-savvy taxpayers enter the system. However, for some taxpayers, such software is never going to substitute for the handholding that a tax preparer can provide. I expect that returns prepared either by employers or tax agencies eventually will be available for lower-income taxpayers.

COMMENT BY
Mark J. Mazur

Chapter 5 demonstrates that the use of tax preparation software is growing at a steady pace but that measures of complexity generally are not among the factors that seem to influence tax software adoption. Instead the degree of comfort with computer use appears to be a major force in determining whether a person will adopt tax preparation software.

One way to address this finding is to recognize that tax complexity in and of itself is not the major focus of taxpayers. Instead taxpayers are concerned about the amount of tax they pay and the burden (time and out-of-pocket costs plus a "hassle factor") they bear. For example, some taxpayers may be apprehensive about doing the arithmetic required to complete an income tax return. This apprehension translates into a burden for these taxpayers, though it really is not a complex activity. Alternatively being subject to the alternative minimum tax may be a major source of complexity and also impose a substantial burden on affected taxpayers. In both cases the use of tax preparation software could help reduce taxpayer burden, but the first instance is not driven by concerns of complexity.

In general, complexity feeds into burden: A more complex tax system tends to increase taxpayer burden in a variety of ways. For example, taxpayers may need to engage in more tax planning to determine if they can benefit from tax provisions. They may need to consult advisors or reference materials to determine eligibility or contact specific parties (such as financial planners) to take advantage of specific tax code provisions. Taxpayers may need to maintain records for specific transactions solely to claim tax benefits offered for specific activities. And the act of filing a tax return may be significantly more complicated for a taxpayer faced with a complex tax system. Tax preparation software generally is focused on the last item, the act of filing the tax return, although elements of tax planning and record-keeping are built into some tax preparation packages.

To the extent that tax preparation software is seen primarily as helping taxpayers navigate the tax filing process, the adoption decision is a rational choice to reduce taxpayer burden, but the decision is not necessarily related to the complexity of the taxpayer's return. In a sense the adoption of tax preparation software can be viewed as a (potentially) lower-cost substitute for certain types of paid tax preparers. And, because paid preparers are responsible for over half the individual income tax returns filed each year, this is an important area to examine. Moreover the use of preparers may have important implications for taxpayer compliance.

The Role of Tax Preparers

In an obvious oversimplification, one can think of the world of paid tax preparers as being made up of two types: those who work on relatively simple returns and those who work on relatively complicated returns. For taxpayers with simple returns, the use of a paid preparer can be viewed as increasing overall taxpayer compliance. In part this occurs because the preparer knows the tax law better than the taxpayer and will help ensure that items are entered correctly and that the arithmetic is correct. In addition, this type of paid preparer is unlikely to permit the taxpayer to obviously underreport income or to overclaim deductions without support, because sanctions could be imposed on preparers who support intentional noncompliance. Taken together, these features may lead to improved compliance for taxpayers using this group of preparers.

For those with complex returns, the use of a paid preparer may actually decrease overall taxpayer compliance. In part this occurs because the preparer knows the tax law (and tax administrative practice) better than the taxpayer and can suggest opportunities for aggressive behavior that may have been unknown to the taxpayer. In addition, taxpayers with complicated financial situations often have opportunities for staking out aggressive tax compliance positions that are unavailable to other taxpayers, and the use of a paid preparer may support this position.

Given this characterization of the paid preparer universe, the adoption of tax preparation software may be a low-cost substitute for the first group of tax preparers, the ones that focus on taxpayers with relatively simple returns. In this world, then, the use of tax preparation software is not directly related to the complexity of the individual's tax situation.

The IRS Taxpayer Burden Model

The Internal Revenue Service would like to reduce unnecessary taxpayer burden.[1] To evaluate various proposals, the IRS and a contractor are in the process of developing a taxpayer burden model. This model is based on survey data and tax return data and will cover all individual taxpayers. The burden model includes a tax calculator and permits the user to engage in "what if" scenarios.[2] The burden model estimates taxpayer burden based on the attributes of the taxpayer's situation and includes items like record-keeping, computations, and

---

1. As part of this effort to reduce burden, the IRS announced in 2002 the appointment of an executive charged with reducing taxpayer burden. This executive is located in the Small Business and Self-Employed Operating Division.

2. See, for example, Stavrianos and Greenland (2002) and Guyton, O'Hare, Stavrianos, and Toder (2003).

gathering materials. These estimates will be more reliable than those currently used by the IRS, which are built on a methodology that relies on the number of lines on a form, the length of instructions, and other factors. A working version of this model was delivered to the IRS in early 2003 and is undergoing testing.

Based on the survey data, however, some interesting observations come out of the burden model. For example, the overall estimate of annual burden for individual taxpayers for 2000 is $16 billion of out-of-pocket costs and 3.1 billion hours (which could be monetized to about $47 billion at a rate of $15 per hour, the approximate average hourly wage in nonagricultural industries). Higher-income taxpayers (say, those with adjusted gross income over $100,000) have greater out-of-pocket costs and greater time burdens imposed by the individual income tax system than their lower-income counterparts.

The survey data from the burden model indicate that both time burden and out-of-pocket costs for taxpayers using tax preparation software are greater than for similar taxpayers preparing their own returns without software. It is unclear what is driving this result. It is possible that taxpayers using tax software require more time to enter data that are not required if the return is prepared by hand. Alternatively, it is possible that taxpayers engage in creating hypothetical scenarios to see what happens to their tax liability if certain items change.

In any event, as the burden model becomes part of the toolkit available to IRS researchers, we can expect to see a fair amount of work that complements or extends Goolsbee's analysis.

Moving toward a Return-Free System

Goolsbee states that significant gains can be achieved by moving taxpayers with simple returns to a return-free income tax system. It is possible to devise such a system for various groups of taxpayers, and it almost surely would reduce the burden on the affected taxpayers. However, such a system might have to sacrifice some precision in the computation of tax liability for these taxpayers.

A return-free income tax system presupposes that the tax authority has a lot of reliable information on a taxpayer's financial affairs prior to the processing of the annual income tax return. In the case of the IRS, the information systems currently in place may not support such rapid processing of financial information.

For the IRS to implement the proposed return-free system for filers of Form 1040EZ, the service would need to process all the information it receives from employers, financial institutions, and other entities prior to the due date of the annual return for the subset of taxpayers who enroll in the return-free system. This would require a major reprogramming exercise for the IRS, which now processes most information documents in the summer—after the April 15th filing date. Moreover the IRS would need information on the filing status of taxpayers in real time in order to process the returns accurately—for example, taxpayers who are married on the last day of the tax year are supposed to file as "married, filing jointly," a filing status that is likely to affect overall tax liability for the household. Getting taxpayers to report this information to the IRS (or to employers who may administer a return-free system) in a timely manner could be difficult.

These hurdles are not insurmountable, but no one should view the move to a return-free income tax system as a trivial exercise that is sure to reduce the burden for the affected taxpaying population. The IRS would likely incur significant costs to administer a return-free system. Taxpayers are likely to see reduced precision in tax liability computation in exchange for removing the filing burden. Taxpayers also may have to give up some of their privacy to permit employers to fine-tune withholding in order to participate in a return-free system. And many taxpayers participating in a return-free system may have to give up the joy associated with receiving an income tax refund.

As with any other policy change, there will be costs and benefits associated with moving toward a return-free income tax system. But cost-effectiveness of such a switch will only be the starting point of a marketing campaign to get taxpayers to participate. It may be more appropriate to consider such a switch in the context of overall tax reform, where there are enough moving pieces in the system to improve the chances of observing a significant take-up rate by the taxpaying public.

References

Akerlof, George. 1978. "The Economics of 'Tagging' as Applied to the Optimal Income Tax, Welfare Programs, and Manpower Planning." *American Economic Review* 68 (March): 8–19.

Arthur D. Little. 1988. *Development of Methodology for Estimating the Taxpayer Paperwork Burden.* Report to the Department of the Treasury, Internal Revenue Service (June).

Becker, Gary S. 1983. "A Theory of Competition among Pressure Groups for Political Influence." *Quarterly Journal of Economics* 98 (3): 371–400.

Becker, Gary S., and Casey B. Mulligan. 2003. "Deadweight Costs and the Size of Government." *Journal of Law and Economics* 46 (October): 293–340.

Bernheim, Douglas, and J. Karl Scholz. 1993. "Private Savings and Public Policy." In *Tax Policy and the Economy*, edited by James Poterba, vol. 7, 73–110. MIT Press.

Berube, Alan, and others. 2002. "The Price of Paying Taxes: How Tax Preparation and Refund Loan Fees Erode the Benefits of the EITC." Center on Urban and Metropolitan Policy, Brookings and Progressive Policy Institute Survey Series (May).

Blumenthal, Martha, and Joel Slemrod. 1992. "The Compliance Cost of the U.S. Individual Income Tax System: A Second Look after Tax Reform." *National Tax Journal* 45 (June): 185–202.

Burman, Leonard. 2002. "Comment." In *American Economic Policy in the 1990s*, edited by Jeffrey Frankel and Peter Orszag, 176–83. MIT Press.

Gale, William, and Janet Holtzblatt. 1997. "On the Possibility of a No-Return Tax System." *National Tax Journal* 50 (September): 475–85.

Goolsbee, Austan. 2000. "In a World without Borders: The Impact of Taxes on Internet Commerce." *Quarterly Journal of Economics* 115 (2): 561–76.

Goolsbee, Austan, and Peter Klenow. 2002. "Evidence on Learning and Network Externalities in the Diffusion of Home Computers." *Journal of Law and Economics* 45 (October): 317–44.

Guyton, John, John O'Hare, Michael Stavrianos, and Eric Toder. 2003. "Estimating the Compliance Cost of the U.S. Individual Income Tax." *National Tax Journal* 56 (September): 673–88.

Kopczuk, Wojciech. 2001. "Redistribution When Avoidance Behavior Is Heterogeneous." *Journal of Public Economics* 81 (1): 51–71.

Orszag, Peter. 2002. "Summary of Discussion." In *American Economic Policy in the 1990s*, edited by Jeffrey Frankel and Peter Orszag, 188–90. MIT Press.

Slemrod, Joel, and Nikki Sorum. 1984. "The Compliance Cost of the U.S. Individual Income Tax System." *National Tax Journal* 37 (December): 461–74.

Slemrod, Joel, and Shlomo Yitzhaki. 1996. "The Social Cost of Taxation and the Marginal Cost of Funds." *International Monetary Fund Staff Papers* 198 (March): 172–98.

Sperling, Gene. 2002. "Summary of Discussion." In *American Economic Policy in the 1990s*, edited by Jeffrey Frankel and Peter Orszag, 188–90. MIT Press.

Steuerle, Eugene. 2002. "Tax Policy from 1990 to 2001." In *American Economic Policy in the 1990s*, edited by Jeffrey Frankel and Peter Orszag, 139–69. MIT Press.

Stavrianos, Michael, and Arnold Greenland. 2002. "Design and Development of the Wage and Investment Compliance Burden Model." Paper prepared for the IRS Research Conference (www.irs.gov/taxstats/article/0,,id=97312,00.html [August 2003]).

U.S. Internal Revenue Service. 2001. *Form 1040EZ Instruction Booklet.* Government Printing Office.

———. 2002a. "Measuring Taxpayer Compliance Burden: A Microsimulation Approach." Unpublished report (November 8).

———. 2002b. Statistics of Income Bulletin, Winter 2001–02 (www.irs.gov/taxstats/article/0,,id=97067,00.html).

———. 2003a. "E-File Demographics Nationwide TY 2001" (www.irs.gov/taxpros/providers/article/0,,id=97377,00.html).

———. 2003b. "Costs Incurred by the Internal Revenue Service, by Budget Activity, Fiscal Years 2000 and 2001" (www.irs.gov/pub/irs-soi/01db29cs.xls[January 2003]).

Yonish, Steve, and others. 2001. "Why Technographics Works." Forrester Online Report (November) (www.forrester.com/er/research/report/0,1338,11797,00.html).

6

JANET HOLTZBLATT
JANET MCCUBBIN

Issues Affecting Low-Income Filers

COMPLEXITY APPEARS TO pervade the U.S. tax system for individuals throughout the income distribution. The alternative minimum tax imposes compliance burdens on high-income taxpayers (and increasingly on middle-income taxpayers as well). Phaseouts of the personal exemption, the child tax credit, and other credits challenge middle-income taxpayers. Subtly different eligibility rules for two refundable tax credits—the earned income tax credit (EITC) and the additional child tax credit—may confuse many low-income working parents who could be eligible for one, both, or neither credit.

To a large extent, the root sources of complexity in the tax code are often the same for all taxpayers, regardless of income. Low-income individuals file tax returns for the same reasons as other taxpayers: They owe taxes or they are owed a refund for taxes that were overwithheld during the year.[1] Fewer than 2 percent of filers with less than $30,000 of adjusted gross income file tax returns solely to obtain refundable tax credits. And, like other filers, low-income individuals may find the tax code complicated, due to conflict among the goals of tax policy. Attempts to achieve other tax policy goals—for example, making taxes fairer—often conflict with attempts to make taxes simpler. Using the tax system to promote social policy goals, such as home ownership, health insurance, or education, may also increase its complexity.

We thank Candice Cromling, William Gale, Dianne Grant, James Nunns, Mary-Helen Risler, and Carolyn Tavenner for helpful discussions throughout the years. We also thank Robert Black and Jennifer Yau for research assistance.
    1. Appendix 6A discusses the reasons low-income individuals file tax returns.

Yet, while many sources of complexity in the income tax system are the same for both high-income and low-income taxpayers, there are sources of complexity that are specific to each group. Higher-income taxpayers often have complicated financial affairs, which are reflected in the extensive rules that govern the tax consequences of their investments. Self-employment income, most capital gains, and losses from passive activities do not appear on the Form 1040A or 1040EZ, the tax return forms used by 58 percent of low-income taxpayers.[2] But the fact that these provisions do not appear on the shorter forms used by low-income filers does not mean that the tax system is simple for them.

The inclusion of low-income filers in the individual income tax system raises unique tax administrative issues because of their particular family and financial circumstances. Provisions that are relatively simple for the majority of filers may be difficult for low-income filers because of their complicated family lives, erratic work histories, or connection to the underground economy. Deficiencies in education and language skills may make it difficult for low-income filers to understand instructions on tax returns or to compute liabilities. These problems affect individuals' abilities to determine if they should file tax returns, how they should compute their withholding allowances, whether they owe income taxes, and if they can claim the refundable child tax credit and the EITC.

Complexity may lead to unintentional errors by low-income filers or the failure to claim tax benefits to which they are entitled. It may also cause the Internal Revenue Service to choose between tolerating a certain amount of noncompliance (both unintentional and intentional) or nonparticipation among low-income filers and devoting resources to low-income filers that may appear to be disproportionate to the amounts of taxes collected or credits paid out.

While the problems faced by low-income filers are not limited to the EITC, most available data regarding the extent of noncompliance and nonparticipation are limited to those who claim or are eligible for the credit. Recent studies suggest that EITC participation among those who are eligible for the credit is high, relative to expenditure programs serving low-income populations, but that noncompliance is also high. The findings of several EITC compliance studies have spurred the IRS to intensify its enforcement activity among low-income filers, thus increasing both compliance and administrative costs. But, given that the IRS does not have comparable data on other tax benefits received by low-income taxpayers (or higher-income taxpayers, either), we cannot determine if noncompliance or participation among low-income filers is especially high. Nor can we determine if the amounts spent by the IRS to administer the EITC (or to handle the tax returns of low-income filers) are disproportionately high relative to its other functions.

2. Authors' tabulations of Statistics of Income individual income tax return data for tax year 2000.

To some extent, reducing complexity for low-income filers may require solutions outside the tax system; for example, stabilizing family lives or expanding educational opportunities could eliminate some sources of taxpayer confusion. Fundamental tax reform could also eliminate many sources of complexity. Within the current income tax system, several options have been suggested as ways to simplify filing for low-income individuals. Removing the EITC from the income tax system would, as some have suggested, reduce IRS administrative costs but would also shift (and possibly increase) burdens to other agencies, third parties, and beneficiaries themselves. The income tax provisions that most affect low-income filers could be simplified, but simplification may be constrained by other goals of the tax system. Finally, the IRS's ability to administer the tax provisions that affect low-income filers could be improved. Improving compliance, without substantially reducing participation, depends on the IRS's ability to identify errors without adversely increasing the compliance costs of eligible filers. It may also require additional resources.

Complexity

For low-income filers, complicated tax affairs may result from complicated personal family lives or instability in their work lives. Relative to other taxpayers, low-income filers are more likely to be single parents or receive means-tested transfers from the government. (See table 6-1.) Census data also suggest that subfamilies (married couples or single parents with children who live in another family's home) are more likely to be poor. In 2001 nearly half of subfamilies with children had incomes below the poverty levels.[3] Complicated family lives give rise to complicated tax lives, as taxpayers must determine if they qualify as a head of household or if they can claim their child for one or more child-related tax benefits.

Subtle distinctions in law and multiple computations may be particularly confusing for low-income filers who, relative to other filers, tend to have less education. Among filers with incomes below 200 percent of poverty, 27 percent did not graduate from high school. Although some publications (including IRS Publication 596, describing the earned income tax credit) are available in other languages (typically Spanish), and the IRS has Spanish-speaking operators on its telephone help lines, most forms, publications, and notices are written in English. Yet nearly one out of five low-income filers was born in a country where English was not the official or primary language.

---

3. "Table 16, Poverty Status of People in Families by Type of Family, Age of Householder, and Number of Children: 2001" (http://ferret.bls.census.gov/macro/032002/pov/new16_000.htm) [October 2002]).

Table 6-1. *Characteristics of Filers, 2000*[a]

Characteristic	Filers (percent)	
	All filers	Filers with family income under 200 percent of poverty
Marital status		
Married	46.5	32.0
Single with dependent	10.6	26.6
Single without dependent	42.9	41.4
Receipt of means-tested transfers		
Temporary Assistance for Needy Families	0.7	3.3
Supplemental Security Income	0.8	1.9
Women, Infants, and Children	2.3	8.8
Food stamps	3.0	13.1
Education[b]		
Not high school graduate	11.6	26.7
High school graduate	31.8	37.8
Some college	28.7	25.9
College graduate	18.9	7.4
Graduate degree	9.0	2.0
Language[b]		
Born in English-speaking country	88.1	79.3
Not born in English-speaking country	11.0	19.4
Unknown	0.9	1.2
Total number of filers (millions)	108.2	20.6

Source: Authors' calculations using March 2001 Current Population Survey.

a. Because the CPS does not ask respondents if they filed tax returns, authors imputed filing status. Filers include individuals and, if married, couples whose income exceeds filing thresholds or who appear eligible to claim the earned income tax credit. The estimates do not include individuals who file tax returns for other reasons, such as to obtain a refund of overwithheld taxes. The estimates of filers do not include individuals claimed as dependents on other filers' returns.

b. Education and language background shown for CPS reference person in filing unit. Estimates may not add to 100 percent due to rounding.

Outside Support

Means-tested transfers, child support payments, and gifts are not taxable and thus are not included in gross income. However, receipt of such income affects the support test for the dependent exemption and the household maintenance test for head-of-household filing status.

For example, taxpayers must provide over half the support of the dependent to claim the dependent's exemption or child tax credit. Publication 501, which explains the rules for exemptions and the standard deduction, contains four pages of instructions on the support test alone, including a twenty-two-line worksheet to help taxpayers determine if they have provided over half the costs of supporting a dependent. The taxpayer must compute the potential dependent's share of the household's total expenses (including expenditures on food, housing, education, medical and dental care, entertainment, and transportation) and determine to what extent the taxpayer financed these purchases. Taxpayers must also keep receipts of expenditures—from rent payments to grocery bills—in order to prove support.

Proving support might not be difficult when the taxpayer's earnings are the sole source of income in his or her household. But low-income taxpayers may be receiving assistance for the support of a dependent from the government (such as Temporary Assistance for Needy Families or food stamps), the child's other parent, or other members of an extended household. When computing support, the taxpayer must subtract amounts provided by the potential dependent and others toward his or her support.

These requirements also add to the administrative burden of the IRS. The taxpayer does not submit these worksheets to the IRS. Nor are data on means-tested benefits like Temporary Assistance for Needy Families (TANF) or expenditures reported independently to the IRS by government agencies or other third parties. Without further (and considerably more expensive) investigation, the IRS cannot obtain information regarding receipt of nontaxable income or expenditures on household and children.

Defining Households

Unmarried taxpayers may be eligible to file as heads of household, entitling them to a more preferential standard deduction and rate schedule than if they were filing as single. To qualify, unmarried filers must demonstrate that they provide over half the costs of maintaining the household in which they and their children or other dependents reside. The tax code, however, does not explicitly define the boundaries of the household unit for which expenditures are being made. Instead the code leaves it to the taxpayer and the IRS to reach their own—and hopefully the same—conclusions.

As *Estate of Fleming* v. *IRS* demonstrates, one, two, or even three or more households may reside at the same address.[4] Jean Foster Fleming, a widow, moved with an adult unmarried daughter into the home of another daughter, who was married and had children. After the IRS denied Fleming's claim of head-of-household filing status, she took the case to tax court, which found in

4. *Estate of Jean Foster Fleming, Deceased, Citizens Fidelity Bank and Trust Company, Executor* v. *Commissioner.* 1974. 33 T.C.M. 619.

her favor. In support of Fleming's claim that she maintained a separate household (consisting of herself and her unmarried daughter), the court noted that she and her unmarried daughter had their own bedroom and bathroom, furnishings, telephone, and magazine subscriptions. Further, they gave Christmas and wedding presents, Christmas cards, and charitable contributions by themselves, without any contributions from the married daughter.

Fleming v. *IRS* suggests that the IRS use a "facts and circumstance" test in audits, to distinguish between groups of individuals who merely reside at the same address from those who share family responsibilities and pool resources. For low-income individuals who live in extended families or with other families at the same address, *Fleming* v. *IRS* implies that they must keep extensive records if they want to support their claim of head-of-household filing status.

Residency

Prior to 1991 filers had to meet the dependency support test and, if not married, the household maintenance test in order to qualify for the EITC. Concern about the compliance and administrative burdens imposed on EITC claimants by these tests led to their elimination in the Omnibus Budget Reconciliation Act of 1990. Instead children qualifying the taxpayer for the EITC must meet three tests: First, they must reside with the taxpayer for over half the year; second, they must be the taxpayer's son, daughter, grandchild, or foster child; and third, they must be under the age of nineteen, unless a full-time student (in which case, they must be under age twenty-four), or permanently and totally disabled.

The residency test was thought to be easier for taxpayers to understand and for the IRS to administer than the support or household maintenance tests. Based on his analysis of the 1988 Taxpayer Compliance Measurement Program (TCMP), Jeffrey Liebman speculates that the replacement of the support test with a residency requirement may have reduced the EITC error rate by as much as 40 percent.[5] Nonetheless some filers may find the residency test confusing, particularly if they share custody of a child (either formally or informally) with another person.

Proving residency rather than support or household maintenance was also thought to be easier. Taxpayers would not be required to retain extensive records documenting how they use their income (nontaxable as well as taxable) to finance expenditures on their children or household. Instead taxpayers might be required to provide only one piece of paper, such as a note from a school, a child-care provider, or a doctor, in the event of an audit.

5. Liebman (2001).

Drawing from interviews with IRS examiners and advocates for low-income taxpayers, the General Accounting Office finds anecdotal evidence indicating that many taxpayers do not understand the documentation requested in the event of an audit.[6] For example, the initial IRS contact letter (Form 886) suggests that filers provide school records containing the child's name, address, and dates of attendance for the entire tax year, and the name and address of the child's parents or guardian. Responding to these letters, filers may obtain school records that show that their child resided with them during a school year. If a taxpayer provides records for a school year (for example, September 2001 through June 2002) that does not coincide with over half the tax year (2001), then the IRS might not accept that documentation as complete. As other evidence of residency, Form 886 suggests a notarized statement from a child-care provider. However, 79 percent of examiners surveyed by GAO said that they would reject a notarized statement from a relative who claimed to be the child's babysitter, even though many working mothers, and particularly low-income mothers, rely on their relatives to care for their children.[7]

Extended Families

Removing the support and household maintenance tests for purposes of determining eligibility for the EITC meant that another rule had to be designed to resolve "ties"—that is, cases where more than one individual in a residence could claim the same child for EITC purposes. Under the 1990 act, the new "tiebreaker" rule awarded the child (and if eligible, the EITC) to the filer with the highest adjusted gross income (AGI). While thought to be simpler than the household maintenance and support tests, the AGI tiebreaker rule also retained the targeting goals of the earlier tests. Thus, for example, if a single mother lived with her wealthy parents, she generally would not qualify for the EITC. Her parents would not be eligible to claim the credit either, because of their high income.

However, several EITC compliance studies conducted during the 1990s found that noncompliance with the AGI tiebreaker rule was a large source of EITC overclaims. In response, Congress simplified the AGI tiebreaker test in two critical ways in the Economic Growth and Tax Relief Reconciliation Act of 2001 (EGTRRA). First, the AGI tiebreaker will now apply only when more than one taxpayer actually claims the same child. Second, a parent's claim will generally supersede any other filer's claim. These changes represent significant simplification, but at some sacrifice of targeting precision.

6. GAO (2002).
7. Smith (2002).

Estranged Couples

Taxpayers who are married at the end of the tax year are generally required to use the "married, filing jointly" or "married, filing separately" filing status. Typically it is more beneficial to file jointly. For example, married taxpayers filing separately are not eligible for the EITC, to ensure that receipt of the credit is based on a couple's combined income.

Married taxpayers may claim head-of-household filing status if they meet three requirements. First, they must live apart from their spouse for the last six months of the year. Second, they must pay over half the costs of maintaining the home in which they and their son, daughter, or stepchild reside during the year. Third, they must be eligible to claim their child as a dependent. If the taxpayer meets these conditions, he or she may file as a head of household and claim the EITC. Even if they understand these tests, many separated individuals may fail at least one test because they receive assistance from the government or family members or they cannot document that they provide over half the costs of maintaining their home or supporting their child.

Lack of Uniformity

Many low-income filers are eligible for more than one child-related tax benefit. In tax year 2003 there will be over 23 million filers with children and adjusted gross income less than $30,000. Of these, 20.8 million taxpayers will claim child dependents. About 10.9 million taxpayers will claim both child dependent exemptions and the child tax credit, 15.3 million taxpayers will claim both child dependent exemptions and the EITC, and 9.7 million taxpayers will claim all three. One million taxpayers will claim child dependent exemptions, head-of-household filing status, the child tax credit, the child and dependent care tax credit, and the EITC.[8] However, the eligibility rules for these provisions, which on the surface appear similar, differ in fundamental ways.

Consider, for example, how the definition of *child* differs among the five provisions. Each provision requires some evidence of attachment between the taxpayer and the child. As noted above, a taxpayer must demonstrate that he or she provides most of the support of a son or daughter to claim the dependent exemption and the child tax credit. To claim head-of-household filing status or the EITC, the taxpayer must demonstrate that he or she resides with the child for a specified period of time. A taxpayer can claim a niece or nephew as a dependent (subject to the support and gross income tests) but can only claim the same child for the child tax credit if he or she cares for the child as his or her

8. Treasury Department Individual Tax Model. See Cilke (1994) for model documentation.

own. A foster child will qualify the taxpayer for the EITC if the child lives in the taxpayer's home for over half the year. But the taxpayer cannot claim the same child for the dependent exemption or the child tax credit, unless the child lives in his or her home for the entire year.

Taxpayers can easily be confused by the subtle distinctions between the household maintenance tests used to qualify for head-of-household filing status and the similar, but not identical, support tests used to determine whether someone is a dependent. For example, mortgage interest expenses and property taxes are counted toward the costs of maintaining a household, but the taxpayer is instructed to factor in the "fair rental value" of a home toward support. To compute household maintenance, taxpayers must measure the costs of food consumed on the premises. But for the support test, the taxpayer must include the costs of all food, regardless of where it is eaten.

The additional child tax credit may also cause confusion. Both the additional child tax credit and the EITC are refundable credits and are primarily targeted to workers with children. Perhaps not surprisingly, over 70 percent of taxpayers who are eligible for the additional child tax credit can also claim the EITC.[9] But despite similarities in the provisions and the overlap between the eligible populations, there are subtle differences between the two credits that may confuse taxpayers. As noted above, a child qualifies a taxpayer for the EITC if he or she resides with the taxpayer, but the taxpayer may claim the same child for the additional child tax credit only if the taxpayer supports the child. Another difference is that the additional child tax credit may be claimed by citizens who reside with their children outside the United States, while the EITC may be claimed only by taxpayers who reside in the United States. The two credits also define earned income slightly differently, requiring some self-employed taxpayers to compute income twice.[10]

Multiple Computations

In 1997, when the additional child tax credit was created, eligibility was limited to taxpayers with three or more children. The formula was designed to ensure that taxpayers with large families and income in roughly the $20,000-to-$30,000 range received some benefit from the child tax credit, even if, after accounting for five or more exemptions, they did not have enough income tax to offset a new, nonrefundable tax credit. When the additional child tax credit was expanded in 2001, a simpler formula was created. But, due to concern that some taxpayers might receive a smaller or no additional child tax credit under the new formula, Congress allowed taxpayers with three or more children to

9. Treasury Department Individual Tax Model. See Cilke (1994) for model documentation.
10. For example, parsonage allowances count toward self-employment income for the EITC but not the additional child tax credit.

compute the credit under either formula and claim the larger of the two credit amounts.

As a result, over 1 million taxpayers with three or more children compute the additional child tax credit amount twice.[11] First, using a formula that was enacted in 2001, they compute the credit as a fraction of earned income in excess of $10,500.[12] Then they compute the credit using the original formula, enacted in 1997, which subtracts the EITC from their Social Security taxes. Finally they compare the two amounts and claim only the larger of the two. But, for most taxpayers, the second computation is unnecessary, because their credit is larger under the first method.

Withholding

While low-income taxpayers may never encounter a corporate inversion, their financial lives may not be free of complexity, either. Low-income taxpayers may have multiple jobs or spells of unemployment during the year. As a result they may find it difficult to adjust withholding (or, if eligible, claim an advance payment of the EITC) to reflect actual tax liabilities during the year, causing them to have to file returns to obtain income tax refunds, even if they do not owe taxes.

Neither the current withholding nor advance EITC payment formulas are designed to be exact for dependent filers, dual-career couples, or taxpayers who do not work all year or have more than one job during the year. In 1999 only 6 million filers with income below $30,000 (including nearly 5 million EITC claimants) met the profile of filers for whom computing withholding or advance EITC payments would be simplest: That is, if married, only one spouse had earnings, those earnings came from only one job during the year, no other income was reported on the tax return, and they were not claimed as dependents by another taxpayer.[13] Even these estimates do not account for changes in family circumstances during the year (such as marriage, divorce, or the birth of a child) that could affect the ease of computing withholding allowances or advance EITC payments.

Indicators of Complexity

Identifying provisions in the tax code that look complicated, as we have done in this section, is admittedly subjective. In the discussion above we sometimes refer to the number of lines of instructions or the number of worksheets as evidence of a provision's complexity. These proxies are imperfect measures of complexity.

11. Treasury Department Individual Tax Model.
12. IRS (2002d, pp. 845–50).
13. Authors' tabulations of Statistics of Income individual income tax return data for tax year 1999.

For example, if the tax return simply stated that taxpayers could claim any child as long as no one else did, many lines would be eliminated from the instructions. But this would not provide either taxpayers or the IRS with any guidance as to how to handle the inevitable onslaught of competing claims.

Tax complexity has many dimensions and could plausibly be defined in different ways. In the following sections we consider four elements of complexity: compliance costs, administrative costs, noncompliance, and participation. Taken separately, none of these indicators provides sufficient insight into complexity. A tax provision, for example, could be so complicated that taxpayers ignore the instructions and the IRS does not enforce it; compliance and administrative costs would thus be low, but noncompliance would be high. Taken together, the indicators provide a more complete view of complexity associated with low-income taxpayers.

Compliance Costs

Compliance costs include the costs associated with maintaining tax records, learning about tax laws, preparing the return, and sending the return to the tax authorities. The Paperwork Reduction Act of 1980 requires the IRS to estimate the average amount of time spent on these four items. These estimates are included in the instructions for every federal tax form. A more comprehensive definition of compliance costs would include expenditures of time or money by the taxpayer solely to avoid taxes, as well as the costs to taxpayers of being audited or corresponding with the tax agency after the return has been filed.

Blumenthal and Slemrod conducted the most recent study of compliance costs, a survey of 2,000 households on their expenditures of time and money for filing federal and state 1989 income tax returns.[14] The survey included questions about the amount of time filers spent arranging their financial affairs to minimize tax liabilities, but it did not ask about their postfiling interactions with the IRS. While absolute expenditures of time and money were greatest among high-income taxpayers, their findings suggest that compliance costs constitute a higher percentage of income for low-income filers.

Although we lack current data on compliance burdens, indications suggest that compliance costs have risen for low-income taxpayers since the late 1980s. First, the IRS estimates that the length of time it takes to complete a Form 1040A or 1040EZ has increased since 1988, the first year that the IRS provided such estimates. In 1988 taxpayers were told that they could anticipate spending about seven hours to complete the basic Form 1040A and only ninety-one min-

---

14. Blumenthal and Slemrod (1992).

utes to fill out a Form 1040EZ. By 2001 these estimates had increased to ten hours for a Form 1040A and four hours for a Form 1040EZ.[15]

Second, more low-income taxpayers are using paid preparers than ever before. Between 1981 and 2000, the share of taxpayers who used paid preparers increased from 41 to 53 percent. Reliance on paid preparers grew even more rapidly among those who used the 1040A and 1040EZ forms: from 17 percent in 1981 to 40 percent in 2000. While EITC filers were as likely as other filers to use paid preparers in the early 1990s, 64 percent reported use of paid preparers in 2000.[16] Berube and others estimate that $1.75 billion of EITC refunds in 1999 were diverted toward paying for tax preparation, electronic filing, and refund anticipation loans.[17]

Third, while audit rates have generally fallen, the odds of being audited have increased for low-income filers relative to other filers. In 1988 the audit rate among 1040A nonbusiness filers with positive income below $25,000 was 1.03 percent, while the average audit rate among all filers was 1.57 percent. By 2000 the audit rate was 0.49 percent for all taxpayers, but it was 0.6 percent among 1040A nonbusiness filers with income under $25,000[18] and 1.4 percent among EITC claimants.[19]

These measures, however, should be used with much caution. Some of the increase in estimated time needed to complete simpler forms may reflect changes in filing requirements that have allowed taxpayers with more complex returns to file a 1040EZ or 1040A instead of a 1040.[20] Further, the IRS burden models used to estimate the amount of time it takes to a file a tax return are derived from a survey of taxpayers who filed tax returns for 1983.[21] Measures based on the survey may not fully account for changes in law or technological advances (like computer software packages that allow taxpayers to complete tax returns online) since then.[22]

To some extent the increased reliance on paid preparers may be due to taxpayers' desires to obtain quicker refunds by filing electronically, especially in conjunction with the EITC, which has expanded over the past decade. While

15. IRS, Instructions for Forms 1040A and 1040EZ.

16. Internal Revenue Service (1985), tables 12 and 13; unpublished IRS data.

17. Berube and others (2002).

18. "IRS Audit Rates by Individual Audit Class: Nonbusiness and Business Returns FY 1988 through 2001" (http://trac.syr.edu/tracirs/findings/national/ratesTab3.html [October 2002]).

19. IRS (2002a) and unpublished data. Disaggregated data on audits of EITC filers are not available prior to 1996. However, it is unlikely that many EITC claimants were selected for audit prior to the EITC compliance initiatives that began in the 1990s.

20. Beginning in 1990, for example, taxpayers with taxable pension and Social Security income were eligible to file a 1040A instead of a 1040. In 2000 the Form 1040A option was extended to filers with certain capital gains distributions.

21. Arthur D. Little (1988).

22. The IRS is currently conducting a new study of taxpayer burden that will address these concerns.

fewer than one-third of all taxpayers filed their tax year 2000 returns electronically, over 55 percent of EITC claimants chose the electronic filing option.[23] As the EITC amount has been increased (which, all other things equal, means higher after-tax income), many families may have chosen to pay professional tax preparers rather than take the time away from other activities to complete the forms on their own.

The data on audit rates provide the most compelling evidence of increasing compliance burdens, but the story is incomplete. On the one hand, the audit data do not reveal the full extent of postfiling contacts between low-income filers and the IRS. Since 1996 the IRS has obtained expanded authority to treat certain types of EITC-related errors that can be detected during initial processing as "mathematical errors." During the 2001 filing season, the IRS issued about 500,000 mathematical error notices to taxpayers who claimed an EITC-qualifying child with a missing or invalid Social Security number or who claimed the childless EITC but were either too young (under twenty-five) or too old (over sixty-four) to qualify for the credit.[24]

Mathematical-error procedures and, increasingly, the timing of EITC-related examinations represent another change in IRS practices toward low-income filers. From the perspective of the tax administrator, the benefits of a prerefund enforcement strategy are obvious. It is difficult to recapture erroneous refunds, once paid, because the target population has few resources to fall back upon to repay refunds. Mathematical-error procedures and prerefund audits limit the government's exposure, because money is not paid out until questions are resolved. But from the taxpayer's perspective, prerefund audits delay refunds if they are, in fact, eligible for the credit. The effect of such a strategy on compliance costs will be a function of how well the independent data sources identify erroneous claims.

The nature of these postfiling contacts has changed in other ways that reduce the burden to affected filers. For low-income filers, office audits have generally been replaced by correspondence audits, in which taxpayers are sent a checklist containing additional information that they must supply to the IRS. Taxpayers are not required to take time off from work in order to meet with an IRS auditor. Instead they can respond to the IRS through the mail or over the telephone.

The scope of contacts has also narrowed, with the IRS investigating fewer items on the returns of low-income filers. Conventional examinations could review every item on tax returns. In contrast, mathematical-error notices tend to focus on one issue, and correspondence audits are also limited, often examining only three issues on the return (dependency, head-of-household filing status, and the EITC).

---

23. Authors' tabulations of Statistics of Income individual income tax return data for tax year 2000.
24. Unpublished IRS data.

Administrative Costs

Administrative costs generally refers to the expenses incurred directly by the government in collecting taxes. (These costs, of course, are ultimately borne by taxpayers.) Although government costs appear explicitly in budgets, measuring the administrative costs of a tax system is not always simple. The IRS does not separate the costs of operating the corporate income tax from the costs associated with administering the individual income tax, let alone the costs associated with a segment of the filing population. However, certain costs associated with low-income filers can be identified.

EITC

Beginning with the 1995 filing season, the IRS intensified EITC enforcement activities. The increasing focus on low-income taxpayers was largely a response to IRS studies in 1993 and 1994 that raised concerns about EITC noncompliance. In 1995 the IRS identified 3.3 million refunds with missing or invalid Social Security numbers for children claimed either as dependents or EITC-qualifying children. Due to limited resources, the IRS could take action on only about one-third of these cases, releasing the other 2 million refunds without further investigation.[25]

Concern about limited resources led Congress to lift the discretionary spending caps for 1998 through 2002 in order to fund a special appropriation for EITC compliance activities. Appropriations over the five-year period totaled $716 million. During this time nearly all EITC activities (including outreach, mathematical-error procedures, and audits) have been charged against this appropriation. The appropriation for fiscal year 2002 was $146 million, or about 0.5 percent of tax year 2001 EITC claims. While the appropriation does not cover all EITC administrative costs, it is likely that the additional costs (such as the costs of processing EITC claims) do not exceed 1 percent.[26]

To target its still-limited resources more efficiently, the IRS has made changes in its enforcement strategies since 1995. As noted above, the IRS is limiting the scope of its enforcement activities either by narrowing the focus of audits or by increased reliance on mathematical-error notices. Audits of low-income filers are generally conducted through the mail rather than in offices.

---

25. GAO (1996).

26. IRS (2002a) and unpublished IRS data. The GAO has estimated that EITC administrative costs are equal to about 1 percent of EITC payments. However, it is not clear how that number is derived. GAO (1995) indicates that 1 percent is an upper-bound estimate based on average return processing costs and assuming that all of the costs of identifying fraudulent refund schemes are EITC-related. GAO (1997) states that the estimate includes only processing costs and excludes enforcement costs.

In addition, the IRS is relying more and more on independent data that can be matched to returns during initial processing to identify questionable claims before refunds are paid out. One step has been the development of a dependent database that uses administrative records, including state child custody records. The IRS began using these data in 2001 to help select questionable EITC claims for prerefund correspondence audits. Beginning in 2004 the IRS will be authorized to deny EITC claims by taxpayers who, according to child custody records, are noncustodial parents. The Treasury Department is currently conducting a study on the accuracy of the child custody records for tax enforcement purposes.

The IRS estimates that EITC enforcement efforts have grossed $5 billion since 1998, or $7 of savings for every $1 expended.[27] The enforcement yield may, in fact, be higher. The estimate does not include savings from outreach and education. It also does not include the effects of changes in taxpayers' behavior in the years following enforcement actions.

Low-Income Tax Clinics

The Internal Revenue Service Restructuring and Reform Act of 1998 authorized the secretary of the treasury to provide matching grants (of up to $100,000) to certain low-income taxpayer clinics. Eligible clinics are those that charge a nominal fee to represent low-income taxpayers in controversies with the IRS or to provide tax information to individuals for whom English is a second language. Ninety percent of their clients must have incomes below 250 percent of the poverty level. In addition, eligible clinics are either affiliated with accredited law, business, or accounting schools or are nonprofit organizations representing low-income filers. Low-income taxpayer clinics must provide matching funds on a dollar-for-dollar basis. In fiscal year 2002, 149 organizations applied for nearly $11 million of grants. The IRS awarded $7 million (the amount appropriated) to 127 organizations.

Noncompliance

Noncompliance may be an important indicator of complexity in the tax system, but little is known about the extent of income tax errors among low- or high-income taxpayers. The IRS has not conducted a comprehensive study of taxpayer compliance since the 1988 Taxpayer Compliance Measurement Program (TCMP) study. However, the IRS undertook four studies of compliance among EITC claimants between 1993 and 1999.

27. IRS (2002a).

There are important questions that the EITC compliance studies, by themselves, cannot answer. First, the causes of noncompliance cannot be ascertained using data on EITC claimants alone. We do not know, for example, how EITC-ineligible taxpayers who erroneously claim the credit differ from their compliant counterparts who do not claim the credit, because taxpayers who do not claim the credit are not studied. Second, we cannot evaluate the extent of EITC nonparticipation, even among tax return filers. Third, we cannot evaluate the importance of the EITC compliance problem relative to other problems in the tax system.[28] Despite the limitations of data collected on EITC claimants only, the EITC compliance studies provide a wealth of information about the size of the EITC compliance problem and the specific EITC eligibility criteria most often associated with erroneous claims.

The 1999 EITC data indicate that between $9.7 billion and $11.1 billion of EITC claims were erroneous.[29] IRS enforcement activities prevented or recovered about $1.2 billion in erroneous claims. Thus between $8.5 billion and $9.9 billion in EITC claims—or between 27.0 and 31.7 percent of total EITC claims—were erroneously paid to taxpayers for tax year 1999. As discussed further below, the difference between the upper- and lower-bound estimates is attributable to alternative treatments of taxpayers who failed to appear for an audit. Unless otherwise noted, the estimates in this chapter are based on the upper-bound set of estimates and on the amount of overclaims prior to any IRS enforcement activities.[30]

The error rate among taxpayers who did not claim an EITC-qualifying child is higher than the rate among taxpayers who claim children. (See table 6-2.)

28. Fortunately, there is now strong consensus within the IRS, the Treasury, and Congress that comprehensive compliance data are critical to ensuring the integrity and fairness of the tax system. The IRS is therefore beginning a new stage of compliance data collection, called the National Research Program. As part of the National Research Program, the IRS is reviewing approximately 50,000 randomly sampled tax year 2001 individual income tax returns. Returns for which reported information cannot be verified using Forms W-2, 1099, and other third-party data will be audited.

29. See IRS (2002b). The study was based on audits of 3,457 randomly selected tax year 1999 returns filed during 2000 and claiming the EITC. The sample represents a population of 18.8 million tax returns and about $31.3 billion in EITC claims. The EITC errors identified in the study include both intentional noncompliance and unintentional reporting mistakes, and the two types of errors are not readily distinguishable in the data. Returns were selected before mathematical and clerical errors were corrected as part of routine IRS processing. Therefore simple computational errors are also counted as noncompliance in this study.

30. The study overstates the net cost of EITC noncompliance to the Treasury, because the sample includes only taxpayers who claimed the EITC and excludes individuals who did not claim any EITC even though they were eligible for the credit. The IRS found that some taxpayers who claimed the credit did not claim the full amount to which they were entitled. These taxpayers failed to claim an estimated $710 million to $765 million, or 2.3 to 2.4 percent of the total EITC claimed for the same period. However, this estimate of unclaimed EITC excludes the amount that should have been claimed by taxpayers who did not claim any EITC at all. See also Plumley and Steuerle (this volume), who argue that the IRS should strive to minimize tax overpayments as well as underpayments.

Table 6-2. *EITC Claims and Overclaims by Presence of Qualifying Child,
Tax Year 1999*

Taxpayer and claim	Amount of total EITC claimed ($ millions)	Amount of excess EITC claimed ($ millions)	Gross overclaim rate (percent)
Upper-bound estimates[a]			
Taxpayers claiming qualifying children	30,500	10,804	35.3
Taxpayers not claiming qualifying children	703	314	44.6
All taxpayers	31,291	11,118	35.5
Lower-bound estimates[a]			
Taxpayers claiming qualifying children	30,527	9,373	30.7
Taxpayers not claiming qualifying children	710	279	39.3
All taxpayers	31,237	9,653	30.9

Source: Authors' calculations from IRS's tax year 1999 EITC compliance study data.

a. Estimates do not account for $1.2 billion in overclaims recovered or not paid due to the correction of mathematical errors during routine processing, examinations, and other enforcement activities. After accounting for IRS enforcement, the upper bound overclaim rate is 31.7 percent and the lower bound rate is 27.0 percent.

About 44.6 percent of the EITC claimed by taxpayers who claimed only the small credit for workers without qualifying children is claimed in error. The overclaim rate among taxpayers who claimed one child was 40.5 percent; the overclaim rate among taxpayers who claimed two EITC-qualifying children was 32.1 percent.[31] However, because most EITC claimants do claim the much larger credit for workers with children, errors by those taxpayers account for the large majority of erroneous claims. The total error among taxpayers who did not claim children is about $314 million. Errors attributable to taxpayers who claimed EITC-qualifying children amounted to $10.8 billion.

Errors Associated with EITC-Qualifying Children

The largest source of EITC errors in 1999 was the failure to meet the age, residency, relationship, or Social Security number tests with respect to a qualifying child.[32] (See table 6-3.) The failure to meet the residency test was by far the most prevalent qualifying-child error. (See table 6-4.) An estimated $2.7 billion in

31. These estimates and subsequent estimates in this section are authors' tabulations of the tax year 1999 EITC compliance data.

32. The child and the taxpayer must have a Social Security number valid for employment in the United States, thus signifying that they are U.S. citizens, are permanent residents, or have a visa authorizing them to work.

Table 6-3. *EITC Overclaims by Type of Error, Tax Year 1999*

Type of error	Number of returns (in thousands)		Dollar amount of overclaim (in millions)	
	Returns with this error only	Total returns with this error[a]	Returns with this error only	Total returns with this error[a]
Qualifying child	1,274	1,828	2,178	3,284
AGI tiebreaker	850	1,082	1,535	1,984
Filing status	1,037	1,663	1,489	2,724
Income[b]	2,946	3,275	1,333	1,710
Other errors	168	458	142	437
Errors corrected in processing[c]	668	958	457	939
Did not appear for audit[d]	1,219	1,375	1,980	2,226
Total	8,162	9,321	9,114	11,118

Source: Authors' calculations from the IRS's tax year 1999 EITC compliance study data.

a. Sum of this column exceeds total, because returns with more than one error appear in more than one row.

b. Excludes cases where income is misreported but had no effect on the final EITC amount because the EITC was denied in full for other reasons.

c. If the entire overclaim is corrected in processing, we do not have information regarding the nature of other errors, except for filing status changed to married, filing separately, or failure to appear for audit.

d. If taxpayer failed to appear for audit, we do not have information regarding the nature of any EITC error, except errors corrected in processing.

Table 6-4. *EITC Qualifying Child Errors by Type, Tax Year 1999*[a]

Type of error	Number of returns (in thousands)		Dollar amount of overclaim (in millions)	
	Returns with this child error only[b]	Total returns with this child error[c]	Returns with this child error only	Total returns with this child error[c]
Residency	675	1,443	1,233	2,698
Relationship	162	820	269	1,447
Age	109	167	145	206
SSN not valid for employment	103	192	167	421
Total	1,050	1,828	1,814	3,284

Source: Authors' calculations from the IRS's tax year 1999 EITC compliance study.

a. Includes returns with qualifying child errors only and with qualifying child errors in combination with other errors.

b. Estimates may not add to total due to rounding.

c. Sum of this column exceeds total because returns with more than one error appear in more than one row. Combinations of child errors occur when two errors are made with respect to the same child or when different errors are coded for two children claimed on the same return.

EITC was erroneously claimed by taxpayers who could not document that they lived with a claimed qualifying child for the required length of time during the tax year. Nearly half the children who failed the residency test were claimed by their own parent. It is likely that in some of these cases the noncustodial parent thought that he (or she) was entitled to the EITC because he provided support for the child or simply because he was the parent of the child. The failure to meet the relationship test was associated with $1.4 billion in excess claims. Relationship errors usually occur in combination with failure of the residency test. Less than $300 million was associated with the failure of the relationship test but no other qualifying-child test.

The AGI tiebreaker rule also accounted for a substantial portion of EITC overclaims. As discussed above, pre-2001 law awarded a child in an extended-family household to the taxpayer with the highest adjusted gross income. Even if the higher-income taxpayer did not claim the child, the lower-income taxpayer was not eligible to claim any EITC. The IRS study counted nearly $2 billion of EITC claims by the lower-income taxpayers as errors, without any adjustment for the amount that should have been claimed by other adults in the household. The EGTRRA modifications to the AGI tiebreaker would have eliminated about $1.4 billion of the tax year 1999 EITC overclaims.

Qualifying Children and Dependents

Evaluating the overlap between dependent and EITC claims provides some additional insight about the effects of maintaining multiple definitions of *child* for tax purposes. At least 97 percent of the qualifying children who were claimed in tax year 1999 were also claimed as dependents by the same taxpayers. (The other 3 percent were not claimed as dependents or could not be matched to dependents because of missing Social Security numbers.)

Of the children who were claimed as both dependents and EITC-qualifying children, about 66 percent met both the dependent and qualifying-child tests (including the AGI tiebreaker). Seventeen percent of children failed both the dependent and qualifying-child tests. The remainder failed one test or the other, but not both. Thus, in most cases where a qualifying child is allowed, the dependent is also allowed, and in most cases where one claim is disallowed, the other is also disallowed. This finding suggests that there is little rationale for maintaining separate EITC-qualifying child and dependent definitions.

In addition, about 700,000 EITC-qualifying children (about 3 percent of all qualifying children) were claimed by more than one taxpayer for purposes of the EITC in tax year 1999. About 1.3 million dependents represented in the EITC study were claimed as dependents more than once. Some of these duplicate claims may occur because taxpayers are confused about the EITC and dependent definitions.

Errors Associated with Filing Status

As noted above, taxpayers who use the "married, filing separately" status are not allowed to claim the EITC. About $2.1 billion in EITC overclaims was attributable to cases where the taxpayer's filing status was changed to "married, filing separately," either alone or in combination with other errors. In addition over $600 million in overclaims was attributable to couples who should have filed joint returns. In these cases the EITC was reduced or eliminated when the income of the two spouses was combined.[33] In about 750,000 cases the taxpayer filed as head of household and appeared to have lived apart from his or her spouse for at least part of the year. These taxpayers might not have understood that they were still considered married for tax purposes.

Filing-status errors were also an important source of errors on returns of taxpayers who did not claim qualifying children. About $90 million in excess EITC was claimed on returns of taxpayers who did not claim qualifying children and who misreported their filing status.[34]

Errors Associated with Misreported Income

About $1.7 billion in EITC overclaims (15.4 percent of the total error) occurred on returns with income reporting errors. Over $1.3 billion of this amount was associated with returns that included misreported income and no other error. Nearly all of the error (87.4 percent of overclaimed amounts associated with income) is attributable to income underreporting. (See table 6-5.) We rarely observe income overreporting, even though very low-income taxpayers could increase their EITC by overstating their incomes.

Farm and nonfarm business income earned by self-employed taxpayers accounts for more than half of unreported income. This is unsurprising, given that most self-employment income is not independently reported to the IRS. However, wages, interest, and unemployment compensation are also underreported, even though these items are reported independently to the IRS.[35]

Income misreporting was the largest single source of error among taxpayers who did not claim EITC-qualifying children, and it was associated with $88 million in error on these returns.

33. These errors are treated as income underreporting errors in the IRS report. See IRS (2002b).

34. Estimates for taxpayers who did not claim children are based on a relatively small sample (601 returns) and tend to be less reliable than estimates for taxpayers who claimed qualifying children. Some of the filing status errors on returns without qualifying children occurred in combination with other errors, especially errors corrected in processing. More detailed estimates cannot be provided, due to the limited sample size.

35. Nontaxable earned income (such as deferred compensation and military housing) accounted for about 6 percent of unreported income. Beginning with tax year 2002, nontaxable earned income is no longer counted in the calculation of the EITC.

Table 6-5. *EITC Overclaims Associated with Misreported Income,*
Tax Year 1999

| Type of error | Number (in thousands) | Amount of income misreported ($ millions) | | Total EITC overclaim ($ millions) |
		Specific item[a]	Total	
Earned income or modified				
AGI underreported	3,060	14,732		1,494
Sources of underreported income				
Wages	942	3,226	4,275	445
Farm or nonfarm business income	1,208	9,512	9,850	854
Interest	521	62	1,604	164
Unemployment compensation	160	232	297	91
Nontaxable earned income	627	924	1,498	201
Other types	453	1,667	3,651	360
Earned income is overreported	144	197		171
Income recategorized, total unchanged	71	0		45
Total	3,275	14,928		1,710

Source: Authors' tabulations from IRS's tax year 1999 EITC compliance study data. Income errors are not coded when the EITC is entirely disallowed for another reason and correcting the income error only would reduce but not eliminate the EITC.

a. While a specific income item may be underreported, other types of income may be overreported. As a result, the sum of the specific items is greater than the total amount of income underreported.

Taxpayers Who Failed to Appear for Audit

In 1999, $2.2 billion in EITC overclaims (or 20 percent of total overclaims) was due to taxpayers whose EITC claims could not be substantiated because they failed to appear for audit.[36] Between 1997 and 1999 EITC claims attributable to taxpayers who were unwilling or unable to appear for the audit more than doubled, and total estimated EITC overclaims grew from $9.3 billion to $11.1 billion. Taxpayers who failed to appear for an audit account for about 72 percent of the difference in the estimated error rates for 1997 and 1999.

Taxpayers might fail to respond to a notice of examination because they know that they should not have claimed the credit. Indeed it is the IRS's standard examination practice to deny the entire EITC whenever a taxpayer fails to appear for an audit. But taxpayers might also fail to appear for an audit because

36. These taxpayers were located and had some contact with the IRS. Taxpayers who could not be located because they had changed addresses, or who could be located but could not be audited because they had moved out of the country, were excluded from the study.

they are confused or intimidated by the IRS. Some taxpayers might not have the time or other resources needed to get to an audit. Taxpayers who claimed only a small amount of EITC might decide that the EITC is not worth the time and expense of an audit. It is difficult to distinguish between taxpayers who failed to appear for an audit because they were intentionally noncompliant and those who failed to appear for other reasons, or to determine why some compliant taxpayers failed to appear for an audit.

If, instead of assuming that all claims of taxpayers who failed to appear for an audit are erroneous, we assume that these taxpayers have the same noncompliance rates as similar taxpayers who did appear for an audit, then we would attribute only $761 million in overclaims to these taxpayers. The estimated total amount of EITC overclaimed would fall from $11.1 billion to $9.7 billion.[37] The amount overclaimed for tax year 1997 would fall from $9.3 billion to $8.7 billion.[38]

Intentional versus Unintentional Errors

The EITC compliance study does not distinguish taxpayer confusion from intentional misreporting. As part of the study, the IRS did ask examiners to ascertain whether the EITC overclaim was attributable to difficulty understanding the law, intentional disregard of the law, or a variety of other possible reasons. However, data are missing or difficult to interpret for over half the EITC overclaims. Moreover previous research using EITC compliance data for tax year 1994 suggests that IRS examiners might not be able to consistently evaluate taxpayer intent.[39]

Another way to evaluate taxpayer intent is to examine the correlation between the size of the EITC and the probability or level of noncompliance. If errors are random, then there should be no correlation between the size of the credit and noncompliance. A correlation between the size of the credit and noncompliance would suggest that errors are nonrandom and perhaps intentional.

37. This assumption is implemented by excluding taxpayers who failed to appear for an audit from the sample and reweighting the remaining observations so that the weighted estimates still sum to the total number of EITC claimants. For information about the sample strata, see IRS (2002b).

38. When all claims of taxpayers who failed to appear for audit are treated as overclaims, the overclaim rate after accounting for IRS enforcement activities is 25.6 percent for tax year 1997 and 31.7 percent for tax year 1999. If taxpayers who failed to appear for audit are assumed to have the same compliance characteristics as similar taxpayers who were audited, then the overclaim rate is 23.8 percent for 1997 and 27.0 percent for 1999. The year-to-year difference in the lower-bound estimates is not statistically significant at the 5 percent level.

39. For example, there are observations in the 1994 data that appear to involve similar circumstances but are coded differently. In addition, some examiners were much more likely than others to code errors as intentional; these differences in examiner determinations remained statistically significant, even after controlling for the size and type of overclaim. In some cases, it appeared that the determinations about taxpayer intent reflect primarily the IRS agent's certainty about the presence of an EITC error, rather than the nature of the taxpayer's behavior.

Using TCMP data for 1985 and 1988, Liebman estimates the probability that a taxpayer erroneously claims a dependent child.[40] He estimates that, in the absence of the EITC, 3.53 percent of taxpayers without children would incorrectly claim a dependent, due to non-EITC tax benefits or inadvertent errors. Given the EITC as it existed under 1985 law, an additional 0.76 percent of taxpayers would claim a child. In the Tax Reform Act of 1986, the size of the EITC and the EITC income thresholds were increased. Liebman estimates that, as a result, another 0.87 percent of taxpayers would claim a child. Liebman therefore concludes that at least 32 percent of the erroneous EITC claims in 1988 that were associated with a dependent error were behavioral responses to the EITC. The remaining EITC claims could be the result of inadvertent errors or errors induced by non-EITC tax benefits.

McCubbin uses EITC compliance study data for tax year 1994 combined with IRS data on low-income taxpayers who did not claim the EITC to estimate the probability that an ineligible taxpayer erroneously claimed an EITC child.[41] The model estimated by McCubbin suggests that at least 28 percent of qualifying-child errors observed for tax year 1994 were intentional responses to the EITC. Some of the remaining errors were caused by intentional responses to other tax benefits of claiming children. McCubbin also finds that the incidence of child misreporting is correlated with lower levels of education, income, and wealth, perhaps because less-educated taxpayers are more likely to make unintentional errors. In addition the size of the EITC, tax rates, and observable taxpayer characteristics in the model explain only a fraction of noncompliance. Unintentional errors might account for a substantial portion of the unexplained variation in the model. It is also likely that some of the unexplained noncompliance is due to unobserved variations in expected penalties, unobserved tendencies to engage in intentional noncompliance, or other factors associated with intentional noncompliance.

The Role of Paid Preparers

About two-thirds of tax year 1999 EITC claimants used a paid preparer to file their return. The overclaim rate among taxpayers whose returns identify a paid preparer is 34.6 percent; the rate among taxpayers whose returns do not indicate paid preparation is 37.8 percent. However, these estimates mask substantial variation among different types of preparers.[42] About 31.1 percent of taxpayers reported that their return was prepared by an attorney, certified public accoun-

---

40. Liebman (1995).

41. McCubbin (2000).

42. The following estimates by reported type of return preparer exclude taxpayers who failed to appear for an examination, thereby reducing the estimated error rates. While we can determine whether a paid preparer is identified on the face of their return, we do not know which type of preparer was used.

tant, enrolled agent, or a nationally recognized tax preparation service. About 25.2 percent of the EITC claimed by these taxpayers was claimed in error. About 35.2 percent of EITC claimants reported that their returns were completed by other types of paid preparers, including individuals who are not attorneys, certified public accountants, or enrolled agents, and who are self-employed or working for smaller, local firms. The error rate among these EITC claims was 36.2 percent. The extent to which the difference in the overclaim rates is attributable to differences in the skills of preparers or to the characteristics of the clients who choose the different kinds of preparers is not known.[43]

Participation

The task of administering the tax system includes ensuring that individuals file returns if they are required to file or have another reason to file (such as to claim a refund of withheld taxes or a refundable credit). Administering the tax system also entails ensuring that taxpayers who file returns claim the tax benefits to which they are entitled. The IRS does not have current data on the characteristics of nonfilers or estimated participation rates for most tax benefits. There are, however, several sets of estimated EITC participation rates and tax return filing rates for EITC-eligible individuals and families. Researchers using somewhat different data sets and methodologies consistently find that EITC participation rates are fairly high, ranging from about 75 percent to about 86 percent.

Scholz uses Survey of Income and Program Participation (SIPP) data matched to tax returns to estimate EITC participation rates for tax year 1990.[44] Using the SIPP data, Scholz identifies 9.6 million EITC-eligible filing units. Using SIPP responses regarding whether or not a taxpayer filed a return, along with SIPP data matched to tax returns, Scholz estimates that 80.5 to 86.4 percent of eligible units claimed the EITC. (See appendix 6B for details.)

Scholz also examines the factors that influence the tax return filing decision (and implicitly the EITC participation decision) among EITC-eligible filers.

43. Erard (1993) finds that self-selection across preparation modes increases the observed level of noncompliance. In response to high error rates among certain preparers of tax year 1994 EITC claims, the Taxpayer Relief Act of 1997 imposed new due diligence requirements for paid preparers. To demonstrate due diligence, a preparer must ask the taxpayer certain questions in order to ascertain his or her eligibility for the EITC. The preparer must retain this information using Form 8867 or other documentation for three years. A preparer who cannot show that he or she was diligent in filing a taxpayer's claim for the EITC may be assessed a $100 penalty, even if the taxpayer's claim is not disallowed. By placing the burden of proof of due diligence on the preparer and allowing the IRS to levy fines without auditing the client's return, the provision makes it less expensive for the IRS to penalize lax preparers. The requirements are also intended to educate preparers about the EITC eligibility criteria, by spelling out the information necessary to evaluate a taxpayer's claim.

44. Scholz (1994).

He finds that (controlling for the size of the EITC benefit) lower-income and self-employed taxpayers are less likely to file returns. As expected, taxpayers who are eligible for a larger EITC are more likely to file. Married individuals and older persons are also more likely to file tax returns. Those less likely to file include respondents reporting receipt of Social Security or public assistance, males, taxpayers with larger families, persons of Spanish origin, persons with some college or a college degree, and taxpayers who reside in states without a state income tax. Occupation appears to play a large role in determining particip. Workers in the private household services occupation (such as house-keepers and child care providers) are 26 percent less likely to claim the EITC than other EITC-eligible workers. Scholz suggests that some of these individu-als may be working "off the books."

The IRS used both SIPP and Current Population Survey (CPS) data to esti-mate the percentage of EITC-eligible taxpayers who filed a tax return for 1996.[45] Using the CPS, the IRS estimates that 17.9 million potential tax filing units were eligible for the EITC in 1996. Actual filers are identified by match-ing Social Security numbers provided by CPS respondents to tax return data provided by the IRS. About 11.5 million EITC-eligible units were matched to tax returns, resulting in a 64.2 percent filing rate. Another 2.3 million EITC-eligible units provided a valid Social Security number that did not match to any tax return, yielding a 12.8 percent nonfiling rate. The remaining 4.1 million CPS respondents, or 23.1 percent, either did not have a valid Social Security number or refused to provide a number to the CPS interviewer. If we assume that some of these individuals filed a tax return, then the filing rate would be higher, perhaps 75 to 80 percent. (See appendix 6B for derivation.)

Using the SIPP data, the IRS estimates that 19.3 million filing units were eli-gible for the EITC in 1996 (1.4 million more than were identified using the CPS). The IRS did not have SIPP data matched to tax returns for estimating the filing rate. However, SIPP respondents are asked whether they filed a tax return. About 14.2 million SIPP respondents who appeared eligible for the EITC reported that they filed a tax return, yielding a filing rate of 73.5 percent (9.3 percentage points higher than initially estimated from the CPS). About 3.4 million reported that they did not file a tax return, resulting in a nonfiling rate of 17.8 percent (5 points higher than the IRS estimated using the CPS). About 1.7 million did not respond or did not know whether they had filed a tax return. The number of EITC-eligible units estimated from the SIPP is likely to include some individuals who did not have a valid Social Security number and were eligible for the EITC. If some SIPP respondents were not eligible to receive the EITC, and if these individuals are less likely to report filing a return, then the true filing rate would be higher than 73.5 percent.

45. IRS (2002c).

Because some taxpayers who filed a tax return nevertheless did not claim the EITC, the filing rate is larger than the participation rate. The IRS also examines taxpayers' responses to notices indicating that they appeared eligible for the EITC but had not claimed the credit on their tax returns. The IRS sent notices to 194,000 taxpayers with children who appeared to be eligible for the EITC, based on the information provided on their 1998 tax return. Of these, only about a third responded, requesting the EITC. Over 680,000 notices were sent to low-wage workers without children, alerting them of their possible eligibility for the EITC, and 45 percent responded, requesting the credit. The reasons for the low response rate, particularly among filers with children, are not known. It is possible that many taxpayers did not initially claim the EITC because they knew they were ineligible.[46]

The IRS uses the SIPP data to examine various characteristics of nonfilers. Taxpayers eligible to receive only the smaller credit for workers without children are less likely to file tax returns. About 28.9 percent of respondents without qualifying children reported that they did not file a tax return, whereas 14.1 percent of taxpayers with children reported that they did not file a return.[47] (There is virtually no difference between the nonfiling rates of taxpayers with one child and taxpayers with two or more children.)

Like Scholz, the IRS finds that the likelihood of filing appears to be increasing with the size of the credit, that lower-income persons appear less likely to file than persons with somewhat higher incomes, and that persons from a Hispanic country of origin are less likely than others to file a tax return. In contrast to Scholz, the IRS finds that nonfiling rates appear to be highest among taxpayers with lower levels of education. An estimated 25.1 percent of taxpayers without a high school degree did not file a return, whereas 16.4 percent of high school graduates and 14.3 percent of EITC-eligible taxpayers with higher levels of education reported that they did not file a tax return.

Using CPS data, the General Accounting Office estimates that there were 17.2 million EITC-eligible households in 1999.[48] The GAO obtained the number of eligible claimants—12.9 million—from the IRS's tax year 1999 EITC compliance study. Combining the two data sources, the GAO estimates a participation rate of 75 percent.[49]

---

46. Note also that some filers who are eligible for the EITC do not receive notices because they do not appear eligible for the EITC, based on the face of the tax return. For example, if a custodial parent does not claim her child as a dependent (possibly because she waives the exemption to the child's noncustodial parent), then the custodial parent will not appear to have an EITC-qualifying child and would not receive a notice.

47. IRS (2002c).

48. GAO (2001).

49. To the extent that some taxpayers who are not authorized to work in the United States appear to be eligible for the EITC in the CPS, the estimated participation rate is too low.

While the estimated participation rate among taxpayers with children is 86.5 percent, it is only 44.7 percent among those without children, who qualify for a much smaller credit. The GAO finds that, while 25 percent of EITC-eligible taxpayers fail to claim the credit, only 11.1 percent of EITC dollars are unclaimed. That is, for both taxpayers with and without children, participation rates increase with the size of the EITC.

The GAO also finds variations in participation rates among taxpayers with qualifying children. Estimated participation rates for taxpayers with one child and taxpayers with two or more children are extraordinarily high, at 96.0 and 93.0 percent. (The difference between these two groups is not statistically significant.) In contrast, the participation rate among taxpayers with three or more children is 62.5 percent. The discrepancy between the findings for small and large families may reflect underreporting of children in the EITC compliance data. Examiners who performed the audits for the IRS compliance study were directed to collect information on all the taxpayer's qualifying children. However, as long as taxpayers have two children, the presence of additional children is irrelevant for calculation of the EITC. Therefore examiners had less incentive to collect data on additional children, and taxpayers had less incentive to provide information about those children. However, the lower participation rate for larger families is consistent with the earlier findings of Scholz.

Improving Tax Administration for Low-Income Filers

Making the current individual income tax system simpler for low-income filers to navigate is an important goal, as is reducing IRS administrative costs. Identifying strategies that achieve these two goals, while maintaining high participation rates and improving compliance, is challenging. In this section, we consider three alternative approaches: first, removing the EITC from the income tax system; second, simplifying the tax provisions that affect low-income filers; and third, improving IRS administrative processes.

Removing the EITC from the Income Tax System

The EITC compliance problems have led some policymakers and analysts to question whether the credit should remain in the income tax system. Some have argued that the EITC is comparable to means-tested transfer programs, because about 85 percent of the credit's costs are payments in excess of income and self-employment tax liabilities (in other words, only about 15 percent of its costs reduce income tax receipts). Thus some policymakers have argued that the EITC should be provided through the transfer system and not the tax system.[50] Others recognize that, while many EITC recipients owe no income tax, most are subject to payroll taxes, which the EITC is also intended to offset. This finding has led some to argue that it makes little sense to subject workers to payroll taxes and then refund those taxes through the EITC.

Shifting Responsibility for Refundable Tax Credits to Other Agencies

Shifting responsibility for the EITC from the tax system to other government agencies (such as state welfare agencies) would reduce tax compliance burdens for millions of filers (including filers who are not eligible for the EITC but who might expend time and money to determine that fact) and would lower IRS administrative costs. But the effects on the overall complexity of the tax and transfer systems are less obvious, for several reasons.

As noted earlier, most EITC claimants would be required to file a tax return even if the credit did not exist. Under current law, individuals attach a six-line schedule to their tax return in order to claim the EITC. The schedule contains basic information about their children, such as their names, Social Security numbers, and ages. (Childless workers are not required to attach any schedule to claim the credit.) Although most do not choose this option, the IRS will compute the EITC for taxpayers who complete Schedule EIC. Thus, once a taxpayer has determined that he or she is eligible for the EITC, the actual filing burden can be relatively small.

Shifting the EITC to another agency would mean that these individuals would have to contact another government office and provide it with the same information on income, marital status, and children that they already provide the IRS. If most EITC claimants already interact with another government agency and provide it with comparable information, shifting responsibility for the credit might be achievable at low cost. However, relatively few individuals who are eligible for the EITC report claiming means-tested benefits. Of individuals who were eligible for the EITC in 2000, only 3 percent appear to have claimed Supplemental Security Income (SSI), 5 percent claimed Temporary Assistance for Needy Families (TANF), and 16 percent claimed food stamps.[51]

One of the reasons that shifting the EITC to state agencies may appear attractive is that the programs operated by them tend to have much lower reported error rates than the EITC. For example, only 6.5 percent of food stamp

---

50. See, for example, statements to the House Committee on Ways and Means (1997) by Representative Rob Portman.

51. These estimates are authors' computations using the March 2001 Current Population Survey. Measurement problems (including underreporting of transfer income) may result in underestimates of program participation.

benefits were paid in error in 2000.[52] But the trade-off for the lower error rate has been higher administrative and compliance costs and lower participation rates, particularly among the working poor.

To claim food stamp benefits, an individual must personally visit a welfare office and provide detailed information on income, assets, and household characteristics. Several aspects of this process impose significant costs on working families in particular. First, with the food stamp application process requiring on average nearly five hours (sometimes spread over two days), applicants may have to miss a day or two from work in order to apply for benefits.[53] Second, the length of the application is due in part to the fact that many states combine eligibility determination for food stamps with other programs that may be irrelevant to working families. Forty-four states and the District of Columbia provide a single initial application for food stamps, TANF, Medicaid, and general assistance.[54] Third, the length of time between the initial application and recertification (and then between subsequent recertifications) depends on how often an applicant's income or family composition is likely to change. Many states consider earnings to be volatile, thus requiring workers to reapply—in person—as often as once every three months.[55]

The ease of claiming the EITC and the lack of stigma associated with the credit likely explain why EITC participation rates are substantially higher than participation rates for means-tested programs. Only about 53 percent of eligible households claimed food stamps in 2000. Among eligible households with earnings, the food stamp participation rate was 43 percent.[56] As we have seen, estimates of the EITC participation rate range from 75 to 86 percent.

Not surprisingly the food stamp program costs considerably more to administer than the EITC. While EITC administrative costs are roughly $145 million, the food stamp program costs the federal and state governments $4 billion a year to operate. Adding direct administrative costs and compliance errors, there appear to be closer equivalence between the costs of administering spending programs and refundable tax credits.[57]

The school lunch program provides an interesting contrast to the food stamp program. Like the EITC, the school lunch program has a simple application process, relatively low administrative costs, and a selective eligibility verification system (only up to 3 percent of applicants are asked to verify eligibility). There is also a large overlap between the school lunch and EITC populations: About

52. Rosenbaum and Super (2001).
53. Ponza and others (1999)
54. O'Brien and others (2000).
55. GAO (1999). In 2000 the Agriculture Department published regulations giving states the option to use semiannual reporting. Semiannual reporting effectively freezes a household's food stamp allotment for six months, thus disregarding changes in income over the certification period.
56. Cunnyngham (2002).
57. Holtzblatt (2000).

45 percent of filing units who appear eligible for the EITC also report that a child in their family participated in the school lunch program.[58] And, like the EITC, the school lunch program appears to have a sizable noncompliance problem.[59]

The food stamp and school lunch program experiences suggest that shifting the EITC into the transfer system is not the magic bullet that some have suggested. Improving compliance may require additional resources, regardless of whether the administering agency is a school district, a welfare office, or the IRS. The tools used by conventional spending programs to detect and prevent noncompliance may also increase compliance burdens on beneficiaries, which in turn may result in a reduction in participation.

Payroll Tax Exemption

As an alternative to the EITC, Yin and Forman suggest that it would be preferable to simply exempt the first $10,000 of annual earnings from Social Security taxes.[60] Under their proposal, all workers would receive this exemption.[61] In addition, families with children, regardless of income, would be eligible for a family allowance benefit. By eliminating income phaseouts, the Yin-Forman proposal may be simpler to compute than the current EITC and child tax credit benefits and may reduce some of the incentives for noncompliance. But, relative to the EITC, the Yin-Forman proposal is less targeted and costlier. It is also not immune to administrative problems (for example, the IRS would have to track workers who change jobs during the year).

Simplification

Throughout the past decade, Congress has taken a number of steps to simplify the EITC eligibility criteria. As noted above, the support and household maintenance requirements were replaced in 1991 with a residency-based test. Beginning in 2002, the AGI tiebreaker test was liberalized, at the cost of some targeting precision, to allow parents' claims to supersede other filers and to apply the test only in cases where more than one filer claimed the same child. Also in 2002 the definitions of *earned income* and *adjusted gross income* were conformed to those used throughout most of the rest of the tax form.

Other tax provisions affecting low-income filers have not been simplified. In 2002 the Treasury Department announced a proposal to create a uniform

58. U.S. Department of Agriculture (2001, p. 59); authors' calculations using March 2001 Current Population Survey.
59. USDA (1999).
60. Yin and Forman (1993).
61. The Social Security earnings cap and tax rates would be increased to pay for the exemption, which would be substantially more expensive than the EITC, because it would apply to all workers.

definition of *child*. Under the proposal, taxpayers would be able to follow the same eligibility rules when claiming a child for five major tax benefits, including the dependent exemption, head-of-household filing status, the child tax credit, the child and dependent care tax credit, and the EITC. The proposal addresses several sources of complexity in the tax provisions affecting low-income taxpayers with children. By replacing the support test with a residency-based test, the proposal reduces record-keeping and audit burdens. By substituting a common definition of *child* for the five definitions currently applicable, the proposal also reduces the multiplicity of rules. If a uniform definition of *child* were adopted, Schedule EIC (whose sole purpose is to obtain information about EITC-qualifying children) could be eliminated.

But the proposal does not eliminate the support test completely, and this aspect has drawn criticism that it retains some of the complexity of current law. For example, the proposal would allow taxpayers to continue to claim the dependent exemption and child tax credit for children they support, as long as no one else claims the children. Further simplification could possibly be achieved by using a strict residency test, as was recommended by the Joint Committee on Taxation.[62] However, a strict residency test would mean that some children could not be claimed by anyone. For example, a taxpayer could not claim his granddaughter as a dependent if the child did not live with him, even if he supported her and no one else could claim the child as a dependent.

Other provisions affecting low-income filers could be simplified. For example, the household maintenance test could be simplified by liberalizing or eliminating the test entirely. Determining filing status for separated spouses could be made easier by relaxing the requirement that taxpayers maintain the household in which they and their dependent children reside. The eligibility criteria for the refundable portion of the child tax credit could be brought into closer conformity with those used for the EITC. Eliminating multiple computations of the additional child tax credit would also reduce compliance burdens. While these options would reduce complexity, they have other effects that may or may not be desirable. Liberalizing or eliminating the household maintenance test, for example, would lose revenues by allowing more single parents to qualify as heads of household, including many who live in extended families or who receive assistance from the state.

Administrative Practices

Since 1990 Congress and the IRS have taken a number of steps to improve EITC compliance. As described elsewhere in this chapter, these steps provided the IRS with additional data and simplified procedures that enable the IRS to

62. JCT (2001).

more easily deny erroneous credits before they are paid out. In recognition of the fact that the IRS can detect far more erroneous claims than it can subject to examination procedures, Congress has also provided the agency with a special appropriation to fund EITC compliance activities since 1998.

Yet despite these steps the recent IRS study of EITC claimants in tax year 1999 shows that noncompliance remains high. The 2001 tax act contains some provisions that should help lower EITC noncompliance, including a simplification of the adjusted gross income tiebreaker and an expansion of mathematical-error authority. We estimate that these provisions could reduce EITC erroneous claims by roughly $2 billion but still leave EITC noncompliance at levels that may be considered too high.

Further reducing EITC noncompliance will require some difficult choices and possibly additional resources. With additional resources the IRS could examine more of the questionable cases that are identified through existing data sources, such as the Federal Case Registry of Child Support Orders. Additional resources would also enable the IRS to develop new data sources to help identify erroneous claims. A long-term goal might be to collect information on marriage licenses and divorce decrees to better enable the IRS to verify filing status. Unfortunately there is no centralized marital status data bank, even at the state level. Some commercial data sets, however, could provide useful information, such as the names of all individuals who live at the same address.

If independent data from third parties are sufficiently accurate in detecting errors, then using such data to target IRS enforcement activities could yield a big bang for the buck: Noncompliance could be reduced, with minimal increase in the compliance burdens of eligible taxpayers. More low-income filers would become subject to audits, but the scope of the audits could be restricted to a few or even one item, in order to minimize their impacts on compliance burdens and administrative costs. Compliance burdens could be further reduced by clarifying documentation requests in correspondence, by improving the training of examiners to ensure that consistent standards are applied to all returns, and by providing notices in Spanish as well as English.

Another option is to require individuals to provide more documentation directly to the IRS in support of their claim of the EITC, either before or when they file a tax return. For example, some or all filers could be asked to supply proof that they meet one or more of the EITC eligibility criteria before they could receive a credit payment. Taxpayers who did not provide such documentation would be subject to an examination.

Collecting data from all EITC claimants directly could improve EITC compliance significantly, but only if the IRS had sufficient resources to absorb such data and use them effectively. Individual filers might have to provide less information than they would if they received a mathematical-error notice or were selected for an examination. However, millions more taxpayers than are currently subject to post-filing activities—including many eligible filers—would be required to provide such information. Because many more filers would be expected to provide documentation than under current examination procedures, total compliance costs would rise, and participation might fall as a consequence. Limiting data requests to taxpayers for whom independent databases provide little if any information would reduce these effects without compromising compliance benefits.[63]

Conclusion

To some extent the administrative issues raised by the inclusion of low-income tax filers are the same as those raised by taxpayers with higher incomes. But the inclusion of low-income filers in the individual income tax system may raise unique tax administrative issues, as well. While they are eligible to file using the forms generally considered to be simple, their tax affairs—mirroring their own lives—may not be simple at all.

Addressing the issues that affect low-income filers may require trade-offs between various administrative goals, as well as with other tax and social policy goals. Shifting responsibility for refundable tax credits like the EITC from the IRS to other agencies would reduce IRS administrative costs but could increase the compliance burden of low-income individuals, with negligible savings to the government. Simplifying certain tax provisions could reduce compliance burdens of low-income taxpayers but could also reduce the extent to which tax relief is targeted to low-income families (and thus reduce tax revenues) or deny tax benefits to current recipients. With greater resources the IRS could improve its administration of the EITC and other provisions that affect low-income filers. But finding a strategy that improves compliance while minimizing administrative costs and compliance burdens presents challenges.

One possible strategy could be to combine simplification with increased resources that could allow the IRS to prevent erroneous refunds from being paid using third-party data sources. In addition, taxpayer assistance programs could be enhanced, consistent standards could be adopted for selecting returns for examination, and the examination process could be streamlined. Such a strategy may achieve balance between the goals of lowering compliance burdens, keep-

---

63. On June 13, 2003, the IRS announced a five-point initiative to improve the administration of the EITC. The initiative includes a pilot certification program. Beginning in 2004, about 25,000 EITC claimants are being asked to provide proof that their child meets the credit's residency requirements prior to receiving the EITC. Taxpayers are selected for certification if IRS research indicates that they have a relatively high risk of claiming a child who does not meet the residency requirements. A second selection criterion is that the IRS has little or no information from existing data sets to determine their eligibility. The IRS will be studying the effects of the certification pilot on both compliance and participation.

ing administrative costs relatively low, maintaining high participation rates, and improving compliance. However, the effectiveness of such a strategy is dependent on the reliability of third-party data. If such data are not reliable or available, then other strategies may merit examination.

Appendix 6A: Filing Behavior of Low-Income Individuals

Individuals are required to file a tax return when their gross income equals or exceeds the sum of the taxpayer's personal exemption and the standard deduction (the filing threshold). Individuals who do not claim dependents, deductions, or tax credits generally incur income tax liabilities when their gross income exceeds the filing threshold. Thus it is unlikely that such individuals would be required to file a tax return unless they owe income taxes. But if, for example, they have dependents, then they are required to file returns even when they have no positive income tax liability. In effect, they must file returns to identify the dependents who, by making them eligible for dependent exemptions and certain tax credits, also wipe out their income tax liability.

As figure 6A-1 demonstrates, the gap between the filing and income tax thresholds has widened in recent years, particularly for families with children. While the Tax Reform Act of 1986 raised both the filing and income tax thresholds by increasing the standard deduction and exemption amounts, more recent tax acts, with their expansions of child-related tax benefits (including the EITC), have lifted income tax thresholds without affecting filing thresholds. By 2002 a married couple with two children did not incur any tax liability until their income exceeded 182 percent of poverty. However, they were required to file a tax return with income about 76 percent of poverty. Beginning in 1994 the gap between filing and tax thresholds also increased for childless workers, as a result of an extension of a small EITC to very-low-income childless workers.

Table 6A-1 shows that over two-thirds of filers with adjusted gross income under $30,000 are required to file a tax return because they have a positive individual income tax liability before accounting for the offsetting effects of the EITC. An additional 6 percent file because they owe Social Security taxes on their self-employment income or other types of "special taxes" (such as payroll taxes on tips not reported to their employers). Seven percent file because their income exceeds the filing threshold, even though they do not have any income tax liability. Thus 81 percent of low-income filers are required to file tax returns. In comparison, 88 percent of all filers are required to file returns.

Low-income individuals may file returns even if they have no positive income tax liability or they are not required to file a return. Fifteen percent file returns to obtain refunds of income taxes that were overwithheld during the year.

Figure 6A-1. *Filing and Tax Thresholds Relative to Poverty Threshold*

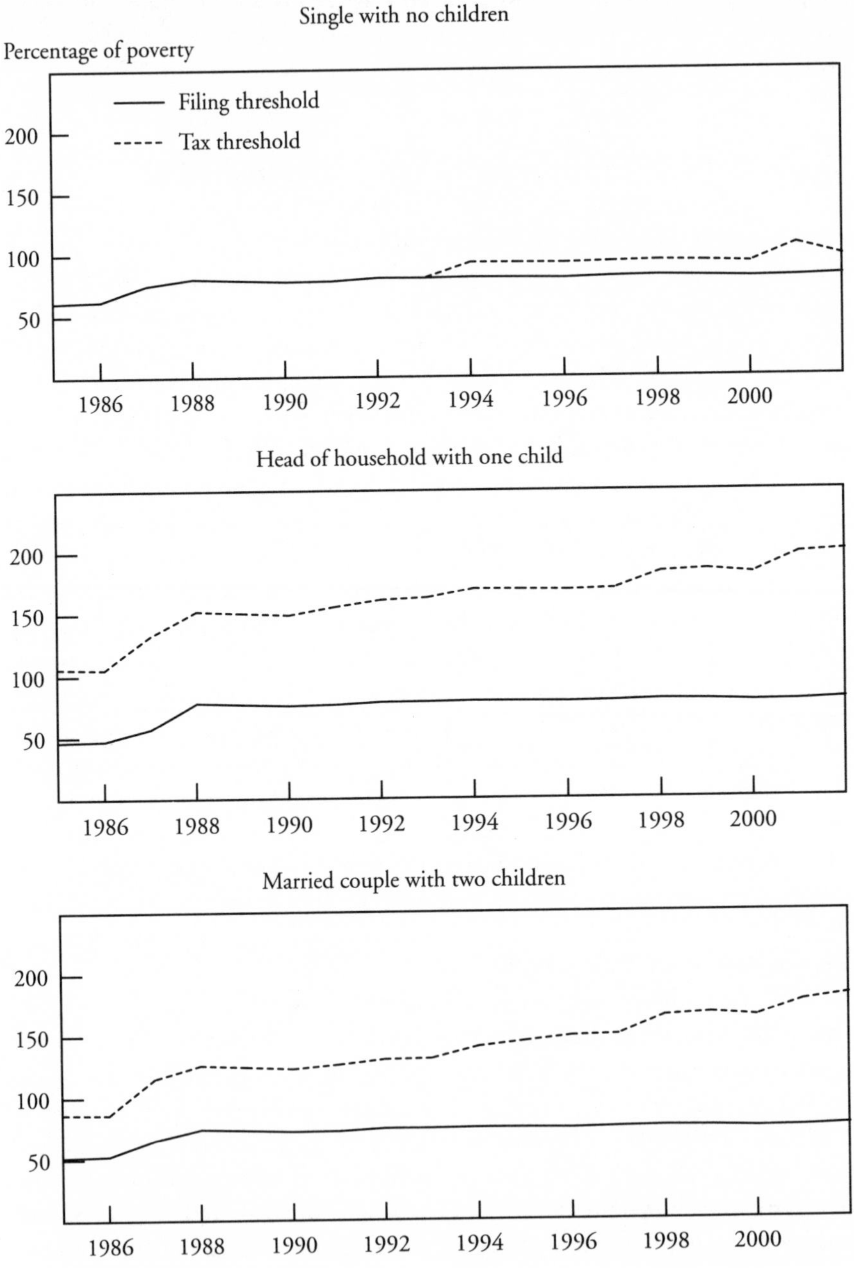

Single with no children

Head of household with one child

Married couple with two children

Source: Authors' computation based on tax parameters published in Internal Revenue Service, Instructions for Form 1040, various years. Poverty thresholds are at www.census.gov/hhes/poverty/threshold.html. Assumes wages are the sole source of income.

Table 6A-1. *Reason for Filing a Tax Return, Tax Year 2000*

Characteristics of filers	Total (percent)	Adjusted gross income under $30,000 (percent)ᵃ
Required to file		
Positive income tax liability before EITC	81.4	67.8
Self-employment taxes or special taxes	2.9	6.0
Income above the filing threshold	3.2	7.1
Required to file return for other reason	0.1	0.3
Subtotal: required to file	87.6	81.2
Other reason to file		
Refund of overwithheld taxes	10.1	14.8
EITC or additional child tax credit	0.6	1.5
Subtotal: other reason to file	10.7	16.3
Subtotal: required or reason to file	98.3	97.5
No apparent reason to file		
Not in any of preceding categories	1.7	2.5
Total	100.0	100.0

Source: Authors' calculations using 2000 Statistics of Income.
a. Returns with AGI under $30,000 do not include dependent filers.

Because a portion of the child tax credit (known as the additional child tax credit) and the EITC are refundable, low-income workers may find it advantageous to file returns and claim credits even if their income is below the filing and income tax thresholds. Most filers with income below $30,000, however, file returns either because they have a positive income tax liability or are required to file a return. Less than 2 percent file solely to obtain refundable tax credits.

When it comes to filing returns, low-income filers have options that many higher-income filers do not. Filers with less than $50,000 of taxable income (adjusted gross income less exemptions and deductions) may be eligible to use the simpler Forms 1040EZ or 1040A. To be eligible to use Form 1040EZ, taxpayers must be single or married, filing jointly, and have taxable income only from wages, salaries, tips, scholarships, unemployment compensation, and, if under $400, interest. Filers of the 1040EZ can claim the EITC, but only if they qualify for the small credit available to workers who do not reside with children. In 2000, 12 million nondependent filers with adjusted gross income less than $30,000 (22 percent of low-income filers) used the 1040EZ.

An additional 20 million low-income filers (36 percent of low-income filers) filed the 1040A form. More types of income can be reported on a Form 1040A, including income from pensions, IRAs, Social Security, interest, dividends, and certain capital gains distributions. Form 1040A filers may report deductions for IRA contributions and student loan interest deductions, as well as claim a number of tax benefits for families with children (for example, the EITC and the child tax credit).

Even though most low-income filers file 1040EZ or 1040A forms, over 24 million (42 percent of low-income filers) with adjusted gross income below $30,000 filed the more complicated 1040 form. In most cases, low-income filers used the 1040 form because they had income from a source not included on one of the simpler forms (for example, self-employment income) or claimed adjustments, credits, or deductions other than those found on the Form 1040EZ or 1040A. However, about 7 million filed the Form 1040 when, in fact, they could have used one of the two simpler forms.

Appendix 6B: Studies of Earned Income Tax Credit Participation

EITC participation rates are difficult to estimate, because no data set contains complete information on both taxpayers who are eligible for the EITC and taxpayers who claim the EITC. IRS data (particularly the EITC compliance studies) contain information on who claims the credit and which of those taxpayers are eligible to claim the credit. IRS data typically do not include information on individuals who do not file tax returns, who are likely to account for the large majority of EITC nonparticipants. Survey data, including the Survey of Income and Program Participation (SIPP) and the March interview for the Current Population Survey (CPS), include information about both persons who do and do not file tax returns. However, they do not include direct information about EITC eligibility. Rather, eligibility must be inferred from self-reported income and household characteristics, which may be subject to reporting errors.[1] Despite these difficulties, researchers using somewhat different data sets and methodologies consistently find that EITC participation rates are fairly high, ranging from about 75 to 86 percent.

Scholz uses SIPP data matched to tax returns to estimate EITC participation rates for tax year 1990.[2] He identifies 9.6 million EITC-eligible filing units. Scholz also computes two alternative estimates of EITC-eligible units to partially compensate for measurement problems in the SIPP. The first ignores the

1. In addition, census surveys may undercount certain populations that are likely to include low-income taxpayers: the homeless, migrant workers, and individuals who move frequently. Simulating EITC eligibility is also difficult because CPS and SIPP household and family units and income concepts are not the same as tax filing units and income tax definitions.
2. Scholz (1994).

support test in evaluating EITC eligibility.[3] Not surprisingly, this increases the estimated number of eligible units to 10.3 million. The second alternative measure uses adjusted gross income, earned income, filing status, and the presence of a dependent child as reported on tax returns matched to SIPP data to determine eligibility. (Eligibility for SIPP units that do not match to tax returns is simulated using the SIPP data only.) This increases the estimated number of eligible units to 10.1 million.[4]

Through filing year 1991 (tax year 1990), the IRS automatically computed the EITC for taxpayers who filed tax returns and appeared eligible for the credit (based on income, filing status, and dependents), even if they did not claim the credit. SIPP respondents were asked whether or not they filed a tax return. They were also asked to provide a Social Security number, and about 69 percent provided a valid number. Scholz assumes that SIPP respondents filed a return (and received the EITC) if a Social Security number for the unit matched a tax return or if the respondent reported filing a tax return. He estimates that 80.5 to 86.4 percent of eligible units claimed the EITC. The variation in the estimate is due to the alternative assumptions about EITC eligibility and about filing rates among taxpayers who did not provide a valid Social Security number or answer the SIPP question about tax return filing.[5]

The IRS uses both SIPP and CPS data to estimate the percentage of EITC-eligible taxpayers who filed a tax return for 1996.[6] Using publicly available CPS data, the IRS estimates that 17.9 million potential tax filing units were eligible for the EITC in 1996. The IRS is authorized to routinely provide certain tax return data to the Census Bureau. The IRS also provided the Census Bureau with a file identifying records of CPS respondents who appeared eligible for the

3. EITC eligibility in 1990 depended in part on the support test, and information on total income (including transfer payments and help from friends and family) and expenses may be mismeasured in the SIPP. In his initial estimate, Scholz assumes that taxpayers fail the support test if the sum of Aid to Families with Dependent Children and child support received by the respondent exceeds the sum of labor and capital income. In the alternative estimate, the support test is ignored, and respondents are assumed to have a qualifying child as long as the filing unit includes a child under age 18 or a child between the ages of 18 and 24 who appears to be a full-time student.

4. Note that this corrects for sources of income that are included in earned income and AGI for tax and EITC purposes but are not reported in the SIPP. However, if income is underreported on tax returns, this measure will tend to understate eligibility for very-low-income tax return filers and overstate eligibility for higher-income tax return filers. In addition, if taxpayers misreport filing status and dependents, EITC eligibility is likely to be overstated in the tax data.

5. In addition, Scholz computes two alternative measures of the number of eligible units that claimed the EITC. The first measure is the aggregate number of EITC claims filed for tax year 1990, reduced by the number of claims filed by ineligible taxpayers, estimated using 1988 TCMP data. By this measure, the participation rate was 85.0 to 89.1 percent. The second alternative measure uses a question in the SIPP about whether or not the respondent claimed the EITC. By this measure, the participation rate was 75 to 80 percent.

6. IRS (2002c).

EITC. Census used Social Security numbers reported by CPS respondents (but not included on publicly available CPS files) to match the tax return records to the CPS. Census then provided tabulations about matches (tax return filers) and nonmatches (nonfilers) back to the IRS. No Social Security numbers or CPS records matched to tax returns were provided to the IRS.

About 11.5 million EITC-eligible units were matched to tax returns, resulting in a 64.2 percent filing rate. Another 2.3 million EITC-eligible units provided a valid Social Security number that did not match to any tax return, yielding a 12.8 percent nonfiling rate.

The remaining 4.1 million CPS respondents, or 23.1 percent, either did not have a valid Social Security number or refused to provide a number to the CPS interviewer. It is not known whether these individuals filed a tax return. About 3.1 million of the individuals who did not provide a valid Social Security number were U.S. citizens, suggesting that they were eligible to receive the EITC and could have filed a tax return. The other 1.0 million individuals were not U.S. citizens. It is likely that many of these individuals were not authorized to work in the United States and were therefore not eligible to receive the EITC. If we assume that noncitizens who did not provide Social Security numbers were ineligible for the EITC, that citizens who did not provide Social Security numbers were eligible for the EITC, and that half the citizens who did not provide numbers nevertheless filed a tax return, then the estimated filing rate rises to about 77 percent. If we instead assume that half the noncitizens who did not provide a Social Security number were eligible for the EITC, and that two-thirds of those who did not provide a Social Security number did file a tax return, then the estimated filing rate would increase to 80 percent.

The IRS did not have SIPP data matched to tax returns for estimating the filing rate. However, SIPP respondents were asked whether they filed a tax return. The IRS used these responses to estimate that 73.5 percent of EITC-eligible taxpayers filed a return. The number of EITC-eligible units estimated from the SIPP is likely to include some individuals who did not have a valid Social Security number because they were not authorized to work in the United States and thus were ineligible for the EITC. Individuals without valid Social Security numbers may appear as filers, nonfilers, or nonrespondents to the filer question. (They are excluded from the known filer and known nonfiler groups in the CPS tabulations.) If some SIPP respondents were not eligible to receive the EITC, and if these individuals were less likely to report filing a return, then the true filing rate would be higher than 73.5 percent.

It is unclear whether the CPS or the SIPP measure is preferable. The CPS data are collected in March of the following tax year. They indicate whether a child resides with the respondent at the time of the interview but not whether the child resided with the respondent for over half the preceding year. The SIPP data are collected three times a year and therefore allow for a more careful measure of the length of time that a respondent and child reside together. Roemer and Coder and Scoon-Rogers find that the SIPP enumerates more wage earners and self-employed workers than the CPS.[7] This suggests that some very-low-income workers with sporadic labor force participation will appear to be eligible for the EITC in the SIPP but not in the CPS, and that the CPS would understate the size of the EITC population. On the other hand, to the extent that the CPS understates amounts of self-employment income and misses sources of unearned income (such as interest and unemployment compensation), the CPS might overstate the size of the EITC population. While the SIPP tends to identify more sources of income, it also yields lower estimated amounts of wages and unearned income. If the SIPP understates the amount of wages and unearned income reported (conditional on some positive amount reported), then more moderate-income workers might appear eligible for the EITC, when in fact they are not. It is difficult to assess the net effect of potential biases in the SIPP and CPS by making these aggregate comparisons, because income may be overreported or underreported, because both overreporting and underreporting can increase or decrease the estimated EITC, and because misreporting might vary across the income distribution.

Using data from the March 2000 Current Population Survey, the General Accounting Office estimates that there were 17.2 million EITC-eligible households in 1999.[8] The GAO obtained the number of eligible claimants—12.9 million—from the IRS's tax year 1999 EITC compliance study. Combining the two data sources, the GAO estimates a participation rate of 75 percent.[9]

The GAO participation rate estimates assume that all taxpayers who failed to appear for an audit were in fact not eligible for the credit, and this raises questions about the plausibility of the results. If we instead assume that taxpayers who failed to appear for an audit have the same compliance characteristics as similar EITC claimants who were audited, then the overall estimated participation rate would be 80.8 percent. Rates for different family sizes would range from 48.9 percent for taxpayers with no qualifying children to 100 percent for taxpayers with two children and 104 percent for taxpayers with one child.

Estimates in excess of 100 percent are obviously incorrect. The overestimate probably arises in part because taxpayers who fail to appear for an examination are more likely than similar taxpayers to be ineligible for the EITC (even though not all taxpayers who fail to appear for an examination are ineligible). The overestimates could also arise if some qualifying children are missed by the IRS, so that some families with three or more children are classified as families with one or two children (biasing participation rates for smaller families upward). In

---

7. Roemer (2000) and Coder and Scoon-Rogers (1996).

8. GAO (2001).

9. To the extent that some taxpayers who are not authorized to work in the United States appear to be eligible for the EITC in the CPS, the estimated participation rate is too low.

addition, errors in identifying EITC-eligible taxpayers in the CPS could bias the participation rate estimates.

Even though surveys may misidentify the EITC-eligible population, participation rate estimates might be fairly accurate if filing rates are measured accurately and if respondents who are erroneously included or excluded from the estimated population of EITC-eligible units have about the same filing rates as units correctly identified as eligible. Potential bias is more problematic in the case of the GAO estimate, where the numerator and denominator of the participation rate are obtained from different data sources. In that case, overestimates or underestimates of the size of the eligible population in the denominator will not be mitigated by similar mismeasurement in the numerator.

COMMENT BY
Leonard E. Burman

Janet Holtzblatt and Janet McCubbin have devoted their professional careers to trying to make the earned income tax credit (EITC) work. Nobody is better qualified to write about the burdens facing low-income people and the challenges facing tax administrators in trying to implement programs aimed at them.

The chapter considers a number of important issues related to low-income families affected by the tax system, including: the characteristics of taxpayers who must file tax returns solely to establish that they do not owe tax, the characteristics of taxpayers who file when it appears that they are not required to do so, special compliance burdens facing low-income tax filers, challenges in administering provisions affecting low-income tax filers, and evidence on noncompliance with provisions targeting low-income filers, especially the EITC.

Noncompliance

The chapter appropriately spends a great deal of time on the compliance and administrative issues related to the earned income tax credit. The EITC is the principal avenue for cash income support for low-income families in the United States. Noncompliance may represent as much as 30 percent of the cost of the program. Thus our assessment of the compliance problem and any solutions can materially affect the well-being of low-income tax filers.

The high rates of noncompliance are troubling, but it is hard to put them in context. As the chapter points out, it is likely, but not provable at present, that much EITC noncompliance reflects compliance problems that are endemic to the income tax. If that is true, then targeting compliance activity at EITC participants alone may not be the most effective use of IRS resources.

The IRS's current compliance initiative, which will for the first time since 1988 collect information about other than low-income taxpayers, should help resolve some of these issues.

EITC Noncompliance in Perspective

Holtzblatt and McCubbin use the data from the IRS's 1999 EITC compliance study to draw out some comparisons between EITC compliance and compliance with other tax provisions in definition of an eligible child. Of children claimed for both the EITC and the dependent exemption (97 percent of qualifying children claimed for EITC were also claimed as dependents), more tax filers failed the test for dependency status than the test for EITC-qualifying child. It is striking that one-third of children were claimed in error for the dependent exemption, the EITC, or both. However, while 6 percent qualified as a dependent but not as a qualifying child, 11 percent (almost twice as many) were eligible for qualifying-child status but not for a dependent exemption. An additional 17 percent of children were ineligible for both.

While this level of noncompliance with both provisions is troubling, the statistics only apply to low-income tax filers who claimed the EITC compliance program. These statistics raise the question of whether higher-income people have the same propensity to claim dependent exemptions for children who do not qualify. There is some historical evidence (from 1986) that people are prone to cheat with dependent exemptions when they think they can get away with it. In that year, seven million children disappeared when the IRS started requiring reporting of Social Security numbers to verify dependent exemptions.[1]

The ineluctable conclusion is that there are likely to be many dependents claimed incorrectly at all income levels—not just among the poor. Thus the relevant policy response would be to study compliance in the entire taxpaying population, not just among low-income people.

Another fascinating set of statistics drawn from the EITC compliance data relates to homemade marriage penalty relief. In 1999, 0.5 million people filed as head of household when they were actually married and living together, possibly to avoid EITC marriage penalties. Another 0.4 million filed as single when they should have claimed another (unspecified) status. Three-quarters of a million filed as head of household when they lived apart from their spouse for at least part of the year but were still married and should have filed as "married, filing jointly"

1. Graetz (1997).

or "married, filing separately." The obvious question is the extent to which this type of roll-your-own marriage penalty relief occurs among higher-income taxpayers (who often have a far greater incentive to misstate their filing status).

Some EITC recipients with income in or beyond the phase-out range of the credit underreported their income and thus increased their tax refund. Half the unreported income was from self-employment, consistent with ancient evidence from the Taxpayer Compliance Measurement Program that self-employment income is an area of rampant evasion. Again, while the noncompliance among EITC recipients is troubling, there is no reason to think that it is any worse than exists among the taxpaying public generally.

How Much Noncompliance Is Intentional?

A key question is how much of EITC noncompliance is intentional and how much inadvertent. If intentional tax evasion is rampant, then the solution is to increase enforcement. However, if a major source of noncompliance comes from taxpayer confusion, then education, assistance in preparing tax returns, and simplification of the tax law would be better-targeted policy responses.

The chapter reports evidence by McCubbin that at least 28 percent of qualifying-child errors are systematic and thus intentional attempts to overclaim the EITC.[2] Some of the remaining 72 percent may be influenced by other elements of the tax code, such as the dependent exemption. How many of the 72 percent are simply confused tax filers?

One approach would be to try deriving an instrument for taxpayer confusion to use in a model of determinants of errors. Chapter 6 hints at a potentially valuable source of information—people who do not claim the EITC but appear eligible. The IRS mailed notices to 194,000 taxpayers who appeared to be eligible for the EITC based on income and the presence of dependent children reported on their 1998 return. About one-third responded requesting the credit.[3] The people who only requested the credit after being notified by the IRS almost surely underclaimed the credit unintentionally.

To create the instrument, compare the postaudit tax return and demographic information about these confused taxpayers (after removing any who were found by the IRS to be ineligible) with similar information about those who claimed the credit and were eligible for it. One could estimate a probit model of confusion (that is, not filing when eligible) as a function of family status, income, and so forth, plus at least one instrument that is correlated with confusion but not the propensity to cheat. One possible instrument would be a

2. McCubbin (2000).
3. The IRS also sent 680,000 notices to low-wage single filers, notifying them that they appeared to be eligible. About 45 percent of them responded requesting the credit.

dummy variable for nonnative English speaker. If education is available, that might also be a useful instrument. Finally, people in states without income taxes may also be less likely to claim the EITC than those in states with income taxes. A dummy variable for those states could be included in the first-stage equation.

The fitted value from that first stage probit equation (estimated probability of confusion) could be used as an explanatory variable in an equation to determine the causes of nonsystematic errors. The coefficient could provide a measure of the extent of noncompliance due to confusion rather than cheating.

Addressing EITC Noncompliance

The chapter discusses some options to address noncompliance. It is a difficult policy issue, because there is a trade-off between administration and compliance costs on the one hand and targeting, compliance, and participation on the other. The question for policymakers is how to strike the right balance. The IRS could audit every return, which would minimize noncompliance but would maximize enforcement and compliance costs. At the other extreme the IRS could make all low-earning families eligible for EITC, without regard to children, which would also reduce noncompliance, but at tremendous cost in terms of tax revenues. In that context one might argue that the current system does not do a bad job of balancing out competing objectives.

The compliance problems with EITC may be viewed as comprising two parts, each of which has a specific policy implication: systemic problems and those specific to the EITC. There are errors and fraud that are endemic to the income tax, such as children claimed incorrectly, understated income, and incorrect filing status. The solution to that problem is system-wide enforcement, not a specific EITC compliance program. Indeed targeting scarce enforcement resources on low-wage returns to catch systemic noncompliance would be a highly inefficient audit strategy, because so much more money is at stake on the high-income returns.[4]

Certain errors are specific to the EITC. For example, a major factor in the 1999 data involves parents who violated the confusing AGI tiebreaker rule or were disqualified because of too much noncash earned income (such as pensions, parsonage benefits, and the like). In these cases Congress ultimately decided that the targeting rule was not worth the cost, and the rules were simplified to reduce chances of inadvertent errors.

A similar example is the inconsistent definition of *child* for different purposes. The Treasury Department has proposed rules to make the definitions

---

4. For example, consider the roll-your-own marriage penalty relief. The maximum marriage penalty under the EITC was about $4,200 in 2003. The maximum marriage penalty for high-income tax returns is almost $19,000.

more consistent and intuitive, although Congress has not yet acted on that proposal.[5] Further simplifications would be possible, such as automatically allowing dependents to be a qualifying child for EITC purposes so long as the other parent does not claim the child for the EITC. These simplifications all involve some cost in terms of tax revenues, but they would significantly reduce confusion for low-income working families that do not tend to think like tax lawyers.

Another promising approach is to enlist the help of those who prepare tax returns for low-income people. Almost two-thirds of EITC returns are prepared by paid preparers. As reported in the chapter, IRS statistics show that more-competent preparers—accountants, lawyers, enrolled agents, major tax preparation firms—produce returns with fewer errors than less-competent preparers. Volunteer tax preparers have the lowest error rate, although the sample is too small to draw firm inference. It is at least possible that spending more time on tax returns reduces the likelihood of errors. It is also possible, as noted in the chapter, that differences in performance among preparers reflect self-selection— that noncompliant taxpayers are more likely to seek the help of disreputable tax preparers—but this conjecture should be tested.

In 1999 the IRS initiated a large-scale outreach program aimed at tax return preparers who had recently prepared at least 100 EITC returns. During those visits, preparers (other than national firms, CPAs, lawyers, and enrolled agents) received one-on-one instruction from IRS agents on EITC compliance and preparers' due diligence responsibilities. Because most EITC claimants use paid preparers, such a strategy could prevent both unintentional and intentional errors on tax returns claiming the EITC. The value of this approach could be measured by comparing the accuracy of trained preparers with similar preparers who did not get training. However, no data are available yet, and it is not clear that the IRS followed up. If not, they lost an important opportunity to improve compliance without adding extra burdens for low-income taxpayers.

The other tool to improve compliance is to strengthen EITC enforcement. The administration's 2004 budget proposes significant new resources to create a precertification program for the EITC. This probably would improve compliance but also could significantly reduce participation and might not save the government much money. The paper reports that cash welfare programs cost about as much to administer as the EITC, including both the administration and compliance costs and the revenues lost due to noncompliance, but EITC participation is much higher than participation in direct transfer programs. The proposed precertification program is supposed to be nonintrusive, but it is not clear how the IRS is supposed to accomplish that. How can they determine that the residency requirement is met in advance, especially for households that are highly

---

5. U.S. Department of the Treasury, "Proposal for a Uniform Definition of a Qualifying Child," 2002 (www.ustreas.gov/press/releases/docs/child.pdf).

mobile? Eligibility for other benefits, such as head-of-household status and dependency exemption, theoretically requires extensive record-keeping, as demonstrated in the chapter. Resolving filing status errors would require fairly intrusive tests, which again might be hard to certify in advance. The fear among those who care about the EITC is that the precertification strategy is tantamount to a 100 percent audit rate (in advance) for some people who claim the EITC.[6]

Conclusion

The lion's share of the cost of administering low-income tax subsidies is the revenues lost to noncompliance, but we have no idea how large noncompliance in EITC and other low-income programs is, compared with noncompliance with higher-income tax provisions. The relatively high EITC noncompliance rate may be evidence either of systemic problems or of problems specific to the tax credit. As a result the IRS's proposed compliance research program, which will monitor noncompliance among the entire taxpaying population, is incredibly important.

COMMENT BY
Nina Olson

Janet Holtzblatt and Janet McCubbin present a comprehensive analysis of what we know about low-income filers and their sources of tax complexity and compliance burden, particularly in the context of the Earned Income Tax Credit. There is, of course, much that we do not know about low-income filers. For example, what are the most effective means of communication between these filers and the tax agency? Does the method differ depending on the message? And much of what we do know about EITC compliance is based on studies that I view as flawed, because they rely on IRS examiners and exam techniques that fail to take into account the financial and familial circumstances of low-income filers, two characteristics that the authors have identified as leading to a greater compliance burden. In many EITC examinations, the best one can conclude is that the taxpayer did not pass the examination, not that the taxpayer was not entitled to the credit. So our knowledge of low-income taxpayers and their compliance burden is incomplete, and this lack of completeness has consequences for all EITC studies.

6. Since this was written, the IRS announced details of their precertification program that confirm early concerns. See Robert Greenstein, "The New Procedures for the Earned Income Tax Credit," Center on Budget and Policy Priorities, 2003 (www.cbpp.org/5-20-03eitc2.pdf), for a discussion.

One of the most interesting observations by the authors is that most low-income filers who had adjusted gross income of less than $30,000 file for a reason other than obtaining refundable tax credits. This fact undermines one aspect of the argument for removing the EITC from the tax system. Because these taxpayers must file taxes for one reason or another regardless of the EITC, removing the EITC from the tax system would not completely eliminate the tax compliance burden for these taxpayers. Given the additional benefits identified by the authors, including ease of delivery and lack of stigma, coupled with the fact that the EITC alone does not impose the threshold burden of entering the tax system, one could reasonably conclude that it makes sense to leave the EITC in the tax system.

Both the EITC and the current family status rules present problems for the tax administrator and impose a compliance burden on the taxpayer. The authors have clearly described the complexity of the family status rules. While taxpayers of all income levels face these issues, the authors correctly point out that low-income taxpayers often have different family structures, which raise difficult eligibility questions. Low-income families also receive government benefits that complicate the determination of eligibility for family status tax provisions. Still, the family status rules are complex for all taxpayers. In fact the EITC definition of a qualifying child, which is based on relationship, residency, and age, is the least burdensome of all of the family status requirements and serves as the model for the uniform definition of a qualifying child.

So what sets low-income taxpayers apart from other taxpayers in dealing with these provisions? It is what happens to them once they are in the tax system; their inability to navigate it creates compliance burdens that are greater for this population than for others.

Here is what we know about the current approach to EITC administration.

—Low-income taxpayers generally do not have access to or cannot afford representation. Representation does have some positive effect on the outcome of a tax dispute.[1] Today there are only 136 low-income taxpayer clinics nationwide available to represent 400,000 potential clients who are selected annually for EITC examination.

—In service center (campus) correspondence examinations, which are what the IRS normally conducts for EITC or family status issues, the no-response rate is 28 percent.[2] The IRS does not know why taxpayers do not respond in correspondence examinations. In 2001 the IRS conducted a study of correspondence

1. A survey of all litigated cases involving tax issues in federal courts from June 1, 2001, to May 31, 2002, revealed that represented taxpayers prevailed in 26 percent of their cases, while taxpayers represented themselves ("pro se") in 15 percent of their cases. IRS (2002e, p. 253).

2. The total EITC no-response and undeliverable percentage rate is 35.4 (EITC Program Office, April 2003).

examination no-reply assessments. Unfortunately, when the IRS tried to explore in focus groups the reasons taxpayers did not respond, only 8 taxpayers out of a sample of 5,600 responded![3]

—Correspondence examinations are particularly ill-suited for obtaining information from low-income taxpayers. It was my experience, in representing low-income taxpayers, that I would have to make seven or eight contacts and follow-up calls before the taxpayer provided me with sufficient information to assist him or her. My experience is similar to that of virtually every other low-income taxpayer clinic. Low-income taxpayers need encouragement, direction, and other forms of assistance. They have so many basic survival demands in their lives, they are afraid of the IRS, they do not understand what is required and why, and, most difficult to overcome, they believe that, whatever they provide, it will not make any difference.[4] Clearly even eligible low-income taxpayers require handholding during an examination, particularly in light of the burdensome documentation required during the audit.[5] Yet standard IRS correspondence examination procedures require only two attempts to contact the taxpayer by telephone in order to obtain additional information.[6]

—If and when the taxpayer responds to the IRS examination, the documentation requests are often excessive and inflexible, particularly in light of the low-income taxpayer's financial and other circumstances. Box 6-1 outlines a recent case that was handled by the Taxpayer Advocate Service.

—In fiscal year 2002 the Taxpayer Advocate Service (TAS) closed 30,554 cases involving EITC revenue protection strategy (RPS) examinations, which represent 8 percent of total fiscal year 2002 EITC correspondence examination closures.[7] More than half the TAS EITC cases resulted in a change from the previous IRS position. This suggests that the 1999 EITC study overclaim rate may be overstated by at least 4 percentage points. The cases required 88.7 to 91.3 days, on average, in the Taxpayer Advocate Service for closure.[8]

The issues outlined above, and so well described in the authors' chapter, create burdens for both the taxpayer and the IRS. They lead the IRS to seek

3. The IRS was able to match telephone numbers for only 21 percent—or 5,600—taxpayers from an extract of 27,000 (IRS 2001).

4. The authors cite a GAO study that interviewed IRS examiners who refused to accept notarized statements from related day care providers, although the day care provider might be perfectly legitimate. There was no indication that such a notarized statement might be acceptable along with additional corroborative statements. There was also no acknowledgment that low-income taxpayers might disproportionately rely on related persons to provide day care or that it was a legitimate arrangement.

5. See also IRS (2002e, pp. 47–63).

6. Internal Revenue Manual 4.19.1.5.1.3.

7. Taxpayer Advocate Management Information System (TAMIS).

8. The IRS closed 367,811 EITC correspondence examinations in fiscal year 2002 (EITC Program Office, April 2003).

Box 6-1. *Taxpayer Assistance Order, EITC Examination*

August 15, 2001

Taxpayer Advocate Service received case. Taxpayer states that he submitted all requested information forty-five days ago and has received no response from examiner. Examiner's position is that the taxpayer has not met the support and residency test. Case was accepted into TAS as a systemic hardship case.

Background: Taxpayer timely filed 2000 tax return claiming head of household, one dependent, and EITC qualifying with one child. Return was selected for examination, and EITC refund check was frozen. Qualifying child is dependent; IRS records indicate no other individual claimed child as dependent or as qualifying child under IRC section 32. Taxpayer offered to forward documentation previously submitted to examiner to TAS.

August 16, 2001

Operation Assistance Request (OAR) was issued to examiner advising that the taxpayer had submitted all requested information and requested status of case. Response date: August 30, 2001.

August 18, 2001

TAS received via fax the following documentation from taxpayer:
    —copy of dependent's birth certificate;
    —Social Security card;
    —court documents granting taxpayer sole legal and physical rights and responsibilities for dependent child;
    —doctor's note indicating that taxpayer is primary caregiver for dependent child;
    —record of electric bill payments for six months;
    —statement from day-care provider indicating that taxpayer was guardian of the dependent child for all of 2000;
    —copy of homeowner's policy taxpayer carried on trailer with same address identified in property tax records. (Taxpayer lived in trailer but maintained address at his mother's house. He explained that this was due to vandals destroying mailboxes in front of his trailer. He has since opened a post office box to receive mail.)

August 25, 2001

Taxpayer contacted TAS advising that he received a notice of deficiency adjusting his filing status, exemptions, and the EITC. Examiner claimed documentation submitted was insufficient to meet support and residency test.

August 30, 2001

TAS received response to OAR from examination indication the following:
    —Note from doctor was insufficient because it did not provide taxpayer's address of record and dates the child was seen in 2000.
    —Taxpayer needs to provide verification of mortgage payments.

August 31, 2001

TAS contacted taxpayer to secure additional documentation required by examiner. Taxpayer indicated that the doctor will not provide any additional information. TAS recommended securing notarized statements verifying that the child lived with him for more than half the year.

September 7, 2001

Taxpayer provided the following additional information:

—affidavit from bank verifying taxpayer paid mortgage for all of 2000 and statement from the bank loan officer indicating she had been at the home of the taxpayer and saw the dependent child there;

—notarized statements from three individuals indicating that the child lived with the taxpayer and he supported the dependent child.

September 8, 2001

OAR was issued to examiner recommending acceptance of additional documentation provided by taxpayer to allow original return as filed and to release refund. Response date: September 15, 2001.

September 9, 2001

Local Taxpayer Advocate (LTA) reviewed case file and considered taxpayer documentation to be sufficient. If examiner does not accept documentation, next step is to issue a Review TAO.

September 15, 2001

TAS received response to OAR from examination indicating they will not accept notarized statement from neighbors or friends; they must be from disinterested third party.

TAS contacted exam manager regarding notarized statements. He suggested getting a letter from social services verifying that the child lived with the taxpayer.

TAS contacted taxpayer to suggest obtaining letter from social services.

September 20, 2001

TAS received letter from state agency of human services verifying that the child lived with the taxpayer and faxed it to exam manager for consideration.

September 21, 2001

Examiner will not accept letter because it does not state that the child lived at the taxpayer's address in 2000.

September 22 through November 25, 2001

TAS continued efforts to obtain documentation requested by examiner to substantiate the support and residency test, even though the LTA already determined that the documentation submitted was sufficient.

November 26, 2001

Review TAO was issued to director of Compliance Services, requesting reconsideration of EITC denial.

December 5, 2001

Examiner complied with Review TAO and allowed the EITC.

third-party data and other indicators that can serve as proxies for eligibility. This approach is only helpful if the original data source is itself accurate. Otherwise the IRS will get false negatives and impose additional burden on eligible taxpayers. The age or accuracy of the data can, to some extent, be ameliorated by creating a hierarchy of data that takes into account the degrees of accuracy of third-party data. A flag based on one data source may be a definitive indicator of ineligibility; another data source may only be used as a corroborator of other data or as an indicator of the need for additional investigation. And of course one must ask how much data on any one person the government should process and store annually. Do we really want our tax administration system to routinely collect or compile certain types of personal information?

The use of third-party databases raises the question of whether the IRS will use its summary assessment authority under IRC section 6213(b) for math errors, with respect to proposed adjustments arising from those data. The use of math error authority—which assesses the tax without first providing the taxpayer the ability to petition the United States Tax Court—is appropriate only where the adjustment is quantitative, not qualitative, in nature.[9] As the IRS looks to third-party databases as a means to identify EITC and other errors, the reduction in taxpayer burden (by avoiding an examination or other postfiling activity) will be undermined, if math error authority is used in conjunction with databases that are merely indicators for questions that essentially require a facts-and-circumstances analysis.

The authors do an excellent job of showing the complexity and compliance burden that certain tax law provisions, most notably the EITC, impose on low-income taxpayers. They also identify and briefly discuss some of the alternatives to administering the EITC through the tax system. The EITC does bedevil the tax administration system. The continuing focus on EITC compliance masks significant issues that low-income taxpayers face on a daily basis, including worker classification issues and cancellation of indebtedness income. Because the EITC is both a social benefit program and a tax program, it generates an uneasy tension between social welfare advocates and the tax administrator. The former are often not knowledgeable about legitimate concerns regarding equity, efficiency, and administrability of the income tax laws; the latter is inflexible and unwilling to bend tax administration procedures to take into account the known characteristics of the EITC population.[10] Until each constituency recognizes and is willing to accommodate the legitimate concerns of both parties, low-income taxpayers will continue to be poorly served.

9. IRS (2002e, pp. 185–99).

10. The IRS routinely designs examination procedures with respect to the particular characteristics of large and midsize taxpayers. Limited Issue Focused Exam, or L.I.F.E., is a recent example of such taxpayer-specific approaches.

References

Arthur D. Little. 1988. *Development of Methodology for Estimating the Taxpayer Paperwork Burden.* Report to the Department of the Treasury, Internal Revenue Service (June).

Berube, Alan, and others. 2002. "The Price of Paying Taxes: How Tax Preparation and Refund Loan Fees Erode the Benefits of the EITC." Brookings (May).

Blumenthal, Marsha, and Joel Slemrod. 1992. "The Compliance Cost of the U.S. Individual Income Tax System." *National Tax Journal* 45 (2): 185–202.

Cilke, James. 1994. The Treasury Individual Tax Model. Mimeo. Department of the Treasury, Office of Tax Analysis.

Coder, John, and Lydia Scoon-Rogers. 1996. "Evaluating the Quality of Income Data Collected in the Annual Supplement to the March Current Population Survey and the Survey of Income and Program Participation." Working Paper 215. Bureau of the Census, Department of Commerce (July).

Cunnyngham, Karen. 2002. "Trends in Food Stamp Participation Rates: 1994 to 2000." Report to Food and Nutrition Services, Department of Agriculture. Washington: Mathematica Policy Research (June).

Erard, Brian. 1993. "Taxation with Representation: An Analysis of the Role of Tax Practitioners in Tax Compliance." *Journal of Public Economics* 52 (2): 163–97.

Graetz, Michael. 1997. *The Decline (and Fall?) of the Income Tax.* W. W. Norton.

Holtzblatt, Janet. 2000. "Choosing between Refundable Tax Credits and Spending Programs." *Proceedings of the 93rd Annual Conference on Taxation.* Washington: National Tax Association.

Liebman, Jeffrey B. 1995. "Noncompliance and the Earned Income Tax Credit: Taxpayer Error or Taxpayer Fraud?" Economics Department, Harvard University (December).

———. 2001. "Who Are the Ineligible Earned Income Tax Credit Recipients?" In *Making Work Pay: The Earned Income Tax Credit and Its Impact on America's Families,* edited by Bruce D. Meyer and Douglas Holtz-Eakin, 274–98. New York: Russell Sage Foundation.

McCubbin, Janet. 2000. "EITC Noncompliance: The Determinants of the Misreporting of Children." *National Tax Journal* 53 (4): 1135–64.

O'Brien, Doug, and others. 2000. "The Red Tape Divide: State-by-State Review of Food Stamp Applications." Chicago: America's Second Harvest.

Ponza, Michael, and others. 1999. "Customer Service in the Food Stamp Program." Report to Food and Nutrition Services, Department of Agriculture. Washington: Mathematica Policy Research (July).

Roemer, Marc I. 2000. "Assessing the Quality of the March Current Population Survey and the Survey of Income and Program Participation Income Estimates, 1990–1996." Bureau of the Census (July 16).

Rosenbaum, Dorothy, and David Super. 2001. "Understanding Food Stamp Quality Control." Washington: Center on Budget and Policy Priorities (April).

Scholz, John Karl. 1994. "The Earned Income Tax Credit: Participation, Compliance, and Antipoverty Effectiveness," *National Tax Journal* 47 (1): 63–85.

Smith, Kristin. 2002. "Who's Minding the Kids? Child Care Arrangements: Spring 1997." *Current Population Reports,* P70-86, U.S. Census Bureau.

U.S. Congress Joint Committee on Taxation. 2001. *Study of the Overall State of the Federal Tax System and Recommendations for Simplification Pursuant to Section 8022(3)(B) of the Internal Revenue Code of 1986.* JCS-3-01 (April).

U.S. Department of Agriculture, Food and Nutrition Service. 1999. *Current Population Survey Analysis of NSLP Participation and Income.* Nutrition Assistance Program Report Series (October).

———. 2001. *Eligibility Guidance for School Meals Manual.* (August).

U.S. General Accounting Office. 1995. *Earned Income Credit, Noncompliance and Potential Eligibility Revisions.* Testimony of Lynda D. Willis before the Senate Finance Committee (June 8). GAO/T-GGD-95-179.

———. 1996. *Earned Income Credit: IRS' 1995 Controls Stopped Some Noncompliance, but Not without Problems.* GAO/GGD-96-172.

———. 1997. *Tax Administration Earned Income Credit Noncompliance.* Testimony of Lynda D. Willis before the House Committee on Ways and Means (May 8). GAO/T-GGD-97-105.

———. 1999. *Food Stamp Program: Various Factors Have Led to Declining Participation.* GAO/RCED-99-185.

———. 2001. *Earned Income Tax Credit Eligibility and Participation.* GAO-02-0290R.

———. 2002. *Earned Income Credit: Opportunities to Make Recertification Program Less Confusing and More Consistent.* GAO/GGD-02-449.

U.S. House of Representatives, Committee on Ways and Means. 1997. *Hearing on the Internal Revenue Service's 1995 Earned Income Tax Credit Compliance Study.* Serial 105-26 (May 8).

U.S. Internal Revenue Service. 1985. *Statistics of Income Bulletin.* Publication 1136 (Winter 1984–85).

———. 2001. *Study of Service Center Correspondence Examination No Reply Assessments.* Project Report 2.08 (April).

———. 2002a. *Earned Income Tax Credit (EITC) Program Effectiveness and Program Management* (www.irs.gov/pub/irs-utl/eitcprogeff_progmgmt.pdf).

———. 2002b. *Compliance Estimates for Earned Income Tax Credit Claimed on 1999 Returns* (www.irs.gov/pub/irs-soi/compeitc.pdf).

———. 2002c. *Participation in the Earned Income Tax Credit Program for Tax Year 1996.* Fiscal Year 2001 Research Project 12.26 (January).

———. 2002d. "Cost-of-Living Adjustments for 2003." Rev. Proc. 2002-70. *Internal Revenue Bulletin* 2002-46.

———. 2002e. *National Taxpayer Advocate FY 2002 Annual Report to Congress.* Publication 2104 (rev. 12-02).

Yin, George K., and Jonathan Barry Forman. 1993. "Redesigning the Earned Income Tax Credit Program to Provide More Effective Assistance for the Working Poor." *Tax Notes* 59 (7): 951–60.

7

MARSHA BLUMENTHAL
CHARLES CHRISTIAN

Tax Preparers

T HE USE OF tax preparers by individual income taxpayers grew by 26.4 percent over the past decade, compared to an overall growth of 13.7 percent in the number of returns filed. Table 7-1 documents the growth by return type over the past decade. It contains the latest statistics available for the 2001 filing season (January 1 through August 30, 2002) compared to the comparable period for 2000. It shows that 59.4 percent of the 128 million individual income tax returns filed for tax year 2001 were signed by a preparer. For filers of the standard Form 1040, two-thirds of all returns were signed by a preparer, and for electronically filed returns almost three-fourths were signed by a preparer. Perhaps more striking is the fact that 21.1 percent of the 10.5 million Form 1040EZ returns, the simplest individual return, were signed by a paid preparer, and the percentage is growing rapidly. That represents over two million taxpayers who use a preparer to file the single-page Form 1040EZ.

In this chapter we explore practitioner use from the perspectives of taxpayers, tax practitioners, and tax administrators. We consider what motivates taxpayers to hire practitioners and review what is known about the characteristics of those who do. We also explore who provides tax preparation services and what we know about their impact on taxpayers and tax revenue. Finally we discuss why

We gratefully acknowledge the comments and suggestions of our discussants, Peggy Hite and Gerry Padwe. We also appreciate comments from Don Goldman, Sanjay Gupta, Steve Kaplan, and Ker-Wei Pei of Arizona State University, and an insightful discussion on electronic filing with Robert Weinberger of H&R Block. We also thank Tom Petska and Mike Strudler, of the Internal Revenue Service's Statistics of Income Division, and Richard Hinkemeyer, of the IRS's Office of Electronic Tax Administration, for providing current statistics.

Table 7-1. *Tax Returns Filed with Paid Preparer Signature, 1990–2001*

Year	1040	1040A	1040EZ	Electronic[a]	Total
1990	49,049	4,801	648	. . .	54,498
1995	52,447	4,754	1,760	. . .	58,961
1998	61,611	4,239	701	. . .	66,551
1999	64,743	3,746	761	. . .	69,250
2000	63,778	4,138	950	. . .	68,866
2000 percent	65.4	31.9	18.0	74.8	57.5
Change, 1999–2000					
(percent)	30.0	–13.8	46.6		26.4
2001 percent	66.5	34.4	21.1	73.2	59.4
Change (percent)	1.6	7.6	17.3	–2.2	3.3

Source: U.S. Internal Revenue Service (2002a, table 23; 2002b).

a. Excluding TeleFile; no data for some years.

tax administrators might regulate practitioners and review the mechanisms for doing so. In that context we look at the current IRS initiatives for electronic filing and also present evidence suggesting that a tax administration's audit policy can affect the proportion of practitioner-prepared returns.

The evidence is clear that taxpayers use practitioners to reduce uncertainty and to save time and effort. The evidence also suggests that practitioners affect taxpayer compliance, but the effect depends on a variety of factors. Compelling evidence exists, in the words of Klepper and Nagin, that practitioners "contribute to compliance by enforcing legally clear requirements and contribute to noncompliance by taking advantage of ambiguous requirements."[1] It is not clear that this finding holds for all types of practitioners.

From the tax administrator's perspective, little evidence exists on the differential effects on practitioners of regulation versus reward. While it is clear that penalties assessed on practitioners have the desirable effect of reducing their aggressive reporting recommendations, it has yet to be seen how effective rewards are in engaging practitioners' help to promote electronic filing. Therefore it is difficult to make policy recommendations.

However, recent experimental evidence is consistent with the prediction that increased enforcement in the form of audit notices does increase practitioner usage. That leads to the recommendation that tax administrators carefully consider the impact of enforcement policies on preparer usage because of the increase in costs to taxpayers and the potential detrimental impact on compliance.

1. Klepper and Nagin (1989, p. 190).

Taxpayer Perspective

Researchers posit two explanations for the use of practitioners, both of which flow from the length and the complexity of the Internal Revenue Code. The first explanation is that taxpayers hire practitioners to determine the amount of tax due. In other words, practitioners help reduce the uncertainty surrounding true tax liability: Can I claim Aunt Sally as my dependent? Am I qualified for the earned income tax credit? May I file as a head of household? Taxpayers also depend on practitioners to identify strategies that reduce their tax liability. While some taxpayers (and perhaps some practitioners) may stretch this into evasion, that is not necessarily so, because the code is complex enough that much of this activity is legitimate.

The second explanation is that taxpayers hire practitioners to avoid spending personal time on tax preparation. A complex code and long forms impose a burden that an experienced, trained practitioner can bear with less time and effort than a taxpayer. For these services, taxpayers willingly pay fees. As one element of taxpayers' compliance costs, one might well wonder about the magnitude of preparation fees.

One study of individual income tax compliance costs, conducted after the Tax Reform Act of 1986, estimated that taxpayers hiring practitioners spent, on average, $132 in preparation fees.[2] A more recent estimate, for the 18.1 million taxpayers who engaged H&R Block during the 2002 filing season, is an average of $122 for tax return preparation and related services, totaling over $2 billion.[3] H&R Block prepares almost one-fourth of all practitioner returns. Their average fees suggest that total fees for practitioner-prepared returns could approach $10 billion annually, or approximately 1 percent of the individual income tax liability. Because H&R Block is not representative of all taxpayers, average fees paid by their clients may well be lower than for a more general taxpayer population.

If the motivation for hiring a practitioner is based on the complexity of the tax code, then one would expect that taxpayers with either more intricate tax situations or less tax knowledge would be more likely to use practitioners. In fact, consistent empirical evidence shows that taxpayers who are self-employed, older, or less educated hire practitioners more frequently.[4] Taxpayers with more complex

---

2. Blumenthal and Slemrod (1992).

3. "H&R Block Reports Record Tax Season Results," press release, May 1, 2002.

4. Slemrod and Sorum (1984) and Collins, Milliron, and Toy (1990) collected data from surveys of taxpayers; Long and Caudill (1987, 1993) and Erard (1990) gathered data from tax returns. Both data sources are subject to bias. Survey data may be biased by inaccurate or incomplete taxpayer recall. Tax return data are less rich—few demographic variables are recorded in tax data (age, for example) and these so-called omitted variables may be correlated with the variables that are included in the data (employment status, for example). Such correlations complicate and potentially bias the statistical analysis.

returns have also been found to use practitioners with greater frequency and to pay higher fees.[5]

At issue is whether taxpayers with greater income or with higher marginal tax rates (MTR) are more likely to hire a practitioner. Because income level and marginal tax rate are strongly correlated, it is difficult to separate their effects statistically. In one study using 1983 tax returns, practitioner use is positively associated with income level and marginal tax rate, ostensibly because high-MTR taxpayers would have more to gain from a practitioner's expertise.[6] In another study, using 1982 Taxpayer Compliance Measurement Program (TCMP) data, no such association was found; on the other hand, certain occupations (for example, chief executive or elected official) were associated with practitioner use.[7] Yet a third study, also using 1982 TCMP data, found that taxpayers with sole proprietorship or farm income use preparers more, and that, within each income source, paid preparers were hired more as income rises.[8]

Confirmation of many of these associations may be found in the results of a controlled field experiment in Minnesota, discussed in detail later. Practitioner use in a random sample of income tax returns was significantly and positively associated with income in excess of $100,000, being married or over 65, and filing Schedules A (itemized deductions), B (interest and dividend income), C (business income), D (capital gains), E (rents and royalties), F (farm income), and ES (estimated tax). Taxpayers with higher marginal tax rates were significantly less likely to use a practitioner. As an example of the magnitude of the influences at the margin, the probability of using a practitioner (a number between 0 and 1) was 0.13 higher for taxpayers choosing to itemize deductions on their 1993 returns, relative to nonitemizing taxpayers. In this study, high income and Schedules C, E, and F had particularly large positive marginal effects.[9]

Practitioner Perspective

The practitioner community is composed of a wide range of businesses and individuals, including attorneys and certified public accountants. Although national tax services, including H&R Block, do prepare a large number of returns, the majority of taxpayers using practitioners do not choose national services, attorneys, or CPAs. They choose other paid practitioners, a group that

5. Erard (1990); Lin (1993); Christian, Gupta, and Lin 1993.

6. Long and Caudill (1993).

7. Erard (1990). The Taxpayer Compliance Measurement Program (TCMP) was an IRS research program based on an intensive line-by-line audit of a random sample of income tax returns.

8. Klepper and Nagin (1989).

9. Complete results of the weighted probit estimation are available from the authors.

includes enrolled agents and general tax preparers, as can be seen from the following statistics:[10]

—Other paid, 52 percent

—CPA, 29 percent

—National tax service, 17 percent

—Attorney, 2 percent

A number of researchers have studied the impact of practitioners on taxpayers and tax agencies, both theoretically and empirically. We begin with the theoretical work, which divides into two strands. In one strand, practitioners allow taxpayers to reduce the uncertainty surrounding their true tax liabilities. In the other strand, practitioners provide tax-preparation services more efficiently than can taxpayers.

Reducing Uncertainty

In theoretical models where taxpayers are uncertain of their true taxable income and face penalties if discovered underreporting, using a practitioner to resolve some uncertainty generally benefits taxpayers.[11] If taxpayers are averse to the risk of an audit, they report more income as their uncertainty rises. Hence, as uncertainty is resolved, the income they report and the taxes they pay both decline.[12] Of course this implies that the tax agency is worse off when taxpayers use practitioners (in other words, that the tax agency is better off when taxpayers are imperfectly informed). In part this is because fines are asymmetric: A dollar of income overreported by a poorly informed taxpayer is worth more to the tax agency than a dollar of underreported income (discovered upon audit and fined) is costly to the taxpayer. In our view, this result also depends on a crucial assumption, namely that the tax agency's objective is to maximize revenue. In contrast the IRS often claims that its objective is to collect the correct amount of tax. To the extent that practitioners help taxpayers resolve their uncertainty so that their returns are more accurate, the tax agency may gain.

Providing Services

In this strand of research, taxpayers who are not averse to risk are assumed to have full knowledge of their true income and the tax law. It is also assumed that taxpayers hire practitioners to reduce the time and effort they spend preparing their returns and to procure expert support in the event of an audit. If we look at taxation as a game, practitioners move first by setting their fees, and taxpayers move

---

10. Based on 1988 TCMP; Christian (1994, table 7).

11. Scotchmer (1989a, 1989b); Beck and Jung (1989).

12. In a model where taxpayers are not averse to audit risk, Beck and Jung (1989b) still conclude that taxpayers benefit from hiring practitioners.

next by deciding whether to hire practitioners and how much of their true income to report. The tax agency has the final move, choosing the probability of audit in order to maximize its revenues (net of enforcement costs). There are penalties on underreported income, both for the taxpayer and for the practitioner, if one is used. In the game's equilibrium, the probability of audit decreases as taxpayer income reports rise, but it increases as the tax rate, penalty rates, and true income increase. The income reports of self-filing taxpayers rise with the costs of responding to an audit. Of particular interest, the tax agency will devote more enforcement to a practitioner-prepared return than to a self-filed return with the same amount of reported income. This result follows from the higher penalty revenue the tax agency earns (per dollar of underreported income) on practitioner-prepared returns.[13]

In addition to this theoretical literature, which seems to suggest that taxpayers may have more to gain from using practitioners than a tax agency, empirical work explores the effects of practitioner use on taxpayer compliance in actual practice. One measure of compliance that researchers have used to study audited (TCMP) returns is the voluntary reporting percentage (VRP) of particular line items. The VRP is the ratio of the amount reported by the taxpayer to the amount determined to be correct by the IRS auditor. Using 1982 TCMP data, Klepper and Nagin found the VRP of practitioner-prepared returns to be significantly higher than the VRP of self-filed returns on line items for supplemental capital gains, partially taxable pensions, moving expenses, and paid alimony.[14] On the other hand, practitioner-prepared returns showed significantly lower VRPs than self-prepared returns on line items for proprietor's income, rent, royalty and partnership income, casualty and theft losses, and the dependency exemption for parents.

Hypothesizing that the direction of a preparer's influence (whether positive or negative with respect to compliance) depends on how ambiguous a line item is in the code, Klepper and Nagin seek to measure the relative ambiguity of different line items. Their two ambiguity measures are the number of revenue rulings and whether the item requires the taxpayer to impute a monetary value. Line items with the highest number of revenue rulings include rent, royalty and partnership income, casualty and theft losses, and business income. Those involving the most substantial imputation include casualty and theft losses. Thus their VRP results are consistent with the hypothesis that paid preparers have a negative compliance effect on the most ambiguous line items and a positive compliance impact on the least ambiguous line items: Practitioners thus are rule enforcers but ambiguity exploiters.

13. Reinganum and Wilde (1991).
14. Klepper and Nagin (1989).

Additional evidence of the influence of preparers on taxpayer compliance is reported by these researchers in the context of a successful 1984 Pennsylvania initiative to increase enforcement of the state's estimated tax payment rules.[15] They find a statistically significant positive impact of preparers on the probability of a liable-tax payer becoming an estimated-tax payer. This supports their hypothesis that preparers play a procompliance, informational role, promoting changes in the priorities of a tax agency.[16]

In another study of the impact of practitioners on taxpayer compliance, Erard used 1979 TCMP data and differentiated between practitioners who are CPAs or lawyers and all other practitioners.[17] His work attempts to control for the possibility that a taxpayer's preparation mode choice (CPA or lawyer, other practitioner, or self) is influenced by the sorts of evasion opportunities that result from the choice. For example, a taxpayer may choose to hire a CPA because he believes he will have better opportunities to evade successfully with a CPA than with other practitioners or by self-preparing. If many taxpayers make their preparation decisions in this way, then taxpayers who use CPAs will be less compliant. This will not be so because practitioners counsel them to evade but rather because these taxpayers have an underlying predilection to evade, relative to taxpayers who either use other practitioners or self-prepare. Eliminating this influence and assuming instead that taxpayers are randomly assigned to a preparation mode, Erard finds that noncompliance would be greater among those self-preparers with business or farm income; returns for taxpayers using a CPA or lawyer would be more noncompliant when, in addition to business or farm income, there are capital gains, rents, or royalties. Strikingly, if a taxpayer randomly assigned to self-prepare her return were to switch and use a CPA or lawyer, noncompliance would increase by a factor of about 4.5. In contrast the noncompliance of a taxpayer switching from randomly assigned self-preparation mode to some other kind of practitioner would increase only 15 percent.

In a series of simulations, Erard then demonstrates that both the predicted frequency and the level of income underreporting rise with income and return complexity, regardless of preparation mode. Furthermore he finds that the highest predicted mean level of noncompliance occurs in CPA- or lawyer-prepared returns, and the lowest predicted mean level occurs in self-prepared returns. These results suggest that some practitioners may have a substantial anticompliance effect, once we control for the underlying inclinations of taxpayers to engage in evasion.

15. Under this system, taxes on quarterly estimated income must be paid during the year in advance of filing.
16. Klepper and Nagin (1989).
17. Erard (1993).

For low-income filers, there is more recent evidence of the correspondence between practitioner usage and compliance. Looking at returns claiming the earned income tax credit, as reported by Holtzblatt and McCubbin in chapter 6 of this volume, the 1999 overclaim rate among taxpayers whose returns identify a paid practitioner was 34.6 percent, while the overclaim rate among presumably self-preparing taxpayers was 37.8 percent. Interestingly, when the practitioner was a lawyer, a CPA, an enrolled agent, or a nationally recognized tax preparation service, the overclaim rate was 25.2 percent. In contrast the overclaim rate for "other" paid practitioners was 36.2 percent.

Tax Administrator Perspective

Both the theoretical and the empirical work described above offer ample motivation for tax administrators to care about whether taxpayers use practitioners and, to the extent that they do, to regulate them. In a nutshell, tax administrators care about practitioner usage because practitioners influence the amount of tax revenue raised; they want to regulate practitioner usage in order to increase taxpayer compliance. Taxpayers who are confused about their true tax liabilities are more likely to overreport than when, using practitioners, they are more fully informed. Some taxpayers may choose to use practitioners in order to obtain greater opportunities for evasion. In this section we first explore the regulations available to the IRS in directly managing practitioner behavior and discuss several current regulatory issues. Then we provide an example of how, in the complex interactions between taxpayers, practitioners, and tax administrators, a policy initiative not aimed at regulating practitioners might still encourage or discourage practitioner use, therefore generating unintended, indirect effects.

Regulating Practitioners

While, as an industry, tax return preparation is largely unregulated, practitioners are subject to both civil and criminal penalties. The Tax Reform Act of 1976 instituted penalties for preparers who understated a taxpayer's tax liability through negligent or intentional disregard of rules and regulations. "Historically, negligence meant the lack of due care or failure to do what a reasonable and prudent person would do under the circumstances." The IRS also may impose criminal sanctions on practitioners who engage in fraud. In the three-year period ending September 30, 2001, the IRS Criminal Investigation Division initiated 468 investigations. Of the resulting 291 indictments, there were 283 convictions, resulting in 263 incarcerations.[18]

---

18. Mathews and Davidson (2002, p. 2).

In 1989 Congress enacted the Improved Penalty Administration and Compliance Tax Act.[19] This act increased the penalties where the refund "is due to a position for which there was not a realistic possibility of being sustained on its merits,"
and the preparer of the return or claim "knew (or reasonably should have known)
of such a position . . . [which] was not disclosed . . . or was frivolous."

In this environment, there is an important distinction between types of practitioners: those who can practice before the IRS and those who cannot. Although all are subject to the penalties provided by the Internal Revenue Code
for fraudulent returns, little if any regulation exists for who may prepare a
return. On the other hand, all professional practitioners, including attorneys,
certified public accountants, enrolled agents, actuaries, and appraisers, do agree
to abide by professional practice standards and codes of ethics issued by their
organizations.[20]

Extensive governmental regulation does exist, however, for those who may
practice before the IRS. At present the practice rules governing these practitioners are contained in Circular 230.[21] The document also establishes the office
of the director of practice within the Department of the Treasury. The primary
responsibility of the director is to act "on applications for enrollment to practice
before the Internal Revenue Service; . . . institutes and provides for the conduct
of disciplinary proceedings relating to attorneys, certified public accountants,
enrolled agents, enrolled actuaries, and appraisers."[22] It is not clear how Circular 230 applies to employees of taxpayers.

What constitutes practice before the IRS is a matter of some debate. According to Circular 230, practice "comprehends all matters connected with a pres-
entation to the Internal Revenue Service or any of its officers or employees relating to a taxpayer's rights, privileges, or liabilities under laws or regulations
administered by the Internal Revenue Service. Such presentations include, but
are not limited to, preparing and filing documents, corresponding and communicating with the Internal Revenue Service, and representing a client at conferences, hearings, and meetings."[23]

It is unclear whether the IRS has adequately enforced these penalties. In 1991
the General Accounting Office conducted a study that concluded that preparer
penalties were not assessed unless more than $5,000 in taxes was owed. They also
concluded that preparers subject to penalty were not routinely referred to the
Treasury's director of practice or the IRS district director, as required by law.[24]

19. P.L. 101-239 sec. 7732[a][a].
20. For example, the American Institute of Certified Public Accountants has a Code of Professional Conduct, as well as an enforceable Statement on Standards for Tax Services.
21. *Code of Federal Regulations* 31, part 10, effective date July 26, 2002, hereafter Circular 230.
Federal Register 67 (144), pp. 48760–80.
22. Circular 230, part 10.2, p. 48766.
23. Circular 230, part 10.1, p. 48766.
24. GAO (1991).

Recently Circular 230 was amended. A final set of new regulations was published in the *Federal Register* on July 25, 2002, as "Regulations Governing Practice before the Internal Revenue Service."[25] It includes new requirements for practitioners that address a dozen areas of practice, effective July 25, 2002. Two of the more important new requirements provide that practitioners identify the person in possession or control of requested documents by imposing a duty to make reasonable inquiry of the practitioner's client, and that they return a client's records that are necessary for a client to comply with federal tax obligations, regardless of a fee dispute. The new regulations also include an additional sanction of "censure," defined as a public reprimand.

While the 2002 amendment to Circular 230 does not include the new regulations on tax shelter opinions that had been discussed, the Department of the Treasury has stated its intention to issue a second notice of proposed rulemaking, with additional regulation of those tax shelter opinions that will be used (or referred to) by third parties in connection with sales promotion efforts. As defined in the Internal Revenue Code, a tax shelter is "any other plan or arrangement, if a significant purpose of such partnership, entity, plan or arrangement is the avoidance or evasion of Federal income tax."[26] Practitioners also face a "more likely than not" standard. The proposed regulations also require practitioners to include a statement that the practitioner has considered the possible application to the facts of all potentially relevant antiabuse authorities, including judicial doctrines and rules prescribed by statute or regulation, and an analysis of whether a tax shelter item is vulnerable to challenge under any of the foregoing authorities, taking into account the relative weight of the taxpayer's nontax and tax purposes for entering into the transaction and structuring it in a particular manner.

In response to the proposal, the American Institute of Certified Public Accountants (AICPA) commented that practitioners "have a right to be reasonably apprised of the applicable circumstances in which they are to be held to a prescribed level of conduct," and that a standard as vague as "a significant purpose of tax avoidance" will not provide meaningful notice to practitioners of the transactions to which proposed sections would apply.[27] Therefore, they oppose any definition of *tax shelter* based on IRC section 6662(d)(2)(C)(iii). The AICPA also opposes applying the "more likely than not" standard for opinions that expressly state they are not to be relied upon for penalty abatement purposes:

In conclusion, we believe the goal should be to define "tax shelter" distinctively enough in the Circular 230 regulations so that legitimate

25. 67 F.R. 48760-80, July 26, 2002, amending *Code of Federal Regulations* 31, part 10, effective date July 26, 2002.

26. U.S.C. Title 26, sec. 6662 [d]BB [C][iiii].

27. AICPA (2001).

transactions are not burdened by unnecessary reporting or other administrative requirements, confining the transactions affected to those where practitioners should reasonably expect to provide a higher level of due diligence. In searching for an acceptable definition, we urge consideration of our alternatives for defining "tax shelter." Regarding alternatives that use "filters" to identify transactions requiring higher standards, we suggest that this approach be rejected.[28]

According to the Tax Executives Institute (TEI), tax shelter "opinions must meet a series of requirements in respect of each item directly or indirectly attributable to a tax shelter, including making an inquiry of the relevant facts, being satisfied that the opinion takes into account these facts, ensuring that all material facts are accurately and completely described in the opinion."[29] In summary they state,

TEI believes that the term "tax shelter" should be more clearly defined and examples of the application of these rules should be provided. The definition of a tax shelter opinion in section 10.33 (c) (4) should be clarified to exclude advice provided by in-house professionals who are communicating with other employees of the taxpayer. Finally, section 10.35 should be limited in application to opinions used to satisfy the standards of the penalty provisions of sections 6662 and 6664.[30]

An additional set of regulatory concerns surrounds electronic filing. The IRS Restructuring and Reform Act of 1998 set an overall goal that 80 percent of all tax and information returns would be filed electronically by 2007. Table 7-2 shows that, as of August 30, 2002, 46.7 million individual income tax returns were electronically filed, accounting for 35.8 percent of all returns filed. Although the rate of electronic filing is 15.1 percent higher than the comparable period in 2001, projections for 2004 suggest that the rate of growth in the number and percentage of electronic filings will decline, and that only 45.2 percent are expected to file electronically.[31] A declining rate of growth in electronic filing is consistent with the notion that it becomes increasingly difficult to persuade a larger and larger proportion of the population to file electronically.

Of more relevance to practitioner issues is the fact that, of the 46.7 million returns filed electronically, 33.2 million, or 71.1 percent, were signed by tax

28. AICPA (2002, p. 4).
29. TEI (2002, p. 5).
30. TEI (2002, p. 9).
31. Unpublished stats from Richard Hinkemeyer of the Office of Electronic Tax Administration, October 2002.

Table 7-2. *Methods of Filing Electronic Returns, 2001–2004*

Year	Total (millions)	Electronic (millions)	Electronic, percent of total	Practitioner, electronic (millions)	Practitioner, percent of electronic
2001	129.4	40.2	31.1	28.9	71.9
2002	130.6	46.7	35.8	33.2	71.1
2003[a]	131.7	54.3	41.2	36.5	67.2
2004[a]	133.9	60.5	45.2	40.1	66.3

Source: IRS Office of Electronic Tax Administration.
a. Projection.

practitioners. This practitioner-filed proportion is projected to fall slightly over the next two years, presumably because of an increase in personal-computer preparation and the growth in electronic filing through electronic return originators who do not prepare returns.

As an interim goal, the 1998 legislation recommends that, to the extent practicable, 100 percent of electronically prepared returns should be filed electronically by 2003. The most recent statistics show that 102.6 million returns filed during 2002 for tax year 2001 were computer-prepared, but only 42.6 million returns (41.5 percent) were filed electronically (excluding TeleFile returns).[32] Given that it is much easier to electronically file an electronically prepared return, one must question the feasibility of achieving the congressionally mandated goals or the IRS strategies for achieving the goals. Even H&R Block, which filed 15.4 million returns electronically from January through April 2002, electronically files only 85 percent of the federal returns it prepares.[33] An apparently common reason for not filing a return electronically is that many clients specifically request paper filing, especially those who have a balance due.[34]

In response to the 1998 Restructuring and Reform Act, the IRS has developed strategies to promote electronic filing, specifically noting the important role of practitioners in achieving Electronic Tax Administration goals:

Tax practitioners authorized to electronically file tax returns to the IRS as Electronic Return Originators must be recognized, supported, and motivated as ETA product and service distributors. Much as the private sector employs storefront operations, whether independent, franchise or corporate owned, the IRS depends upon tax practitioners to promote electronic filing and payment to taxpayers. In support of this vital chan-

32. IRS (2002a, 2002b).
33. "H&R Block Reports Record Tax Season Results," press release, May 1, 2002.
34. Personal communication from Robert Weinberger, vice president, government relations, H&R Block.

nel and based on their input, ETA will assist EROs by expanding the marketing support available including national advertising and promotional kits; implementing a program of product and service incentives, rewards and special recognition depending upon an ERO's success in marketing ETA products and services; developing an ERO website; and establishing an ETA account management program. In this vein, the IRS intends to establish an incentive program for practitioners. Consideration will be given to differing tiers of e-services based on the percent of eligible returns.[35]

These programs in support of practitioners stand in stark contrast to the regulatory environment previously described, and it is not clear which will be more effective for tax administrators: regulation, reward, or sanctions.

Some theoretical research has explored how practitioners would react to increased sanctions. In one investigation using an experimental simulation, as might be expected, practitioners responded to greater sanctions by recommending fewer aggressive income reporting strategies to their clients and raising their fees. Surprisingly, however, practitioners also responded by spending less time finding tax-reducing opportunities for which the rules are clear. Additional results suggest that these responses to increased sanctions would be moderated if practitioners faced only a few competitors in the market or if their clients were unable to observe their efforts and were unaware of the penalties they faced.[36]

Indirect, Unintended Effects

In the following, we offer an example in which an increase in a tax agency's audit rate, intended to increase voluntary taxpayer compliance, generated, as a side effect, an increase in practitioner usage.

Early in the filing season for tax year 1994, the Minnesota Department of Revenue conducted a controlled experiment in which one randomly assigned group of taxpayers was informed that its returns would be audited, while a second randomly assigned group was not. The objective of the experiment was to find out whether a heightened audit threat would lead taxpayers to voluntarily report more income; the expectation was that it would, an expectation grounded in the work of a number of researchers.[37] However, as has been discussed here, a heightened audit threat might also enhance the appeal (to taxpayers) of hiring tax practitioners. Then, as has also been discussed, greater practitioner usage might depress compliance. While we cannot yet separately

---

35. IRS (2001, p. 23).

36. Anderson and Cuccia (2000).

37. See, for example, Allingham and Sandmo (1972) and Becker (1968).

identify both the procompliance and the anticompliance effects of the audit initiative, we do demonstrate here the unintended rise in practitioner usage.

The Minnesota Department of Revenue sample was drawn from the population of 1993 full-year Minnesota residents who filed income tax returns for that year and for whom matching federal income tax data were available. No amended returns were included. Taxpayers in the sample were randomly assigned to either a treatment group or a control group. The department sent taxpayers in the treatment group a letter in early 1995, just as they were about to file for tax year 1994. The letter informed them that their 1994 return would be "closely examined." No letter was sent to the control group.

The sample was stratified by income and by a set of characteristics believed to proxy for evasion opportunity. There were three income strata based on 1993 adjusted gross income (AGI): low (less than $10,000), medium ($10,000 to $100,000), and high (above $100,000). There were two opportunity strata: high (taxpayers filing either a 1993 federal Schedule C [business income] or Schedule F [farm income] and paying 1993 Minnesota estimated tax), and low (all other taxpayers). A Minnesota taxpayer in 1993 was required to file and pay estimated tax quarterly if his or her tax liability was expected to exceed withholding and expected tax credits by $500 or more. The $500 estimated tax threshold effectively eliminated taxpayers from the high-opportunity stratum if they filed a Schedule C or F but expected to have little reported income from their businesses. The population count, sampling rate, and resulting sample frequency for each stratum are presented for the treatment group (letter recipients) in table 7-3 and for the control group in table 7-4.[38]

The treatment group received a letter by first-class mail from the commissioner of revenue in January 1995. Note that this treatment was administered after the tax year, and at the beginning of the filing season. Thus, with a few exceptions, it could not have affected nonreporting behavior with tax consequences.[39] The taxpayers were told: first, that they had been selected at random to be part of a study "that will increase the number of taxpayers whose 1994 individual income tax returns are closely examined"; second, that both their state and federal tax returns for the 1994 tax year would be closely examined by the Minnesota Department of Revenue; third, that they would be contacted about any discrepancies; and fourth, that if any "irregularities" were found, their returns filed in 1994 as well as in prior years might be reviewed, as provided by

38. The control group from this "audit notice" experiment was combined with the control group from a second "appeal to conscience" experiment to increase precision. See Blumenthal, Slemrod, and Christian (2001). Both groups were randomly selected, and neither was contacted by the Department of Revenue during the experiment.

39. This aspect of the experiment is consistent with the Allingham and Sandmo (1972) assumption of a fixed "true" taxable income.

Table 7-3. *Treatment Group Sample Selection, Minnesota Study, 1993*

Stratum	Population	Sampling rate (percent)	N	Weight
Low income, low risk[a,c]	449,017	0.10	460	976.1
Low income, high risk[a,b]	2,120	2.69	57	37.2
Medium income, low risk[d,c]	1,290,233	0.04	567	2,275.5
Medium income, high risk[d,b]	50,920	0.84	429	118.7
High income, low risk[e,c]	52,093	0.22	114	457.0
High income, high risk[e,b]	8,456	1.03	87	97.2
Total	1,852,839		1,714	

Source: Minnesota Department of Revenue.
a. Low income: Federal AGI less than $10,000.
b. High risk: Filed a federal Schedule C (trade or business income) or Schedule F (farm income), and paid Minnesota estimated tax in 1993.
c. Low risk: All other returns.
d. Middle income: Federal AGI from $10,000 to $100,000.
e. High income: Federal AGI over $100,000.

law. The taxpayers were given department phone numbers to call for information and assistance with their taxes.

The overall impact of the experimentally induced audit notice on taxpayers' reported income and tax liability has been analyzed previously.[40] In summary, low- and middle-income taxpayers in the treatment group on average increased tax payments compared to the previous year. The effect was much stronger for those with more opportunity to evade. We focus here on the effect of the audit notice on practitioner usage. The weighted proportion of taxpayers across all six strata who used a practitioner in 1993 is roughly the same for the treatment and control groups: 50.4 percent of the treatment group and 50.1 percent of the control group, a difference that is not statistically significant. In contrast, in 1994, after the audit notice was sent, the proportion for the treatment group increased to 53.8 percent versus 50.7 percent for the control group, a statistically significant difference. Table 7-5 reports the weighted sample proportions and their standard errors. This modest difference provides evidence that the audit notice caused taxpayers in the aggregate to seek the services of a practitioner.

As an alternative test for an effect, we compared the proportions of treatment versus control taxpayers who initiated preparer use in 1994 after receiving the audit notice. Almost 16 percent of the treatment group began using a practitioner in 1994, while only 10.6 percent of the controls did so, a statistically significant difference.

40. See Slemrod, Blumenthal, and Christian (2001).

Table 7-4. *Control Group Sample Selection, Minnesota Study, 1994*

Stratum	Population	Sampling rate (percent)	N	Weight
Low income, low risk[a,b]	449,017	1.30	5,821	77.1
Low income, high risk[a,c]	2,120	6.56	139	15.3
Medium income, low risk[d,b]	1,290,233	1.15	14,817	87.1
Medium income, high risk[d,c]	50,920	2.76	1,403	36.3
High income, low risk[e,b]	52,093	1.42	739	70.5
High income, high risk[e,c]	8,456	3.15	266	31.8
Total	1,852,839		23,185	

Source: Minnesota Department of Revenue.
   a. Low income: Federal AGI less than $10,000.
   b. Low risk: All other returns.
   c. High risk: Filed a federal Schedule C (trade or business income) or Schedule F (farm income) and paid Minnesota estimated tax in 1993.
   d. Middle income: Federal AGI $10,000 to $100,000.
   e. High income: Federal AGI over $100,000.

Next, to explore the characteristics of those taxpayers who initiated practitioner use in 1994, we used a multiple regression analysis.[41] We found that taxpayers with incomes in excess of $100,000, as well as those filing Schedules B (interest and dividends) or C (business income) were significantly more likely to initiate practitioner use, with the high-income characteristic increasing the likelihood of practitioner usage by 0.20. Moreover, filing a Schedule A had a differentially stronger positive impact for those in the treatment group, relative to controls (that is, an itemizing taxpayer "threatened" with an audit had a higher

Table 7-5. *Increase in Preparer Usage, Minnesota Study*[a]

	Treatment group		Control group	
Year	Sample proportion	Standard error	Sample proportion	Standard error
1993	0.504	.168	0.501	.004
1994	0.538	.167	0.507	.004
Added	0.160	.178	0.107	.003

Source: Minnesota Department of Revenue.
   a. N = 20,980.

41. A probit regression was used because the dependent variable takes on only two values (0 if the taxpayer continued to self-prepare in 1994 or 1 if she initiated practitioner use in 1994).

probability of using a practitioner than an itemizing taxpayer in the control group). Filing a Schedule B, on the other hand, had a differentially stronger negative impact among treated taxpayers.[42] Missing here is an assessment of the indirect impact of the rise in practitioner usage on compliance, a complicated task that is the subject of future work. One also wonders to what extent policy initiatives such as this influence taxpayer and tax practitioner behavior over a longer period.

Conclusions and Recommendations

The evidence is clear that taxpayers use practitioners to reduce uncertainty and to save time and effort. The effect of practitioners on taxpayer compliance is less clear, but compelling evidence exists that they are "rule enforcers but ambiguity exploiters." In general the evidence suggests that the effect may be reduced compliance, but it is likely that the effect differs across types of preparers.

While it is clear that penalties assessed on practitioners have the desirable effect of reducing their aggressive reporting recommendations, it has yet to be seen how effective rewards are in engaging practitioners' help in promoting electronic filing. Therefore it is difficult to make policy recommendations. However, recent experimental evidence is consistent with the prediction that increased enforcement in the form of audit notices does increase practitioner usage. That leads to the recommendation that tax administrators consider the impact of enforcement policies on preparer usage.

Before implementing any new tax policy intended to affect voluntary compliance (for example, changes in audit rates, penalties, or rule interpretation), we recommend that tax administrators consider how the new policy might affect both practitioner use and practitioner fees. This is important for two reasons. First, and most obviously, practitioner fees are an important element of taxpayers' compliance burden. Any policy change that results in higher fees (either on average or in the aggregate) also increases compliance costs. This should be weighed against the expected benefit of enhanced compliance. Second, policy changes may affect the propensity of taxpayers to use practitioners. The evidence reviewed here suggests that, in some cases, greater practitioner use is associated with reduced compliance.

While there is much that we still do not know about this indirect link between policy and compliance, we do now know that it matters. And that should lead administrators to think especially carefully about their options.

---

42. Complete results of the weighted probit regression are available from the authors.

COMMENT BY
Peggy A. Hite

Blumenthal and Christian discuss the relationship between practitioners and tax administration, presenting several components affecting that relationship, such as electronic filing, preparer penalties, Circular 230, tax shelters, criminal sanctions, taxpayer compliance costs, prior compliance research on the effect of practitioners, and preparer usage. Presumably the latter topic, preparer usage, is a significant focus of the chapter, as it presents tables analyzing data on preparer usage in 1994 as compared to 1993.

In January 1995 a stratified random sample of taxpayers received letters indicating that the Minnesota Department of Revenue would closely examine their forthcoming 1994 returns. These returns were then compared to a control group who did not receive the letters. The authors report that use of paid preparers was significantly higher in 1994 for those who received the letter, 53.8 percent versus 50.7 percent for the control group. However, when a multivariate model is used, controlling variables for income level, type of income, marital status, age, marginal tax rate, and schedules included in the tax return, the treatment variable for receiving the letter is no longer significant.

The authors' data show that taxpayers who in 1993 had income greater than $200,000, were over 65, and filed Schedules A, B, C, D, E, F, or ES tended to use a paid preparer. This is consistent with prior research showing that taxpayers with higher incomes, sole proprietorships, and complex returns tend to use paid preparers.[1]

In addition, the authors find a significant negative association between marginal tax rates and use of a paid preparer. This result suggests that tax returns with a paid preparer tend to have lower marginal tax rates, and this is consistent with prior research showing that paid preparer returns tend to have lower tax liabilities, lower tax prepayments, and larger refunds.[2]

Comparison of 1993 and 1994

The authors compare preparer use by Minnesotans in 1994 and 1993. The only difference between 1994 and 1993 is that paid-preparer usage in 1994 is associated with two additional levels of income, below $20,000 and between $20,000 and $50,000. In other words, taxpayers with incomes between $50,000 and $200,000 were less likely to begin to use a paid preparer in 1994 than those with lower or higher incomes. Receiving an audit letter from the

1. Christian, Gupta, and Lin (1993); Blumenthal, Slemrod, and Christian (2001).
2. Christian and others (1994).

Minnesota Department of Revenue did not affect the 1994 results, so why did these significant effects for low- and middle-income taxpayers occur in 1994 and not in 1993?

A highly probable answer is the Revenue Reconciliation Act of 1993 (RRA). This act contains some major tax law changes that affected lower- and upper-income taxpayers. For lower-income taxpayers, the RRA drastically changed the earned income credit, but the changes did not become effective until 1994. For example, in 1993 a taxpayer with earned income below $23,050 could get the credit, while in 1994 the earned income ceiling was $25,250. Moreover the maximum credit in 1993 was $1,508, but it increased to $2,528 in 1994. Clearly the change in the earned income credit was one of the incentives for lower- and middle-income taxpayers to seek preparer assistance in 1994.

New Use of Preparers

For upper-income taxpayers, the 1993 RRA changed the federal tax rates from 15, 28, and 31 percent in 1992 to 15, 28, 31, 36, and 39.6 percent for 1993. Thus it is not surprising that upper-income taxpayers in 1993 and 1994 increasingly hired paid preparers. This is confirmed when the authors analyze only those who added a paid preparer in 1994. High-income taxpayers, with incomes greater than $200,000, were significantly associated with initiating the use of a paid preparer.

Taxpayers who initiated preparer use in 1994 tended to file Schedules B and C and tended to have lower marginal tax rates. Although the Department of Revenue "audit" letter did not significantly affect the decision to begin use of a preparer in 1994, it did interact with Schedules A and B. Those receiving a letter were more likely to initiate preparer use in 1994 when they filed a Schedule A in 1993. When they filed a Schedule B in 1993 but then received the Minnesota letter, they were less likely to use a paid preparer in 1994. The authors offer no explanation as to why these two seemingly contradictory results exist. Moreover the results are only marginally significant (using two-tailed tests because no specific hypotheses were posited); thus the strength of the results is questionable.

Discussion of Results

Overall, those receiving a letter that their returns would be closely examined were not more likely to use a paid preparer. Instead, paid preparer usage may have been driven by changes and complexity in the tax law. Statistics of Income data show that approximately 49 percent of all individual returns used a paid preparer in 1993 and 1994.[3] Thus increased preparer use is not evident in the total population. However, from 1993 to 1994 there was a 67 percent increase in the number of telephone inquiries received by the IRS.[4] The lag for switching to a preparer may surface in subsequent years.

The study by Blumenthal and Christian does not provide strong evidence that taxpayers forewarned of a close examination are more likely to hire a preparer, but it does confirm prior research findings that taxpayers who use a paid preparer tend to have higher incomes, more complex returns, and lower tax liabilities.

In addition the study does not provide any evidence of increased noncompliance among paid preparer returns. In a previous paper, Slemrod, Blumenthal, and Christian analyzed the same Minnesota data and found that the taxpayers who tended to increase their income tax liabilities in 1994 after having received the audit letter were those in the low- and middle-income categories who either filed a Schedule C or F or made estimated tax payments to the state of Minnesota.[5] The results did not differ between self-prepared and paid-preparer returns.

Preparer or Practitioner

Although the Blumenthal-Christian chapter does not distinguish the potential effects for each type of preparer, the authors do discuss two prior studies on preparer mode, one suggesting that CPA-prepared returns are more noncompliant[6] and one suggesting that they are more compliant.[7] Additional evidence does exist. For example, a recent study by Hite and Hasseldine analyzes data from a random sample of 1998 IRS office audits and finds that tax returns with CPA-preparer assistance are significantly less likely to have audit adjustments and penalties than are self-prepared returns.[8] Furthermore CPA assistance is associated with fewer audit adjustments than other paid preparers. The latter study cannot be generalized to all individual tax returns, but it provides valid data for analyzing preparer behavior on audited returns, which are the returns supposedly identified as problematic.

Conclusion

Chapter 7 is an excellent resource for synthesizing some of the prior literature and current data on paid-preparer usage. The authors demonstrate that upper-

3. IRS (1996).
4. IRS (1996, table 22).
5. Slemrod, Blumenthal, and Christian (2001).
6. Erard (1993).
7. Holtzblatt and McCubbin, this volume.
8. Hite and Hasseldine (2003).

income taxpayers, as well as low- to middle-income taxpayers, tended to use a
paid preparer in 1994. Preparer use is also associated with complex returns, marital status, and age, which is consistent with prior research. This study, however,
does not test for differences between types of preparers. Future research on tax
return assistance should examine the impact of preparer mode on return preparation, tax liability, and likelihood of audit adjustments and penalty assessments.
At the same time, researchers need to explore how taxpayer attitudes are being
affected by the use of paid preparers and practitioners. Hite finds that taxpayer
attitudes are significantly lower after an IRS audit when a paid preparer assists
with the audit than when no paid prepaper is involved.[9] No significant attitude
differences are found between CPA-assisted and non-CPA-assisted audits.

The authors provide a clear and concise summary of the study by Klepper
and Nagin.[10] The oft-cited conclusion of that study is that paid preparers are
"rule enforcers but ambiguity exploiters." Klepper and Nagin report that paid
preparers had fewer errors on some types of items but had more errors on items
that either require imputation of monetary values or have lots of related revenue
rulings (for example, proprietor's income, rent, royalties and partnerships,
dependency exemptions, and casualty and theft losses) than did self-prepared
returns. The study is frequently cited as evidence of aggressive paid-preparer
behavior. However, the result is based on 1982 data that may no longer be relevant, and noncompliance on the ambiguous items could have been a result of
efficiency, not necessarily intentional noncompliance.

For example, calculating a casualty loss requires data on the fair market value
of the assets before and after the casualty, cost basis of all the assets, and their date
of purchase. Not many taxpayers have all those data, yet clearly a deduction is
"deserved." A self-preparer may have become frustrated with all the requirements
and deducted only a portion of the losses. A paid preparer may not have insisted
on getting all the supporting data because of the costs of collecting and verifying
the information. Thus estimates could have been used to minimize compliance
costs. Shortcuts in practice lead to inaccuracies, but future research needs to consider whether increased accuracy is worth the increase in compliance costs. Blumenthal and Christian make this point. They argue that new compliance and
enforcement policies should not be implemented until the increased compliance
costs are weighed against the benefits of enhanced compliance.

The trend is toward more paid-preparer assistance. Last year 59.4 percent of
the individual income tax returns had paid-preparer or practitioner assistance.
The United States is not alone. In Australia 75 to 80 percent of annual tax
returns have paid-preparer assistance. If tax law complexity continues, the
growth in preparer use will continue. The end result is increasing costs for the

9. Hite (2002).
10. Klepper and Nagin (1989).

taxpayer, which may be viewed as indirect taxes. E-filing will not necessarily decrease the economic burden, as 70 percent of electronically filed returns are paid-preparer returns. If filing electronically is efficient and economically advantageous for the tax administration, then perhaps e-filing should be encouraged by making the cost a refundable credit for the taxpayer. The recent decision to offer free e-filing for some taxpayers sends a positive signal.

COMMENT BY

Gerald W. Padwe

Marsha Blumenthal and Charles Christian have written a thoughtful and challenging essay looking into the role of tax practitioners in the tax administration process. My view, as a discussant of their chapter, is that of a former "big six" practitioner and current executive of a major practitioner membership association. As such I confess to being swayed less by regression analyses than by thousands of real-life interactions with clients and, subsequently over ten years, by working with others (primarily certified public accountants) who are sole practitioners or members of small firms. As practitioners ourselves, we view with alarm the dramatic increase in paid-preparer involvement with individual taxpayers, because we see this as a direct reflection of the growing complexity of the tax law and the inability of ordinary taxpayers to comprehend or comply with those laws without professional assistance.

Taxpayer Perspective

Table 7-1 of the Blumenthal-Christian chapter reveals that the number of individual returns filed over a paid preparer's signature grew from 54.5 million in calendar 1990 to 68.9 million in calendar 2000—an increase of 26.4 percent. The total number of individual income tax returns filed in those two years was 112.6 million in 1990 and 127.7 million in 2000, an increase of 13.38 percent.[1] Clearly the growth rate of individual taxpayers seeking assistance with filing their returns is significantly outstripping the growth rate of individual returns filed. Indeed the percentage of individual returns utilizing paid preparers has been marching inexorably upward: 48.4 percent in 1990 (as noted by Blumenthal and Christian) to 59.4 percent in 2001. The 60 percent mark may well be surpassed in the 2002 filing season, and there is no clear end to this trend in sight.

1. IRS (2002a, table 22).

Chapter 7 summarizes much of the research on why taxpayers seek practitioner assistance by citing two primary explanations: to reduce taxpayer uncertainty about true tax liability, and to avoid spending personal time on tax return preparation. Both explanations are consistent with the growing complexity of the tax system. The continually increasing number of taxpayers using professional preparers is evidence of this complexity.

Equally interesting, but substantially more difficult to ascertain, would be to see how this complexity is reflected in the fees charged by preparers. Obtaining meaningful information about what an "average" CPA charges individual clients for return preparation work would be difficult, particularly getting the information to compare, say, 1990 to 2000. Chapter 7 does present information from H&R Block, which, they note, prepares about one-quarter of all practitioner-prepared returns. The Block average charge during the 2002 filing season was $122 "for tax return preparation and related services."[2] An analysis of 1992 information, if available, would help to see whether growth in return preparation charges has outstripped inflation.

Practitioner Perspective: Providing Services

Chapter 7 refers, in some detail, to studies during the past fourteen years that have analyzed the effect of practitioners on voluntary compliance.[3] Although different studies come to different conclusions, the two analyzed in the most detail lead to these authors' view that, first, paid preparers have a negative compliance effect on the most ambiguous line items of an individual return (that is, rent, royalty, business and partnership income, casualty and theft losses); and second, some practitioners may have a "substantial" anticompliance effect (based primarily on the Erard study's view that the highest predicted mean level of noncompliance occurs in CPA- or lawyer-prepared returns and the lowest in self-prepared returns).

Perhaps it is time to update this type of study. While both Klepper and Nagin and Erard used taxpayer compliance measurement program information, the former was based on 1982 data and the latter on 1979 data. The tax law has subsequently become substantially more complex and, although I suspect that more current research would only emphasize these conclusions, I suggest that these studies still leave open questions.

Noncompliance is a fairly pejorative term and leads the reader to conclude that the practitioner has done something wrong. Using a practitioner (particularly a

2. It is not clear whether "related services" includes per-return revenue from refund anticipation loans, which is a significant part of Block's business model today but which was likely less significant in 1992.

3. Primarily Klepper and Nagin (1989) and Erard (1993).

CPA or an attorney) may indeed result in lower reported taxable income and tax liabilities, but this results largely from the more detailed and sophisticated knowledge of the law and the tax system that these practitioners bring to their clients. Further, as recognized by Klepper and Nagin, the tax law is incredibly complex, with any number of ambiguities. Thus much of the work done by practitioners involves interpretations of complex issues rather than bright-line determinations easily entered on a return.

Using TCMP (and therefore audited) data to conduct these studies gives a significant level of credibility to their conclusions. Nonetheless it is somewhat unclear that, simply because an IRS auditor includes additional amounts on a return line, the practitioner has allowed or persuaded the taxpayer to be non-compliant. Precisely because of the inherent ambiguities, practitioners are likely—indeed, are ethically bound—to interpret these ambiguities in favor of the taxpayer. Further, taxpayer willingness to accept an audit adjustment in favor of the government may be more closely related to a dispassionate analysis of the future costs to contest the audit change (in appeals or in litigation) in light of the size of the proposed adjustment, or to accepting an adjustment of one item on the return in exchange for not making one to another item.

Tax Administrator Perspective: Regulating Practitioners

The relationship between regulating tax practitioners and levels of compliance should be of great interest to tax administrators, particularly given Blumenthal and Christian's suggested general conclusion that the effect of regulating preparers may be reduced compliance. Their discussion of the statutory preparer penalty provisions and of Circular 230 discloses a tightening band of regulation, presumably providing direct regulators (the IRS) and indirect regulators (state bars or state boards of accountancy) with an expanding array of tools to force preparers and other practitioners into a compliance-oriented mind-set.

The chapter notes that it is "unclear whether the IRS has adequately enforced these penalties" (presumably referring both to sanctions under Circular 230 and to statutory penalties under Internal Revenue Code section 6694). To the extent that IRS enforcement is lacking, I suggest that this results, in large part, from human and financial resource allocation issues within the IRS. For example, it is interesting that the recently renamed Office of Professional Responsibility[4] is in the process of more than doubling its staff, thus presumably providing the opportunity to substantially increase inquiries into practitioner behavior. However, it has been made clear that a primary focus of the office will be on tax shel-

---

4. Formerly the Office of the Director of Practice.

ter activities, thereby leaving uncertain the extent to which nonshelter investigations will increase.

Regardless of past enforcement success or lack thereof, we may be about to undergo a sea change in practitioner regulation, in large measure due to increased legislative and regulatory concern about the proliferation of abusive tax shelter transactions. Should this occur, academic researchers will find fertile ground for their attempts to measure changes in compliance behavior due to new and increased constraints on practitioners—including whether the use of practitioners decreases as taxpayers conclude that they may have greater opportunities for "flexible" reporting if they revert to being self-filers.

Chapter 7 notes that income tax return preparers were first subject to penalties in 1976, for "negligent and intentional disregard of rules and regulations" ($100) and "willful attempt to understate liability" ($500).[5] In 1989 the definition (and the monetary risk) was expanded: A preparer knowing or having reason to know that there was not a "realistic possibility" of being sustained on the merits became subject to a $250 penalty, and a "willful attempt" to understate liability, or "reckless or intentional disregard of rules or regulations," exposed the preparer to a $1,000 penalty.[6]

Provisions contemplated in the 107th Congress[7] and under consideration in 2003 by the 108th Congress[8] would expand even further the definition of preparer misconduct and increase the monetary sanctions for violations. Rather than a "realistic possibility" of a nondisclosed return position being sustained on the merits in a subsequent dispute, a preparer would have to have a "reasonable belief" that the return position is "more likely than not" the correct tax treatment of the transaction. The penalty for failure to have such a reasonable belief would increase to $1,000, and the penalty for willful or reckless conduct would become $5,000.

As noted in Blumenthal and Christian, Treasury's 2002 amendments to Circular 230 created a new sanction on practitioners: censure.[9] The effect of censure on practitioner behavior will have to be carefully evaluated. Prior to this regulatory change, the director of practice tended to use a private reprimand as the primary Circular 230 sanction (certainly for first-time offenders). By definition, this was a private matter between the practitioner and the IRS, and imposition

5. P.L. 94-455, sec. 1203(a), amending section 6694 of the Internal Revenue Code.

6. Omnibus Budget Reconciliation Act of 1989, sec. 7732(a).

7. S. 2498, the Tax Shelter Transparency Act, approved by the Senate Finance Committee, June 18, 2002; not acted upon further.

8. S. 476, CARE Act of 2003, sec. 711, passed by the Senate on April 9, 2003; not acted upon further.

9. Impetus for this provision may be found in the Tax Shelter Transparency bill of 2002, S. 2498, since that proposed legislation specifically authorized Treasury to adopt censure as an additional sanction under Circular 230. Ultimately Treasury determined it already had statutory authority to create this sanction and adopted it even without enactment of S. 2498.

of the reprimand did not become known to the general public. With the adoption of censure (described in the regulatory preamble as a "public reprimand") three of the four sanctions presently in use against practitioners (censure, suspension, disbarment) will be matters of public record.

The IRS has never articulated the criteria by which it determines which sanction is appropriate to impose in given factual circumstances. To the extent that censure is applied primarily to those who would formerly have been subject to a private reprimand, a larger number of disciplined practitioners will have their names publicly listed. To the extent that censure is applied to those who earlier would have been sanctioned with a suspension from practice, there may be a distinction in the level of sanction, but the affected practitioner's name will be a matter of public record in any event.

Public disclosure of a disciplined practitioner can be significant, even if censure is involved rather than suspension or disbarment. If, for example, the practitioner is a member of the American Institute of Certified Public Accountants, public disclosure of a sanction by the IRS will trigger an automatic ethics investigation by the AICPA (often in conjunction with the practitioner's state CPA society). There is also the potential for inquiry and action by the practitioner's state bar or state board of accountancy, should he or she be an attorney or a CPA. In short, publication of a disciplined practitioner's name has consequences and, at the margin, the increased potential for exposure would be expected to influence behavior.

In addition to the new censure rules, the proposed tax legislation would also authorize Treasury to impose monetary sanctions—on practitioners and their firms—of up to the gross income derived (or to be derived) from the conduct giving rise to the penalty, in addition to other Circular 230 sanctions.

Interestingly both the new section 6694 penalty definitions and amounts and the enhanced Circular 230 sanctions and penalties are included in proposed legislation that is specifically anti-tax-shelter. However, these increased penalties and sanctions are not limited to tax shelter transactions. Rather they apply to any item subject to the income tax return preparer statutory rules or any aspect of practice before the IRS.

Finally, the IRS is looking into the possibility and the propriety of bringing a substantially larger group of return preparers (those not attorneys, CPAs, enrolled agents, or enrolled actuaries) into its practitioner regulatory scheme. In an advance notice of proposed rulemaking, the IRS has requested public comment on whether return preparation by an "unenrolled return preparer" should be considered to be practice before the service, such that the unenrolled preparer would be fully subject to the Circular 230 rules.[10]

---

10. IRS Announcement 2003-5 IRB 397 (January 31, 2003).

At this writing, it is not clear which, if any, of the above-proposed changes to legislation or regulation will be adopted. However, if first, the standards for advising on or signing a client return are increased to "more likely than not," second, the penalty levels for preparers advance to at least $1,000, and third, the new IRS Office of Professional Responsibility is authorized to impose monetary penalties on practitioners and firms, we should anticipate significant changes in practitioner interactions with taxpayers. This could take the form of substantially increased return disclosure or significantly more conservative positions being advised or reflected on returns.

It will likely take several years for practitioner behavior to reflect these legislative or regulatory changes. Nonetheless it would not be premature to start considering what research projects might be undertaken to measure future changes in compliance behavior, as well as in taxpayer and practitioner attitudes.

References

Allingham, Michael G., and Agnar Sandmo. 1972. "Income Tax Evasion: A Theoretical Analysis." *Journal of Public Economics* 1(November): 323–38.

American Institute of Certified Public Accountants. 2001. "Comments on Proposed Regulations, REG-111835-99 Regarding Modifications to Treasury Department Circular No. 230" (www.aicpa.org/letters/comments.htm).

———. 2002. "Supplemental Comments on REG-11835-99, Proposed Amendments to Circular 230." Letter to Eric Solomon, Deputy Assistant Secretary of the Treasury for Regulatory Affairs (www.aicpa.org/letters/circ_230_jan7_02.htm).

Anderson, Susan E., and Andrew D. Cuccia. 2000. "A Closer Examination of the Economic Incentives Created by Tax Return Preparer Penalties." *Journal of the American Taxation Association* 22 (1): 56–77.

Beck, Paul J., and Woon-Oh Jung. 1989. "Taxpayer Compliance under Uncertainty." *Journal of Accounting and Public Policy* 8 (1): 1–27.

Becker, Gary S. 1968. "Crime and Punishment: An Economic Approach." *Journal of Political Economy* 76 (2): 169–217.

Blumenthal, Marsha A., and Joel B. Slemrod. 1992. "The Compliance Cost of the U.S. Individual Income Tax System: A Second Look after Tax Reform." *National Tax Journal* 45 (2): 185–202.

Blumenthal, Marsha A., Joel B. Slemrod, and Charles W. Christian. 2001. "Do Normative Appeals Affect Tax Compliance? Evidence from a Controlled Experiment in Minnesota." *National Tax Journal* 54 (1): 125–36.

Christian, Charles W. 1994. "Voluntary Compliance with the Individual Income Tax Results from the 1988 TCMP Study." *IRS Research Bulletin*. Publication 1500 (rev. 9-94).

Christian, Charles W., Sanjay Gupta, and Suming Lin. 1993. "Determinants of Tax Preparer Usage: Evidence from Panel Data." *National Tax Journal* 46 (4): 487–503.

Christian, Charles, and others. 1994. "The Relation between the Use of Tax Preparers and Taxpayers' Prepayment Position." *Journal of the American Taxation Association* 16 (1): 17–40.

Collins, Julie H., Valerie C. Milliron, and Daniel R. Toy. 1990. "Factors Associated with Household Demand for Tax Preparers." *Journal of the American Taxation Association* 12 (Fall): 9-25.

Erard, Brian. 1990. "Tax Practitioners and Tax Compliance: A Microeconometric Analysis of the Decision to Engage a Tax Preparer and Its Consequences." Ph.D. dissertation, University of Michigan.

———. 1993. "Taxation with Representation: An Analysis of the Role of Tax Practitioners in Tax Compliance." *Journal of Public Economics* 52 (2): 163–97.

Hite, Peggy. 2002. "The Preparer Effect on IRS Customer Satisfaction." In *Advances in Taxation*, vol. 14, edited by T. Porcano, 159–84. JAI Press.

Hite, Peggy, and John Hasseldine. 2003. "Tax Practitioner Credentials and the Incidence of IRS Audit Adjustments." *Accounting Horizons* 17 (1): 1–14.

Klepper, Steven, and Daniel Nagin. 1989. "The Role of Tax Preparers in Tax Compliance." *Policy Sciences* 22 (2): 167–94.

Lin, Suming. 1993. "Income Tax Return Preparation Fees and Tax Savings of Using Tax Return Preparers." Ph.D. dissertation, Arizona State University.

Long, James E., and Steven B. Caudill. 1987. "The Usage and Benefits of Paid Tax Return Preparation." *National Tax Journal* 40 (1): 35–46.

———. 1993. "Tax Rates and Professional Tax Return Preparation: Reexamination and New Evidence." *National Tax Journal* 46 (4): 511–17.

Matthews, Mark, and Marilyn Davidson. 2002. "IRS Criminal Investigation: Enhancing Compliance in the Return Preparer Community." *Tax Practice and Procedure* (April-May): 1–3.

Reinganum, Jennifer F., and Louis L. Wilde. 1991. "Equilibrium Enforcement and Compliance in the Presence of Tax Practitioners." *Journal of Law, Economics and Organization* 7 (Spring): 163–81.

Scotchmer, Suzanne. 1989a. "Who Profits from Taxpayer Confusion?" *Economic Letters* 29: 49–55.

———. 1989b. "The Effect of Tax Advisors on Tax Compliance." In *Taxpayer Compliance*, vol. 2: *Social Science Perspectives*, edited by Jeffrey A. Roth and John T. Scholz, 182–99. University of Pennsylvania Press.

Slemrod, Joel B., Marsha A. Blumenthal, and Charles W. Christian. 2001. "Taxpayer Response to an Increased Probability of Audit: Evidence from a Controlled Experiment in Minnesota." *Journal of Public Economics* 79 (2): 455–83.

Slemrod, Joel, and Nikki Sorum. 1984. "The Compliance Cost of the U.S. Individual Income Tax System." *National Tax Journal* 37 (4): 461–74.

Tax Executives Institute. 2002. "Comments on Proposed Regulations Amending Circular 230 Governing Practice before the Internal Revenue Service REG-111835-99" (www.tei.org/230comments.html).

U.S. General Accounting Office. 1991. "Effectiveness of IRS' Return Preparer Penalty Program Is Questionable." GAO/GGD 91-12.

U.S. Internal Revenue Service. 1996. *Statistics of Income Bulletin.* Publication 1136 (Summer).

———. 2001. *Electronic Tax Administration: A Strategy for Growth.* Publication 3187 (rev. 12-00).

———. 2002a. *Statistics of Income Bulletin,* vol. 22, no. 1.

———. 2002b. *Taxpayer Usage Study.* Report 14. August 30.

8

FRANK COWELL

Carrots and Sticks in Enforcement

THIS CHAPTER IS about the role of economic analysis in understanding the tax-compliance problem. The carrots and sticks in the title suggest a recalcitrant beast that needs to be seduced into cooperation by an elusive, dangling incentive or beaten into unwilling compliance. The story is, however, somewhat richer than that. The discussion shows that economic theory can play an important part in explaining the underlying mechanisms relating to the economic engagement of the citizen in the funding of public programs and why such engagement—or lack of it—may be an endemic problem for tax administration. It also shows what the natural limitations of the carrot-and-stick analogy may be and what alternative paradigms of compliance could usefully be employed.

The standard microeconomic approach to tax compliance helps us understand the basic schizophrenia that lies at the heart of public economics. This has little to do with like or dislike of government or with approval or disapproval of the way in which the government raises funds or with the mix of goods and services it provides. To appreciate how the standard approach can be useful in designing empirical investigations into tax noncompliance and in formulating policy, it is important to understand what can reasonably be expected from pertinent economic models and what can be expected by way of evidence.

I am grateful for the research collaboration of Ralph Bayer and Carlo Fiorio and for helpful comments from Henry Aaron, John Scholz, Douglas Shackelford, and Joel Slemrod.

No overall modeling framework can be expected to offer an all-encompassing story of the compliance problem, although particular models can provide particular economic insights that illuminate particular aspects of the compliance problem, allowing a piecemeal appreciation of tax administration. Microeconomic models have a further role in showing what may be the consequences of the successful establishment of specific institutions and norms or, indeed, the breakdown of these institutions and norms. Predictions from these models are always conditional upon the appropriateness of the particular institutional set that is assumed.

By definition, evidence is bound to be limited and imperfect; however, data arising from the audit process or from activities collateral to noncompliance activities can be expected to reveal information about subsets of the compliance problem.

I begin by introducing the standard paradigm.

The TAG Model

The taxpayer-as-gambler (TAG) model is perhaps the benchmark economic approach of modeling tax noncompliance.[1] It is important to understand the ground rules of this approach and, thereby, its limitations in indicating the way official incentives work on individual decisions to conceal taxable income and, in some cases, to generate taxable income.

The model is based on the elementary choice facing an individual in an atemporal environment. It is nonstrategic, in that no account is taken of the possible conditioning of taxpayer behavior on beliefs about the tax authority's reaction to its information signals. Government or tax authority actions may be conditioned on personal attributes, but there is not enough information in the system to build in assumptions about best response.

Foundations

Taxpayers are confronted by a classic economic problem of choice under risk. They know the tax legislation, the taxes they are liable for, and the penalty for failing to pay (if they are caught and convicted). Taxpayers also know that the tax authority is not psychic: The authority cannot know their true tax liability unless they report it or unless the authority spends the time and trouble to find

---

1. The model was pioneered by Allingham and Sandmo (1972) and is widely discussed in the literature. For an introduction see, for example, Andreoni, Erard, and Feinstein (1998, pp. 823–24); Cowell (1990, pp. 50–59); Franzoni (1999, sec. 3.1); Slemrod and Yitzhaki (2002, chap. 4).

out for itself. So taxpayers could get away with concealing part of their resources, falsifying reports made to the tax authority, or even making no report at all. Being without moral scruples, they are tempted to take the opportunity of evasion.

THE INDIVIDUAL. At the heart of the analysis is a simple and familiar lottery: Is it worth the taxpayer's taking a chance on being caught and suffering a financial penalty? Assume that the taxpayer's initial resources and all gains and losses can be measured in terms of a single consumption good, which can be termed *income*. To further simplify the discussion, make two important assumptions about time and uncertainty: First, time is compressed into a single period within which the taxpayer has to make a decision on whether to attempt to evade paying tax and, if so, how much to evade. Second, once the decision to evade tax has been taken, one of two possible states occurs: Either the taxpayer is not audited and enjoys a consumption level c' or is audited, convicted, and punished, in which case consumption is c'', and $c'' < c'$.

If the taxpayer has chosen not to evade tax, then $c'' = c'$.

The exact nature of the lottery is determined by the taxpayer's financial resources, the tax system, and the penalty system in force. The model assumes that the tax system is based on income and the following three axioms:

Axiom 1: The individual has a fixed gross income, y, which is liable to tax.

Axiom 2: There is a proportional income tax at rate t.

Axiom 3: There is a fixed probability, p, of tax evasion being discovered and punished, and the tax on any concealed income is subject to surcharge at a rate s.

Viewed this way, noncompliance is just another risky activity with a known distribution of returns. The rate of return, r, to a dollar of evaded tax takes the value $-s$ with probability p and the value 1 with probability $1 - p$. So the expected rate of return is $\bar{r} = 1 - p - ps$.

But if the taxpayer has behaved honestly and declared y, disposable income would be $(1 - t)y$. Otherwise, disposable income would depend on the amount of evasion: If an amount of income e is concealed (so that the taxpayer reports $y - e$), then consumption is given by the random variable:

$$(1) \qquad\qquad\qquad c = (1 - t)y + ret.$$

An analysis of the taxpayer's optimal evasion decision, given the above budget constraint, shows that the exact decision that the taxpayer makes depends on his or her personal attributes, a, which may include willingness to take risks and innate honesty. However, it is conventional to assume that all taxpayers of whatever a type have the same structure to their preferences over the state-contingent consumption levels c' and c''. The standard assumption is

Axiom 4: Each a-type taxpayer's preference is represented by an expected utility function:

(2) $$[1 - p] u^a(c') + p u^a(c''),$$

where u^a is an increasing, concave function.

What this means is that the utility derived from disposable income (consumption) is increasing but that marginal utility increases at a decreasing rate. It rules out the phenomenon of the risk lover: Everyone is assumed to be either risk averse (in which case the indifference curves are strictly convex to the origin) or risk neutral. Furthermore the slope of any indifference curve in the neighborhood of perfectly honest behavior is fixed at $-(1 - p)/p$ (the betting odds on the taxpayer succeeding in his evasion), irrespective of income.[2]

With c determined by the rate of return to evasion r and by equation 1, if the taxpayer conceals some but not all income, then

(3) $$\frac{1 - p}{p} \frac{u^a_c(c')}{u^a_c(c'')} = s,$$

where $u^a_c(c')$, $u^a_c(c'')$, denotes the a type's marginal utility in the two possible cases (not-caught and caught), respectively. The simple interpretation is

Marginal rate of substitution = proportional penalty.

In principle, one should also consider two special cases that modify this conclusion. If the taxpayer reports completely honestly, then,

Marginal rate of substitution ≤ proportional penalty.

If the taxpayer completely evades, then,

Marginal rate of substitution ≥ proportional penalty.

Equation 3 can be used to derive optimal evasion e^* as a function of the tax enforcement parameters (p, s, t) and the personal characteristics (y, a). The properties of this function are inherited directly from the assumptions about the utility function, and it can be used to derive a number of specific behavioral predictions.

THE AGGREGATE. If the economy is large, the government may take as determinate the total amount of revenue it receives through the penalties imposed on proven tax evaders, although the amount each taxpayer has to pay (tax plus surcharges) is random.

The appropriate budgetary constraint upon government might be modeled several ways. The standard version is as follows. The government has a specific net revenue target, R_0, and it faces an aggregate resource cost of enforcement that is increasing in the detection probability, p. Actual revenue raised, R, is

2. This the point at which $c'' = c'$, because $e = 0$.

given by total legal tax burden minus the total leakage through evasion and the resource cost of enforcement. The constraint that the government faces is simply $R \geq R_0$: Tax receipts, net of any leakages to the underground economy and administration costs, must be at least as great as revenue. Given an appropriate objective function and a specification of the resource-cost function, this constraint can form the basis for the design of an optimal tax enforcement policy. But uncritical application of this apparently commonsense criterion in a normative model can lead to unfortunate prescriptions.

Results

The following is a brief review of what can be deduced immediately from the basic assumptions of the simple TAG model and the attempts to implement it empirically.

THEORETICAL OVERVIEW. Although three possible outcomes of individual optimization (equation 3 and the two modifications that follow it) are described, only two are relevant. Given that the taxpayer is an expected utility maximizer and that the marginal utility of consumption is positive, then the first outcome drops out if $\bar{r} > 0$, that is, if the taxpayer always conceals some income.[3] Equation 3 also shows that increasing the probability of detection, p, or the surcharge, s, will shift the equilibrium in such a way that e^* is reduced.[4]

Furthermore, there is an intuitively reasonable result to be obtained that characterizes taxpayer behavior across different attribute classes of taxpayers. An a type's risk aversion is defined to be the proportion rate at which the a type's marginal utility falls with consumption:

$$(4) \qquad\qquad -\frac{u_{cc}^a(c)}{u_c^a(c)},$$

---

3. See Cowell (1990, p. 56), for an explanation. However, this may not apply in richer models of taxpayer choice. Andreoni (1992). Of course if the taxpayer's preferences in the face of risk do not conform to that of the expected utility model, then the taxpayer may comply more than the conventional theory would suggest. Bernasconi (1998).

4. Equation 3 can be rewritten as

$$\frac{u_c([1-t]y + et)}{u_c([1-t]y - set)} = \frac{ps}{1-p}.$$

Check the left-hand side of this equation: Remembering that $u_c(\cdot)$ is everywhere decreasing or constant, one can see that an increase in e will decrease the numerator and increase the denominator; the LHS is decreasing in e. Now increasing p or s obviously increases the right-hand side. So the only way the equation can still hold if p or s increases is if e falls.

where $u_{cc}^a(c)$ is the slope of the marginal utility function (negative in the case of risk aversion). If a taxpayer's risk aversion for all values of c is dependent on personal attributes, then certain taxpayers will always conceal more income than other taxpayers.[5]

To obtain other results, a fifth axiom is usually introduced:

Axiom 5: Absolute risk aversion is a decreasing function of c. This implies that a risk-averse individual who holds a portfolio containing a safe asset and a risky asset will increase the holding of the risky asset were the endowment to increase. So for any particular a type and any given set of tax enforcement parameters (p, s, t), if the individual's taxable income, y, increases, then so too does e, the absolute amount of income concealed. Decreasing absolute risk aversion does not permit anything definite to be said, however, about the proportion of taxable income that is being concealed.

So the elementary analysis of behavior in the face of risk results in four simple propositions about the incidence of tax evasion in the community (also see appendix 8A):

—If the rate of return to evasion is positive, everyone evades tax.

—Those with higher risk aversion tend to evade less.

—Those with higher personal income tend to evade more.

—Increasing any of the tax enforcement parameters (p, s, t) will reduce the amount of concealed income.

The TAG model is remarkably robust, in that the above propositions are established for a wide class of individual preferences. However, only the second proposition and two-thirds of the fourth proposition seem to chime with common sense. It seems strange to assert that all taxpayers will evade; and although one would expect compliance to increase with the probability of audit, p, and with the size of the surcharge, s, why should it also increase with the nominal tax rate, t? Many would argue that common sense suggests the opposite. As for the third proposition, who knows? Clearly this is an area where common sense is not adequate, and we need empirical evidence.

EMPIRICAL MODEL SPECIFICATION. The TAG model gives aggregate evasion, which suggests that an appropriate econometric version of the model ought to have tax and enforcement parameters, personal income, and indicators of type of income recipient as explanatory variables; the dependent variable would be some measure of underreported income. The model could be estimated for different categories of taxpayer or for taxpayers in general. The empirical model could be used to test the empirical validity some of the propositions on the shape of the e function raised earlier.

5. See Cowell (1990, pp. 57, 58).

A number of difficulties arise, however, with appropriately specifying an empirical model. There may be underlying problems of sample-selection bias; for example, even a carefully conducted review of taxpayer audits may nonetheless exclude individuals who do not file a tax return at all. Furthermore a particularly tricky difficulty is the specification of the variable characterizing the probability of audit. Usually some proxy for evasion opportunity (such as the presence of business income) has been used to categorize audit classes, and the probability of audit can be expected to differ across these classes.[6] Finally there is a "rationing" problem: Individuals' opportunities for participating in evasion differ greatly among occupations and social groups, although one might suppose that the membership of rationed and nonrationed groups is largely self-selected. The appropriate margin of choice for an individual may not be to change the amount of evasion undertaken within the context of a particular group but rather to migrate among groups in response to changes in tax enforcement parameters.

TAXPAYER AUDITS.   In the United States the Tax Compliance Measurement Program (TCMP), a program unmatched in other countries, provides the empirical researcher a preeminent data source.[7] Here I briefly summarize some of the empirical work based on taxpayer audit data, principally from the TCMP.[8]

—Tax compliance differs according to income type and socioeconomic group. For example, it is lower for married people than for single persons, lower for younger people than for older people.

—Source of income rather than income level is a significant determinant of evasion. A much higher proportion of wage and salary income than self-employment income is reported. Those paying taxes on nonfarm business have a lower value (about 0.3) on the income elasticity of underreporting than those paying taxes on farm business income (about 0.65).

—Income level and enforcement parameters generally have the expected effects on evasion behavior. Higher income is associated with higher amounts of underreported income. Although taxpayer compliance is usually positively associated with the probability and severity of criminal penalties, the relationship is weak. This is broadly confirmed by a Minnesota experiment, in which taxpayers were informed that they were likely to be subject to close scrutiny (high-

6. See, for example, the approach in Andreoni, Erard, and Feinstein (1998).

7. The last TCMP was done in 1988, although a limited successor was announced in 2002 as the National Research Program.

8. The results on taxpayer characteristics and income sources are drawn from the studies by Beron, Tauchen, and Witte (1992); Clotfelter (1983); and Feinstein (1991). The main sources for the role of income and the impact of enforcement parameters are Beron, Tauchen, and Witte (1992); Poterba (1987); and Witte and Woodbury (1985). For an authoritative account of the inherent econometric problems, see Feinstein (1991). The Minnesota audit experiment is reported in Slemrod, Blumenthal, and Christian (2001).

income taxpayers appeared, however, to behave differently from low- and middle-income taxpayers).

—Early studies suggest less taxpayer compliance in groups with higher marginal tax rates. However, in any sample of taxpayers taken at any particular time, those facing different marginal tax rates may belong to groups that have different economic opportunities or that have significantly different preferences for risk and attitudes toward evasion. More recent work shows greater insight on the important relationship between the marginal tax rate and evasion, separate from income: While income has only a weak effect, the marginal tax rate has a negative impact.

—Detection is imperfect: Variation in detection rates is at least as important as variations in personal characteristics.

INDIRECT EVIDENCE. The microdata on tax evasion are, perhaps understandably, limited in availability and coverage, so some researchers infer underground economic activity by using an indirect indicator, including monetary variables or apparent differences between income and expenditure at the aggregate level.

Unfortunately many of the more ambitious attempts to obtain indirect evidence are of dubious value, since they are only sketchily based on economic theory and suffer from severe econometric shortcomings. What is needed is a careful empirical model of the relationship between observables that appropriately takes account of the influence of unobservables in its specification and that provides a plausible basis for distinguishing between the impact of noncompliance and other unobservables.[9]

LABORATORY EXPERIMENTS. The questions that either microdata or indirect evidence allow the researcher to pursue usually concern issues such as the possible role of specific personal or job characteristics as factors predisposing to tax compliance, the impact of changes in tax rates, and the relationship between compliance and the tax structure. It is not usually possible to focus clearly on taxpayer motivation, which may be of immediate concern for those who want to judge the effects of incentives—the carrot and the stick—on compliance.

Experimental methods suggest themselves as a possible way of filling this gap. It is not often that circumstances permit experiments with real taxpayers, so it is not surprising that several economists and psychologists have used laboratory

9. An example of the aggregate approach is Crane and Nourzad (1986), who use a synthetic series of an "adjusted gross income gap" as a measure of tax evasion. Modeling this as a function of tax rates, enforcement parameters, income, and the inflation rate, they suggest that aggregate evasion falls with the tax rate, in line with the early cross-section TCMP evidence. Thomas (1999) provides a good overview of the methodological pitfalls in many of these aggregate approaches. A good example of appropriate micromodeling of behavioral relationships is Pissarides and Weber (1989), who use the Family Expenditure Survey (United Kingdom) to model the differential relationship between expenditure and income for the employed (with very low evasion opportunities) and for the self-employed, who clearly have substantial opportunity for noncompliance.

experiments. The results are not encouraging for the TAG model: An early study concludes that subjects do not act like gamblers in the tax compliance setting, and it is not even clear that they act in conformity with the basic economic model of risk taking. Furthermore it appears that the structure of taxation is important, over and above the levels of tax rates and exemptions. However, the evidence on the responses to tax enforcement parameters is broadly in line with what one gets from econometric analysis of the microdata. A higher probability of audit is associated with greater compliance (although it may have its principal impact on whether one chooses to evade at all rather than on the amount evaded) conditional on noncompliant behavior.[10]

WHAT IS WRONG WITH THE MODEL? Some aspects of the TAG model are distinctly unsatisfactory, especially the implication in axiom 5 that, as long as the expected rate of return to evasion is positive, everyone will conceal some income. The structure of the model might be reformed in three areas:

—The nature of taxpayer motivation. The assumption is usually made that the objective function should be in the form of expected utility. But what is a more appropriate characterization of risk?

—The nature of the economic interaction. Because of the inherently non-strategic nature of compliance, some essential features determining compliance and the possibility of manipulation by the tax authority may have been assumed away. Furthermore the atemporal setting arguably leaves out some of the crucial aspects of the interaction between taxpayer and tax authority (for example, it completely misses the issues associated with tax amnesties).

—The nature of the economic agent. The model assumes gamblers endowed with exogenously fixed incomes. While this assumption has been relaxed in some models to include labor supply, the productive economy is usually ignored.[11] In particular, focusing on the TAG model typically neglects a key feature of tax noncompliance: the behavior of firms. Given that the firm is constrained only by the size of the market and its ability to undercut the costs of competitors, the consequences of successful individual attempts at noncompliance may be enormous.

Rethinking Taxpayer Motivation

Underlying the TAG model is the simple greed assumption conventionally made in economics, but this assumption may tell only a partial story about the

---

10. See Baldry (1986, 1987); Cowell (1991); Spicer and Thomas (1982). But see Alm, Bahl, and Murray (1990) for contrary evidence.

11. See, for example, Baldry (1979); Cowell (1985); Pencavel (1979).

relationship between citizens and the state. The question as to what motivates taxpayers deserves to be addressed. For example, some people may pay taxes and refrain from evasion out of civic duty. In reviewing taxpayer motivation one may examine a number of issues that affect the structure of the model.

Expected Utility

The TAG model, rooted in conservative economic theory, assumes rational individuals with stable preferences who, given specific economic opportunities and probabilities, maximize their expected utility. The expected utility (EU) paradigm may be good as a device for simplified model building, but it may miss important nuances about people's preferences in the face of uncertainty.

Indeed the use of EU assumptions to characterize these preferences is arguably restrictive. It rules out state-dependent utility and hence any feeling of shame (or delight) at successful evasion. It also rules out regrets and misperceptions on the part of the taxpayer about the probabilities of alternative possible states of the world—for example, the probability of audit. However, there is evidence that individuals make systematic mistakes when attempting to maximize their expected utility. Would relaxing the expected utility assumption to consider other models—such as rank-dependent utility or prospect theory—result in a more promising underlying story?

Rank-dependent utility is unlikely to be a fruitful approach in the present context given the typically uncomplicated nature of the risk involved: The possible outcomes are usually taken to be the simple pair (income-if-not-caught, income-if-caught) rather than a structure of possible payoffs. However, prospect theory incorporates features that may be relevant to the problem of appropriately modeling taxpayer choice, in particular the following:

—Individuals "edit" information about gambles before they evaluate them so as to simplify the representation of the prospect with which they are faced.

—Individuals use a reference point from which to measure outcomes in terms of changes.

—The value function is defined over gains and losses relative to the reference point rather than to absolute values of wealth or income.

—In evaluating gambles, individuals assign decision weights different from the actual probabilities.

The first three of these features lead to a version of the framing phenomenon, in which risk choices are evaluated according to the way they are presented to the decisionmaker; in particular, gains may be evaluated quite differently from losses, relative to a particular reference point.

Several studies that examine tax evasion in the light of prospect theory suggest support for the framing hypothesis, whereby the response to a particular economic incentive (carrot or stick) differs according to the context. But direct tests of conformity of behavior with prospect theory are inconclusive.[12] It is not clear that prospect theory receives overwhelming support in comparison with expected utility theory, although the framing issue remains important for the issue of the effectiveness of incentives and sanctions.

Range of Goods

The range of goods in the utility function is also simplified in the TAG model. Individuals are concerned only with their own private consumption and so of course care nothing for the goods and services produced by the resources raised through the tax system. This issue is relevant to economies with a small public sector as well as to those that supply a lot of goods publicly. One would expect to see a positive relationship between marginal tax rates and the overall size of the underground economy if, on average, public goods were perceived to be underprovided, with the reverse effect if there is overprovision of public goods.[13]

The Temporal Model

The TAG model ignores time. It assumes that, each year, essentially the same gamble takes place, without there being any "memory" in the system. Some contributions to the literature attempt to correct this by allowing the tax authority to use information from multiple time periods. Even if the tax authority uses only information from the current period for an audit, the outcome of the audit may be used to trigger retrospective investigation.[14] This clearly weights the "stick" wielded by the tax authority. A rational taxpayer's current tax evasion is a decreasing function of evasion in previous periods. The reason for this is that if the taxpayer is audited and caught evading this year, penalties for earlier noncompliance may be incurred.

12. On the general issues of prospect theory, see Kahneman and Tversky (1979); Tversky and Kahneman (1981); and Schepanski and Shearer (1995). For a review of experimental evidence on the expected utility model and other paradigms of individual decisionmaking, see Camerer (1995). Support for the framing hypothesis is found in the studies by Chang, Nichols, and Schultz (1987); Robben and others (1990); and Schepanski and Shearer (1995). King and Sheffrin (2002) investigated whether individual behavior conforms to the standard results of prospect theory, given a scenario that incorporates a perception of inequity, using a questionnaire with student respondents. The responses to the control questions are consistent with expected utility theory in that they do not display the phenomenon of loss aversion (risk taking when faced with losses and risk averse when faced with gains) characteristic of prospect theory.

13. Note that this phenomenon is, nonetheless, consistent with the free-rider problem associated with public good provision; it follows from the impact of income levels on risk-taking behaviors associated with noncompliance. Cowell and Gordon (1988).

14. This is the argument in Engel and Hines (1999).

Interdependence

Among the aspects of taxpayer interdependence that can affect the overall compliance problem is trust and the concept of a climate of behavior. This climate can be represented by an externality in the individual utility function—people may care about their own behavior relative to that of their peers; the stigma or the nonmonetary penalty associated with discovered evasion may be endogenously determined by the behavior of others.[15] This consumption externality may be supplemented by a production externality; the growth in individual noncompliance may facilitate the development of a kind of infrastructure of noncompliance—finding a corrupt accountant for one's own tax cheating will lower the search costs of other potential noncompliers.

The endogeneity of interdependence in the economic model is crucial. One of the contributions of the economic model that incorporates such interdependence is its explanation of epidemics of noncompliance. The maintenance of a culture of compliance is one example of the government or tax administration creating a "carrot"—a positive incentive for taxpayers to act in their broad social interest rather than in their narrow self-interest.

Donkeys, Mice, and Ghosts

Are taxpayers donkeys? The carrot-and-stick approach to modeling the interaction between taxpayer and tax authority assumes that the tax authority views economic incentives in a fairly simplistic fashion. The reason for this is the simple nature of the economic interaction in the basic TAG model: The tax authority lays down ground rules for the mass of taxpayers; each taxpayer then assumes that the probabilities in the fundamental gamble are uninfluenced by his or her own actions.

Strategic Models

An alternative view of economic interaction between the two parties sees them as cat and mouse, or cat and dog. Each party is aware of the other's motivations and interests (the taxpayer wants to maximize utility, the tax authority to maximize net tax revenue) and takes these into account in selecting its own strategy. The outcome is an equilibrium in which each party makes the best response to the other's strategy in the light of the available information.

15. On trust, see Scholz and Lubell (1998b). The stigma model is attributable to Benjamini and Maital (1985). Note that it only requires an aggregate level of externality to be generated by the taxpayers as distinct from the near-neighbor model of Glaeser, Sacerdote, and Scheinkman (1996), in which the position of other economic agents is important.

This approach resolves into two classes of model according to whether one assumes that it is reasonable for the tax authority to precommit to an audit strategy, that is, to set the agenda for the interaction.[16] Which model is the more appropriate depends on factors such as the type of institutions and laws present in the economy and the nature of the information available to the parties.

PRECOMMITMENT. In a model characterized by a simplified distribution of income (just rich and poor in known proportions) and in which the tax authority moves first strategically, the optimal policy of the tax authority is stark. It should audit all low-income tax reports and ignore all high-income tax reports. However, under such circumstances no high-income person would ever dare to report a low income; so in fact the only people who would ever get audited are those who are genuinely low income! The statement of the model may seem extreme, but it contains an inner truth about the regressive nature of such carefully tailored audit schemes.

NO PRECOMMITMENT. By contrast consider a model in which precommitment to such an extreme policy is not credible. Again there are two income levels, but the personal characteristics of the population are such that some will always report truthfully and others will not if they have the opportunity and find it profitable. Let the probability that the tax authority decides to audit a particular low-income report be p and the probability of a potentially dishonest taxpayer not complying be q. Each party takes fully into account the other's strategy in this game of noncompliance and investigation. The outcome will be a Nash equilibrium characterized by a pair (p^*, q^*) representing the "best response" of each party (the tax authority and the taxpayer) to the other's strategy. Each of these equilibrium values depends on, among other things, the tax rate, t, the penalty surcharge, s, and the cost of an individual audit. The following generalizations can be made:

—Decreasing the marginal cost of audit (that is, making the investigation and enforcement system more efficient) reduces the probability of noncompliance, q^*, but leaves the optimal probability of audit, p^*, unchanged.

—Increasing the surcharge, s, reduces both the optimal probability of noncompliance and the optimal probability of audit. The first of these is attributable to the usual marginal deterrent effect of higher punishment.[17] The second emerges because the tax authority does not need to put in so much effort to achieve a given net revenue.

—Increasing the tax rate reduces the probability of noncompliance, q^*, and will either increase or leave unchanged the optimal probability of audit.

16. See Reinganum and Wilde (1985) for the model with precommitment and Graetz, Reinganum, and Wilde (1986) and Reinganum and Wilde (1986) for the no-commitment case. The specific no-commitment model discussed here is briefly outlined in the appendix to this chapter.

17. A word of caution: This argument about the marginal deterrent effect in this and other models cannot be pressed too far. See remarks under "Guidance for Policymakers," below.

Note that, despite the different premises of this model, the impact of the key parameters s and t on compliance is in the same direction as in the TAG model.

Ghosts

Ghosts are individuals who fail to comply with their income tax filing requirements in an extreme form: They disappear from the system. From the point of view of economic modeling there is an essential difference between those who make a zero-income report and those who make no report at all. What do we know, or what could be known, about ghosts and the way they can be expected to respond to economic incentives designed by the tax authority?

Unfortunately, information about the behavior and characteristics of ghosts is sparse, although enough is known to suggest that they are quantitatively important: The U.S. ghost population in 1988 is estimated at nearly 8 million (compared with 110 million who filed tax returns); the tax shortfall for ghosts is estimated at $11 billion, or some 15 percent of the known tax shortfall of those who file returns.[18]

A Hybrid Model

The role of ghosts in the tax enforcement story may, however, be more important than their numbers suggest. Typically, both ghosts and strategic players are present in the same population. The margin between the two types of behavior may be crucial from the point of view of policy design: An overzealous approach to enforcement in the sector populated by strategic players may encourage them to migrate to the ghost sector, which is, in essence, nonstrategic and in which the costs of detection and enforcement are typically higher.[19]

Firms

Why consider corporations and businesses separate from individual taxpayers in economic models of tax compliance? Some theorists have adopted an essentially pragmatic approach, arguing that to distinguish corporate and personal sectors is a way to understand the overall distortional impact of tax evasion.[20] However,

---

18. The results come from Erard and Ho (2001), who extend the standard TAG model to account for nonfilers and use a special subset of the TCMP data containing detailed tax and audit information for both filers and nonfilers of U.S. federal income tax returns.

19. See Cowell and Gordon (1995).

20. Fullerton and Karayannis (1994).

this is distinct from the issue of whether the underlying economic analysis of tax evasion is, or should be, different according to the sector considered.

A brief look at the economics literature on compliance and tax enforcement as it relates to the behavior of firms reveals the key issues that might characterize a theory of compliance by firms. This theoretical approach could then form the basis of appropriate empirical models for the corporate sector and enable policymakers to develop a quantitative model for analyzing the effectiveness of tax compliance regimes.

In principle, firms can evade by misreporting or making false declaration about profits, sales, or input use and other costs. Does the assumed market environment of the firm make a difference to its compliance behavior?

A Simplified Model

Let us take a simplified model of a firm with constant average and marginal cost, producing a single output subject to tax at a uniform rate.[21] The tax is enforced in the same way as described earlier, and so again there is an implied expected rate of return to noncompliance $\bar{r}$. Checking through the formal specification of this model in appendix 8A, it can be seen that this could be reinterpreted as a model in which profit is the tax base. The firm has two types of decisions to make: the quantity of output and the extent to which it conceals output or hides profit.

In analyzing the solution to this double problem, it is useful to introduce two new concepts. The first is the expected tax rate on output $\bar{t}$, which is given by the nominal tax rate, t, multiplied by a factor of 1, minus the proportion of output concealed times $\bar{r}$. The expected tax rate is under the control of the individual firm (through the choice it makes on concealment) as well as the tax authority. The second concept is the average concealment cost per unit of output, g, which is a function of the amount of concealment (amount of tax evasion) undertaken.

Assume that the firm chooses the output and level of evasion to maximize expected profits. Because the model is so simple, expected profits can be written as

$$(P - m - g - \bar{t}) \times \text{output},$$

---

21. The simplified model is based on the standard approach in the literature. The main references are Cremer and Gahvari (1993) and Virmani (1989), who focus on a competitive industry; Marrelli (1984) and Marrelli and Martina (1988), who deal with noncompetitive firms that are assumed to be risk averse.

where P is the price, m is marginal cost, and the components g and $\bar{t}$ (but not others) depend on the amount of concealment. A number of conclusions immediately follow:

—If the firm conceals output, it will do so up to the point where the marginal cost of concealment equals the marginal reduction of expected tax rate.

—The firm will always conceal some output if $\bar{t} < t$. This is equivalent to the requirement that the expected rate of return $\bar{r}$ be positive.

—There is a fundamental separability property between the concealment decision and the output decision. Here the concealment decision is independent of the output decision.

—Output decisions for the competitive firm are determined by a modified "price = marginal cost" rule.

The solution to the maximization problem can be used to derive comparative statistics results in the usual way. In the case of the competitive model we then find:

—Reported sales decrease as the tax rate increases.

—An increase in tax increases the price but by less than the amount of the tax, since some of the tax increase is absorbed in increased evasion.

—An increased probability of detection, p, or an increased surcharge, s, will raise the proportion of sales declared, expected tax, and the market price.

So, as in the TAG model, enhanced deterrence will have the appropriate effect on evasion; in addition it moves expected taxes in the direction that we might have anticipated. But in contrast to the TAG model, there is an unambiguous prediction of a rise in tax evasion with a rise in the tax rate.

Moreover the results are not special to the competitive model. Under risk neutrality the separability property holds, and so it is not surprising to find that basically the same conclusions apply to the monopolistic case as those for the case of perfect competition. The only real difference in the equilibrium is that the "price = adjusted marginal cost" rule is replaced by a condition involving the elasticity of demand.

However, the separability issue is potentially more problematic once one drops the assumption of risk neutrality. This matters both because it clarifies the factors that determine equilibrium compliance by firms in a variety of market environments and because it allows for clearcut conclusions about the impact of policy parameters.[22]

---

22. Wang and Conant (1988) study the expected utility function when a monopolist overstates production costs in order to reduce taxable profits. The uncertain monopolist's optimal rate of output is not affected by either the profit tax or the penalty rate. Yaniv's (1995) model of tax evasion covers different types of taxes that can be evaded by the firm, showing that these taxes do not alter the separability conclusion. Yaniv (1996) extends the analysis of separability to cases in which both the probability of detection and the penalty rate vary with the amount of cost overstatement. Lee (1998)

An Empirical Analysis

Unfortunately the empirical analysis of corporate tax evasion is extremely limited. In the main it consists either of a compilation of rather obvious results (for example, tax evasion depends on the preferences of the person who has the power over declaration) or of procedures that could be considered as methodologically very weak. The main reasons are the lack of theoretical models, since theory mainly focuses on personal income tax evasion; the lack of corporate income tax compliance microdata; and the lack of confidence in microdata on tax compliance and relevance of measurement error.

However, some evidence is available, again drawn from the TCMP.[23] Of special interest are two main results that have no counterpart in the literature on personal income tax compliance:

—A firm's compliance is positively associated with being publicly traded and with belonging to a highly regulated industry.

—Having low profits relative to the industry median is correlated with higher corporate tax noncompliance.

Clearly both of these findings have potentially important implications for the design of policy.

An Assessment

What makes the simple microeconomic model of the firm essentially different from the TAG model as it is applied to the individual? Three features stand out: the nature of the taxpayer, the assumption about risk preferences, and the determinants of responsiveness to economic incentives.

THE TAXPAYER. It is reasonable to argue that individuals—and perhaps even families and households—exist as exogenously given entities; the set of potential taxpayers could be imagined as exogenously given. This is not the case with firms. Firms are born and dissolved, they merge and change their shape, and they do all this in response to economic incentives. The tax system and its enforcement mechanism are essential components of those economic incentives, and so a reasonable model of firm behavior has to be established before the impact of tax and enforcement policy on firms can be understood. Of course the

---

shows that the separability property and the neutrality of profit taxes depend on how the audit probability and penalty rate are formulated.

23. Rice (1992) uses a corporate subset of TCMP based on an examination of the tax and financial records of a stratified random sample of about 30,000 U.S. corporations out of a total of 1.5 million corporations with assets less than $10 million.

contrast with the household sector is somewhat overstated, but this contrast may contain an important component of the problem.[24]

RISK PREFERENCES. A major feature of the model of personal noncompliance is the role of risk aversion in the equilibrium. Although several studies using the cat-and-mouse tradition of strategic models assume risk neutrality, a reasonable amount of risk aversion is required in the TAG model in order to get interesting answers. Risk neutrality or extremely high risk aversion would always yield an extreme solution: The individual either evades all the tax or none at all.

By contrast, in modeling noncompliance among firms it is common to assume risk neutrality. An assumption of neutrality is often important for the separation result, which allows predictions to be established from the theory.

RESPONSIVENESS TO INCENTIVES. Following on from the difference in conventional assumptions about risk preference is the question of what drives the taxpayers' responsiveness (or lack of it) to sticks and carrots. In the case of individual taxpayers, differences in risk preference characterize the differential: the differing responsiveness of different groups to penalties or to the probability of detection. In the case of the firm, it is quite different. Equilibrium is determined by a first-order condition involving the marginal concealment cost and the rate of return to tax evasion. This essential difference gives rise to, among other things, the different relationship between compliance and the tax rate in the models of the personal and the corporate sector.

Understanding the nature and the determinants of the cost-of-concealment function, g, is essential to understanding what is going on in firms' noncompliance and to understanding the economic incentives that may usefully be applied by a tax enforcement agency. The academic literature on this point is rather sparse, but one could conjecture that the following are key factors:

—The nature of the product. The output or sale of a highly visible physical good is harder to conceal than some services, for example. Just as the opportunities for evasion in the individual sector differ strongly across occupational categories (employment versus self-employment), so also one would expect to find systematic differences across industry categories.

—The size and organizational structure of the firm. Firms with a more complex organization are likely to have higher concealment costs: The more people brought into the plot, the greater the security problem and the greater the risk of discovery.

24. In particular one would expect to find a relationship between the individual personal motivations of those running firms and firm behavior. An interesting example of this is Joulfaian (2000), who finds a positive and significant correlation between managers' preferences and firm compliance using U.S. data.

—The role of reputation. Firms with a respected brand name have much to lose by exposure of illegal activity and therefore have high concealment costs.

—Degree of concentration of the industry. There are two counteracting effects. On the one hand, an industry with a large number of firms may be easier to police by an external agency: Those deviating from the norm in terms of reporting will be easier to spot, leading to higher concealment costs for each firm. On the other hand, the presence of a large number of similar firms could encourage the spread of concealment technology among them.

Guidance for Policymakers

Unsurprisingly, the appropriate guidance for policymakers depends on the specific model considered. Alternative models can yield useful policy lessons.

The TAG Model

If noncompliant taxpayers are, in economic terms, indistinguishable from gamblers, then they should be responsive to the same kind of economic incentives as are gamblers. There may be enough information about individual a types to tailor an audit policy conditioned on personal attributes. Of course, such a policy would have to use proxies for the true values of the components of a, which are unobservable, but reasonable proxies may well be available. Obviously this approach rests on the assumptions that the TAG model is appropriate, that individuals' perceptions of the gambles involved are accurate, and that these individuals are rationally pursuing a policy of ex ante utility maximization. But as we have seen, the evidence on this is not particularly convincing.

However, let us take the TAG model at face value for a moment: What recommendations does it suggest? Suppose the objective of the tax authority is simply to raise revenue. Intuition would then suggest (and formal analysis confirms; see appendix 8A) that enforcement should be intensified until the probability of audit satisfies that the marginal revenue raised equals the marginal resource cost.

Marginal revenue raised includes both direct revenue (tax uncovered plus surcharge) and the indirect revenue yielded by the effect on compliance of a higher audit probability. Allowing for the problem that the computation of marginal revenue raised relies on taxpayer perceptions of probabilities that may be inappropriate, the above condition seems to have a commonsense appeal. Moreover, this marginalist rule can be adapted and extended to other versions of the objective function.

There is a snag, though, a result of focusing on just the audit probability as a policy variable. If parameter s is also chosen, then it appears as though the tax authority can do better; that is to say, it can achieve its objective at lower resource cost by raising s and cutting p (as long as p remains positive). Indeed, given this greater flexibility, there is an obvious method of guaranteeing total compliance: choosing s and p to ensure that the expected rate of return to compliance is not positive. If one presses the simple logic of the TAG model, then it is clear that the tax authority should save resources by using a (very) big stick version of deterrence.[25]

But uncritical application of the big stick approach can lead to ridiculous outcomes. One cannot assume that such ridiculous outcomes will be prevented by the common sense of legislators or administrators, or one could reach the extraordinary situation of eighteenth-century London, described by Charles Dickens in *A Tale of Two Cities*:

> But indeed, at that time, putting to death was a recipe much in vogue with all trades and professions and not least of all with Tellson's [Bank]. Death is Nature's remedy for all things, and why not Legislation's? Accordingly, the forger was put to Death; the utterer of a bad note was put to Death; the unlawful opener of a letter was put to Death; the purloiner of forty shillings and sixpence was put to Death; the holder of a horse at Tellson's door, who made off with it, was put to Death; the coiner of a bad shilling was put to Death. . . . Not that it did the least good in the way of prevention—it might almost have been worth remarking that the fact was almost exactly the reverse—but it cleared off (as to this world) the trouble of each particular case and left nothing else connected with it to be looked after" [book 2, chap. 1].

Of course it is a cheap shot to thus picture the outcome of the simplified economic model. What is more useful is to identify the economic reasons behind the ridiculous outcome of a high s and a low p and, perhaps, the way to derive a more useful model. Four faulty characteristics of the simplified model—unreasonableness, ineffectiveness, inequity, and misspecification—are considered.

UNREASONABLENESS. At first glance the obvious objection to the big-stick approach is that it is just not reasonable. Do we really want to see extreme penalties for minor infringement of the tax law? At the very least, legislators and those implementing the law need a sense of proportion as to what is appropriate in the context of taxation relative to, say, fraud and theft elsewhere in society.

INEFFECTIVENESS. The TAG model also ignores the issue of appropriately structured punishment. If for a terrible moment one imagines the death penalty for tax noncompliance, we might well also comment, "not that it did the least

---

25. On the welfare consequences of the simple TAG approach, see Cowell (1989); Kolm (1973).

good in the way of prevention." Taxpayers would, with impeccable economic logic, conclude that they might as well be hung for a sheep as for a lamb.

INEQUITY. Ex post inequities are almost bound to occur, but it is the job of a sensible tax administration to make sure that the consequences are not grotesquely magnified. An obvious source of potential inequity are errors by taxpayers and auditors. Although the standard model assumes that noncompliance is a result of optimization amoral on the part of taxpayers who desire the public benefits of the state without paying the private cost, a substantial amount of noncompliance could be attributable to mistakes or the outcome of inertia or laziness.

A more sensible approach to the normative analysis of compliance is to allow that errors are entirely possible; indeed this seems reasonable in the light of the evidence from the psychological literature. Taxpayers can be encouraged by appropriate incentives to take care in reporting, while the design and implementation of the penalty structure can distinguish between minor infractions and serious violations, even if this were to be at the apparent cost of some expected revenue.[26]

MISSPECIFICATION. Although the TAG model has the advantage of conformity with mainstream economic analysis, and although it may be useful as a starting point for discussion among those raised in a neoclassical tradition of applied welfare economics, it takes the wrong direction because it is built of the wrong components. Let us consider what might be learned from some of the alternatives that have been mentioned previously.

Modified Motivation

A better understanding of how individuals reach decisions under uncertainty can help in the design or modification of a policy to enhance tax compliance.

NON-EU MODELS OF RISK. One of the main reasons for the failure of the TAG model is a popular misperception of the probability of audit. The use of decision weights that differ from the actual audit probabilities may give the tax authority an opportunity to induce greater compliance by exploiting this misperception, since it is in its interest that taxpayers overestimate their chances of being caught.

However, the non-EU risk model also suggests that there could be fruitful and low-cost possibilities for administrative innovation. If we take the framing phenomenon seriously there may be considerable scope for imaginative redesign

---

26. On the role of inertia, see Smith and Kinsey (1987). Boadway and Sato (2000) examine the effects of unintentional errors on the design of tax enforcement and tax policy. Maximal sanctions are not applied, unlike the Dickensian model. Although intentional evasion can be deterred by carrots, inadvertent tax evaders are not protected by either the carrot or the stick.

of conditional payments associated with tax enforcement. Even though two payment schemes may be formally equivalent in terms of a taxpayer's conditional budget constraint, they may be viewed differently by the taxpayer making the choice under uncertainty. For example, should the tax authority consider prizes for promptness instead of penalties for late payments? One might even suggest that bonuses for an excellent compliance record may be more effective in some cases than surcharges for underreporting.

Finally, since there is evidence that, contrary to the TAG assumptions, taxpayer perceptions are important, the structure of taxation as well as the magnitude of the incentives should be taken into account.

INTERACTION MODELS. Interaction models pick up on an important externality present in the economic problem of compliance. The message of the "epidemic" model is that the impact of a modification in tax enforcement policy should not be judged just in terms of its marginal impact on the compliance of a representative taxpayer. The tax authority also has a role—if not a duty—in fostering a climate of compliance.

Unfortunately the message is mainly negative. The right climate can be lost through careless implementation more easily than it can be built from scratch through group effects and socially responsible behavior. Insofar as the externality is generated by an infrastructure of noncompliance, it makes sense to regulate the activities and institutions associated with this infrastructure. Other forms of regulation in the economy may be crucial for effective regulation of tax compliance.

STRATEGIC MODELS AND HYBRIDS. The strategic, or cat-and-mouse, model is informative for the design of enforcement strategy in a reporting context. However, it assumes a well-defined and rather limited set of possible outcomes and a highly simplified distribution of unknowns (for example, in the implementable versions of such models there is usually a simple representation of the income distribution from which the taxpayer is assumed to be drawn). This model of the compliance problem seems more appropriate to the one-on-one negotiation between the tax authority and large taxpayers, personal or corporate, rather than to the masses.

Even where the simple cat-and-mouse model is applicable, the model can lead to some uncomfortable conclusions. Typically the kind of tailored policy that emerges from the model generates a regressive application of the tax law: Reports from the poor are audited much more intensively than those from the rich, but for good economic reasons. But these good economic reasons may not be sufficient to recommend a strategy that could be socially divisive.

Furthermore, the lesson of the hybrid model indicates the possibility of spillover: an induced migration by taxpayers from the reporting sector to the ghost sector. Overzealous enforcement in areas with relatively low-cost information may exacerbate the problems in high-cost areas (where the ghosts are).

The Firm

The simplified model of the firm outlined above can yield optimal tax enforcement rules for noncompliance by the firm.[27] But the more interesting use of the model is to provide working guidelines for those who design tax compliance schemes. Here concealment costs and their relationship to characteristics of the firm seem crucial and will determine the responsiveness to incentives of all firms for which the expected rate of return to noncompliance is positive. It suggests that the right approach to the empirical modeling of compliance and to the practical enforcement of tax payments by corporations should be piecemeal. The appropriate piecemeal approach will depend on the type of market in which the firm operates, the nature of its products, and the size of the firm itself.

Several points from the analysis of the individual sector play an important part in tax enforcement policy toward firms.

—The time component is, possibly, more important for firms than for individuals. One can expect reputation to be relevant for the effectiveness of enforcement mechanisms.

—As with individuals, audit data on firms are bound to be limited, in that they have relatively little to say on ghosts. For many developed economies an important contribution to the understanding of firms' noncompliance is a suitable model of the underground economy.

—Sometimes practical economic inquiry has to proceed by stealth. The tax authority needs to identify observables that are correlated with profit (as consumption with income) and that firms have an incentive to reveal.

—This suggests that, as with the control of the infrastructure of personal noncompliance, an appropriate compliance policy will go hand in hand with effective regulation of industry.

A Final Word

Although the standard economic model of the carrot-and-stick approach to tax enforcement is flawed in many ways, it is a useful starting point for understanding the mechanics of individual decisionmaking. But it can be misleading as a guide to policy advice. However, this should not make one skeptical of the contribution that theory can make to tax administration: Careful microeconomic analysis of the role of incentives can reveal a lot, if the model is selected with prudence.

27. See the derivations in Cremer and Gahvari (1993) and Etro (1998).

Appendix 8A

Elements of the theoretical models that undergird some of the principal assertions in the text are presented here.

The TAG Model

Given the model in axioms 1–4, the first-order condition for maximizing equation 2 with respect to e is given by

(A1) $$E[ru_c^a(c)] \leq 0 \text{ if } e^* = 0,$$

(A2) $$E[ru_c^a(c)] \geq 0 \text{ if } e^* = y,$$

(A3) $$E[ru_c^a(c)] = 0 \text{ otherwise,}$$

where $u_c^a(c)$ denotes the first derivative of u^a and E denotes the expectations operator. Inequalities in equations A1 and A2 represent, respectively, the cases in which the person reports truthfully (conceals no income) and in which the person conceals everything. Equation A3 gives the case in which the person conceals just a part of his or her income from the authorities. First-order conditions (equations A2 and A3) can be solved to yield the taxpayer response function,

(A4) $$e^* = e(\tau, y, a),$$

where $\tau: = (p, s, t)$ is the collection of tax and enforcement parameters.

COMPARATIVE STATISTICS. If the person is risk averse and at an interior equilibrium, then equation A3 characterizes the optimum, and differentiation can be used to obtain the way e changes in response to policy parameters. For example, differentiating equation A3 with respect to p and using equation 1, gives

(A5) $$E[r^2 u_{cc}^a(c)] \frac{\partial e(\tau, y, a)}{\partial p} - u_c^a(c') - s u_c^a(c'') = 0.$$

The expectation term on the left-hand side must be negative, in view of the concavity of u^a, and so

(A6) $$\frac{\partial e(\tau, y, a)}{\partial p} = \frac{u_c^a(c') + s u_c^a(c'')}{E[r^2 u_{cc}^a(c)]} < 0.$$

Likewise, one can derive

(A7)
$$\frac{\partial e(\tau, y, a)}{\partial s} < 0,$$

and, if axiom 5 holds and if s is a constant independent of t and y, then

(A8)
$$\frac{\partial e(\tau, y, a)}{\partial t} < 0.$$

Note that equation A8 holds if the penalty is proportional to the tax evaded (as in my interpretation of the TAG model) rather than to the income concealed.[1]

THE AGGREGATE. If the number of taxpayers is effectively infinite and the distribution of individuals in the community by (y,a)-type is given by a continuous distribution function $F(y,a)$, then aggregate income is

$$Y: = \int y \, dF(y, a) \text{ (the tax base)},$$

aggregate evasion is

(A9)
$$E: = \int e(\tau, y, a) \, dF(y, a),$$

and revenue raised is

(A10)
$$R: = tY - \overline{rEt} - \Phi(p),$$

where $\overline{rEt}$ is the expected aggregate loss through tax evasion and $\Phi(p)$ is the dollar cost to the government of enforcing the probability of detection p everywhere.

A rule for public policy can then be derived by differentiating with respect to p:

(A11)
$$\frac{\partial R}{\partial p} = -\frac{\partial(\overline{rE})}{\partial p} t - \frac{\partial \Phi(p)}{\partial p}.$$

So if the objective were simply to maximize revenue, R, setting equation A11 to zero would yield:

(A12)
$$\underbrace{[1 + s] et}_{\text{direct effect}} - \underbrace{\overline{rt} \frac{\partial e}{\partial p}}_{\text{indirect effect}} = \frac{\partial \Phi(p)}{\partial p}.$$

Cat and Mouse

Consider a world in which there are exactly two levels of income, y_0 and $y_0 + \Delta y$, and three groups of taxpayers with characteristics known to be as in the following table:

1. Yitzhaki (1974).

Group	Income	Personal attribute	Proportion of population
0	y_0	—	f_0
1	$y_0 + \Delta y$	Always honest	f_1
2	$y_0 + \Delta y$	Potentially dishonest	f_2

Consider first the taxpayers' position. The behavior of those in groups 0 and 1 is fixed; and those in the group 2 get expected utility

(A13) $\qquad pu^a[(1 - t)y_0 + (1 - t - st)\Delta y] + (1 - p)u^a[(1 - t)y_0 + \Delta y]$

if they cheat and

(A14) $\qquad\qquad\qquad u^a([1 - t][y_0 + \Delta y])$

if they do not cheat, where p is the assumed probability that a low-income report will be audited. The value of p that equates equations A13 and A14 is given by

(A15) $\quad p^* := \dfrac{u^a[(1 - t)y_0 + \Delta y] - u^a[(1 - t)(y_0 + \Delta y)]}{u^a[(1 - t)y_0 + \Delta y] - u^a[(1 - t)y_0 + (1 - t - st)\Delta y]}.$

If the person were risk neutral, then equation A15 becomes $p^* = \dfrac{1}{1 + s}$.

Let q be the proportion of group 2 who cheat on taxes. If they believe that $p < p^*$, then all will cheat ($q = 1$). If they believe that $p > p^*$, then none will cheat ($q = 0$).

Now consider the tax authority. It knows that group 0 has to report y_0, that the group 1 people feel bound to report $y_0 + \Delta y$, and that each person in group 2 could report low (y_0) or high ($y_0 + \Delta y$); it assumes that a proportion, q, of this group will report low. If the authority aims to maximize net revenue and audits a proportion, p, of the low-income reports, then the probability of catching an evader is

$$\frac{f_2 q}{f_0 + f_2 q}\, p.$$

So if the cost of an individual audit is φ, the expected net revenue from the policy is

(A16) $\qquad [f_1 + (1 - q)f_2]\, t\Delta y + \dfrac{f_2 q}{f_0 + f_2 q}\, p(1 + s)t\Delta y - \varphi p,$

which may be rewritten as

(A17)
$$\text{const} + p\,\frac{\varphi f_0}{f_0 + f_2 q}\left[\frac{q}{q^*} - 1\right],$$

where

(A18)
$$q^*: = \frac{\varphi f_0}{f_2(1 + s)\,t\Delta y - \varphi}.$$

From equation A17, if $q > q^*$, then expected net revenue would increase everywhere with p, in which case the authority would investigate all low-income reports ($p = 1$); but if $q < q^*$, then expected revenue would decrease with p, and the authority would choose $p = 0$.

The Nash equilibrium is given by the point at which the beliefs of the tax authority and those of the taxpayers are consistent. This is the point at which $p = p^*$ and $q = q^*$. To see how this equilibrium is affected by public policy, one would differentiate equations A15 and A18 with respect to the parameters φ, s, t, giving

(A19)
$$\frac{\partial p^*}{\partial \varphi} = 0, \frac{\partial q^*}{\partial \varphi} > 0,$$

(A20)
$$\frac{\partial p^*}{\partial t} \geq 0, \frac{\partial q^*}{\partial t} > 0, \text{ and}$$

(A21)
$$\frac{\partial p^*}{\partial s} < 0, \frac{\partial q^*}{\partial s} < 0.$$

The Firm

The simplified model uses the following assumptions:

—Proportional cost function: Average and marginal cost are a constant, m.

—Proportional tax: Output, x, is taxed uniformly at rate t.

—Determinate demand: The firm faces a demand function, $x(P)$, or, equivalently, can command a known price, $P = P(x)$, for its product, where $P(\cdot)$ is the inverse demand function. This includes as a special case the situation of perfect competition, where $P = \text{constant}$.

—Costly concealment: A proportion β of sales are concealed by the firm; that is, a proportion, $1 - \beta$ of sales are declared to the tax authority, where $0 \leq \beta \leq 1$. The unit cost of concealing is given by $G(\beta)$, where $G(\cdot)$ is an increasing convex function.

—Fixed detection probability. The probability of discovery by the tax authority and subsequent conviction is fixed at level p.

—Fixed proportional penalty. The penalty rate on evaded tax is s.

Hence the expected tax rate per unit of output is

$$\bar{t} := [1 - \beta + \beta p(1 + s)]t = (1 - \beta \bar{r})t,$$

where $\bar{r} := 1 - p - ps$, as before. Expected profits are

(A22) $$\left[P - m - \beta G(\beta) - \left[\underbrace{(1 - p)(1 - \beta)t}_{\text{"notcaught"}} + \underbrace{p(1 + s\beta)t}_{\text{"caught"}}\right]\right] \times (P)$$

$$= [P - m - g(\beta) - \bar{t}] \times (P),$$

where $g(\beta) := \beta\ G(\beta)$ is the average concealment costs per unit of output. For any given output level, $x > 0$, equation A22 implies that the firm chooses β to minimize concealment costs (as a proportion of total output) plus the expected tax rate, $g(\beta) + \bar{t}$.

The first-order condition for a maximum is

$$\frac{dg(\beta)}{d\beta} + \frac{\partial \bar{t}}{\partial \beta} = 0,$$

which simplifies to

(A23) $$\frac{dg(\beta)}{d\beta} = [1 - p(1 + s)]t$$

(A24) $$= \frac{t - \bar{t}}{\beta}.$$

From equation A23 a necessary condition for an interior solution for β is that

(A25) $$1 - p(1 + s) > 0,$$

or, equivalently, $\bar{t} < t$ for $0 < \beta \leq 1$.

Note that equation A25 is exactly the same as the requirement that the expected rate of return to evasion be positive in the simple TAG model. If equation A25 is violated, then clearly no evasion issue will arise, and the firm will report honestly.

Market equilibrium for a competitive firm occurs at $P = m + g + \bar{t}$, implying that expected profits are zero; actual profits are positive if the firm is not audited, negative if audited.

Differentiating equation A23 with respect to t, gives

$$\frac{d^2 g(\beta)}{d\beta^2} \frac{\partial \beta}{\partial t} = [1 - p(1 + s)],$$

so

$$\frac{\partial \beta}{\partial t} > 0.$$

The same method gives

$$\frac{\partial \beta}{\partial p} < 0, \frac{\partial \beta}{\partial s} < 0.$$

COMMENT BY
John T. Scholz

Frank Cowell's analysis provides an insightful, expansive summary of the advantages and limitations of the utility-maximization framework, which underlies much of the current thinking about administrative approaches to tax compliance. My comments underscore some of his main points but primarily expand on one critical limitation of the carrot-and-stick approach—the inattention to the role of justice, or "just deserts," in maintaining a system of tax compliance. Specifically I argue that the current "crisis" of tax administration rests in part on confusion about the appropriate roles of deterrence and justice in maintaining tax compliance. How can tax administrators integrate the relatively new concerns about taxpayer rights and customer service with the established concerns about audits, sanctions, and criminal prosecutions? Building on Cowell's argument, I suggest that positive motivations do indeed play a critical role in maintaining taxpayer compliance, but that taxpayers, like most people, prefer just deserts to carrots.

Cowell presents a simple (at least as formal models go) yet sophisticated model of taxpayer-as-gambler and shows how it can be extended to probe a wide range of enforcement and compliance problems relevant to deterrence. He demonstrates that the basic model can be used to derive the assumptions necessary for the standard conclusions of deterrence theory: Compliance increases with the increase of enforcement and sanctioning activities, particularly among risk-averse taxpayers. Of course Cowell also points out that these standard beliefs have only modest empirical support at present. Furthermore he shows that, under reasonably innocuous assumptions, the model predicts that all taxpayers will evade if there is any positive return to evasion, and that higher income is associated with greater evasion, conclusions that he notes are not necessarily intuitively reasonable or empirically supported.

This balance between optimism about the range of tax compliance behavior the model could explain and skepticism about the restrictive assumptions and limited empirical support for current models is one of the strengths of his chapter. Cowell emphasizes that models based on the taxpayer-as-gambler model can indeed clarify many problems relevant to administrative concerns with maintaining tax compliance, but to do so they generally require less-restrictive assumptions about motivations, greater sensitivity to context, and greater empirical verification to ensure that the model's predictions indeed reflect the reality of the compliance problem being analyzed. Basing policy decisions on untested, overly simplistic models is a recipe for unhappy surprises and short careers. It is easy to support Cowell's call to apply the taxpayer-as-gambler model judiciously and to work harder at empirical verification of the model's implications.

Three sections of the chapter suggest promising directions for further development of the basic model and consider the policy implications of these potential developments. The section on firms contains the best-developed suggestions. By including the cost of concealment as a choice variable and noting that this cost varies systematically across different industries, market sectors, and types of organization, Cowell shows that deterrence effects (and hence deterrence policies) should vary systematically, depending on the type of market in which the firm operates, the nature of its products, and the size and structure of the firm. This direction provides perhaps the most natural extension for economic models of deterrence, particularly since the simplifying assumptions of utility maximization appear to be most relevant for studying business behavior as opposed to individual tax behavior. Given the relative lack of corporate compliance studies, Cowell's chapter would provide a major contribution to the compliance literature if it succeeds in fostering further studies of these important issues.

The section on strategic behavior reviews a few tax studies that have already begun to incorporate the strategic interaction between taxpayers and the tax collector into deterrence models. The models Cowell reviews do not appear to provide as a strong case for the relevance of this line of work as one might expect, but he suggests some interesting conclusions that caution against overly simple approaches to deterrence that ignore the agency's behavior. In particular, increasing enforcement stringency may induce strategic taxpayers to migrate to the "ghost" sector, or the underground economy, where their tax noncompliance may be even more costly and difficult to control.

The least developed but potentially most important new direction is provided in the section on rethinking taxpayer motivation. This section explores the possibility of including taxpayer motivations that have been found to be important in a wide range of compliance studies but that are traditionally excluded from economic analyses or treated as residual effects. Cowell briefly reviews four promising approaches: Utilize concepts like "framing" from behavioral decisionmaking studies, which can be used to relax behaviorally questionable assumptions of full-information utility maximization; include the value of public goods in individual utility functions; expand the time dimension of the ongoing relationship between taxpayer and tax collector; and explicitly model the endogenous interactions among taxpayers to reflect that "people may care about their own behavior relative to that of their peers." Cowell goes on to note that "The maintenance of a culture of compliance is one example of the government or tax administration creating a 'carrot'—a positive incentive for taxpayers to act in their broad social interest rather than in their narrow self-interest."

This concern with incorporating a more relevant motivational framework for understanding taxpayer behavior is widely shared among compliance scholars. For example, a recent comprehensive review of tax compliance research concluded that "adding moral and social dynamics to models of tax compliance is as yet a largely undeveloped area of research. There seems to be little dispute [that] these factors are important in individual compliance decisions, but little is known or agreed upon about how best to include these effects in a theoretical or empirical analysis of tax compliance."[1] My remaining comments expand on Cowell's suggestions, in an attempt to incorporate concerns with justice into the utility-maximizing model, to make the model directly relevant to the current crisis of tax administration.

Deterrence or Assurance?

Although the extensions of utility-maximization models presented by Cowell can conceivably help tax administrators design and improve enforcement policies that enhance deterrence, the major changes in IRS procedures in the past decades are oriented more toward assurance than deterrence. The expansion of taxpayer services, taxpayer problem resolution offices, the taxpayer bill of rights, and the customer service orientation toward taxpayers are all intended to assure honest taxpayers that they will be treated fairly as long as they carry out their responsibilities as citizens. Combined with the IRS's traditional enforcement activities intended to punish those who do not meet their tax obligations, the new activities are intended to assure that taxpayers receive their just desserts. The implicit assumption behind the growth of these new IRS activities is that the primary role of deterrence is to support assurance. Honesty is treated with respect, while dishonesty is punished. We need a model of compliance that recognizes both assurance and deterrence and that links both types of taxpayer motivations to tax policy and tax administration.

The emphasis on assurance is implicit in many of the views of practicing enforcement officials. Consider, for example, Chester Bowles's perspective as director of the Connecticut Office of Administration Control during the Sec-

1. Andreoni, Erard, and Feinstein (1998, p. 852).

ond World War.[2] He noted that the agency had little effect on 20 percent of people that would always obey the agency's laws and a smaller group of "bad apples" that would never comply unless dragged into court. However, the large majority of people could be convinced to comply voluntarily, but only if the law were rigidly enforced enough to assure the average person that they were not "suckers" if they met their legal obligation to obey. Translating into the tax context, deterrence is most relevant for minimizing violations among the small group of hard-core evaders, whereas assurance is critical for maintaining voluntary compliance levels for the broadest group of taxpayers.

The model of compliance we need to develop is not really concerned with positive rewards (a lottery ticket as a reward for a clean audit), but rather with ensuring that taxpayers get what they deserve. "Just deserts" provides a better metaphor than the traditional image of a carrot as a positive incentive. To fully develop the model requires an extension into the literatures on clubs, contracts, collective action, and evolutionary psychology. I provide a brief overview here of the intuition behind the argument developed more fully elsewhere.[3]

Contractual Compliance

The basic argument is that taxpayers obey the terms of an implicit tax contract as long as other taxpayers and the government meet their expected roles. The role of the general government is to produce worthwhile public goods, but the more specific role of the IRS is to ensure that other taxpayers cannot free-ride by shirking their tax obligations. This important assurance role requires the coercive powers of the deterrence model. But taxpayers also need to be assured that the coercive powers delegated to ensure the compliance of other taxpayers will not be misused to exploit honest taxpayers, whether from malevolence or organizational ineptitude. Administrative activities associated with customer service for taxpayers and the taxpayer bill of rights can be designed to fulfill this function.

How plausible is this model? Consider first the extreme case in which a predatory government attempts to extract the maximum possible tax from an understandably reluctant population. This is indeed the assumed model behind deterrence theory, since only the threat of punishment is expected to induce compliance. The problem with this model is that deterrence is expensive for both ruler and ruled, given the taxpayer's incentive and ability to hide whatever is being taxed. Levi has argued that even in this extreme case, both rulers and the ruled can be better off if they can agree to reduce the deadweight loss involved in deterrence.[4] If the king reins in the intrusive tax collector in return for

2. Bowles (1971).
3. Scholz (2003).
4. Levi (1989).

the barons' "voluntary" contributions of taxes, both can be better off under this new contractual arrangement than they were under the repressive deterrence system. The king saves the cost of maintaining the coercive tax mechanism, while the barons save the costs of hiding their taxable assets from the intrusive tax collector.

Of course the new tax contract will be worthless unless both sides can provide some credible commitment toward fulfilling the contract. Levi argues that contingent compliance provides the critical foundation of this contractual system. If the king imposes additional taxes based on the now-visible assets of the barons, the barons can react to this breach of contract by withdrawing their voluntary contribution. The anticipated loss of revenue during these battle periods must be sufficient to cure the king of the temptation to cheat the barons. Similarly the king must maintain sufficient coercive powers to be able to punish barons if they fail to live up to their contractual obligation. In game theoretic terms, it is the contingent withdrawal of cooperation in repeated play of the game that provides the credible commitment to maintain compliance with the contract on both sides.

The predatory government perspective on contingent compliance, like the model of deterrence, captures only part of the picture of tax compliance for democratic governments, since democratic governments presumably provide desired public goods of value to taxpayers. To the extent that this is true, democratic taxation is closer to the theories of teams and clubs than to theories of predatory government. Both clubs and teams impose obligations on members in exchange for benefits derived from joint activities, just as democratic governments impose tax obligations in exchange for desired public goods. Thus teams, clubs, and government suppliers of public goods can be conceived of as implicit or explicit contracts that define the benefits and obligations of members or taxpayers.

The necessary condition for such a contract is that benefits exceed obligations for each member. But joint gains are insufficient without some means of assuring members that the contract will be enforced for all other parties, and the deadweight loss of costs required to enforce the contract is perhaps the greatest barrier to the broader provision of public goods. Thus the central problem in club and team theories is to devise efficient mechanisms for overcoming the problem of free riding that would otherwise prevent members from enjoying the benefits of joint production.

When members who fail to meet their obligation can be readily identified and excluded, as in some private clubs, there is little problem in obtaining the public goods. The problem arises when obligations are difficult to monitor and punish. An internal IRS could be set up to monitor and enforce the contract, but the cost of this deterrence approach is generally high and not necessary. For example, a simple strategy of shirking whenever team production falls below some threshold can provide the necessary credible commitment to enforce a joint production contract without requiring the expense of monitoring individual behavior.[5] As long as shirking has a sufficient probability of causing below-threshold production, and as long as the drop in joint production when everyone shirks is sufficient to overshadow the short-term gains of free riding, no team member would have an incentive to shirk his obligations.

Axelrod and others have demonstrated the power of reciprocity for maintaining cooperation, and have pointed out the importance of such contingent, reciprocal behavior in supporting a broad array of cooperative arrangements.[6] As noted earlier, the baron's contingent compliance with the king's tax allows both king and baron to minimize the deadweight costs of enforcing their implicit tax contract. Miller applies this same argument to the relationship between managers and workers.[7] He argues that corporate managers rely on reciprocity to maintain higher levels of productivity than could be achieved by more elaborate and costly enforcement mechanisms and incentive schemes. Managers eschew nit-picking monitoring and punishment of minor lapses, in return for expected efforts and flexibility on the part of the worker.

The advantages of cooperation have been so fundamental to human society since its early beginnings, according to Cosmides and Toobey, that specialized human cognitive mechanisms have evolved to support the gains of contractual compliance.[8] By developing cognitive mechanisms of trust, commitment, reciprocity, vengeance, and other behavioral strategies that can increase the credibility of contractual commitments, contemporary citizens are "better than rational" in their ability to resolve free-rider problems in ways that are beyond the reach of "rational fools."[9]

Are Taxpayers Better than Rational?

Taxpayers have generally been treated as rational fools because of the apparent intractability of the free-rider problem as applied to millions of taxpayers. For most analysts the rationality of contingent compliance is just too implausible, because taxpayers are unlikely to believe that their own behavior can have any impact whatsoever on other taxpayers. Without the IRS to provide a plausible assurance that other taxpayers will fulfill their obligations, any other concerns of the taxpayer are unlikely.

5. See, for example, Radner (1986).
6. Axelrod (1984).
7. Miller (1992).
8. Cosmides and Tooby (1994).
9. See also Frank (1988) for a delightful analysis of the instrumental utility of moral sentiments.

The work of Scholz and Lubell suggests the implausibility that citizens use cognitive mechanisms for tax obligations that are different from the mechanisms they use for the broad array of obligations from the many teams, clubs, and governing institutions they encounter in the rest of their lives.[10] Think, for example, of the way individuals determine their obligation to keep implicit contracts with friends, teams, or clubs they belong to. Instead of storing every incident relevant to the obligation, people simplify the cognitive task by translating each incident or any relevant information into a series of overall attitudes and evaluations about the friend or club. When required to fulfill the relevant obligation, these attitudes determine the likelihood that the obligation will be met. The general evaluation of obligation for the particular friend or club provides an efficient decisionmaking process, leading to compliance when others are fulfilling their contractual obligations and noncompliance when they are not.

For tax compliance, this suggests a model in which taxpayers unconsciously process relevant incidents and information related to their income tax obligations into compliance-related beliefs and attitudes, just as they do with other laws. These attitudes subsequently lead to different probabilities of compliance in reporting taxes. For example, Scholz and Lubell interviewed taxpayers before and after they filed their first tax return affected by the 1986 Tax Reform Act (TRA). Taxpayers with large increases in tax due to the TRA systematically reduced their perceived obligation to pay taxes, suggesting that they are sensitive to the relative costs and benefits derived from the collective.[11] Furthermore, they found that self-reported tax compliance fell when obligation and trust in other taxpayers to pay their full share fell.[12]

While we know little about the actual cognitive mechanisms relevant for determining compliance with tax or other governmental obligations, Tom Tyler's studies of compliance with police and court orders provide evidence of one particular mechanism that is directly related to the current crisis in tax administration.[13] Controlling for the outcome of their case, individuals subjected to police and court orders who feel that they have been treated with fairness and dignity are much more likely to comply than those who feel ill-treated by the system. Expectations about procedural justice provide one plausible mechanism by which individuals can evaluate the extent to which large, distant organizations like police, courts, and tax collectors have lived up to their contractual obligations.

Just as the medieval baron's compliance may have been contingent on the expected behavior of the monarch, so also may the less-exalted taxpayer in con-

---

10. Scholz and Lubell (1998a,b).
11. Scholz and Lubell (1998a).
12. Scholz and Lubell (1998b).
13. Tyler and Huo (2002).

temporary democracies respond contingently when IRS behavior falls short of socially determined expectations of procedural fairness. In contemporary society at least (and probably for the barons as well) the response is not a reasoned, conscious attempt to restrain the power of the tax collector. But the unconscious heuristic triggered by perceived breaches of procedural justice is part of a repertoire of cognitive and social mechanisms that provide the function of supporting contractual compliance by making compliance contingent on the behavior of others.

There is a good reason why procedural justice may be a critical part of citizenship responses, particularly for obligations imposed by large state agencies. Barzel argues that the consolidation of coercive enforcement powers in the state provides tremendous efficiency by enforcing standardized "contracts" that can be used by teams, clubs, and other organized joint production efforts in order to avoid the costs of creating their own coercive enforcement mechanism.[14] However, a state enforcement agency with coercive power capable of ensuring compliance of even the most powerful individual is also capable of using that power to exploit members. Thus a critical problem for democratic governments is how to design effective constraints on the power of coercive enforcement agencies without destroying their ability to assure the credibility of contracts. Congressional oversight, judicial review of administrative procedures, the separation of tax enforcement from military and police agencies, and mandatory internal appeals processes are some of the institutional constraints on IRS authority. Taxpayer responses to procedural justice issues may provide a less familiar constraint that may be equally important in maintaining a tax system capable of supporting contractual compliance with tax obligations.

Implications for Tax Administration

If contractual compliance is relevant to tax compliance, we would expect that the level of compliance among taxpayers would be contingent on the perceived activities of the government and of other taxpayers. Compliance would decline if the tax collector became too intrusive or the government too exploitative. Thus an overzealous IRS would reduce compliance, and the reforms from taxpayer service to the taxpayer bill of rights would provide a means of redressing the balance and restoring the conditions of contingent compliance. On the other hand, if other taxpayers appear to be cheating on their taxes and the IRS appears to be too weak to catch and punish them, compliance would also fall. Critics of the customer-service orientation toward taxpayers argue that the past

14. Barzel (2002).

decade of reforms has emasculated IRS enforcement capabilities to the point that it will soon be incapable of providing the needed assurance that other tax-payers will pay their taxes, resulting in a dramatic drop in compliance rates.

What is the appropriate balance between reforms favoring procedural justice and those that enhance enforcement effectiveness? The model of contractual compliance would suggest that the balance depends on which threat to assurance is causing the greatest concern among taxpayers. Unfortunately too little is known empirically about factors affecting contractual compliance to provide clear resolution of the current uncertainty between enhancing procedural justice and increasing enforcement effectiveness. The cautious note that Cowell emphasizes for his suggested extensions of compliance models applies even more fully for the contractual compliance model.

However, it is tempting to speculate about what a fully developed and empirically tested model of contractual compliance might offer in the way of advice to tax administrators. Use the "sticks" of deterrence where they are most appropriate—among subpopulations in which there is little support for contractual compliance. This ensures "just deserts" by providing maximal deterrence where contractual compliance has failed. But it also ensures that those willing to comply with the implicit tax contract are not discouraged from doing so by perceived injustices in their treatment by the IRS. Reduce compliance costs and burdens but in particular ensure that expectations about procedural justice are met as fully as possible whenever taxpayers are contacted. The appropriate balance of deterrence and procedural justice required for optimal assurance evolves over time with the nature of both the government and the governed and must be adjusted accordingly. Empirical and theoretical analyses of assurance and contractual compliance could help understand current challenges and provide a broader foundation for debate.

COMMENT BY

Douglas A. Shackelford

Chapter 8 reviews the prevailing economic model for noncompliance, details its weaknesses, and then discusses some possible improvements. It highlights the assumptions that underlie the model and explicitly details the propositions that fall out. Besides the theoretical model, the review also discusses the difficulties and weaknesses in empirical archival studies (for example, sample-selection bias) and includes a brief survey of tests conducted by experimentalists in economics and psychology. It is an excellent introduction for anyone trying to understand noncompliance.

The fundamental model, which the author terms TAG (taxpayer-as-gambler), treats the compliance decision as a classic trade-off between risk and taxes. The taxpayer opts either for a certain tax today or an uncertain tax tomorrow, after a possible government audit. Tomorrow's tax may be lower, because the taxpayer intends to understate his taxable income. However, there exists a possibility that tomorrow the government will discover the understatement and not only force the full tax to be paid but add an additional penalty. I have found this model to be useful in structuring my thinking about compliance and, like many others, including several in this volume, I have used it in my own research.

The model, however, is not limited to compliance choices. You could imagine many settings where taxpayers face either a certain tax today or an uncertain (potentially lower) tax tomorrow. For example, consider a model where the taxpayer faces either a certain short-term capital gains tax today or a potentially lower long-term capital gains tax tomorrow. Although waiting until the property qualifies for the more favorable long-term treatment lowers the tax bill, it may result in a drop in after-tax profits, because there is a possibility that the value of the property will fall in the interim. In other words, the TAG model is a special case of a more general model that grapples with the coordination of taxes and risk.

As the author states, TAG assumes "rational individuals with stable preferences who, given economic opportunities and probabilities, maximize their expected utility." It is amoral; it is nonstrategic; it ignores time. Like all theory, abstraction is necessary in order to construct a tractable, useful model. TAG ignores much of the economic, social, and philosophical richness that makes the compliance decision so interesting and so difficult to understand. The question is not whether TAG captures the "real world." It clearly does not. The question is whether the more salient features of the compliance decision are included in the model.

The author identifies three "distinctly unsatisfactory" problems with the TAG model: its reliance on expected utility as the taxpayer motivation; its nonstrategic, atemporal nature; and its omission of the behavior of firms. I concur with the author that the model is both missing these features and would be improved if they could be added. Clearly compliance involves more taxpayer motives than simply expected utility. My observation is that some individuals take unusual pleasure in saving tax dollars, while others find legal tax avoidance vaguely inappropriate.

Likewise compliance decisions clearly are strategic. Both taxpayers and the government consider the multiperiod nature of compliance. The compliance model would be strengthened if it could be expanded to incorporate all economic agents. By not including these important aspects, the TAG model is clearly an incomplete, imperfect window on the world.

Besides these three arguably obvious limitations, the author adds that the nature of the product, the size and organizational structure of the firm, the role of reputation, and the degree of concentration of the industry also may affect compliance. Raising these more subtle considerations, which have been largely ignored in the literature, is a particularly useful contribution of the chapter.

Of course, if it were easy to incorporate these features into the noncompliance model, we would not be having this discussion. Thus apparently including these features comes at a high cost. So the real question is: What are the analytical costs of incorporating these benefits of realism in the model?

My disappointment with the chapter came at this point. It is unclear to me what to do with these problems or how to do it. If the purpose of the essay is simply to tell us that the TAG model is incomplete, that may be an important contribution. But I already knew that; I was looking for more guidance on where to go from here.

Since I do not know the way home either, I will join in the TAG bashing. In particular, I would like to see three improvements in the ultimate compliance model.

The Role of the Tax Preparer

Tax returns (personal or business) of any level of complexity involve a preparer. A complete model of noncompliance needs to consider the preparer's role. One can argue that preparers improve compliance: They know the law better; they know the penalties (including special penalties on them) better; they know where to find answers to questions better. So one could argue that introducing a preparer lowers the level of noncompliance.

Alternatively preparers may increase noncompliance. Presumably they are paid with the proceeds from the tax savings they create. For example, corporate tax shelters are prima facie evidence that preparers increase noncompliance. Preparers know the legal ways to restructure transactions to achieve lower taxes; they know which options are likely to trigger audits and which are not. Consequently they can carefully select from a menu of avoidance options, choosing those that are most effective at lowering taxes and avoiding those that are most likely to be detected under an audit. The result is that the game is not between the government and the taxpayer. It is between the government and the taxpayer's agent, who is an expert at playing the game.

The preparer's role in compliance leads to classic principal-agent problems. For example, preparers face special preparer penalties if returns are found to be fraudulent. Thus, two penalties are considered in the production of the return—the taxpayer's penalty and the tax preparer's penalty. Also preparers face both the cross-temporal issues raised in the chapter (choosing an avoidance option this year affects previous and future options), but also cross-client problems. Providing an avoidance option for one client affects the risk of audit for other clients using the same technique.

This relates to problems with property rights associated with tax plans. For example, the shelf life for corporate tax shelters is short. With each application of the shelter, the probability of its continuing usefulness diminishes. Presumably preparers ration noncompliance options across taxpayers in a manner that maximizes the preparers' profit.

One promising option for improving TAG is to incorporate findings from the accounting literature concerning the role of tax preparers. Academic accountants have a long-standing interest in the role of tax preparers (who, of course, are often practicing accountants). Roberts and Cloyd and Spilker provide examples of the research in this area.[1] Not surprisingly these studies find the taxpayer-preparer-government triangle to be complex.

The Political Environment

The second dimension that I would like to see incorporated into the ultimate compliance model is the political environment. I have no idea how to do this, but it is a major factor in understanding the seemingly increasing level of noncompliance.

What is the genesis of corporate (and increasingly personal) tax shelters? Any discussion of noncompliance requires an inquiry into these shelters. Their size alone demands attention. The *New York Times* quotes a tax attorney at Sullivan and Cromwell who states that "the government needs to devote ten times as many resources as it does now if it wants to tax capital effectively."[2] Where did this monster come from? If we want to understand corporate tax shelters, we must understand the political environment in which they have arisen. Many will point to changes in the federal government over the past decade, such as the IRS-bashing of 1997 and 1998, for a political explanation for the emergence of these shelters (and I would not disagree). However, I think it is useful to move back a few more years to some unintended consequences of deregulation.

One group that many label as a primary source of the noncompliance problem is the Big (or Final) Four accounting firms. The financial statements of all

1. Roberts (1998); Cloyd and Spilker (1999).
2. David Cay Johnston, "Departing Chief Says the I.R.S. Is Losing Its War on Tax Cheats," *New York Times*, November 5, 2002.

publicly traded firms must be audited annually. The size and scope of large multinationals limit their potential auditors to the largest multinational accounting firms (of which only the Final Four remain). Let me briefly review the evolution of these firms.

In the late 1970s the auditing industry, as well as several other professions, initiated what I will call deregulation. Until then, the code of professional conduct for the American Institute of Certified Public Accountants had forbidden all forms of advertising, including soliciting business from another firm's client without first asking their auditor's permission. Over the quarter century since these barriers to entry began to be reformed, the profit margins on audits have shrunk considerably. (Bankman's chapter in this volume terms these returns "unspectacular.") The result has been less auditing and movement into higher-margin businesses, such as consulting. It is a long story, but a line can be drawn from deregulation to lower fees to Enron, WorldCom, and other debacles that have left the auditing industry in shambles.

What does this have to do with tax noncompliance? Conducting an audit requires the collection of much of the same information that is required to complete an income tax return. Over time the accounting firms began to provide tax advice and complete tax filings for their audit clients. After deregulation, firms began to compete for audit and tax assignments, driving down the fees for both services. Firms also began to compete for profitable tax consulting assignments for nonaudit clients. This competition led to a further reduction in the profit margins on traditional tax work. Thus, in the same way that auditors began to look for higher-margin activities to replace the diminishing returns from auditing, tax advisers began to look for more profitable tax plans.

Twenty-five years later, the most profitable tax product for multinational corporations is a loose collection of tax plans known as corporate tax shelters. These shelters generally meet the letter but not the spirit of the law. I would term them legal noncompliance. To some extent noncompliance attributable to the large accounting firms is an unintended consequence of deregulation from a quarter century ago. This should not be construed as regret that trade restraints were lifted but rather recognition that the lifting indirectly changed tax compliance. I present the evolution of the tax industry as evidence that a complete model of noncompliance needs a thorough dose of political economics.

Public Disclosure of Tax Liability

Finally, to fully understand compliance for publicly traded corporations, we need to consider the information about taxes that the public receives. Consider Enron or WorldCom. Did they pay taxes on the profits they reported but never earned?

If so, then we have noncompliance that results in tax overpayment. Erickson, Hanlon, and Maydew attempt to address this question.[3] They show that companies actually paid taxes on allegedly fraudulent earnings. That is, the profits they reported, but never actually earned, were reported as taxable income. Their paper builds on a long line of studies showing that publicly traded companies often forgo tax avoidance opportunities that result in reduced earnings, because they value the accounting earnings (and their impact on share price) more than the cash outlay associated with the taxes.[4] So, if we wish to understand tax compliance for publicly traded companies, we need to consider the information about profits and taxes paid that these companies must provide investors and recognize that the public nature of this information may lead to increased tax revenue.

In short, this chapter is an excellent primer for understanding compliance issues. Both theorists and empiricists can benefit from its insights and its guidance for future compliance research. The challenge is to develop models that better capture the richness of the compliance decision.

References

Allingham, M., and A. Sandmo. 1972. "Income Tax Evasion: A Theoretical Analysis." *Journal of Public Economics* 1: 323–38.

Alm, J., R. Bahl, and M. N. Murray. 1990. "Understanding Taxpaying Behavior: A Conceptual Framework with Implications for Research." *Review of Economics and Statistics* 72: 603–13.

Andreoni, J. 1992. "IRS as Loan Shark: Tax Compliance with Borrowing Constraints." *Journal of Public Economics* 49: 35–46.

Andreoni, J., B. Erard, and J. Feinstein. 1998. "Tax Compliance." *Journal of Economic Literature* 36 (2): 818–60.

Axelrod, R. 1984. *The Evolution of Cooperation.* Basic Books.

Baldry, J. C. 1979. "Tax Evasion and Labour Supply." *Economics Letters* 3: 53–56.

———. 1986. "Tax Evasion Is Not a Gamble." *Economics Letters* 22: 333–35.

———. 1987. "Income Tax Evasion and the Tax Schedule: Some Experimental Results." *Public Finance* 42: 357–83.

Barzel, Y. 2002. *A Theory of the State: Economic Rights, Legal Rights, and the Scope of the State.* Cambridge University Press.

Bayer, R.-C., F. A. Cowell, and C. Fioro. 2003. "Tax Compliance and Firms: An Integrated Analysis." Distributional Analysis Discussion Paper 65, STICERD, London School of Economics.

3. Erickson, Hanlon, and Maydew (2002).
4. See review in Shackelford and Shevlin (2001).

Benjamini, Y., and S. Maital. 1985. "Optimal Tax Evasion and Optimal Tax Evasion Policy: Behavioral Aspects." In *The Economics of the Shadow Economy,* edited by W. Gaertner and A. Wenig. Berlin, Germany: Springer-Verlag.

Bernasconi, M. 1998. "Tax Evasion and Orders of Risk Aversion." *Journal of Public Economics* 67: 123–34.

Beron, K. J., H. V. Tauchen, and A. D. Witte. 1992. "The Effects of Audits and Sociological Variables on Compliance." In *Why People Pay Taxes,* edited by J. Slemrod, 67–89. University of Michigan Press.

Boadway, R., and M. Sato. 2000. "The Optimality of Punishing Only the Innocent: The Case of Tax Evasion." *International Tax and Public Finance* 7: 641–64.

Bowles, C. 1971. *Promises to Keep.* Harper & Row.

Camerer, C. 1995. "Individual Decisionmaking." In *The Handbook of Experimental Economics,* edited by J. H. Kagel and A. E. Roth, 587–673. Princeton University Press.

Chang, O. H., D. R. Nichols, and J. J. Schultz. 1987. "Taxpayer Attitudes toward Tax Audit Risk." *Journal of Economic Psychology* 8: 299–309.

Clotfelter, C. T. 1983. "Tax Evasion and Tax Rates." *Review of Economics and Statistics* 65: 363–73.

Cloyd, C., and B. Spilker. 1999. "The Influence of Client Preferences on Tax Professionals' Search for Judicial Precedents, Subsequent Judgments and Recommendations." *Accounting Review* 74 (3): 299–322.

Cosmides, L., and J. Tooby. 1994. "Better than Rational: Evolutionary Psychology and the Invisible Hand." *American Economic Association: Papers and Proceedings* 84 (2): 327–32.

Cowell, F. A. 1985. "Tax Evasion with Labour Income." *Journal of Public Economics* 26: 19–34.

———. 1989. "Honesty Is Sometimes the Best Policy." *European Economic Review* 33: 605–17.

———. 1990. *Cheating the Government.* MIT Press.

———. 1991. "Tax-Evasion Experiments: An Economist's View." In *Tax Evasion: An Experimental Approach,* edited by P. Webley and others, 123–29. Cambridge University Press.

Cowell, F. A., and J. P. F. Gordon. 1988. "Unwillingness to Pay: Tax Evasion and Public Good Provision." *Journal of Public Economics* 36: 305–21.

———. 1995. "Auditing with Ghosts." In *The Economics of Organised Crime,* edited by G. Fiorentini and S. Peltzman, 185–96. Cambridge University Press and CEPR.

Crane, S. E., and F. Nourzad. 1986. "Inflation and Tax Evasion: An Empirical Analysis." *Review of Economics and Statistics* 68: 217–23.

Cremer, H., and F. Gahvari. 1993. "Tax Evasion and Optimal Commodity Taxation." *Journal of Public Economics* 50: 261–75.

Engel, E. M. R. A., and J. R. Hines. 1999. "Understanding Tax Evasion Dynamics." Working Paper 6903. Cambridge, Mass.: National Bureau of Economic Research.

Erard, B., and C.-C. Ho. 2001. "Searching for Ghosts: Who Are the Nonfilers and How Much Tax Do They Owe?" *Journal of Public Economics* 81: 25–50.

Erickson, M., M. Hanlon, and E. Maydew. 2002. "How Much Will Firms Pay for Earnings That Do Not Exist? Evidence of Taxes Paid on Allegedly Fraudulent Earnings." Working Paper. University of North Carolina.

Feinstein, J. S. 1991. "An Econometric Analysis of Income Tax Evasion and Its Detection." *Rand Journal of Economics* 22: 14–35.

Frank, R. 1988. *Passions within Reason: The Strategic Role of Emotions.* W. W. Norton.

Franzoni, L. A. 1999. "Tax Evasion and Tax Compliance." In *Encyclopedia of Law and Economics,* edited by B. Bouckaert and G. De Geest, 52–94. Cheltenham, U.K.: Edward Elgar.

Fullerton, D., and M. Karayannis. 1994. "Tax Evasion and the Allocation of Capital." *Journal of Public Economics* 55: 257–78.

Glaeser, E. L., B. Sacerdote, and J. A. Scheinkman. 1996. "Crime and Social Interactions." *Quarterly Journal of Economics* 111: 507–48.

Graetz, M. J., J. F. Reinganum, and L. L. Wilde. 1986. "The Tax Compliance Game: Toward an Interactive Theory of Law Enforcement." *Journal of Law, Economics, and Organization* 2: 1–32.

Greenberg, J. 1984. "Avoiding Tax Avoidance: A Repeated Game-Theoretic Approach." *Journal of Economic Theory* 32: 1–13.

Joulfaian, D. 2000. "Corporate Income Tax Evasion and Managerial Preferences." *Review of Economics and Statistics* 82: 698–701.

Kahneman, D., and A. Tversky. 1979. "Prospect Theory: An Analysis of Decision under Risk." *Econometrica* 47: 263–92.

King, S., and S. Sheffrin. 2002. "Tax Evasion and Equity Theory: An Investigative Approach." *International Tax and Public Finance* 9: 505–21.

Kolm, S.-C. 1973. "A Note on Optimum Tax Evasion." *Journal of Public Economics* 2: 265–70.

Landsberger, M., and I. Meilijson. 1982. "Incentive-Generating State-Dependent Penalty System." *Journal of Public Economics* 19: 333–52.

Landsman, W. R., D. A. Shackelford, and R. J. Yetman. 2002. "The Determinants of Capital Gain Tax Compliance: Evidence from the RJR Nabisco Leveraged Buyout." *Journal of Public Economics* 84: 47–74.

Lee, K. 1998. "Tax Evasion, Monopoly, and Nonneutral Profit Taxes." *National Tax Journal* 51: 333–38.

Levi, M. 1988. *Of Rule and Revenue.* University of California Press.

Marrelli, M. 1984. "On Indirect Tax Evasion." *Journal of Public Economics* 25: 181–96.

Marrelli, M., and R. Martina. 1988. "Tax Evasion and Strategic Behaviour of the Firms." *Journal of Public Economics* 37: 55–69.

Miller, G. J. 1992. *Managerial Dilemmas: The Political Economy of Hierarchy.* Cambridge University Press.

Pencavel, J. H. 1979. "A Note on Income Tax Evasion, Labor Supply, and Nonlinear Tax Schedules." *Journal of Public Economics* 12: 115–24.

Pissarides, C., and G. Weber. 1989. "An Expenditure-Based Estimate of Britain's Black Economy." *Journal of Public Economics* 39: 17–32.

Poterba, J. M. 1987. "Tax Evasion and Capital Gains Taxation." *American Economic Review, Papers and Proceedings* 77: 234–39.

Radner, R. 1986. "Repeated Partnership Games with Imperfect Monitoring and No Discounting." *Review of Economic Studies* 53 (1): 43–57.

Reinganum, J. F., and L. L. Wilde. 1985. "Income Tax Compliance in a Principal-Agent Framework." *Journal of Public Economics* 26: 1–18.

———. 1986. "Equilibrium Verification and Reporting Policies in a Model of Tax Compliance." *International Economic Review* 27: 739–60.

Rice, E. M. 1992. "The Corporate Tax Gap: Evidence on Tax Compliance by Small Corporations." In *Why People Pay Taxes*, edited by J. Slemrod, 125–61. University of Michigan Press.

Robben, H. S. J., and others. 1990. "Decision Frame and Opportunity as Determinants of Tax Cheating: An International Experimental Study." *Journal of Economic Psychology* 11: 341–64.

Roberts, M. 1998. "Tax Accountants' Judgment/Decision-Making Research: A Review and Synthesis." *Journal of the American Taxation Association* 20 (1): 78–121.

Schepanski, A., and T. Shearer. 1995. "A Prospect Theory Account of the Income Tax Withholding Phenomenon." *Organizational Behavior and Human Decision Processes* 63: 174–86.

Scholz, J. 2003. "Contractual Tax Compliance." *Journal of Law and Policy* 13.

Scholz, J. T., and M. Lubell. 1998a. "Adaptive Political Attitudes: Duty, Trust, and Fear as Monitors of Tax Policy." *American Journal of Political Science* 42 (3): 903–20.

———. 1998b. "Trust and Taxpaying: Testing the Heuristic Approach to Collective Action." *American Journal of Political Science* 42 (2): 398–417.

Shackelford, D., and T. Shevlin. 2001. "Empirical Tax Research in Accounting." *Journal of Accounting and Economics* 31 (1–3) (September): 321–87.

Slemrod, J., M. Blumenthal, and C. Christian. 2001. "Taxpayer Response to an Increased Probability of Audit: Evidence from a Controlled Experiment in Minnesota." *Journal of Public Economics* 79: 455–83.

Slemrod, J., and S. Yitzhaki. 2002. "Tax Avoidance, Evasion, and Administration." In *Handbook of Public Economics*, edited by A. J. Auerbach and M. Feldstein, vol. 3: 1423–70. Amsterdam: North-Holland.

Smith, K. W., and K. A. Kinsey. 1987. "Understanding Taxpaying Behavior: A Conceptual Framework with Implications for Research." *Law and Society Review* 21: 639–63.

Spicer, M. W., and J. E. Thomas. 1982. "Audit Probabilities and the Tax Evasion Decision: An Experimental Approach." *Journal of Economic Psychology* 2: 241–45.

Thomas, J. 1999. "Quantifying the Black Economy: 'Measurement without Theory' Yet Again?" *Economic Journal* 109: F381–90.

Tversky, A., and D. Kahneman. 1981. "The Framing of Decision and the Psychology of Choice." *Science* 211: 453–58.

Tyler, T., and Y. Huo. 2002. *Trust in the Law: Encouraging Public Cooperation with the Police and Courts*. Russell Sage.

Virmani, A. 1989. "Indirect Tax Evasion and Production Inefficiency." *Journal of Public Economics* 39: 223–37.

Wang, L. F. S., and J. L. Conant. 1988. "Corporate Tax Evasion and Output Decisions of the Uncertain Monopolist." *National Tax Journal* 41: 579–81.

Witte, A. D., and D. F. Woodbury. 1985. "The Effect of Tax Laws and Tax Administration on Tax Compliance: The Case of the U.S. Individual Income Tax." *National Tax Journal* 38: 1–13.

Yaniv, G. 1995. "A Note on the Tax-Evading Firm." *National Tax Journal* 68: 113–20.

————. 1996. "Tax Evasion and Monopoly Output Decisions: Note." *Public Finance Quarterly* 24: 501–05.

Yitzhaki, S. 1974. "A Note on Income Tax Evasion: A Theoretical Analysis." *Journal of Public Economics* 3: 201–02.

9 WILLIAM G. GALE
   JEFFREY ROHALY

Effects of
Tax Simplification Options:
A Quantitative Analysis

ALTHOUGH PLEAS TO simplify the tax system are ubiquitous, quantitative
analyses of simplification options are rare.[1] The difficulties in simplifying
taxes are well known. Policymakers and the public care about economic performance, the level of revenues, the distribution of tax burdens, and other items,
as well as the complexity of the tax system. As goals, however, these areas of concern are often in conflict. Efforts to fine-tune the tax system to provide more
precisely targeted fairness inevitably make taxes more complex and create a
trade-off between simplicity and horizontal equity. Rules that tax people different amounts at different income levels also increase complexity, creating a trade-
off between simplicity and vertical equity. Policies that target particular forms of
saving or investment in the hope of spurring economic activity also make tax
planning more difficult, causing a potential trade-off between simplicity and
growth.

This chapter explores the effects of tax simplification proposals on selected
aspects of equity, efficiency, and complexity. As Slemrod emphasizes, quantitative
analyses of the effects of simplification options are essential if such options are to
receive the same serious scrutiny as other proposals.[2] Our analysis uses the tax

We thank Matt Hall and Manijeh Azmoodah for outstanding research assistance and Henry
Aaron, David Glickman, Michael Graetz, Joseph Minarik, Deborah Schenk, and Joel Slemrod for
helpful comments.
    1. Pechman (1987) proposes a base-broadening, rate-lowering set of changes to the income tax
and examines the impact on marginal tax rates and the distribution of tax burdens. Slemrod (1984)
estimates the reduction in the resource cost of complying with and filing income taxes from alternative simplification options.
    2. Slemrod (1984).

microsimulation model developed at the Tax Policy Center. We use the model to examine changes to the individual income tax and alternative minimum tax and a partial replacement of the income tax with a value-added tax (VAT).

We evaluate the effects on equity by considering the distribution of tax burdens, holding revenues constant by adjusting marginal tax rates. We evaluate the efficiency effects by examining the impact on the effective marginal tax rate on consumption financed by labor supply and by savings in interest-bearing assets. We evaluate the impact on tax complexity by using regression analysis of taxpayers' likelihood of using a tax preparer.

Our goal is not to advocate or oppose any particular simplification proposal. Rather we believe the chapter makes two broad contributions. First, we subject some prominent simplification proposals to the type of analysis regarding equity, efficiency, and revenues that other proposals routinely receive. Second, we provide new evidence on the way in which these simplification proposals would affect the use of tax preparers.

Our results show that simplification proposals differ dramatically with respect to their effects on revenue, distribution, marginal tax rates, and indeed on simplification per se. As a result, a focus on simplification options does not eliminate the need to make judgments regarding the distributional, efficiency, or revenue consequences of tax changes.

We begin by describing the tax model and the simplification options considered, after which the following three sections examine the impact on distribution, marginal tax rates, and tax preparer usage.

Background

The version of the Urban-Brookings Tax Policy Center microsimulation model used here is based on data from the stratified, random sample of tax returns in the 1996 public use file produced by the Statistics of Income division of the Internal Revenue Service.[3] The data contain virtually complete information from the income tax filings of approximately 112,000 returns.

Earlier versions of the model incorporated major provisions of the individual income tax and the individual alternative minimum tax (AMT).[4] In this chapter we expand the model to incorporate a consumption tax. The model assumes that individual income tax and AMT liabilities are borne by the individuals who are liable for the taxes, and that consumers bear the burden of consumption taxes. We allocate consumption expenditures across filing units as a function of the number of people in the unit and after-tax income, based on data

---

3. Weber (2001).
4. See, for example, Burman and others (2002).

from Sabelhaus and Groen and our own extrapolations based on those data for very-high-income households.[5] The appendix contains details on the model specification and the incidence assumptions and compares our results to those reported by the Treasury and the Congressional Budget Office.

The income tax system is projected to change significantly over the next decade. The tax cuts enacted in 2001 are slated to phase in slowly and then to expire at the end of 2010. The tax legislation passed in 2003 accelerates some of the 2001 tax cuts, at least temporarily, and reduces the tax rates applied to long-term capital gains and dividends through 2008. In addition the AMT is projected to grow rapidly, because the 2001 tax cuts reduced regular income tax liability without sustained cuts in AMT liability and because the AMT is not indexed for inflation.[6] Because of uncertainty regarding the way in which these issues will be resolved, we focus our analysis on projections for calendar year 2010. This is late enough to capture the massive projected growth in AMT coverage and liabilities and to allow the 2001 tax cut to phase in fully, but it still predates the legislated expiration of the 2001 tax cut. Under this specification, all features of the 2003 tax cut, including the dividend and capital gains rate reductions, have expired.

There is an unending variety of ways to simplify the tax system.[7] In this chapter we focus on policies that can be examined usefully in the tax model, that mirror recent or well-known proposals, and that are likely to be significant. We begin by examining the following proposed changes to the income tax and the AMT:

—Raise the AMT exemption to $100,000 or repeal the AMT.[8]

—Raise the standard deduction by $1,000 or by $5,000.

—Exclude the first $500 or the first $1,000 of interest and dividend income.

—Tax capital gains as ordinary income.

We model combinations of the first option in each case above (called combination A) and the second option in each case above (combination B). Both combinations tax capital gains as ordinary income.

We also consider replacing much of the income tax with a value-added tax.[9] One of the notions underlying this idea is that the income tax has an inexorable tendency toward complexity and that the only way to significantly and perma-

---

5. Sabelhaus and Groen (2000).

6. Burman and others (2002).

7. See Burman and Gale (2001) and JCT (2001) for recent discussions.

8. The $100,000 amount is for married couples filing a joint return. The exemption for singles and married individuals filing separately would rise to $50,000; for heads of household the exemption would be $75,000.

9. This option is inspired by the work of Graetz (1997, 1999, 2002). But we emphasize both that our proposal considers only a fraction of the sweeping changes Graetz advocates and that, even for just the VAT replacement combined with the wage and child credits, a variety of results can be obtained, depending on the details of the specification. Thus, our results in no way should be taken to reflect estimates of the impact of Graetz's proposals per se.

nently simplify taxes for the vast majority of households is to remove them entirely from the need to file returns or collect information for tax purposes. To model this idea, we make the following modifications to the tax system, as of 2010:

—Raise the exemption to $85,000 for joint filers, $42,500 for singles, and $63,750 for heads of households.

—Repeal all credits other than the foreign tax credit.

—Add a credit based on wages and the number of children, described below.

—Repeal the AMT.

—Impose a flat 25 percent income tax rate on all taxable income, including capital gains and dividends.

—Impose a broad-based value-added tax of 17.5 percent (tax-exclusive) to make up the lost revenue.[10]

We retain the foreign tax credit because it would continue to serve its current role in ensuring that foreign-source income is not taxed twice. The other credits are repealed because they would require low- and moderate-income households to file income tax returns.

As a partial replacement for the lost credits and in order to offset the burden of the VAT on low- and moderate-income households, we include a refundable wage subsidy program and child credit. Both subsidies are based on the individual's earnings level. The wage credit is equal to 40 percent of earnings up to $15,000, yielding a maximum credit of $6,000, and would phase out at a 15 percent rate on earnings above $20,000. The credit would be exhausted when earnings reached $60,000. The child credit would be $1,500 per dependent child but would phase out at a rate of 5 percent on earnings above $15,000. For a two-child family, the credit would be exhausted when earnings reached $75,000.

Since low- and moderate-income individuals would no longer have to fill out income tax returns under the consumption-tax proposal, the credits would be on an individual rather than a tax return basis and would be based solely on earnings.[11] This has several implications. Although each working spouse would

10. This rate is revenue-neutral but not budget-neutral. If a switch from an income tax to a consumption tax raises the consumer price level (including the consumption tax), then nominal government transfer payments must be raised to maintain their real value. If the consumer price level including the consumption tax remains constant after the replacement of an income tax with a VAT, then nominal pretax prices and wages must fall, implying lower tax revenues than if they did not fall. Either way, the budget-neutral consumption tax rate would be about 21 percent. See Gale (1999) for details. Unfortunately, incorporating a budget-neutral change is beyond the scope of this chapter, because it would require information on the allocation and taxation of government transfer payments by income class. By using a 17.5 percent VAT rate with no changes to government spending, we are understating the needed consumption tax rate. However, using a 21 percent tax rate with no change in government spending would significantly overstate the revenues needed.

11. Earnings are defined as wage and salary income plus income from self-employment. Since, under the consumption-tax proposal, individuals would still be required to pay self-employment taxes, they would still need to calculate income from self-employment.

be entitled to the wage credit, a married couple would have to choose which spouse would claim the child credit.[12] In addition, unlike the current earned income and child credits, the new subsidies would not be restricted to low-income families. The spouse of an individual with millions of dollars of income could still obtain a wage and child credit if he or she had a small amount of wage or self-employment income. Similarly an individual with substantial investment income but only a small amount of wage or self-employment income would be eligible for the credit.[13]

We acknowledge that the VAT would likely create significant administrative costs and tax complexity, but we have no way of estimating those costs in the context of the current modeling framework. Also we ignore all transition costs.

Distributional Effects

We use several alternative measures of the distributional impacts of tax simplification options, all of which are reported on an overall basis by adjusted gross income class. First is a simple tabulation of the share of tax filers that would obtain increases or reductions in tax burdens under the proposals. This gives a simple metric for measuring the number of "winners" and "losers" under each option. Second, we examine the changes, in dollars and percent, in mean after-tax income. Although controversy exists regarding whether absolute dollar changes or percent changes in income are most useful, we find both measures informative. The percent change in after-tax income is probably the most useful measure of how the progressitivity of the tax system changes.[14] A change that altered everyone's after-tax income by the same percent would leave the distribution of after-tax income unchanged. The change in dollar liabilities provides a basic reality check on the interpretation of tax proposals, since trivial differences in the change in taxes as a percent of income often mask huge differences in changes in tax liability in dollars across income groups. The VAT proposal is constructed to be revenue-neutral. For the income tax reform proposals, we obtain revenue neutrality by increasing all marginal tax rates (including those that apply to capital gains) in the regular income tax by an equal proportion. As noted above, all of our distribution results are obtained using 2010 law at 2010 income levels, with income classes and mean tax change figures quoted in 2001 dollars.

12. In the revenue and distribution estimates of the VAT proposal, we assume that the couple makes the optimal choice that results in the highest possible amount of child credit.

13. Under current law in 2003, if an individual has investment income of more than $2,600 (indexed for inflation), he or she is disqualified from receiving the EITC. In addition, the phaseout of the EITC is based on either earnings or AGI, whichever results in a smaller credit value.

14. See Cronin (1999); Gale and Potter (2002); and Gravelle and Smetters (2001).

Examined in isolation and without offsetting marginal tax rate adjustments to maintain revenue neutrality, each of the components of income tax simplification has plausible estimated effects (which are not shown in the tables). Repealing the AMT or raising the AMT exemption to $100,000 would provide tax cuts for about 24 percent of filers, but the distributional impacts and costs would differ significantly. Repeal would help almost all high-income taxpayers, whereas increasing the exemption to $100,000 would provide almost no help to those with income above $500,000, because the AMT exemption phases out at lower income levels. Dividend and interest exemptions would cut taxes for almost 50 percent of all filers, but the change in tax liability would be tiny for the vast majority of households. Raising the standard deduction would cut taxes for just over 40 percent of taxpayers, including a sizable majority of those with income between $15,000 and $50,000.[15] About 11 percent of taxpayers would be worse off if the taxation of capital gains were increased, with the share rising dramatically with income.

Table 9-1 shows the distributional effects of the two combined income tax reforms and the VAT proposal, all estimated under conditions that generate revenue neutrality.[16] The distributional effects of these simplification options differ considerably. Income tax reforms A and B would raise taxes for between 15 and 30 percent of tax filers, with the share growing with income. The VAT proposal would raise tax burdens for about half of filers overall, with the likelihood of experiencing a tax increase varying markedly by income class. Middle-income taxpayers would be most likely to experience an increase in their tax burden; two-thirds of those in the $30,000–$50,000 income group would see their taxes increase (not shown in table). The effects of the consumption tax are partially offset for many lower-income individuals by the wage and child credits; upper-income taxpayers are helped by the lower-income tax rates and the fact that they consume a proportionately smaller amount of their income than those in the lower ranges.

The lower two panels of table 9-1 report the actual tax change in dollars and the percentage change in after-tax income. All three panels tell the same story. Relative to current law, the income tax proposals would be progressive with respect to current income. The VAT proposal hits the middle class the hardest and provides the largest benefit to those at the top of the income scale. Although we do not

15. One caveat to the estimates involving the standard deduction is that the Statistics of Income file does not contain information on itemized deductions for filers who choose to take the standard deduction. If itemized deductions grow with nominal income, or at any rate faster than inflation—which is the rate of growth of the standard deduction—records that were nonitemizers in our 1996 data could have itemized deductions greater than our increased standard deduction when aged to 2010 income levels. These individuals would thus not benefit in reality from the increased standard deduction. We would not capture this effect, since we would continue to assume that they take the standard deduction.

16. Table 9A-3 shows the marginal tax rates required for revenue neutrality.

Table 9-1. *Effect of Broad-Based Simplification Options on Distribution of Tax Burdens, 2010*

Option	Adjusted gross income (AGI) class, in thousands of 2001 dollars[a]				
	All	15–30	75–100	200–500	> 1,000
Filers with tax increase (percent)					
Combination A (revenue neutral)[b]	29.7	26.6	30.2	21.6	98.5
Combination B (revenue-neutral)[c]	15.9	3.2	31.6	36.0	96.6
Value-added tax (VAT) proposal[d]	51.0	45.2	37.7	26.5	23.5
Change in mean after-tax income (2001 $)					
Combination A (revenue neutral)[b]	0	32	916	3,173	−152,137
Combination B (revenue neutral)[c]	0	368	1,117	1,085	−199,260
VAT proposal[d]	36	−40	612	2,498	48,688
Change in mean after-tax income (percent)					
Combination A (revenue neutral)[b]	0.0	0.1	1.2	1.4	−6.9
Combination B (revenue neutral)[c]	0.0	1.7	1.5	0.5	−9.1
VAT proposal[d]	0.1	−0.2	0.8	1.1	2.2

Source: Urban-Brookings Tax Policy Center microsimulation model.

a. Returns with negative AGI are excluded from the lowest income class but are included in the totals.

b. Raise the alternative minimum tax (AMT) exemption to $100,000, raise the standard deduction by $1,000, exclude $500 interest and dividends, and tax capital gains as ordinary income.

c. Repeal the AMT, raise the standard deduction by $5,000, exclude $1,000 interest and dividends, and tax capital gains as ordinary income.

d. Raise the personal exemption to $85,000 for "married, filing jointly," to $42,500 for singles and "married, filing separately," and to $63,750 for heads of household; retain current-law dependent exemptions as well as standard and itemized deductions; tax capital gains as ordinary income; repeal all tax credits other than the foreign tax credit; repeal the alternative minimum tax, impose a 17.5 percent VAT rate and a single 25 percent income tax rate; give wage and child credits, as outlined in text.

report a range of results, it is worth noting that by varying the parameters of the wage and child credits, and the associated VAT rates, a wide variety of distributional results can be obtained. We focus on the specification above because we think it would be representative of the type of proposal that might emerge.

Effects on Marginal Tax Rates

Because the proposals involve changes to the tax rate on wages, capital gains, and consumption, determining "the" marginal tax rate is difficult. To provide a sense of these changes, we focus on incentives to work and to save in interest-bearing assets. Define *tw* as the marginal income tax rate on wage income, *tcons* as the marginal consumption tax rate (in a tax-exclusive form), *tcorp* as the marginal tax rate on taxable corporate income, and *tint* as the marginal tax rate on taxable interest income. We examine two composite sets of marginal tax rates:

The marginal tax rate on wages used for consumption is given by

$$1 - (1 - tw) / (1 + tcons).$$

For example, a worker who earns $1, pays 10 percent in income taxes, and then faces a 25 percent tax-exclusive sales tax, is able to spend 72 cents on private consumption and thus faces an effective tax rate of 28 percent, where

$$0.28 = 1 - (1 - 0.1) / (1.25).$$

The marginal tax rate on taxable interest that is used for consumption is given by

$$1 - \{(1 - tint)\,(1 - tcorp) / (1 + tcons)\}.$$

The corporate rate appears because we assume that capital income generally bears the burden of the corporate tax.

Table 9-2 shows the effects of the proposals on these incentives. The income tax reforms would provide modest reductions in marginal tax rates on consumption financed by wage earnings for low- and middle-income households and raise marginal tax rates for high-income households. The VAT proposal would raise marginal tax rates on wages sharply for lower-income households because they either are currently not subject to the income tax or face statutory rates of 10 or 15 percent but would now have to face the 17.5 percent VAT. Marginal tax rates would also rise, but less dramatically, for higher-income households. Many upper-middle-income households, particularly in the $50,000-to-$75,000 income range, who would no longer be subject to the income tax, would see their marginal rates fall (not shown in table). The VAT proposal has similar effects on marginal tax rates on consumption financed by interest earnings. The income tax reforms would raise the marginal tax rate significantly more for higher earners.

Effects on the Use of Tax Preparers

The use of preparers is by no means an ideal metric for measuring tax complexity.[17] People use preparers for reasons other than the complexity of the tax system—for example, to save time or to receive rapid-refund loans. Likewise, the

17. See the discussion in Slemrod (1992) and Gale and Holtzblatt (2002).

Table 9-2. *Effect of Broad-Based Simplification Options on Mean Effective Marginal Tax Rates on Consumption, 2010*
Percent

	AGI class, in thousands of 2001 dollars[a]				
Option	All	15–30	75–100	200–500	> 1,000
Financed by wage income[b]					
Combination A (revenue neutral)[c]	0.0	0.6	–0.5	3.3	3.1
Combination B (revenue neutral)[d]	0.6	–1.2	–0.2	5.6	5.6
VAT proposal[e]	2.4	6.4	0.6	6.0	2.0
Financed by interest income (percent)[f]					
Combination A (revenue neutral)[c]	1.1	–0.1	–0.3	3.8	5.8
Combination B (revenue neutral)[d]	1.7	–3.2	–0.9	5.5	8.6
VAT proposal[e]	3.0	2.0	0.9	3.6	3.0

Source: See table 9-1.

a. Returns with negative AGI are excluded from the lowest income class but are included in the total.

b. Returns are weighted by the amount of wage and salary income.

c. Raise the AMT exemption to $100,000, raise the standard deduction by $1,000, exclude $500 interest and dividends, and tax capital gains as ordinary income.

d. Repeal the AMT, raise the standard deduction by $5,000, exclude $1,000 interest and dividends, and tax capital gains as ordinary income.

e. Raise the personal exemption to $85,000 for "married, filing jointly," $42,500 for singles and "married, filing separately," and $63,750 for heads of household; retain current-law dependent exemptions as well as standard and itemized deductions; tax capital gains as ordinary income; repeal all tax credits other than the foreign tax credit; repeal the AMT; impose a 17.5 percent VAT rate and a single 25 percent income tax rate; give wage and child credits as outlined in text.

f. Returns are weighted by the amount of interest income.

use of a preparer does not directly measure the extent of complexity. Nevertheless, use of preparers is a simple and straightforward measure and provides evidence on how one threshold of tax complexity—whether people feel they can or want to do their tax returns by themselves—would be affected. As a result, holding other factors constant, such as households' valuation of their time, changes in the use of tax preparers induced by changes in the tax code can provide some useful information on the impact of simplification options.[18]

To determine the impact of the reforms on the extent to which filers use tax preparers, we proceed in two steps (see appendix 9A for details). First, we estimate a regression equation that explains tax preparer usage as a function of income and other factors. For income, we use a series of indicator variables cor-

18. For additional research on this topic, see Long and Caudill (1993); Erard (1993); Mills (1999); Frischmann and Frees (1999); Blumenthal and Christian (this volume); and Christian, Gupta, and Lin (1993).

responding to different income groups (for example, $20,000 to $30,000). The income variables capture the fact that, controlling for taxes, households in different income groups face different incentives or may have different preferences for use of paid preparers.

Other variables that affect preparer usage, but are not altered in the simulations, include indicators for married, filing jointly; claiming the EITC; and presence of business income. Each of these variables is interacted with income in order to allow the effect of each item to vary by income class. The EITC variable is interacted only with income groups that have AGI up to $30,000. Other variables that affect usage and are altered in the simulations include indicators for positive AMT liability; being required to fill out the AMT forms; dividend and interest income that is below $500, between $501 and $1,000, or above $1,000; short-term capital gains, long-term capital gains, or both; and itemizer status.

Appendix table 9A-7 reports the results and shows that, holding other factors constant, preparer use rises significantly with income level, the presence of business income, and the EITC.[19] Having AMT liability or having to file the AMT form, even with no liability, has a large impact on the use of preparers at all income levels. The presence of less than $1,000 of dividend and interest income has a relatively small impact on the likelihood of using a preparer, except for filers with negative or low AGI and those with very high AGI. Taxpayers with long-term capital gains but not short-term gains are significantly more likely to use paid preparers in almost every income class, compared to those with short-term gains, but not long-term gains. A seemingly paradoxical result is that those with both types of gains are less likely to use paid preparers than those with just long-term gains.[20] Itemizing deductions raises the likelihood of using a preparer by about 10 percentage points for households with income below $50,000, by 2 to 5 percentage points for filers with income between $50,000 and $100,000, and by negligible amounts for filers with higher income.

Our methodology for estimating the effects of policy changes on tax preparer usage is described in appendix 9A, with the results in table 9-3. In the base case, 56.8 percent of filers use tax preparers, with the share rising sharply with income. However, even for households with AGI between zero and $50,000, between 44 and 52 percent use preparers.

The two income tax reforms would reduce tax preparer usage by between 8 and 10 percent (4.4. to 5.7 percentage points). These are significant declines,

19. It is possible, of course, that it is the use of a preparer that raises the likelihood of claiming the EITC. We do not evaluate that possibility here, since we include the EITC only as a control and focus on other variables.

20. One possible explanation is that taxpayers with both types of gains are more financially sophisticated than others and thus more able to complete their own tax forms.

Table 9-3. *Effect of Broad-Based Simplification Options
on Tax Preparer Usage, 2010*
Percent, unless otherwise noted

Option	AGI class, in thousands of 2001 dollars[a]				
	All	15–30	75–100	200–500	> 1,000
Current law probability	56.8	51.0	73.4	90.6	95.1
Combination A					
Probability	52.4	49.7	59.0	89.3	92.0
Change (percentage points)	–4.4	–1.3	–14.4	–1.3	–3.1
Reduction	7.7	2.6	19.6	1.4	3.3
Combination B					
Probability	51.1	49.0	57.8	78.0	85.3
Change (percentage points)	–5.7	–2.0	–15.6	–12.5	–9.8
Reduction	10.0	3.9	21.2	13.9	10.3
VAT proposal[b]					
Probability	20.0	0.0	57.7	78.6	85.5
Change (percentage points)	–36.8	–51.0	–15.7	–12.0	–9.6
Reduction	64.8	100.0	21.4	13.2	10.1

Source: Urban-Brookings Tax Policy Center microsimulation model and authors' calculations.
a. Returns with negative AGI are excluded from the lowest income class but are included in the totals.
b. Filers with AGIs less than personal exemption are assigned a 0 percent likelihood of using a preparer.

representing about 35 to 45 percent of the increase in use of preparers since 1980, but would still leave over half of all filers using preparers.

The VAT proposal has a substantial impact on the use of tax preparers. We estimate that only 20 percent of the would-be filers would use tax preparers under this system. The proposal would reduce the use of preparers by 100 percent for AGI groups below $30,000.[21] Even in higher-income groups, the proposal would reduce the likelihood of filing by between 10 and 13 percentage points. These significant declines suggest that the proposal would be effective in reducing filing burdens. However, the proposal would not be entirely successful in removing the income tax from the day-to-day lives of middle-class households. About 18 percent of households with income between $30,000 and $50,000 and 32 percent with income between $50,000 and $75,000 would still use preparers. In addition, the proposal would create an entirely new tax system, a value-added tax, with presumably significant administrative costs.[22] There could also be

21. For simplicity, we have assumed that the 0.7 percent of taxpayers with negative AGI would not have to file. In practice, many of them probably would be required to file.
22. Slemrod (1996); Gale and Holtzblatt (2002).

significant costs associated with the administration of the wage and child credits that would be necessary to reduce the burden of a consumption-based tax on low- and moderate-income households.

Conclusion

We view the principal contribution of this chapter as providing a unified set of quantitative estimates of the impact of simplification proposals on selected aspects of equity, efficiency, and complexity. Our results suggest that simplification proposals that fall well short of fundamental tax reform nevertheless can have a significant impact on the distribution of average tax burdens, the level of marginal tax rates, and the use of tax preparers. That is, different ways of simplifying taxes provide widely disparate benefits to different income groups and can have significantly different effects on tax complexity and the incentives to work and save. Our methodology and results should provide at least a first step in the direction of more quantitative analysis of simplification proposals.

Appendix 9A

We use a large-scale microsimulation model of the U.S. federal income tax system, developed at the Tax Policy Center (TPC). The model is similar to those used by the Congressional Budget Office (CBO), the Joint Committee on Taxation (JCT), the Treasury's Office of Tax Analysis (OTA), and private-sector tax analysts.

The model uses data from the 1996 public-use file produced by the Statistics of Income (SOI) division of the Internal Revenue Service. The file contains 112,186 records with detailed information on federal individual income tax returns filed in the 1996 tax year.[1] In some cases, imputations from other sources, such as the Current Population Survey of the U.S. Census Bureau, supplement the SOI tax data. For example, imputations for education expenses are necessary to estimate the Hope and lifetime learning credits. We also use data from the Urban Institute's TRIM (transfer income) microsimulation model—which uses CPS data—to impute the ages of dependent children in order to estimate the child tax credit. These imputations are necessary because the 1996 public-use file does not contain information on either the education or child credits.

---

1. Weber (2001) describes the SOI public-use data file, including the sampling methodology and disclosure avoidance procedures used to maintain taxpayer confidentiality.

The model incorporates EGTRRA (Economic Growth and Tax Relief Reconciliation Act of 2001) provisions for changes in marginal tax rates, the 10 percent tax bracket, credits for children and dependent care, itemized deduction limitations, personal exemption phaseouts, the alternative minimum tax (AMT), and the standard deduction, 15 percent bracket, and earned income tax credit provisions for married couples. It does not currently incorporate EGTRRA's education and retirement saving provisions. The model also incorporates the individual income tax measures in the Job Creation and Worker Assistance Act of 2002.

Aging and Extrapolation Process

To produce a representative sample of filers in years beyond 1996, the input data are first extrapolated to 1999 based on published SOI data and then "aged" to future years based on CBO aggregate forecasts and projections. The extrapolation to 1999 occurs in two steps. First, the dollar amounts for income, adjustments, deductions, and credits on each record are grown by their actual per capita 1996–1999 growth rate. To capture the large growth in income at the top end of the distribution that occurred between 1996 and 1999, we employ a separate wage-skewing factor for high-income returns. For items where SOI provides the necessary information, separate per capita growth rates are used for each filing status. Record weights are grown by the actual growth rate in the number of returns by filing status over the 1996–1999 period. Second, the weights on each record are adjusted via a large linear programming problem to ensure that, for the major income items, adjustments, and deductions, the model hits aggregate targets and for some items—including wages and AGI—distributional targets as well. The extrapolated outcomes closely resemble published aggregate and distributional results for 1999.

For years 2000 to 2012, we age the data based on forecasts and projections from the CBO for variables such as wages, personal income, capital gains, and inflation.[2] Where possible, we use actual 2000 and 2001 data instead of projections. Again we use a two-stage routine, this time for each future year. In the first stage, dollar amounts for the items on each record are grown by the appropriate forecasted per capita growth rate, with per capita personal income serving as the default growth factor for many items. Record weights are increased each year by the average annual growth rate for each filing status over the last decade. In the second stage, the record weights are further adjusted to ensure that the model hits a limited number of aggregate targets. For years beyond 1999, we do not

---

2. CBO (2002).

target distributions for any item; wages and salaries, for example, are grown by the same per capita growth factor for all records.

Calculating the AMT

Many of our simplification options entail changes to, or repeal of, the AMT, and we therefore need to include these variants as well as current-law AMT projections in our tax model. The SOI data file provides information on AMT adjustment and preference items for taxpayers who filed Form 6251 in 1996. However, when we simulate tax law and income levels for future years, individuals who were not subject to the AMT in 1996 could potentially be affected by the tax. This requires calculating AMT adjustments and preferences for all individuals in future years. Using the public-use file, we calculate the major AMT items: state and local tax deductions, personal exemptions, miscellaneous deductions above the 2-percent floor, the standard deduction, the additional disallowance of medical deductions, and state and local tax refunds. Together these provisions account for over 95 percent of the projected reconciliation between AMT and regular taxable income by 2010 in Tempalski.[3] Our measure of lost credits includes disallowed amounts for the following credits, where appropriate: child, child and dependent care, elderly, Hope, lifetime learning, general business, and prior year minimum tax.

The TPC model estimates for AMT taxpayers and revenue are similar to those in the Treasury's Office of Tax Analysis model and the JCT (see table 9A-1).[4] Table 9A-2 shows our projected distribution of AGI, the regular income tax, and the AMT for the 2010 calendar year.

Revenue-Neutral Reform Options

As discussed in the text, we look at paying for the individual income tax and AMT simplification options by changing all statutory tax rates (including the rates on long-term capital gains) by the same proportion. Table 9A-3 summarizes the marginal income tax rates that would prevail under each revenue-neutral option. All the options other than the taxation of capital gains as ordinary income would require tax rate increases; repealing the AMT, for example, would require across-the-board tax rate increases of about 11 percent. Taxing capital gains as ordinary income would allow rates to fall by about 8.5 percent.

3. Tempalski (2001).
4. Tempalski (2001); JCT (2001).

Table 9A-1. *Treasury, Joint Committee on Taxation, and Tax Policy Center Alternative Minimum Tax Projections, 2001–2012*

| Year | AMT taxpayers[a] | | | | | | AMT revenue[b] | | | |
| | Pre-EGTRRA law | | | Current law[c] | | | Pre-EGTRRA law | | Current law | |
	Treasury[d]	JCT[d]	TPC	Treasury	JCT	TPC[e]	Treasury	TPC	Treasury	TPC
2001	1.8	1.5	2.0	1.7	1.4	1.9	10.2	10.9	10.3	11.1
2002	3.6	3.5	4.8	2.7	2.7	2.6	12.6	14.7	12.6	13.0
2003	4.7	4.3	5.5	3.5	3.3	3.0	14.6	16.5	14.5	14.4
2004	5.8	5.6	6.5	5.6	5.3	5.5	16.8	18.8	20.4	20.7
2005	7.5	7.1	8.1	13.4	13.0	13.8	19.7	21.8	34.9	36.4
2006	9.1	8.7	9.9	20.4	19.6	20.3	22.9	25.5	59.2	60.7
2007	11.1	10.5	11.4	25.3	23.9	25.0	27.2	29.4	72.7	74.2
2008	13.1	12.8	13.4	29.0	29.1	29.9	32.4	34.6	96.0	100.0
2009	15.7	14.9	15.5	32.1	32.1	32.9	38.4	40.6	111.4	117.9
2010	18.0	17.5	17.9	35.1	35.5	35.6	45.0	47.0	133.2	141.4
2011	20.8	20.7	20.5	n.a.	n.a.	38.3	53.2	55.3	n.a.	162.5
2012	n.a.	n.a.	23.3	n.a.	n.a.	41.0	n.a.	64.9	n.a.	185.6

Source: Tempalski (2001); JCT (2001); Urban-Brookings Tax Policy Center microsimulation model.

a. Includes those with AMT liability from Form 6251 and those with lost credits.

b. Includes direct AMT liability and lost credits. JCT has not published projections of AMT revenue.

c. Assumes EGTRRA is extended and includes the effects of the Job Creation and Worker Assistance Act of 2002.

d. Does not include the effects of the Job Creation and Worker Assistance Act of 2002.

e. Assumes that the provisions in EGTRRA that expire after 2010 are extended through 2012.

Table 9A-2. *Distribution of Alternative Minimum Tax and Regular Income Tax by Adjusted Gross Income, 2010*

AGI class, by thousands of 2001 dollars	Returns (thousands)		Percent of returns		Percent of AGI		Percent of tax liability	
	AMT taxpayers[a]	All returns	AMT taxpayers	All returns	AMT taxpayers	All returns	AMT[b]	All income tax[c]
Less than 0	8	1,040	*	0.7	−0.1	−1.1	0.2	*
0–15	1	41,681	*	28.3	*	3.9	*	−1.9
15–30	136	31,730	0.4	21.6	0.1	8.8	0.1	1.0
30–50	2,220	25,401	6.2	17.3	2.1	12.6	1.4	7.0
50–75	7,815	18,082	22.0	12.3	11.4	14.1	8.1	10.5
75–100	8,926	11,364	25.1	7.7	17.7	12.5	14.7	11.1
100–200	13,036	13,862	36.7	9.4	39.7	23.2	38.2	27.1
200–500	3,052	3,156	8.6	2.1	19.8	11.5	28.5	18.6
500–1,000	287	531	0.8	0.4	4.2	4.5	3.9	8.0
1,000 and more	72	267	0.2	0.2	5.1	10.1	5.0	18.5
All	35,554	147,114	100.0	100.0	100.0	100.0	100.0	100.0

Source: Urban-Brookings Tax Policy Center microsimulation model.
* Less than 0.05 percent.
a. Includes those with AMT liability from Form 6251 and those with lost credits.
b. Includes direct AMT liability and lost credits.
c. Sum of regular income tax net of refundable credits plus direct AMT liability.

Consumption Tax

In order to estimate the revenue, distributional, and incentive effects of the VAT proposal, which includes the introduction of a broad-based tax on consumption, it is necessary to impute consumption expenditures for each filing unit on the SOI tax file.[5]

We allocate consumption to each record on the tax file based on after-tax income and the number of individuals in the filing unit. We first rank filing units by a measure of family-size-adjusted income. Our measure of income is expanded to include AGI plus the nontaxable portion of Social Security benefits, nontaxable pension income, and tax-exempt interest income. This measure of income is then adjusted for family size by dividing by the implicit adjustment factors in the 2001 federal poverty thresholds. The poverty threshold adjustment factors imply, for example, that a family of two requires about 28 percent

5. Nonfilers would also be subject to the consumption tax but are not in the current version of the model.

Table 9A-3. *Revenue-Neutral Income Tax and Alternative Minimum Tax Options: Statutory Marginal Tax Rates, 2010*
Percent

	Individual income tax bracket					
Option	Lowest	Second	Third	Fourth	Fifth	Top
Current law	10.0	15.0	25.0	28.0	33.0	35.0
Repeal AMT	11.1	16.6	27.7	31.0	36.5	38.8
Increase AMT exemption to $100,000	11.0	16.4	27.4	30.7	36.2	38.4
$500 interest and dividend exemption	10.1	15.2	25.3	28.4	33.5	35.5
$1,000 interest and dividend exemption	10.2	15.3	25.6	28.6	33.7	35.8
Increase standard deduction by $1,000	10.2	15.3	25.5	28.5	33.6	35.7
Increase standard deduction by $5,000	10.8	16.2	27.1	30.3	35.7	37.9
Tax capital gains as ordinary income	9.2	13.7	22.9	25.6	30.2	32.1
Combination A[a]	10.7	16.0	26.7	29.9	35.3	37.4
Combination B[b]	11.3	17.0	28.3	31.7	37.3	39.6

Source: See table 9A-2.
a. Raise the AMT exemption to $100,000, raise the standard deduction by $1,000, exclude $500 interest and dividends, and tax capital gains as ordinary income.
b. Repeal the AMT, raise the standard deduction by $5,000, exclude $1,000 interest and dividends, and tax capital gains as ordinary income.

more income than a single individual to be equally well off; a family of three requires 50 percent more income.[6] The filing units are then divided into percentile classes, based on our measure of family-size-adjusted income.

We then use results from Sabelhaus and Groen to impute a level of consumption expenditure to each return.[7] Sabelhaus and Groen use data from the 1992 Consumer Expenditure Survey to construct ratios of average consumption to average after-tax income by family-adjusted income decile. Their results show that families in the bottom income decile spend more than two times their income; families in the 80th to 90th percentile spend a little less than three-quarters of their income (table 9A-4). Families in the bottom half of the income

6. The CBO has recently begun adjusting by dividing by the square root of family size (CBO, 2001), arguing that it is more consistent and less arbitrary than using the adjustments implicit in the federal poverty thresholds. Our method allows us to use the estimates provided by Sabelhaus and Groen (2000), as described below.
7. Sabelhaus and Groen (2000).

Table 9A-4. *Consumption-Income Ratios, by Family-Adjusted Income Percentile, 2010*

Income class (in percentiles)[a]	Ratio of average consumption to average income[b]	Average income (2001 dollars)
0–10	2.30	2,839
10–20	1.37	8,043
20–30	1.34	13,613
30–40	1.12	20,183
40–50	1.00	27,634
50–60	0.95	35,913
60–70	0.90	46,784
70–80	0.81	61,050
80–90	0.74	83,157
90–95	0.69	117,642
95–98	0.62	172,703
98–99	0.54	270,144
99–99.5	0.48	403,230
99.5–99.8	0.42	665,899
99.8–99.9	0.36	1,157,964
99.9–100	0.25	4,108,537
All	0.75	52,315

Source: Sabelhaus and Groen (2000), based on data from the 1992 Consumer Expenditure Survey; Urban-Brookings Tax Policy Center microsimulation model; and authors' calculations.

a. Before-tax family income divided by the family size adjustment implicit in the federal poverty thresholds.

b. Represents the ratio of average consumption to average income within income deciles, not average consumption-income ratios across families.

distribution spend more than their income on an annual basis. These results are consistent with other analysis of the consumption to income ratio. Feenberg, Mitrusi, and Poterba report a consumption-income ratio of about 2.3 for households with incomes less than $10,000.[8]

In order to impute consumption for those at the top of the income scale, we estimate separate consumption-to-income ratios for various percentile classes within the top decile. Formally, we run the following regression:

$$ln\ (C/Y)_i = \alpha + \beta lnY_i + \epsilon_i,$$

where $(C/Y)_i$ is the consumption-to-income ratio for each decile as reported by Sabelhaus and Groen, and Y_i is average family-size-adjusted income for each

8. Feenberg, Mitrusi, and Poterba (1997) use a broad-based measure of income that includes the imputed value of owner-occupied housing and medical expenses that are paid by a third party.

Table 9A-5. *Distribution of 17.5 Percent VAT by AGI Class, 2010*

AGI class, in thousands of 2001 dollars	VAT revenue		Average tax rate (percent)[a]	Consumption base for VAT		
	Dollars (billions)	Percent of total		Dollars (billions)	As percent of expanded income	As percent of after-tax income[b]
0–15	120.3	9.5	28.8	687.3	164.7	129.6
15–30	179.8	14.3	19.7	1,027.7	112.7	100.0
30–50	202.9	16.1	15.7	1,159.8	89.9	88.0
50–75	193.4	15.3	13.3	1,105.0	76.0	77.9
75–100	156.2	12.4	12.1	892.7	69.2	72.6
100–200	250.5	19.8	10.3	1,431.2	59.0	66.8
200–500	92.3	7.3	7.6	527.5	43.7	54.6
500–1,000	27.8	2.2	5.8	158.8	33.4	43.8
More than 1,000	38.3	3.0	3.7	218.9	21.4	27.9
All	1,261.9	100.0	12.1	7,211.1	69.4	74.6

Source: See table 9A-2.

a. Consumption tax liability divided by expanded income, which is AGI plus nontaxable Social Security and pensions and tax-exempt interest income.

b. After-tax income is expanded income less individual income tax net of wage and child credits.

decile, as calculated by the tax model. We then use the estimated coefficients from this regression, together with the average income levels for the percentile classes at the top of the income distribution, to construct fitted values for the corresponding consumption-to-income ratios. These values, along with Sabelhaus and Groen's reported values for the first nine deciles, are shown in the table. The result is a plausible pattern of gradually declining consumption-to-income ratios within the top decile. Households in the top 0.10 percent of the income distribution—who have average income of $4.1 million—are estimated to consume one-fourth of their after-tax income.

After filing units are assigned to the appropriate percentile class, we calculate each record's consumption expenditures by multiplying after-tax income (expanded income less individual income taxes net of refundable tax credits) by the corresponding consumption-expenditure ratio for that class.[9] The resulting distribution of consumption subject to the VAT and the distribution of a 17.5 percent VAT is shown in tables 9A-5 (by AGI class) and 9A-6 (by AGI percentile). In comparison to the individual income tax, the consumption tax is regressive: Individuals in the bottom quintile face an average consumption tax rate of 33.2 percent; those in the top quintile have an average rate of only

9. Returns with negative after-tax income are ignored in the analysis; they are treated as having zero consumption.

Table 9A-6. *Distribution of 17.5 Percent VAT by Percentiles, 2010*

AGI class, in thousands of 2001 dollars	VAT revenue		Average tax rate (percent)[a]	Consumption base for VAT		
	Dollars (billions)	Percent of total		Dollars (billions)	As percent of expanded income	As percent of after-tax income[b]
Bottom quintile	64.6	5.1	33.2	369.2	189.7	147.5
Second quintile	138.2	10.9	22.6	789.6	129.1	107.1
Middle quintile	201.2	15.9	17.6	1,149.6	100.4	94.4
Fourth quintile	289.5	22.9	13.8	1,654.2	78.8	80.1
Top quintile	568.1	45.0	8.8	3,246.4	50.4	58.9
All	1,261.9	100.0	12.1	7,211.1	69.4	74.6
Top 10 Percent	359.7	28.5	7.6	2,055.6	43.7	53.3
Top 5 Percent	231.8	18.4	6.7	1,324.4	38.1	47.9
Top 1 Percent	91.3	7.2	4.9	521.6	27.9	36.4

Source: See table 9A-2.

a. Consumption tax liability divided by expanded income, which is AGI plus nontaxable Social Security and pensions and tax-exempt interest income.

b. After-tax income is expanded income less individual income tax net of wage and child credits.

8.8 percent.[10] This pattern of results is broadly consistent with others who have examined the distributional implications of a broad-based consumption tax.[11]

Regression Estimates

We use a base case specification that uses the 1996 public use file to estimate a linear probability regression of the form:

$$P = a1^*Y + a2^*Y^*JOINT + a3^*Y^*EITC + a4^*Y^*BUSINESS +$$
$$a5^*Y^*AMTLIABILITY + a6^*Y^*AMTFORM +$$
$$a7^*Y^*DIVINT001500 + a8^*Y^*DIVINT5011000 + a9^*Y^*DIVINTHIGH +$$
$$a10^*Y^*CGLONG + a11^*Y^*CGSHORT + a12^*Y^*CGBOTH +$$
$$a13^*Y^*ITEMIZE + u.$$

We also estimate the same equation as a logistic and a probit model, with similar results. Because calculating the marginal effects of tax changes is simpler with the linear model, we focus on those results here.

10. These figures do not include the partially offsetting effects of the wage and child credits targeted to low- and moderate-income households.

11. See, for example, Feenberg, Mitrusi, and Poterba (1997).

P takes the value 1 if the filer used either a paid preparer, voluntary income tax assistance, or tax counsel for the elderly, and 0 otherwise. About 61 million filers used a paid preparer, and a total of 1 million additional filers used one of the other two options. *Y* is a mutually exclusive and exhaustive vector of indicator variables for different income groups. The *Y* vector captures the fact that, controlling for taxes, households in different income groups face different incentives or may have different preferences for use of paid preparers. *JOINT, EITC,* and *BUSINESS* are indicator variables for whether the unit files jointly, files for the EITC, or has business income or loss (defined as filing Schedule C, E, or F), respectively. These are included to help control for general determinants of propensity to use a preparer, aside from income. The variables are interacted with income in order to allow the effect of each item to vary by income class. The EITC variable is interacted only with income groups that have AGI up to $30,000.

AMTLIABILITY takes the value of 1 if households had AMT liability on their Form 6251, and 0 otherwise. *AMTFORM* takes the value of 1 if the filer had to fill out the AMT form but did not have AMT liability, and 0 if either the filer did not have to fill out the form or had positive AMT liability. *DIVINT001500, DIVINT5011000,* and *DIVINTHIGH* take the value of 1 if dividend and interest receipts are between $1 and $500, $501 and $1,000, and greater than $1,000, respectively. *CGSHORT, CGLONG,* and *CGBOTH* take the value of 1 if the filer has short-term gains but no long-term gains, long-term gains but no short-term gains, or both, respectively. *ITEMIZE* takes the value of 1 for filers who itemize their deductions.

Methodology for Estimating Effects of Reform of Tax Preparer Usage

To estimate the effects of repealing the AMT, we set the *AMTFORM* and *AMTLIABILITY* variables equal to zero and recalculate the aggregate likelihoods of using a preparer. To examine the effects of raising the AMT exemption to $100,000, we determine whether each filer has to pay AMT under the new rule and adjust the *AMTLIABILITY* variable accordingly. We stipulate that anyone with AMT income below $100,000 need not fill out the AMT forms (unless they have certain types of income that automatically trigger AMT calculations).[12]

To simulate the effect of taxing long-term capital gains as ordinary income, we assume that the effect on the use of preparers of having long-term capital gains (but no short-term gains) and having both short-term and long-term gains

---

12. See Burman and others (2002).

becomes the same as the effect estimated in the base regression of having short-term gains (but no long-term gains).

To measure the impact of raising the standard deduction, we examine which taxpayers would choose to change their itemization status. Those that do have the value of *ITEMIZE* changed from 1 to 0. Then aggregate probabilities of using preparers are recalculated using the equation estimated in table 9A-7.

To measure the impact of allowing dividend and interest exemptions, we simply zero-out the coefficients on the terms that indicate whether the household has between $1 and $500, or between $500 and $1,000 of interest and dividend income, as appropriate.

To analyze the VAT proposal, we set *EITC, AMTLIABILITY,* and *AMTFORM* equal to zero for all taxpayers, remove the effects of preferential capital gains treatment as noted above, and set the likelihood of filing a return at zero for anyone whose adjusted gross income is below the exemption level, given the filing status.

Table 9A-7. *Estimates of the Likelihood of Using a Preparer*

	AGI class in thousands of 2001 dollars[a]									
	< 0	0–15	15–30	30–50	50–75	75–100	100–200	200–500	500–1,000	> 1,000
Intercept	38.7 (32.9)	31.4 (45.4)	39.0 (49.1)	39.2 (40.7)	47.8 (31.3)	52.7 (19.2)	63.5 (25.0)	70.1 (24.9)	62.1 (12.0)	75.4 (14.0)
JOINT	1.6 (1.9)	2.0 (2.1)	5.7 (6.4)	3.6 (4.1)	-1.3 (-1.2)	-3.0 (-2.0)	-4.2 (-4.1)	-0.4 (-0.4)	-1.5 (-1.7)	-1.8 (-4.1)
BUSINESS	31.9 (24.1)	24.3 (27.6)	20.7 (22.3)	23.4 (25.2)	20.9 (21.9)	21.0 (17.8)	15.4 (18.9)	12.5 (16.0)	11.7 (12.5)	7.4 (13.4)
EITC	11.5 (6.0)	17.1 (18.8)	13.7 (13.5)	8.6 (2.2)	—	—	—	—	—	—
AMTLIABILITY	6.5 (4.3)	13.3 (1.6)	15.0 (1.5)	12.2 (2.1)	16.7 (6.0)	18.3 (7.4)	16.7 (13.4)	10.8 (12.8)	6.4 (7.0)	5.6 (10.5)
AMT form only	7.5 (8.4)	28.2 (13.3)	22.5 (10.9)	20.3 (11.2)	26.0 (16.6)	26.9 (17.0)	23.0 (26.0)	13.6 (19.4)	7.7 (11.0)	6.6 (18.7)
DIVINT $1–$500	15.6 (11.2)	3.4 (3.5)	2.3 (2.3)	2.1 (1.9)	-0.8 (-0.6)	-1.5 (-0.6)	-0.1 (0.0)	1.6 (0.5)	11.3 (1.9)	1.1 (0.2)
DIVINT $500–$1,000	16.9 (8.8)	15.2 (8.7)	6.6 (3.4)	6.7 (3.7)	2.8 (1.4)	-2.4 (-0.8)	0.3 (0.1)	-0.1 (0.0)	16.7 (2.9)	5.2 (0.9)
DIVINT $1,000+	17.0 (12.8)	16.3 (13.7)	12.1 (9.7)	6.1 (4.7)	3.1 (2.0)	1.0 (0.4)	1.0 (0.4)	2.7 (1.0)	13.6 (2.7)	8.8 (1.6)
CG long only	5.0 (4.8)	13.8 (9.2)	10.2 (6.8)	8.9 (6.2)	9.7 (7.0)	8.7 (5.6)	4.3 (4.4)	-0.1 (-0.1)	4.8 (4.4)	0.2 (0.2)
CG short only	3.5 (1.7)	11.4 (3.4)	1.2 (.4)	7.4 (2.6)	4.6 (1.6)	-1.6 (-0.5)	1.9 (1.0)	-2.6 (-1.7)	0.2 (0.1)	-4.0 (-3.3)
CG both	2.5 (2.2)	9.4 (4.4)	4.0 (1.9)	4.3 (2.3)	3.2 (1.9)	1.5 (0.9)	2.5 (2.5)	-1.3 (-1.7)	3.4 (3.6)	-0.5 (-0.8)
ITEMIZE	—	12.7 (8.3)	9.9 (9.3)	10.7 (12.0)	4.9 (5.2)	2.4 (1.9)	-1.5 (-1.6)	0.7 (0.7)	0.2 (0.2)	0.5 (0.7)

Source: Urban-Brookings Tax Policy Center microsimulation model and authors' calculations.

a. Estimates obtained using a linear probability model. Numbers in parentheses are *t* statistics. *N* = 112,186.

COMMENT BY
David Glickman

As a tax lawyer and a nonacademic, what I bring to this discussion is a tax practitioner's view, perhaps expanded by my past government and teaching experiences. Through the Tax Section of the American Bar Association, I have been involved in simplification efforts for many years. The ABA has had a longstanding position strongly recommending that the tax laws be simplified. The Tax Section has joined forces with the Tax Executives Institute (TEI) and the American Institute of Certified Public Accountants (AICPA), three somewhat diverse and divergent groups, to push for simplification. Thus, like Don Quixote, I have been jousting with this windmill for a long time. If we do not continue these efforts, the law will become evermore complicated and possibly, at some point, fall by its own weight.

The Tax Section, TEI, and AICPA started with certain fundamental assumptions. First, although we understood the basic tenets of a sound tax system— simplicity, equity, efficiency, and administrability—we concluded that our approach needed to focus solely on simplicity. Second, we moved forward on the assumption that we could not determine winners and losers. This left some of the most difficult questions unanswered. However, we believed that our highest calling was to point out some of the most complex provisions in the law, based upon our collective experiences, and let the powers that be make the other decisions. Obviously, administrability by the Internal Revenue Service is of great import, and thus we viewed that as part of our charge.

I do not believe that tax simplification has a true constituency in Congress. It is easy to pay lip service to simplification, but most such attempts have been unsuccessful, with some exceptions. In the late 1970s the rules concerning installment sales were addressed and made simpler in application. In 1982 the rules concerning subchapter S corporations were made simpler. The only real effort at broad-based simplification came with the enactment of the Tax Reform Act of 1986, our present Internal Revenue Code. It broadened the base and reduced the rates. I recollect that, when the 1986 act was passed, the members of Congress committed to doing their best to not violate the fundamental underpinnings of that law. As we know, this commitment was short-lived. Of course Congress is not solely at fault. There is ample blame to go around. As Pogo said, we have met the enemy and it is us. It has been suggested that perhaps the best simplification would be a moratorium on tax bills for five years. It will not happen, but at least it is an idea.

If it is to succeed, tax simplification must be strongly supported by all the tax staffs: the Office of Tax Policy, the staff of the Joint Committee on Taxation, and the tax staffs of the minority and majority leaders in both houses of Congress.

Bills directed at simplification have been introduced by various members, but the staffs have to push the idea, or the members lose interest. A former chair of the Tax Section of the ABA once stated that, when you are thinking of tax simplification, think small. Others have amended that statement by saying think small, but when the window of opportunity opens, push as many things through as you possibly can. I believe this is the way to go.

The Bush administration, through the secretary of the treasury, has announced its interest in moving the simplification process forward. The Treasury Department is in the process of preparing, or has issued, white papers on a variety of simplification issues. The assistant secretary, deputy assistant secretary, and the tax legislative counsel have been deeply involved with the Tax Section's simplification efforts. Thus, although they are limited in what they can say, there are "friends in court." It would appear that there has never been a better opportunity for simplification.

The study by the staff of the Joint Committee on Taxation, which was at the direction of Congress, focuses attention on many of the problems in the present law. However, if we are not careful, that study will go the way of many studies, collecting dust on the shelf. The problem is that, although there is agreement that something needs to be done, the approaches for solving the problem vary dramatically. And, as chapter 9 illustrates, different solutions have widely different results. The principal problem is what complexity does to the perception of the system. A survey that took place in the 1980s asked people why they cheated on their income tax. A number of people suggested that the rich have their tax shelters, and failing to report some interest and dividends or taking greater itemized and charitable deductions was their method of tax shelter.

Gale and Rohaly discuss the effect on the use of tax preparers under a simplified system. I have long wondered how many resources are directed to either the preparation of the tax return or, possibly even more important, attempting to avoid paying taxes. From my experience, an enormous amount of time is expended by tax lawyers who do not prepare tax returns. Under a simplified system, in which the perceived need to avoid taxes was reduced, what would these resources do? Perhaps we would see a reverse of the many past bills that have been referred to as "tax lawyers' full employment acts."

Four simplification issues call for more specific remarks: the alternative minimum tax, marginal rates and capital gains, the earned income tax credit, and phaseouts.

Alternative Minimum Tax

With respect to the AMT, unless we are prepared to repeal the income tax, leaving the AMT in place, there is broad agreement that it must go. Chapter 9 analyzes two assumptions: increasing the exemption and total repeal. Although total repeal would seem the best approach, any approach that would stem the flow of persons covered by the AMT would add greatly to simplification. Undoubtedly in 1969 there were people using the preferences to "zero out" their tax liability. Although the number was small, the public perception was bad. Perhaps the provision should not have been enacted in the first place. In any event, times have changed. The number of people that will be subjected to the provision in the future is mind-boggling. I once said that this was a train wreck waiting to happen, and I still feel that way. Obviously the 2001 EGTRRA could have solved this problem. Although funds were available to completely eliminate the AMT, a different approach was taken. Since lower marginal rates are a great plus for simplification, I cannot disagree with the overall direction of the 2001 act. However, from a complexity standpoint, we would have been much better off eliminating the AMT with a lesser reduction in the marginal rates.

EGTRRA did attempt, in a small way, to simplify the law. The ultimate elimination of PEP and Pease, the minor adjustments to the AMT (although they increased its coverage), and the minimal changes to the earned income tax credit were helpful. But it seems that whenever something is given, something is taken back. The phase-in of most of the provisions, including the rate reduction, added complexity, and grandfathering the bill starting in 2011 was a mistake. The repeal of the transfer tax in 2010 and its reinstatement in 2011 has been referred to as a "pull-the-plug provision." Although no one expects that this will in fact take place, what does one do in the interim?

Marginal Rates and Capital Gains

With respect to rate reduction, a broader base and flatter rate is the best answer. It has been suggested that capital gains preferences should be eliminated, so that people will not have an incentive to convert ordinary income into capital gains. Obviously the problem would be ameliorated if the maximum marginal rate were reduced to a figure closer to capital gains. In the early 1980s a client of mine, who had regularly entered into tax shelters, stated that if the rates were ever brought down to 25 percent, he would never again go into a tax shelter. He lived by those words until the rates were once again pushing 40 percent.

Obviously, repeal of the capital gains preference is contentious, since many people believe that capital gains should not be taxed at all. However, from a pure simplification standpoint, the elimination of the differential would make life simpler. At the very least, something must be done with the inordinate complexity of the present law and its various rates and holding periods.

To add a footnote to this point, Emily Parker, who is deputy chief counsel for operations at the IRS, recently pointed out that tax shelters are much more than a corporate problem. My experience confirms this, for individuals with large capital gains. People are intent on saving tax dollars, even though the marginal rate in question is 20 percent. If the dollars are large enough, even a 20 percent marginal rate is too hard to swallow, at least for some. Or do people have such a disregard for our tax system that they believe any action is acceptable?

Earned Income Tax Credit

Although initially my interest in the EITC was purely academic, recently I had to review the substance of the provision with respect to a pro bono matter. A woman had gone to a storefront tax-return preparer and had received a refund. Upon audit, the IRS contended that her refund was greater than what she was entitled to. Going through the provisions, I was forced to call for help from Nina Olson and Janet Spragens. It turned out that the IRS was correct. The real problem was that her refund was long gone. Now she owed taxes plus interest, and she simply did not have the funds to satisfy the liability. The bottom line is that the complexity in the earned income tax credit can have devastating effects on the segment of society that can least afford it.

Phaseouts

Finally, I have long been concerned with the phaseout provisions in the law. Hopefully PEP and Pease are on their way out, albeit slowly, but there are numerous others. Perhaps from a pure simplification standpoint, the best answer would be to eliminate all means-testing provisions in the IRC. This suggestion will make some people uncomfortable, as did the suggestion that the AMT should replace the income tax. It might fly in the face of other tenets of sound tax policy—principally, equity. But we have known for years that a simple system may not be a fair system.

Perhaps it is time to look at the state of our present system and decide what is most important. Is a fair system that no one respects better than a simple system that may not be perceived as fair and has redistribution potential? After all, a consumption tax is regressive, yet many people seem to favor it. Could that be because they understand it?

I have no magic elixir for an ultimate solution. We can pay lip service to simplification, but until we make true believers of the people who have the power to do something about it, nothing will be accomplished. Perhaps, as bills move forward that are directed to other matters, small changes can be made to the law that provide some minor degree of simplification. Such changes could have a revenue impact. The question always is, who will be the loser? Anything we do is better than nothing, assuming that we are not already a day late and a dollar short.

A Final Note

Since I wrote this response, a number of events have transpired that could affect simplification. First, the treasury secretary has changed and, while the previous secretary seemed to be a clear proponent of simplification (although what he may really have wanted was major change in the approach of federal taxation), it is not clear what the present secretary's interest is in this arena. Second, the administration has presented its budget for fiscal year 2004, which includes a number of provisions directed at simplification, one of which is adopting a uniform definition of *qualifying child*. In addition, the linchpin of the administration's positions, and the most expensive element thereof, is directed at integrating the corporate and individual systems by use of the dividend exclusion. While the concept of eliminating the double tax on corporate earnings is supported by many individuals and groups, and has been endorsed by economists on both sides of the political spectrum, the methodology being adopted certainly is not free from complexity. Despite this, the proposal would result in certain types of simplification, such as the elimination of the accumulated earnings and the personal holding company taxes, and it probably would take some of the tension off the debt-equity dichotomy. The administration also has proposed revisions to the retirement savings provisions and has even floated the idea of replacing the income tax with a consumption tax. But despite this evolution, the issues outlined here must be continually addressed.

COMMENT BY
Deborah H. Schenk

Chapter 9 makes an important contribution, both in urging that simplification proposals be subjected to quantitative analysis and in attempting to do so. Equally important is the assumption underlying their work: that the distributional and efficiency impact should be analyzed and weighed in evaluating simplification proposals, just as it is with any other tax reform proposal. The authors correctly point out that these reform efforts usually are supported or evaluated only on simplification grounds, with little regard to their distributional or efficiency effects. This failure is an aspect of the familiar second-best problem that attends all tax system reform (as contrasted to tax system design). Changes that in the abstract might be efficient, for example, may decrease efficiency in a second-best world. That is no less true of simplification proposals than it is of any other type of reform.

The simplification effects of simplification proposals are in some respects even more important than the equity and efficiency effects. The whole point of the proposals that the authors study is simplification and, in some cases, supporters sell a proposal accepting a sacrifice of some equity and perhaps efficiency in order to gain less complexity. Thus, measuring the simplification benefits of these proposals is critical. For this reason I direct my remarks to the authors' effort to quantify simplicity effects.

I want to make two general points. First, I have some doubt about the possibility of quantifying the simplification effect of a simplification proposal. While I am generally critical of the model's ability to quantify decreases in complexity, it has one very important function: It nicely illustrates that measuring simplification effects is not straightforward and that a proposal that may appear to be simplicity-enhancing may have secondary complexity effects.[1] Second, assuming that the simplification effect can be quantified, it is doubtful that this microsimulation model measures that effect.

To measure the simplification effect of a particular proposal, the authors accept the likelihood of using a tax preparer as a proxy for complexity. They explain that "use of preparers is a simple and straightforward measure and provides evidence on how one threshold of tax complexity—whether people feel they can or want to do their tax returns by themselves—would be affected." But they also assert that "holding other factors constant . . . changes in the use of tax preparers induced by changes in the tax code can provide some useful information on the impact of simplification options." The implication is that if a proposal increases the number of taxpayers who would use a preparer, it has a negative simplification effect. If the number who would use preparers declines, it has a positive effect. It is those propositions that I question.[2]

Some of the results do not make sense—that is, they fail to capture some commonsense notions about complexity. To take one example: Table 9-3 indicates that if combination B were adopted, the probability of use of a tax preparer by taxpayers with AGI exceeding $1 million who use a preparer would fall from 95.1 to 85.3 percent, a 10.3 percent reduction. Combination B repeals the

---

1. A good example is taxing capital gains as ordinary income without other changes on a revenue-neutral basis. This change would increase the number of filers who use preparers because the necessary cuts in marginal tax rates to offset the increase in the capital gains tax rate would move more filers onto the AMT.

2. The authors are aware that use of a preparer provides limited information. They begin their discussion with the caveat: "The use of preparers is by no means an ideal metric for measuring tax complexity. . . . Likewise, the use of a preparer does not directly measure the extent of complexity."

AMT, taxes capital gains as ordinary income, raises the standard deduction by $5,000, and excludes the first $1,000 of interest and dividend income. The last two changes should have an extremely limited effect on taxpayers with income exceeding $1 million. Thus, the repeal of the AMT and the capital gains structure would reduce complexity for wealthy taxpayers by only 10 percent. The authors themselves note this and comment: "These are significant declines, representing about 35 to 45 percent of the increase in use of preparers since 1980, but that would still leave over half of all filers using preparers." The implication is that combination B would not significantly decrease complexity. That strikes me as perplexing, because it generally is believed that repeal of the AMT and the capital gains preference would have a major impact on simplification. The authors acknowledge that the use of a preparer is not a perfect proxy for complexity, and I want to explore why I think that is right.

There are several ways in which changes in the use of a paid preparer may fail to capture an increase or decrease in complexity. One relatively unimportant point is that preparers include paid preparers, voluntary income tax assistance, and tax counsel for the elderly. I assume that the authors included only these groups because that is what the public use file denominates. This measure fails to incorporate other external sources for preparation assistance, such as the IRS, friends, other pro bono assistance, and most important, tax return preparation software. In other words, if the metric is the extent to which taxpayers cannot prepare their own returns without assistance, the proxy is too narrow. This is a topic about which I say more below.

Much more important, I question the metric itself. Despite the strong correlation between complexity and preparer use, I doubt that use of a preparer is a robust enough proxy for complexity or that an increase or decrease in the use of a preparer is sufficiently calibrated to measure a change in complexity accurately. The data produced may not provide rich enough information on which to make a judgment about the contribution to simplification that a proposal might make. My concern is with the ease with which it could be misused. The authors make no statement about the use to which the quantitative data might be put or how to interpret them. A policymaker might decide that a mere change of two percentage points in the use of a paid preparer on adoption of a specific proposal was a robust indication of a decline in complexity. Conversely, a decisionmaker might decide that a 25 percent decline was required. The larger the change required, the more concerned we should be about whether the metric used accurately measures the decline in complexity.

I have two concerns: false negatives and false positives. By false negatives I mean that many simplification options will produce no or a statistically insignificant change in the number of taxpayers who use preparers, when in fact there would be a significant decrease in complexity. There are at least two groups for which the use of a preparer may be so relatively inelastic that no reform would result in a decline in the need for assistance. One might infer then that there is no potential for simplification for these groups, which indeed would be depressing.

The first group is low-income taxpayers, who mostly file simple returns. For example in 1998, 35 percent of taxpayers who filed a 1040EZ or a 1040A used paid preparers.[3] A significant percentage of those may have done so to get a rapid refund through electronic filing, to get a refund loan, or for other reasons that have nothing to do with complexity. But surely a significant percentage of those who used a paid preparer to file a 1040EZ did so because they either could not or believed they could not file their own returns, due to complexity.

Short of repealing the system altogether, Congress can do little to ensure that no one who files a 1040EZ needs to use a preparer. And not surprisingly, table 9-3 shows that only small changes are predicted in the use of preparers by income classes under $30,000 for all proposals except Michael Graetz's. The significant drop in the number of low-income taxpayers who use preparers in the Graetz system is because they drop out of the system altogether. This is a robust result and illustrates my conclusion that removing these taxpayers from the system may be the only way to eliminate their need to use a preparer, but it may not be the only way to curb complexity. For example, changes in the EITC that would decrease complexity probably would not change the number of EITC-eligible taxpayers who use a paid preparer. So long as they are in the system, they will need help in obtaining refunds or benefits. Yet there would be simplification benefits from streamlining the EITC.[4]

The use of a preparer at the upper end of the spectrum is also quite inelastic.[5] At a certain income level, use of a preparer is preordained, and there is no change that can be plugged in to the model (short of total and complete reform) that would produce a positive simplification effect. There are several possible reasons for this inelasticity at upper-income levels. With the exception of the indicator variable for business income, the model does not note other complexities that might swamp the proposed changes.[6] For example, a high-income tax-

---

3. Gale and Holtzblatt (2002, p. 190).

4. Since the complications in the EITC presumably arose in response to equity concerns for some political purpose that Congress thought important, one reasonably might ask, Why undertake the simplification if the taxpayer's use of a preparer will not be affected? The answer lies in difficulties faced by third parties—tax preparers and the IRS.

5. The figures in table 9-3 indicate that there is some elasticity. They show that the probability that a taxpayer with over $1 million in adjusted gross income will use a preparer is only 95 percent, and each of the reform proposals results in some (although minor) changes in the use of a preparer. My intuition is that the only plausible explanation is that the 5 percent is due to the use of tax preparation software or the use of "a brother in the business."

6. By definition the model considers only simplification effects on individual taxpayers. Much of what tax professionals consider so complex (financial instruments, corporate reorganizations, international transactions) applies primarily to corporations, particularly multinationals.

payer with a K-1, passive activities, or foreign income, all of which probably would require a paid preparer, would not be likely to show any change in the use of a preparer under the reforms evaluated. Another reason that use of a preparer may be inelastic is that higher-income taxpayers probably use a preparer in part for reasons that have nothing to do with complexity, such as comparative advantage. Just as a billionaire could drive his own car but instead uses a chauffeur, he also may find it more efficient to have a professional prepare the return rather than do it himself. A second possibility is that he values leisure more than the cost savings.

Thus, at least with respect to these two groups, the reforms will register false negatives, that is, none of the reforms would show much, if any, effect on the use of a preparer. If this implies there are no simplification benefits, it seems clearly wrong.

A second reason to question the use of a preparer as the metric for complexity is that it may produce false positives. A false positive occurs where the model shows that a proposal results in a simplification benefit due to a decrease in paid preparers but fails to take into account offsetting complexity costs. For example, I do not believe it is a robust conclusion that the Graetz proposal would significantly decrease complexity based on these data and this model. It shows substantial changes in preparer use by taxpayers in income classes from $30,000 to $50,000 (and even the upper two classes show sizable changes), but it does not measure other changes in complexity arising from the proposal. For example, as a class, taxpayers with income in the $75,000 range would significantly decrease their use of preparers, but some who currently do not use a preparer would be subject to the VAT and might switch to a paid preparer; in other words, within a class there will be winners and losers. The Graetz proposal also fails to indicate that those who were using paid preparers under the current system and would continue to use paid preparers under the Graetz proposal might find the tax system much more complex because of the need to operate under two tax systems, one of which is entirely new. This may be a transitory cost that will disappear as people learn the new system, but it is a compliance cost that needs to be taken into account. Finally complexity of the tax system cannot be measured in the abstract. Although the Graetz proposal would eliminate many incentives, one would expect at least some to resurface as direct subsidies with their attendant complexities.

The metric also fails to capture other important sources of complexity that might change under either combination A or B. Scholars often speak of three kinds of complexity—rule complexity, transactions complexity, and compliance complexity.[7] Using a tax preparer as a proxy for complexity most directly speaks to a particular aspect of compliance complexity. To what extent would a change

7. See, for example, Bradford (1986, pp. 266–67).

in the use of a paid preparer measure changes in other aspects of compliance complexity or transactions complexity?

Unquestionably compliance complexity includes the need to choose forms, make calculations, and file a return. This model measures changes in the extent to which a taxpayer must rely on an outsider to perform those tasks, but it does not necessarily measure changes in the necessity to perform the tasks or the time needed to do so. Compliance complexity also includes the need to keep records and to manipulate those records. A change in the use of a preparer does not measure the extent to which a particular proposal would increase or decrease the record-keeping burden. It also does not measure transactions complexity—that is, the extent to which people organize their affairs to minimize taxes. Elimination of an incentive or a rule change might decrease opportunities for avoidance or even evasion while not affecting the choice to use a preparer.[8] Thus a simplification proposal might produce significant swings in transactions complexity that are not measured by a change in preparer usage.

Finally the authors do not indicate how to weigh the data produced by their model. Suppose there is a significant decrease in the use of paid preparers in income classes under $75,000, ranging from 49 to 100 percent. Standing alone, that is simplification by any measure. But what if the decline in the $75,000-and-up cohorts is much lower, ranging from 4 to 6 percent, but in all cases the cost of preparing the return increases because the law for those groups has become more complex. How do we weigh decreases in the use of paid preparers by different classes? How can we measure changes in the cost of compliance?

I close with a broader point. Not only does the use of a preparer not correlate strongly with complexity, the use of a preparer is not necessarily a bad thing. Many years ago I suggested that most people will use a preparer no matter what and that simplification mavens should aim at moving the tax system to a state where most individuals could afford to pay what a preparer would charge to prepare a return.[9] I do not think that tax preparation fees are necessarily a bad allocation of resources.[10] Equity concerns and Congress's apparently insatiable desire to use the Internal Revenue Code to provide incentives preclude a tax system in which the vast majority of taxpayers can prepare their returns unassisted. That holy grail is unobtainable and should not be the focus of simplification. The

8. These changes might be thought of as efficiency gains, but I do not believe this type of efficiency gain is captured by the model and, in any event, the authors model simplicity separately rather than as an aspect of efficiency.

9. Schenk (1979, p. 130).

10. Switching from using a paid preparer to preparing one's own return is not a zero sum function. It fails to take into account the time taxpayers will spend doing their own returns. It also fails to take into account lost opportunity costs. Even if filing a return became an incredibly simple act, some people would still find it more efficient not to do the return, perhaps because their wage rate exceeded the preparer's.

introduction of tax preparation software and return preparation by the IRS is a major step toward making the preparation aspect of compliance complexity less of a problem. Changes in the law that would reduce the costs of preparation should be the focus rather than eliminating the need for assistance, because much of the complexity of the tax system has nothing to do with return preparation. From that perspective, a change in the use of tax preparers is largely irrelevant.

The authors are to be commended for their work in attempting to quantify the simplification benefits of simplification proposals. The model is a step forward. My conclusion is that the use of a paid preparer is not a satisfactory metric for measuring effects on tax complexity. A better metric would correlate with the cost of tax return preparation and would include other aspects of compliance complexity and the more troubling transactions complexity. I do not know what metric could be used as a proxy for those aspects of complexity. I am unsure therefore whether some of the model's results do not make sense because the metric is imperfect or because simplification effects simply cannot be quantified.

References

Bradford, David F. 1986. *Untangling the Income Tax*. Harvard University Press.

Burman, Leonard E., and William G. Gale. 2001. "A Golden Opportunity to Simplify the Tax System." Brookings Policy Brief 77 (April).

Burman, Leonard E., and others. 2002. "The Individual AMT: Problems and Potential Solutions." Urban-Brookings Tax Policy Center, Discussion Paper 5 (August).

Christian, Charles W., Sanjay Gupta, and Suming Lin. 1993. "Determinants of Tax Preparer Usage: Evidence from Panel Data." *National Tax Journal* 46 (4): 487–503.

Cronin, Julie-Anne. 1999. "U.S. Treasury Distributional Analysis Methodology." Office of Tax Analysis, Paper 85 (September).

Erard, Brian. 1993. "Taxation with Representation." *Journal of Public Economics* 52 (2): 163–97.

Feenberg, Daniel R., Andrew W. Mitrusi, and James M. Poterba. 1997. "Distributional Effects of Adopting a National Retail Sales Tax." In *Tax Policy and the Economy*, vol. 11, edited by James M. Poterba, 49–89. MIT Press for the National Bureau of Economic Research.

Frischmann, Peter J., and Edward W. Frees. 1999. "Demand for Services: Determinants of Tax Preparation Fees." *Journal of the American Taxation Association* 21 (Supplement): 1–23.

Gale, William G. 1999. "The Required Tax Rate in a National Retail Sales Tax." *National Tax Journal* 52 (3): 443–57.

Gale, William G., and Janet Holtzblatt. 2002. "The Role of Administrative Issues in Tax Reform: Simplicity, Compliance, and Administration." In *United States Tax Reform in the 21st Century*, edited by George R. Zodrow and Peter Mieszkowski, 179–214. Cambridge University Press.

Gale, William G., and Samara R. Potter. 2002. "An Economic Evaluation of the Economic Growth and Tax Relief Reconciliation Act of 2001." *National Tax Journal* 55 (1): 133–86.

Graetz, Michael J. 1997. *The Decline (and Fall?) of the Income Tax.* W.W. Norton.

———. 1999. *The U.S. Income Tax: What It Is, How It Got That Way, and Where We Go from Here.* W.W. Norton.

———. 2002. Testimony before the House Subcommittee on Select Revenue Measures, Committee on Ways and Means. April 10.

Gravelle, Jane G., and Kent Smetters. 2001. "Who Bears the Burden of the Corporate Tax in the Open Economy?" Working Paper 8280. Cambridge, Mass.: National Bureau of Economic Research (May).

Long, James E., and Steven B. Caudill. 1993. "Tax Rates and Professional Tax Return Preparation: Reexamination and New Evidence." *National Tax Journal* 46 (4): 511–18.

Mills, Lillian F. 1999. "Discussion of 'Demand for Services: Determinant of Tax Preparation Fees.'" *Journal of the American Taxation Association* 21 (Supplement): 24–37.

Pechman, Joseph A. 1987. "Tax Reform: Theory and Practice." *Economic Perspectives* 1 (1): 11–28.

Sabelhaus, John, and Jeffrey A. Groen. 2000. "Can Permanent-Income Theory Explain Cross-Sectional Consumption Patterns?" *Review of Economics and Statistics* 82 (3): 431–38.

Schenk, Deborah H. 1979. "Simplification for the Average Taxpayer." In *Federal Income Tax Simplification,* edited by Charles H. Gustafson, 115–35. Philadelphia: American Law Institute–American Bar Association.

Slemrod, Joel. 1984. "Optimal Tax Simplification: Toward a Framework for Analysis." *Proceedings of the Seventy-Sixth Annual Conference on Taxation,* 158–62. Baltimore, Md.: National Tax Association-Tax Institute of America.

———. 1992. "Did the Tax Reform Act of 1986 Simplify Tax Matters?" *Journal of Economic Perspectives* 6 (1): 45–57.

———. 1996. "Which Is the Simplest Tax System of Them All?" In *Economic Effects of Fundamental Tax Reform,* edited by Henry J. Aaron and William G. Gale, 355–91. Brookings.

Tempalski, Jerry. 2001. "The Impact of the 2001 Tax Bill on the Individual AMT." *Proceedings of the Ninety-Fourth Annual Conference on Taxation,* 341–48. Baltimore, Md.: National Tax Association.

U.S. Congress Joint Committee on Taxation. 2001. "Estimated Budget Effects of the Conference Agreement for H.R. 1836 [1]." JCX 51-01.

U.S. Congressional Budget Office. 2001. "Effective Federal Tax Rates, 1979–1997." Government Printing Office (October).

———. 2002. "The Budget and Economic Outlook: Fiscal Years 2003–2012." Government Printing Office (January).

Weber, Mike, 2001. "General Description Booklet for the 1996 Public Use Tax File." Statistics of Income Division, U.S. Internal Revenue Service.

10

ALAN H. PLUMLEY
C. EUGENE STEUERLE

Ultimate Objectives for the IRS: Balancing Revenue and Service

ALTHOUGH IT IS widely understood that the Internal Revenue Service has the mission to collect federal taxes, there is some debate as to whether that is its only mission. If there is a crisis in tax administration, it may be one of identity. There is consensus that the IRS must collect revenues, but there is little agreement on how and sometimes even whether it should pursue its many other functions. Even members of Congress have waxed and waned between demanding that almost all effort be put into pursuing noncompliance as opposed to emphasizing service and taxpayer rights.

A crucial unifying factor is limited resources. Decisions routinely have to be made weighing one IRS activity against another, and without some idea of a comprehensive objective for all of the IRS, those decisions cannot be consistent or optimal. Consider some of the expectations citizens have of the IRS. Most taxpayers want the IRS to issue refunds speedily each spring. Many of them look to the IRS to answer their questions about the increasingly complicated Internal Revenue Code. Some even believe the IRS to be the source of the complexity, failing to draw a distinction between lawgivers and law enforcers. Others want the IRS to do a good job as tax cop—helping to direct the "traffic" and assisting those who "break down," while also catching and punishing those who violate the laws. The image that businesses have of the IRS is often colored by the significant record-keeping and information-reporting burden imposed on

The authors wish to thank Michael Graetz for his collaboration on an earlier summary of much of the IRS information presented herein and Eric Toder for his comments on an earlier draft.

them. But the IRS does not just collect taxes; it pays out money under a vast array of subsidy programs. Both lawmakers and the public expect the IRS to implement social programs, just as would the Departments of Energy or Health and Human Services, and to ensure that federal funding reaches targeted purposes or people.

In the midst of these many public expectations, the IRS has had trouble balancing its many roles over the past thirty years. Certainly, even though the Internal Revenue Service has always pursued both revenue and service (just look at the agency's title), remarkable shifts have taken place. These shifts illustrate the tension that exists between the IRS's mission when defined narrowly as collecting revenue and more broadly as providing service. Our view is that meeting citizens' demands for justice under the laws is a service that entails collecting revenues that are owed, as well as providing subsidies that are due, and so the two goals are not as incompatible as they may seem. Still, the challenge remains: to identify and to implement the proper balance for all aspects of tax administration.[1]

This chapter examines how this challenge has been met from a historical perspective and then offers a framework for identifying the proper balance. Once established, it can be used both to critique past performance and to provide some guidance for future resource allocations. Without a comprehensive understanding of its objective (or one that relates goals to one another), the IRS will not be able to make consistent choices in its allocation of resources. We believe that some of the changes in emphasis that took place over the past thirty years reflect this inconsistency.

Historical Perspective

Determining objectives and policies for the IRS requires that we first draw on lessons from the past. In this section we summarize trends in revenue, workload, taxpayer noncompliance, IRS size, resource allocation, enforcement results, and taxpayer service. These data reveal how the preferences of presidents, legislators, and administrators have played out against each other; at the same time they show the extraordinary difficulty the IRS has had in meeting multiple, conflicting, and shifting political demands with limited resources.

1. That challenge is highlighted by a lively debate among authors, editors, commentators, and reviewers of our chapter over whether (1) service is merely a means to the ultimate end of collecting revenue; (2) service is one of several goals in its own right; or (3) collecting revenues is perhaps the principal service. Regardless, it is our hope that this chapter will stimulate thoughtful debate about the proper role of the IRS and how that role should influence IRS decisionmaking in allocating resources.

Revenue

The IRS collects a growing amount of federal tax revenue. In the past thirty years, annual government receipts have grown tenfold, from under $200 billion in 1971 to roughly $2 trillion in 2001. Individual income tax and Social Security and related taxes have accounted for the largest share of government receipts, increasing from about 71 percent of all government receipts in 1971 to almost 85 percent in 2001. Almost all the growth in federal receipts has arisen from the growth in the economy. However, federal revenues as a percentage of GDP have usually fallen in the range from 16 percent in 1971 to 19 percent in 2001.

Workload

From a tax administration perspective, it is workload that must be allocated—from prefiling telephone assistance, to the processing of returns and refunds, to postfiling enforcement activities. Since 1974, for example, the number of individual income tax returns has increased by 60 percent by 2001, while the population has grown by less than 35 percent. This per capita growth in the number of returns is due largely to a shift from married-joint returns to other filing statuses (for example, single and head of household) as couples are getting married later (if at all) and are getting divorced more frequently.[2] Some growth is due to the increase in children being required to file, even though they are on their parents' returns already. The number of returns of corporations, fiduciaries, and partnerships has also been outpacing population growth (growing from 24 to 40 per thousand of population), although employment tax returns have held roughly constant with respect to the population. Fortunately for the returns processing function, the growth in electronic filing has exceeded the growth in returns; however, this shift toward electronic returns has not diminished the workload for prefiling and postfiling activities.

Taxpayer Noncompliance

The Internal Revenue Code imposes three basic obligations on taxpayers: to file timely returns, to report the correct amount of tax liability on those returns, and to pay that amount of tax timely. An obvious influence on the IRS workload, therefore, is the extent to which taxpayers do not fully comply with these obligations. Noncompliance not only drives most of the IRS's postfiling activities (audits, collection actions, criminal investigations, and so forth), but it also

2. The percentage of all individual "married, filing jointly" returns declined from 53.1 percent in 1974 to 39.1 percent in 2001.

Table 10-1. *Selected Federal Tax Compliance Estimates, Tax Year 1992*
Billions of dollars, except as indicated

	Individual income tax	Corporation income tax	Employment taxes	Total income and employment taxes
Total tax liability	558.7	113.5	431.6	1,103.8
Tax paid voluntarily and on time	457.0	92.6	381.5	931.1
Gross tax gap[a]	100.7	20.9	50.1	172.7
Nonfiling	13.8	0.0	0.0	13.8
Underreporting	73.1	19.4	42.8	135.3
Underpayment	14.8	1.5	7.3	23.6
Enforced and late payments	19.2	7.7	6.1	33.0
Net tax gap[b]	82.5	13.2	44.1	139.7
Noncompliance rate (percent)[c]	18.2	18.4	11.6	15.6

Source: Author's calculations based on IRS (1996) and unpublished IRS material.
a. Total tax liability minus tax paid voluntarily and on time.
b. Gross tax liability minus enforced and late payments.
c. Ratio of gross tax gap to total tax liability.

greatly influences filing and prefiling activities (for example, freezing or disallowing refunds and educating taxpayers to avoid noncompliance).

The amount of tax liability that is not paid voluntarily and timely is called the gross tax gap. The most recently published estimates of the entire tax gap are summarized in table 10-1. In 1992 nonfiling accounted for 8 percent of the gross tax gap and was concentrated among individuals. Underreporting on timely filed returns accounted for over 78 percent of the gap, while the remaining 14 percent arose when taxpayers did not timely pay the amount of tax that they reported on their returns as due. These estimates, which are somewhat old and inevitably subject to error, indicate that the noncompliance rate has been roughly the same for individual and corporation income tax and slightly lower for employment tax. Even though about 84 percent of all these taxes are estimated to be paid voluntarily and timely, the remaining gross tax gap was over $172 billion in 1992. This presents an enormous challenge for the IRS. In fact, estimates indicate that over 80 percent of that $172 billion will never be collected.[3]

Although more recent compliance data are not available, and comprehensive estimates are always subject to error (people do not report on how much they do

---

3. Although previous estimates of the gross tax gap suggest that compliance rates have been relatively stable over time, how the IRS administers the tax law presumably influences voluntary compliance and therefore the size of the tax gap.

not report, and nonfilers are not anxious to identify themselves), it is clear that noncompliance is greatest where the opportunity is greatest. In figure 10-1 the IRS estimates are broken down according to the level of withholding and information reporting involved. Both the amount of individual income tax that is not reported timely (the underreporting gap) and the corresponding net misreporting percentage are inversely proportional to the extent to which a reported amount is subject to third-party information reporting, such as Form W-2 and Form 1099; the more completely an amount is covered by information reporting, the lower the noncompliance rate. When the amount is also subject to withholding by the payer, noncompliance drops even more. Clearly the greatest opportunities for significant gains in voluntary compliance are where taxpayers currently have the greatest opportunity to make errors—whether inadvertently or intentionally—and those errors cannot easily be checked on someone else's books (payer's or payee's).

One of the areas of noncompliance that has received much IRS attention in recent years is the earned income tax credit (EITC) for individuals. According to a targeted study of tax year 1999 returns (see table 10-2), just over half of all returns claiming EITC claimed an incorrect amount, with returns claiming too much accounting for 86.0 percent of the erroneous returns and 92.6 percent of the erroneous dollar amounts. Of the entire amount of EITC claimed, almost one-third should not have been. On the other side, there is also significant underclaiming of this credit by those eligible, but the IRS compliance studies (because they examined only EITC claimants) could not estimate the extent to which eligible people do not claim it at all.

IRS Size

How has the IRS coped with increasing workloads and the enormous challenge of taxpayer noncompliance? Comparing 1974 to 2001, the IRS has stayed roughly the same proportionate size—both in terms of its budget (roughly 0.1 percent of GDP) and in terms of its work force (approximately 0.04 percent of the population). However, there was a significant cycle of increase from 1982 to 1993 and decline thereafter. The challenge has been to accommodate the increase in the number of returns and number of programs administered, by becoming more productive. The growth in electronic filing has certainly increased the IRS's ability to process returns, but what about productivity in other aspects of tax administration? The next sections highlight recent trends in IRS resource allocation and productivity, with particular attention to enforcement programs and customer service activities. This dichotomy between enforcement and service, however, is somewhat misleading. In a sense, even enforcement activities can be thought of as service—particularly to honest taxpayers who benefit when tax evaders are forced to pay their fair share of the tax

Figure 10-1. *Underreporting of Individual Income by Visibility Categories, Tax Year 1992*

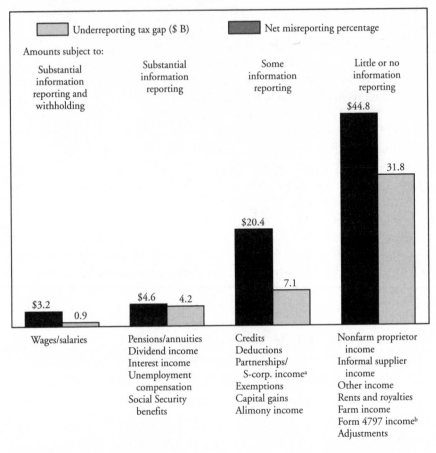

Source: IRS (1996).
a. S-corp. refers to corporations that are structured so their income "flows through" to the owners.
b. Form 4797 relates to gains from sales of business property.

burden. However, when we use the terms *taxpayer* and *service* together, we follow the IRS convention of defining taxpayer service more narrowly as those (generally prefiling) activities in which the IRS provides assistance to taxpayers in understanding and meeting their tax obligations.

Resource Allocation

The three basic taxpayer obligations (filing, reporting, and payment) create three phases of tax administration: prefiling (predominantly helping taxpayers

Table 10-2. *EITC Compliance, Tax Year 1999*[a]

	Over-claim returns	Correct returns	Under-claim returns	Total	Alternative error definitions	
					Net (overclaims – underclaims)	Total (overclaims + underclaims)
Returns claiming EITC (millions)	9.2	8.2	1.3	18.8		
Amount claimed (billions of dollars)	14,572	14,785	1,880	31,237		
Correct amount (billions of dollars)	4,920	14,785	2,646	22,351		
Amount of error (billions of dollars)[b]	9,653	0	–765		8,886	10,418
Overclaim and under-claim (percent)[c]	66.2	0.0	–40.7		28.5	33.4
Misreporting (percent)[d]	196.2	0.0	–28.9		39.8	46.6

Source: IRS, 1999 EITC Compliance Study.

a. Based on audits of a representative sample of EITC claimants. Estimates are lower bound, in that they assume that taxpayers who failed to appear for an audit have the same compliance (overclaims, correct, underclaims) as taxpayers who were audited.

b. Amount claimed minus correct amount.

c. Ratio of amount of error to amount claimed.

d. Ratio of amount of error to correct amount.

to understand and meet their obligations), filing (processing returns, payments, and refunds and maintaining taxpayer accounts), and postfiling (mostly enforcement). Although all three categories of IRS activity involve taxpayer assistance or service, and all three help to generate revenue, prefiling is dominated by taxpayer service, and postfiling is dominated by enforcement. The general rule in our system of voluntary[4] compliance with the tax laws is that both taxpayers and tax administrators prefer to emphasize the prefiling phase. Contrary to what might be predicted by the TAG model presented in chapter 8 in this volume, comprehensive compliance studies have suggested that most individuals seek to meet their tax obligations fully. (Less than half the taxpayers could be found to have understated their tax, and many of the understatements that were made were small amounts, many of which were likely inadvertent. One way to use the TAG model to explain these findings is to

4. At first glance it may be hard to understand how a system that requires withholding and information reporting and that uses enforcement actions to deter noncompliance can be considered

characterize most individuals as risk averse.) Most taxpayers appreciate all the help they can get in understanding their obligations, while the IRS realizes that it is usually much more effective to help taxpayers before they file than it is to collect delinquent taxes after they are due.

A minority of taxpayers, nonetheless, are intentionally noncompliant, necessitating at least some enforcement action by the IRS. This raises one of the most important questions for tax administrators: What is the appropriate balance between their prefiling, filing, and postfiling activities? That is, how should they allocate their limited resources to these three needs (or even within them)? Is it possible to know if one of them is being emphasized (or deemphasized) to the detriment of overall agency performance? How can we judge the performance of the IRS, anyway?

As background to answering these questions, let us examine how the IRS has allocated its resources in the past. The chief IRS resource is its employees. About 69 percent of the IRS budget is devoted to personnel costs, although this is down from almost 77 percent in 1975.[5] Figure 10-2 illustrates how the IRS has allocated its employees to three major categories of work: taxpayer service, the processing of tax returns and related data, and enforcement. Although these categories do not correspond exactly to prefiling, filing, and postfiling, they are close.[6]

Although enforcement may be a last resort, it nonetheless consumes the greatest share of IRS personnel, while taxpayer service activities have traditionally employed the least. Ignoring the period from 1995 onward for a moment, the mix of employees at the IRS has fluctuated somewhat since 1974 (due in part to enforcement hiring initiatives in the late 1980s), but the shares allocated to enforcement, returns and data processing, and general management and overhead remained roughly stable with respect to the number of returns filed, while the staff allocated to taxpayer service has been increasing over time—even as a percentage of returns filed. The traditional mix then changed dramatically in the period from 1996 to 2000: Enforcement and processing personnel were cut dramatically, while those allocated to taxpayer service more than doubled.[7] Notice that this change began at least two years

---

voluntary. In reality even these measures cannot force everyone—or even most people—to comply fully with the law. Unless they are compelled individually (and the data contained in this chapter confirm that only a few are), the extent to which taxpayers comply with their tax obligations is based on their own voluntary choice. This does not mean that everyone complies completely—only that the extent to which many comply is by choice.

5. As we understand it, this decline was due in part to increased investments in automation and to an increasing reliance on outside contractors.

6. Taxpayer service, for example, includes answering taxpayer inquiries about refunds that are pending during processing, and a significant portion of data processing supports enforcement activities.

7. According to conversations with IRS officials, this literally involved the reassignment of enforcement personnel to taxpayer service duties.

Figure 10-2. *IRS Staffing, Fiscal Years 1975–2000*

Number[a]

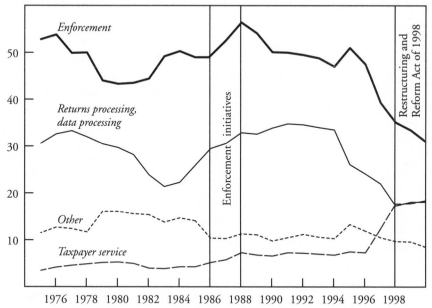

Source: IRS, *Commissioner's Annual Report*, fiscal years 1975–92; IRS, *Data Book*, fiscal years 1993–2000.
a. Positions per 100,000 individual income tax returns filed.

before the Restructuring and Reform Act of 1998 (RRA98), legislation that mandated this shift in emphasis.

Most enforcement personnel are allocated to three primary functions: the examination of tax returns, the collection of delinquent taxes (and securing delinquent returns), and criminal investigation (in that order of size). As illustrated in figure 10-3, examination personnel declined slightly, relative to the number of returns, even before the late 1990s.

The IRS has generally treated the processing of tax returns as mandatory, with enforcement and taxpayer service competing for the discretionary part of the budget. With processing put to the side for the moment, it is instructive to see how the measured outputs from enforcement and taxpayer service have changed over time.

Enforcement Results

The IRS uses the term *examinations* to refer to its scrutiny of tax returns to determine their accuracy. Although sometimes called audits, most examinations

Figure 10-3. *IRS Enforcement Staffing, Fiscal Years 1975–2000*

Number[a]

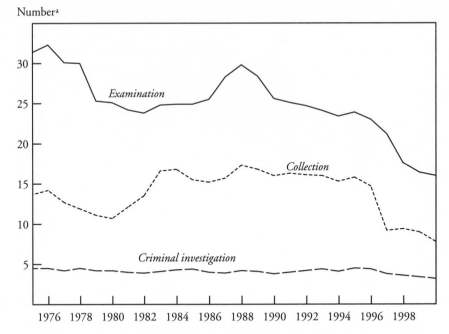

Source: IRS, *Commissioner's Annual Report*, fiscal years 1975–92; IRS, *Data Book*, fiscal years 1993–2000.

a. Positions per 100,000 individual income tax returns filed.

generally focus on just a few items that seem questionable and are not full audits, as accountants would use the term. While most examinations historically have involved direct meetings with the taxpayer, a growing share of examinations are conducted through semiautomated correspondence.[8] Given the decline in enforcement resources in recent years, we should expect the corresponding decline that we see in examination coverage rates (see figure 10-4). What is more surprising is that coverage rates (particularly among corporations) have been declining significantly for a long time—with the exception of the early 1990s, when the impact of the enforcement initiatives was being felt, and more recently, with the rise in EITC-related correspondence exams.

At the same time, direct enforcement revenue (the tax, penalty, and interest paid by taxpayers as a direct result of their being contacted by an IRS enforce-

8. Neither of these types of examinations, however, includes the numerous enforcement contacts that arise from mismatches between third-party information documents and what taxpayers report on their tax returns.

Figure 10-4. *IRS Examination Coverage Rates, Fiscal Years 1978–2001*

Number[a]

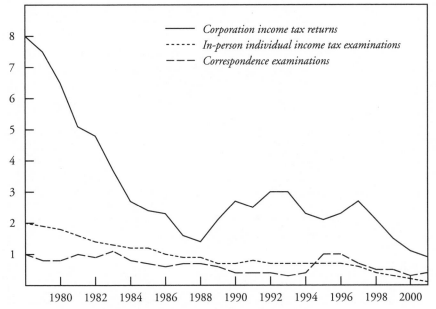

Source: IRS, *Commissioner's Annual Report*, fiscal years 1978–92; IRS, *Data Book*, fiscal years 1993–2001.
a. Examinations closed per 100 returns filed the previous calendar year.

ment program) fell from 2.5 percent of net dollars collected in 1995 to 1.8 percent in 2001. This decline may be associated with a decrease in examinations per examiner, as suggested by figure 10-5. With the exception of the late 1990s (which saw a significant shift in focus toward correspondence examinations of relatively simple issues, most notably the earned income tax credit), examiners' productivity (as defined by returns examined per staff year[9]) has been declining steadily and significantly for over twenty years.

Undoubtedly many factors have contributed to this decline, including the increasing complexity (and variability) of the tax laws and the increase in time spent by examiners fulfilling the mandates of two major taxpayer bills of rights (which impose many rules and restrictions on how taxpayer contacts are conducted). And it is entirely possible that the expansion of computer-generated contacts based on the matching of information returns led to improved compliance

9. Note that this does not account for the possibility of greater productivity *within* any given examination, such as probing more intensively.

Figure 10-5. *IRS Examination Staff Resources and Output, Fiscal Years 1978–2000*

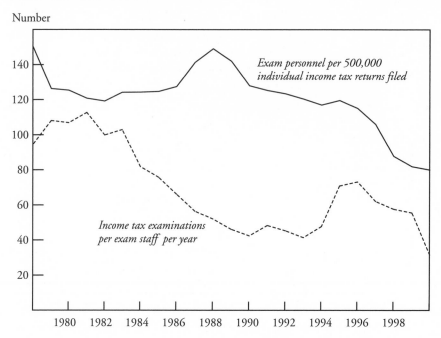

Number

Exam personnel per 500,000 individual income tax returns filed

Income tax examinations per exam staff per year

Source: IRS, *Commissioner's Annual Report*, fiscal years 1978–92; IRS, *Data Book*, fiscal years 1993–2000.

in areas easier to track, such as interest, dividends, and to some extent capital gains. This trend could lead to lower measured productivity (though not necessarily actual productivity, if indirect effects on compliance were measured). But whatever is going on, it is clear that a relatively stable allocation of resources to the examination of tax returns does not necessarily yield a correspondingly stable output of examinations or direct revenues from those exams.

Another challenge for IRS enforcement is that less than half of what is assessed by either in-person or correspondence examinations is eventually collected—even after seven years! Amounts assessed by the matching of information documents against what is reported on tax returns generally are twice as collectible, but even those amounts are not paid in full. Clearly, identifying noncompliance is only part of the challenge facing tax administration.

The collection function seeks to collect delinquent taxes, penalties, and interest, and to secure delinquent returns. The three primary enforcement tools it uses are liens (legal claims to property as security or payments for tax debts), levies (seizures of taxpayers' assets held by others to satisfy the taxpayers' tax debts), and

Figure 10-6. *IRS Collection Enforcement, Fiscal Years 1978–2001*

Number

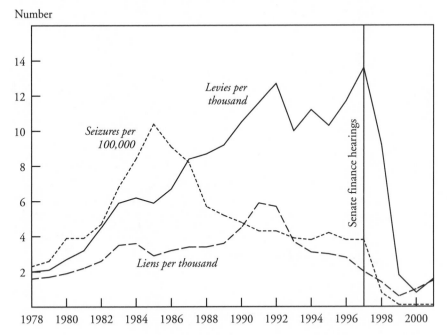

Source: IRS, *Commissioner's Annual Report*, fiscal years 1978–92; IRS, *Data Book*, fiscal years 1993–2001.

seizures (taking control of taxpayers' property that they hold, with the purpose of selling the property to satisfy their tax debts). Interestingly, although the use of all three grew from the early to the mid-1980s, each peaked at a different time (see figure 10-6): The use of liens has been declining since 1991, and seizures began declining in 1986. The use of levies continued to grow until 1998, when they (and seizures) dropped precipitously, after charges of IRS enforcement misconduct were made at hearings held by the Senate Finance Committee. It seems likely that the provisions of section 1203 of RRA98, which followed soon thereafter, also had an adverse effect on collection activities. This code section lists ten categories of misconduct (sometimes called the Ten Deadly Sins) for which an IRS employee can be fired, the first of which deals specifically with seizures of property in collection enforcement cases.

The criminal investigation (CI) function pursues tax crimes related to legal-sector income (for example, fraud), but it also investigates illegal-source and narcotics-related financial crimes. In fiscal year 2001, each of these three categories accounted for roughly one-third of all CI cases, though illegal-source financial crimes represented a larger share. Although the number of new investigations has

Figure 10-7. *IRS Criminal Investigations, Fiscal Years 1980–2001*

Number per million population

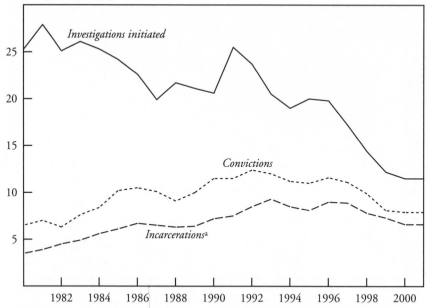

Source: IRS, *Commissioner's Annual Report,* fiscal years 1980–92; IRS, *Data Book,* fiscal years 1993–2001; and unpublished tabulations from the IRS Criminal Investigations Management Information System, 1980–89.

a. Incarcerations may include prison time, home confinement, electronic monitoring, or a combination thereof.

declined steadily over the past two decades (particularly relative to population growth), convictions and incarcerations have not fallen off until recently (see figure 10-7). The decline seems to be partly due to the gradual decline in CI staffing in recent years (see figure 10-3) and to a slight reduction in investigations started per staff year (falling from around 1.6 to about 1.0). However, the apparent increase in time per case seems to have contributed to a higher conviction rate. According to conversations with CI staff, their recent efforts have focused mainly on cooperating with financial and narcotics-related investigations, not with more traditional tax noncompliance, and this may also affect time allocation and conviction rates.

By virtually every measure (both inputs and outputs), IRS enforcement of the tax laws outside of computer-generated document matching programs has been in decline for many years, but particularly so from about the mid-1990s to the beginning of the new century.

Taxpayer Service

The growth in the resources allocated to taxpayer service activities[10] (see figure 10-2) has resulted in more taxpayers being assisted in a variety of ways: getting an answer to an account or tax law question on the telephone; walking into an IRS field office to get a tax form, publication, or help preparing a return; attending an educational seminar for new businesses, and so on. In fact, since 1995, the IRS has on average responded each year to a number of requests approximately equal to the number of individual tax returns (of course, some taxpayers have multiple requests).

It is noteworthy, however, that the dramatic shift of resources to taxpayer service positions from 1996 to 2002 did not result in a corresponding growth in the number of taxpayers assisted. In fact, as figure 10-8 illustrates, the infusion of taxpayer service personnel in recent years has been accompanied by a dramatic drop in taxpayers assisted per staff year. This trend could have several explanations. For example, new employees can be expected to take a while to be as productive as seasoned workers. Moreover, the increased time per taxpayer contact may have resulted in an increase in the quality of those contacts, even if the ratio of contacts has not risen greatly. However, there is little evidence that this is the case for toll-free telephone assistance. The measured quality of the answers given to technical tax law questions has remained fairly stable. From the data, then, the net result from assigning more people to provide taxpayer service is not clear. Although there has probably been some gain, the data do not reveal whether any such gain has been cost-effective.

A Framework for Resource Allocation

The 1996–2002 shift of resources from enforcement to taxpayer service (assistance) activities was accompanied by a corresponding revision of the IRS mission statement. In 1984 the declared purpose of the IRS was "to collect the proper amount of tax revenue at the least cost to the public, and in a manner that warrants the highest degree of public confidence in our integrity, efficiency, and fairness. To achieve that purpose, we will: encourage and achieve the highest possible degree of voluntary compliance in accordance with the tax law and regulations; advise the public of their rights and responsibilities; determine the

---

10. Again, for clarity, we need to emphasize that the IRS and others often use the terms *taxpayer* (or *customer*) *service* synonymously with *taxpayer* (mostly prefiling) *assistance*. That is the sense in which we use the term here, even though we also want to emphasize that filing and postfiling activities are essential to serving taxpayers effectively.

Figure 10-8. *IRS Service Staff Productivity, Fiscal Years 1979–2001*

Number

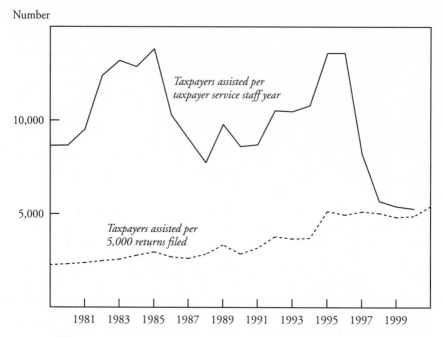

Source: IRS, *Commissioner's Annual Report*, fiscal years 1979–92; IRS, *Data Book*, fiscal years 1993–2001; and unpublished IRS data.

extent of compliance and the causes of noncompliance; . . . do all things needed for the proper administration and enforcement of the tax laws; and continually search for and implement new, more efficient, and effective ways of accomplishing our Mission."[11]

In the 1998 revision, the stated mission was to "provide America's taxpayers top-quality service by helping them understand and meet their tax responsibilities and by applying the tax law with integrity and fairness to all."[12]

Although they overlap significantly with respect to how the mission is to be implemented, the statements reflect much different emphases. The earlier statement characterizes the fundamental role of the IRS as collecting the revenue, while the current one emphasizes the role of providing service. Again, at one level these two goals are not contradictory. Better service can improve revenue collection by facilitating voluntary compliance, while enforcement activities serve compliant taxpayers by ensuring that all pay their required tax. Yet the new mission statement was, in part, a reaction to a perception in Congress that the

11. IRS (1984, cover).
12. IRS (1998, p. 2).

IRS had emphasized revenue collection to the detriment of taxpayer rights and with insufficient sensitivity to taxpayer needs, even though the earlier language also emphasized the need for integrity, fairness, and respect for taxpayer rights.

The 1984 statement is written from the perspective that enforcement and taxpayer service are both means to the ultimate end of collecting "the proper amount of tax revenue." In contrast, the 1998 statement describes service not as a means to an end but rather the end itself, while suggesting that tax law enforcement is a means toward that end. Looking only at the words, the later statement leaves ambiguous whether service is defined narrowly in the traditional sense of taxpayer service or assistance, more broadly as public service, or something in between. However, the later statement only makes sense if the definition of service is broader and means much more than taxpayer service as defined on the organizational chart; it must include applying the tax law as a component of service.

Internal documents and public briefings elaborated on the new mission statement by emphasizing "balanced measures," using the analogy of a three-legged stool. In this paradigm, the IRS mission is supported by three legs (business results, customer satisfaction, and employee satisfaction), which must be balanced if the mission is to be achieved. According to this model, business results (for example, collecting taxes) are not a means to the end of providing top-quality service, but it is one of three objectives, together with customer satisfaction (which is not really the same as service, either) and employee satisfaction. In order to balance these separate objectives, then, the IRS must trade off some of one to strengthen one or both of the others. Revenue collection, for example, might need to be de-emphasized in order to satisfy customers, employees, or both. Although this model appears to have origins in the private sector, the reality is that businesses pay attention to customer satisfaction and employee satisfaction because these are means to maximizing profits—the bottom line. They are not ends in and of themselves, nor are they even coequal with or "balanced" against profits. Nor is customer satisfaction meant to imply public service for a profit-making organization. This is borne out in the American Customer Satisfaction Index (ACSI), which the IRS uses to measure customer satisfaction. According to the ACSI Methodology Report, a "basic tenet underlying the ACSI is that satisfied customers represent a real, albeit intangible, economic asset to a firm. By definition, an economic asset generates future income streams to the owner of that asset. . . . [The] model links satisfaction to economic returns in the form of customer retention and price tolerance."[13]

This statement acknowledges that firms do not seek to balance customer satisfaction with profits; rather, they improve customer satisfaction to the extent that it increases long-term profits. "The customer is always right" because that

13. National Quality Research Center (1998, pp. 4–5).

maximizes customer loyalty and market share and, hence, profits. Likewise businesses seek to improve employee satisfaction because that improves the productivity and retention of employees and therefore increases profits.

Therefore the analogy to a three-legged stool is best viewed as a recognition that a significant factor in taxpayer satisfaction is the perception that the IRS enforces the law fairly and effectively—ensuring that, to the extent possible (given IRS resources and constraints), all pay their fair share. This is much closer to a definition of public service than of simple customer satisfaction, or, in other words, a broad definition of customer service.

Traditional Direct Revenue Maximization

In general the traditional IRS approach to resource allocation placed the highest priority on filing (that is, the "required" tasks of processing returns and refunds and managing taxpayer accounts), with "discretionary" resources devoted mostly to enforcement (postfiling), and a smaller share allocated to taxpayer service (prefiling). Enforcement programs have traditionally pursued the objective of maximizing the revenue that they produce from the taxpayers whom they contact, subject to their budget constraint. However, various enforcement programs have had different interpretations of that objective. The examination function and the document-matching program, for example, defined *revenue* as the amount of additional tax and penalties assessed, with no regard for the amount of revenue actually collected. The collection function has defined *revenue* as the amount of tax, penalty, and interest actually collected, but it has not had a strong ability to distinguish among cases on the basis of how cost-effective it would be to pursue them. The appeals and tax litigation functions do not have much discretion as to which cases to work, and the decision to pursue litigation is dictated more by the precedent being sought than by the dollars at risk in the case in question. Therefore these last functions are not as revenue-driven as the others. Criminal investigation is also less focused on the revenue at risk in the particular cases they pursue. Instead they seek to enforce the law against criminals as a deterrent to noncompliance (and, as noted, have recently spent more time on nontax financial and narcotics functions than on more traditional tax functions).

Notwithstanding these differences, and the difficulty in allocating enforcement resources according to a unified objective, it is still true that the prevailing enforcement objective has been to maximize direct enforcement revenue. The appeal of direct revenue maximization is that, for the most part, it is measurable, and it provides a basis for making resource allocation decisions. For any given budget and absent other constraints, enforcement revenue can be maximized by working the cases with the highest expected revenue-to-cost ratios. Net revenue is maximized only if the revenue-to-cost ratio at the margin is the same across all programs. In other words, if this optimality condition were not true, then revenue could be increased by reallocating resources from workload having lower revenue-to-cost potential to other workload having a higher revenue-to-cost ratio.[14]

There are several problems with maximizing direct enforcement revenue as an objective—particularly as it has been applied historically in the IRS. The most significant of these is obvious: It views enforcement in isolation from voluntary compliance. To the extent that IRS activities—whether enforcement or nonenforcement—indirectly affect the voluntary compliance of the general population, it is the combination of direct and indirect revenue that is important.[15] Some types of enforcement cases, although yielding little enforcement revenue directly, probably have a large indirect effect on compliance and should therefore be expanded at the expense of cases with higher direct yields. Likewise some nonenforcement activities, although they produce no revenue directly, nonetheless contribute greatly to voluntary compliance—surpassing the combined direct and indirect effect of some traditional enforcement programs at the margin. Hence, if the IRS were to account for the impact of each of its activities on voluntary compliance, then both enforcement and nonenforcement resources could be allocated according to a common objective.

The second problem is that several enforcement functions (for example, examination and document matching) have attempted to maximize dollars assessed instead of dollars actually collected. In the case of the document matching program, the error is probably not large, but it has likely caused noticeable inefficiencies in the examination program, since the difference between the amount assessed and what is collected is significant and widely varied across the many examination categories.[16] For years the IRS could not even trace by major taxpayer categories what dollars of assessments were actually collected.

A third problem has been that enforcement cases have been selected for many programs according to the amount of revenue at risk, rather than according to the expected revenue-to-cost ratio (here we are referring only to IRS costs). A

---

14. To the extent that there is discretion as to how intensively to pursue any given case (for example, how many lines on a tax return to examine), then this optimality condition applies to both the intensive margin (that is, how many line items to examine on any given return) and to the extensive margin (how many returns to examine).

15. The examination function has historically recognized this by requiring at least some minimum level of activity in each work category. Although these minimum constraints have been set somewhat arbitrarily, they recognize an impact on voluntary compliance.

16. To some extent this could be rationalized, along with the minimum coverage constraints, on the theory that voluntary compliance is improved by pursuing some cases among those likely to be uncollectable. However, if we were able to account for indirect effects on compliance explicitly, then what is important is not what is assessed but what is collected.

large amount of expected revenue is not attractive if it takes a disproportionate expenditure of resources to collect it. Although the most common guide for selecting returns for examination, the discriminant function (DIF) score, attempts to discriminate between returns that are profitable to audit and those that are not, it is not designed to reflect the degree of profitability. Therefore examining the returns with the highest DIF scores undoubtedly does not result in maximizing even the direct enforcement revenue at any given budget level.

The fourth major problem with maximizing direct enforcement revenue is that it does not reflect the value of getting to taxpayers the benefits to which they are entitled or refunding to them any amounts that they have overpaid. The overassessments uncovered in an examination, for example, have been subtracted from the additional tax and penalties assessed, thus reducing the apparent aggregate results. Ideally some value should be placed on those refunds and added to the enforcement collections, since both adjustments move taxpayers closer to their true tax liability.

The final difficulty is that various quantitative and qualitative costs must be taken into account, including the time of the taxpayer and the cost society would place on an unjustly administered tax system independently from its level of revenues.

Attempts to Operationalize the IRS Objective

After the recent reorganization of the IRS into four principal operating divisions, configured according to taxpayer characteristics, the remaining examination function was re-engineered. Although much of the effort centered on work flow and the division of responsibilities, it also sought to reconsider the traditional objective of maximizing direct enforcement revenue. What resulted was a list of seven objectives for the examination function, which could be "balanced" by decisionmakers:

1. Maximize dollars assessed (the traditional examination objective).

2. Maximize dollars collected (that is, the revenue arising directly from the examinations).

3. Maximize presence (that is, examination coverage within each category of taxpayer).

4. Reflect population distribution.

5. Reflect noncompliance distribution.

6. Minimize taxpayer burden.

7. Maximize relative change in dollars assessed (compared to the amount originally reported on the return).

These objectives are to be measured by the overriding values of efficiency, fairness, and coverage, which leaves them rather opaque. What does it mean to "reflect" a distribution? And where is the objective to get to taxpayers the benefits to which they are entitled?

Although it is worthy to try to juggle more than one objective simultaneously, it must be done in a way that does not leave out legitimate objectives and has some mechanism to weight alternative objectives. Taken together, the seven objectives are incomplete. Maximizing dollars collected might be better than maximizing dollars assessed, particularly if the dollars collected include the indirect effect on voluntary compliance. Maximizing dollars assessed is clearly wrong in cases where taxpayers overpay their taxes. The "presence" objective presumably addresses the traditional approach to accounting for indirect effects on compliance (through minimum coverage constraints). If indirect effects were accounted for explicitly, however, this would not be necessary as a separate objective. "Fairness" means very different things in objectives 4 and 5 but, most important, there is a more basic aspect of fairness, which complements efficiency instead of competing with it. When taxpayers fail to pay their fair share of the overall tax burden, this shifts the burden unfairly to honest taxpayers. IRS enforcement efforts seek to rectify that imbalance as much as possible. However, to the extent that enforcement is conducted inefficiently (that is, less total revenue is collected than could be the case with the given budget), then the effective tax burden is distributed less fairly than it could be.

Taxpayer Burden

Six of the objectives proposed above seem to be closely related to the traditional enforcement objective of maximizing the total revenue collected. Minimizing taxpayer burden (objective 6), however, does go beyond the more narrow revenue objective. Here once again we see a reflection of the tension between revenue and service that faces the IRS as a whole. A key point is that minimizing taxpayers' burden is one part of minimizing costs more generally, which in turn is part of the broadly defined mission of service.

If we define taxpayer burden as the time, expense, and inconvenience incurred to comply with the Internal Revenue Code and regulations, it becomes clear that a large source of burden is the tax code itself, and part of the IRS's mission is to help taxpayers understand what is required of them by the law and to facilitate their calculations and payments. If we had the current tax code, for example, but there were no IRS (no tax forms, instructions, publications, toll-free numbers, and so on), taxpayers would still face the enormously burdensome task of determining and fulfilling their tax obligations. In the aggregate, they would also end up paying a much smaller fraction of the tax liability imposed on them by law—both out of confusion and from the opportunity to cheat. Clearly much of what the IRS does (forms, publications, and so forth) decreases unnecessary burden, where little trade-off is involved with compliance. At other times it imposes a necessary burden to try to minimize some other cost, such as an inequitably enforced tax code. It is easy to be against waste, inefficiency, and unnecessary burdens; the more difficult task is to figure out what necessary burdens in the end best serve the public interest as a whole.

The lesson here is that it is too simplistic, and is often counterproductive, to act as if a particular form of taxpayer burden should be minimized on one front without considering the trade-offs on other fronts. The remainder of this chapter proposes a practical framework for examining those trade-offs more rigorously and offers several directions for the future.

An Objective Function to Guide Resource Allocation

We suggest that most of its goals can be accomplished if the IRS were to seek to allocate resources so as to collect the right amount of tax from each taxpayer at the least cost (including inconvenience) to the people. Unfortunately many taxpayers do not pay the amount of tax that is imposed on them by law. Some pay too much, and many pay too little—if any at all. Some of the error is unintentional but much is willful. All the error, however, causes the tax burden to be distributed in a way that is contrary to the intentions of Congress, which the IRS must assume represents the public will. With noncompliance, the tax burden is shifted from those who pay too little to those who pay too much. In both a relative and real sense, therefore, deficiencies are borne by the compliant, either in the form of higher taxes or lower benefits from programs financed by taxes. (Even this expression does not fully incorporate all services required of any agency to ensure that its programs are well run.) This characterization of the objective recognizes several critical factors:

—The ultimate intent is that each taxpayer (and this includes those who currently pay no tax or get "negative" tax payments from programs run through the IRS) pays the correct amount of tax, when it is required to be paid.

—The IRS must recognize its role in reducing overpayments and performing the other program objectives (getting out subsidies, enforcing charity tax laws, and so forth) that Congress builds into IRS programs.

—All IRS activities, whether service-oriented or enforcement-oriented, should pursue a consistent objective. Therefore resources should be allocated to all activities and programs on the basis of how effectively they contribute to this objective at the margin. Prefiling programs, for example (which help taxpayers avoid paying too little and too much), must compete at the margin with postfiling programs (which collect tax underpayments, refund overpayments, and promote voluntary compliance).

—In pursuit of this objective at any level, the IRS must minimize its own costs, as well as the time, expense, and inconvenience it (and the law) imposes on taxpayers. Even if all taxpayers were perfectly compliant, the IRS would still incur costs for enabling them to understand and meet their tax obligations, for processing their returns and payments, and for maintaining their accounts. Likewise these perfectly compliant taxpayers would bear a significant compliance burden (the time, expense, and inconvenience necessary to understand and meet their tax obligations) in addition to the tax burden itself. In other words, some taxpayer burden is inevitably imposed by the law, while other burden may be imposed by the IRS for the purpose of ensuring that the misallocation of the tax burden is minimized.

—Finally some consideration must be given to the economic cost of using up resources in the economy vis-à-vis transferring resources, as from noncompliant to compliant taxpayers. It is unlikely that a society would find it worthwhile to reduce output by a dollar to collect a dollar from a noncompliant taxpayer.[17]

In simple form (but not simple use), this approach can be expressed mathematically as an objective function for a constrained optimization problem as follows:

$$\text{Minimize: } \Sigma_i W_i \left[\theta_i(T_i^+), \Gamma_i(T_i^-), \Lambda_i(C_i) \right],$$

subject to IRS budget = B (constraint operates only after budget appropriation is set). The subscripts, i, refer to the range of taxpayers, W is a welfare weight, + and − refer to over- and underpayments of tax (T), C is the compliance costs for each filer, and the Greek letters are functions for the person i.

More simplified forms of this equation are possible. For instance one that gives equal weights to overpayments and underpayments and a separate but equal weight to all costs is:

$$\text{Minimize: } \Sigma_i \mid T_i^* - T_i \mid + w \Sigma_i C_i \text{ subject to: IRS budget} = B$$

where, for each taxpayer i:

T = the amount of tax actually paid;

T^* = the amount of tax that should be paid under current law;

C = the cost of complying with the tax code and regulations, including the time, expense, and inconvenience required to understand and meet those tax obligations; and

w = a weighting factor that expresses the value of reducing taxpayer compliance costs relative to the value of minimizing the misallocation of the tax burden.

The simplified form can then be expanded by adding in differences that take into account whether the IRS wants to treat overpayments differently from

17. Steuerle (1986).

underpayments, count errors differently according to the income or other circumstances of the taxpayer, or apply different weights to different costs.

Whether in simplified or more complex form, the advantage of this type of objective function is that it allows one to be more explicit about assumptions used to allocate resources. Overpayments are bad, just as underpayments are. (There is broad disagreement among experts as to whether the IRS should pay less attention to overpayments, but few would say they should be ignored.) Weighting factors recognize that a dollar reduction in taxpayers' compliance costs may be valued differently from a dollar reduction in the overall misallocation of tax. One reason is that the misallocations involve transfers (for example, to noncompliant taxpayers), whereas the costs reduce overall product and income in the economy. This has led some observers to imply that only the latter are important, but we believe that ignores the fundamental fact that taxpayers are willing to pay for a fair system of justice—that it is a real service with a positive value.

Considered in efficiency terms defined narrowly, Joel Slemrod questions how many resources should be devoted to enforcement of the tax laws and concludes that "the appropriate condition is that, at the margin, the resource cost of increasing enforcement should equal the saving of the excess burden attributable to the decline in exposure to risk."[18] In lay persons' terms, the efficiency gain at the margin should equal the efficiency loss, but simple pickup of revenue means nothing, since government taxes at that level simply involve a net transfer from some taxpayers to other persons. Unfortunately this rule gives no weight to such issues as equal justice under the law. In fact, people are willing to pay considerable sums of money to ensure a fair administration of justice. That is, equity has value and people are willing to pay for this service. People do care if government arbitrarily takes from one person's pocket without reason, and it is not simply because of risk.

A related issue over which there is much disagreement is how much weight to give to each type of taxpayer error. We believe that the public, through its representatives, wants people to pay the taxes they owe but not to pay taxes they do not owe. Others argue that overpayments should receive almost no weight at all. We believe that this view cannot be consistently held throughout the budget. That is, if the public cares so little about overpayments of tax, then it seems that they would care equally little about whether spending programs reach their targets (indeed many IRS overpayments are due to just that: People inadequately applying for their share of some subsidy program that just happens to be administered by the IRS rather than some other agency).

Note that giving more weight to a dollar of overpayment than to a dollar of underpayment does not by itself tell us a great deal about how the IRS should

18. Slemrod (2002, p. 11).

allocate its internal resources. Another part of the full equation takes into account the marginal cost of various types of actions to minimize deviations from true tax liability. It turns out that, for many issues, the least-cost way of preventing overpayment comes from the use of private advisors and tax preparers, rather than, say, IRS audits. The average (but not necessarily marginal) dollar spent on audit, then, is more likely to be cost-effective in preventing underpayment rather than overpayment.

The IRS can take the objective function listed here and make more explicit how much attention it wants to pay to overpayments versus underpayments. Sometimes the issue cannot be avoided. It will come up both in the development of broad discriminant functions for selecting workload and in assessing the success of auditors at their jobs (for example, will they be rewarded as much for helping taxpayers?).

On a practical level each year, the IRS often allocates its budget as if it is fixed. We recognize that B in fact is endogenous, and one should remove the constraint if the objective function were being considered by Congress or the president.

Among the many other issues to be addressed is the timeliness of taxpayer payments. Since late payments introduce costs to the IRS and often to the taxpayer, this objective can be handled by thinking of the equation in present-value terms. One can also give different weights to different taxes or tax subsidies, as well as to different costs.

Finally, some expansion of the equation is required to recognize programmatic responsibilities that are not fully related either to collecting revenues or to getting out payments to taxpayers. For instance the IRS plays a major role in monitoring receipts for macroeconomic planning purposes, and it essentially regulates the charitable sector's use of tax subsidies for charitable purposes, despite there being little revenue consequence. More broadly any agency has responsibility for seeing that all aspects of the programs under its supervision are efficiently run. As in many other areas, when these responsibilities do not show up easily in the categories of revenue raising or taxpayer service, narrowly defined, they are in danger of receiving too little attention by the IRS. Indeed we suggest that neglect of these programmatic responsibilities has been among the most serious of IRS failures over the years.

Direction for Decisionmakers

At first this type of objective function may seem to be more tractable for enforcement programs than it is for taxpayer service efforts, because some enforcement results are observable and quantifiable, while that is generally not true of taxpayer service activities. However, since the impact of each on the voluntary compliance of the general population must be accounted for, it is not a simple matter to apply it to either type of work. Moreover the weight applied to taxpayer compliance costs relative to taxpayer error is difficult to assess. Nonetheless this formulation of the IRS objective makes it possible to make several practical and sometimes operational suggestions for improvement—particularly in the context of the trends of the past thirty years.

—Incorporate indirect effects: Strive to quantify the extent to which each IRS activity is effective (at the margin) in prompting taxpayers (both those contacted and those not directly contacted) to pay the right amount of tax in a voluntary and timely manner, and then reflect that in resource allocation and workload selection models. Obviously, since these compliance impacts are not observed in isolation, quantifying them is extremely difficult—but it is not impossible. A couple of studies have already made preliminary estimates for individual income tax.[19] Perhaps one of the most significant things the IRS can do to foster this type of research is to identify and compile the necessary data. Even if the data were not needed for any other purpose, their value in estimating these compliance effects would be enormous.

—Minimize conflicting objectives: Even an arbitrary assumption might still be informative when the IRS, for instance, decides to allocate some enforcement efforts to all classes of taxpayers. Once such an allocation is made, one can work backward through the equation to figure out the implicit gains being presumed if all marginal efforts yield the same benefit to cost. For instance if we assume that actual resource allocations take all factors into account, then an effort with a lower direct revenue-to-cost ratio at the margin generally implies a higher indirect revenue-to-cost ratio, which could be quantified to see if it passes some litmus test for feasibility. We can easily discard alternative objectives that clearly work well only on occasion or by accident—such as allocating examination resources in proportion to the population distribution, or selecting for audit the cases likely to result in the largest percentage of tax change. As stated, these fail any realistic benefit-to-cost criterion.

—Pursue overpayments: Prefiling activities help taxpayers determine their correct tax liability, alerting them not just to what is taxable but also to obtain benefits for which they might be eligible. The IRS has no less responsibility to get EITCs to taxpayers, for instance, than does the Agriculture Department to deliver food stamps.[20] By the same token, many types of taxpayer programs and subsidies in the Internal Revenue Code are handled on a cost-effective basis by the private sector, and the IRS's role is more to provide simplified instructions

---

19. See Dubin, Graetz, and Wilde (1990); Plumley (1996).

20. Actually the task of helping taxpayers take advantage of all the tax benefits to which they are entitled cannot be borne entirely by the IRS. The private sector has a significant role to play in prefiling, just as they do in providing filing assistance and fostering greater compliance. The point is that the IRS cannot abdicate its role in this area either.

and regulations than to devote significant audit resources to tracking down remaining overpayments. Still, enforcement workers need to be as recognized for reducing overpayments of tax as they are for collecting underpayments. This should be reflected in how enforcement workload is selected and in how the results are portrayed.

—Manage taxpayer burden: The IRS needs to evaluate burden reduction proposals to determine how consistent they are with the ultimate objective. For example, changes that simultaneously decrease costs (or burdens) and tax errors are almost always good. However, changes that decrease burdens but also increase errors require explicit attention to the weight placed on different taxpayer compliance costs.

—Identify needed changes to the law: A necessary part of pursuing this mission is translating IRS experience in administering the law into studies that could inform legislative proposals and help to decrease the misallocation of the tax burden, the cost of tax administration, and the compliance burden borne by taxpayers. While Congress and the Treasury Department should consult with the IRS on the administrability of proposed changes to the Internal Revenue Code, IRS responsibility cannot be dodged when they fail to do so. It is one thing to be ignored; it is another to provide so little information that being ignored is easy.

—Research better methods: The IRS should continually attempt to be more cost-effective in all of its prefiling, filing, and postfiling activities. Sometimes doing more of the same thing will not be the most effective use of resources. When areas of low compliance are not addressed effectively by current enforcement approaches, the IRS needs to research new approaches—documenting their cost-effectiveness at the margin so they can compete for operational resources with existing approaches. The research approach may be the most cost-effective of all.

Conclusion

There is both good news and bad news. The good news is that taxpayers' compliance is much greater and their compliance costs are much smaller than if there were no IRS at all. In many ways the IRS has been doing a lot of things right. Compliance, after all, is much higher in areas where there is document matching and withholding. The bad news is that significant opportunities for greater effectiveness still remain. At the beginning of the twenty-first century, enforcement efforts in some areas (in particular, where there is little or no separate reporting by payers) were so low that many believe that noncompliance is or will be on the upswing.

have not always sought the right outcomes, and resource allo-
have not always been based on the marginal effectiveness of
to collect the right amount of tax from each taxpayer at the least
(including inconvenience) to the people. Mission statements incorporate
many important objectives, but they are inherently vague and do not give much
guidance on how to relate one objective to another. It is not surprising that the
IRS (and Congress) has shifted emphasis from revenue to taxpayer service in
recent years. In reality neither is an appropriate objective in and of itself, they are
not mutually exclusive, and service incorporates far more than traditional taxpayer service functions. Although collecting tax revenue is an important purpose
of a tax agency, more broadly it should be collecting the right amount of revenue
from the right taxpayers, helping to get program benefits to the right taxpayers
(often through use of the private sector), and minimizing productive losses to
the economy as a whole from filing, enforcement, and compliance efforts. Fortunately there are several practical ways that the IRS can progress toward fulfilling that mission.

COMMENT BY
Donald C. Alexander

This thoughtful and excellent chapter provides much useful information, much
sound evaluation of competing needs, and many recommendations for a sound
system of tax administration. It is indeed refreshing to an old-timer concerned
about the precipitous drop in the IRS's enforcement activity after the 1997 and
1998 hearings to see a recommendation that the IRS should allocate its resources so as "to collect the right amount of tax from each taxpayer at the least
cost (including inconvenience) to the people."

I must quibble somewhat, however, with the heavy emphasis that the authors
place on prefiling services to taxpayers and seeking out taxpayers who should get
refunds and delivering such refunds to them. While I agree that the IRS has a
special responsibility (which should not have been given to it) to try to deliver
earned income tax credits to those who deserve them and have not claimed
them, I do not believe, for example, that the IRS has any postfiling responsibility to try to find those individuals who would have saved money had they itemized deductions but chose not to do so.

The chapter's heavy emphasis on taxpayer service does not seem to recognize
the vast array of taxpayer services rendered by the private sector. Many practitioners make their living through taxpayer services and through representing
taxpayers. According to H&R Block's 2002 annual report, Block served nearly
21 million tax clients in its fiscal year ending April 30, 2002. Community Tax

Aid and other taxpayer clinics and organizations do a fine job in assisting low-income taxpayers, those for whom English is a second language, and EITC recipients. While the IRS should not abdicate the taxpayer service field to professional preparers and organizations like Community Tax Aid, it should do its best to encourage the latter through grants, and it should supplement the activities of the former for those taxpayers who need help. It should not misuse resources, however, by removing revenue agents from their compliance duties and putting them on telephones to answer taxpayer prefiling questions. The private sector does not supplement the IRS's enforcement efforts.

The chapter vividly demonstrates the precipitous decline in IRS enforcement actions but, in my view, it does not spell out the basic reason for this. Commencing with the 104th Congress, increasing in 1997, and culminating with the Senate Finance Committee's beautifully staged hearings in 1998, the IRS was blasted by Congress and the media, and it found little support in the Treasury. The IRS was ordered to reorganize, to change its attitude toward taxpayers and nontaxpayers, and to change its processes and procedures, particularly in collection actions. IRS employees who commit what Congress regards as impermissible actions became subject to summary dismissal.[1] The result of all this bashing and overkill was to reduce collection actions and to reduce examinations today by more than 40 percent of the level roughly maintained prior to the 104th Congress. It is ironic that some of the members of Congress who were shouting at the IRS for being overaggressive several years ago are now claiming that it is not tough enough. Many are concerned, and rightly so, that compliance with our nation's tax laws has dropped substantially and will drop further. Common sense tells us that this is the case; if the public is fully aware that those who run red lights will not be arrested, the public will run more red lights. To me it is foolish hypocrisy to pretend otherwise.

Despite substantial increases in IRS budgets since 1998, the outgoing commissioner recently complained about inadequate IRS resources, and indeed this complaint has some justification. The chapter points out that only about 69 percent of the IRS budget is now devoted to personnel costs, down from almost 77 percent in 1975. This indicates that the IRS is using its appropriated funds for purposes other than hiring revenue agents, revenue officers, tax auditors, and taxpayer service representatives. Instead the IRS has recently been spending substantial sums on consultants. As I understand it, Booz Allen Hamilton received a $200 million contract from the IRS to help it reorganize. I hope that such diversions will cease in the future.

In allocating the IRS's resources, more emphasis should be placed on enforcement and somewhat less on taxpayer service. A strong and useful taxpayer

---

1. The ten impermissible actions or omissions listed in section 1203 of the IRS Restructuring and Reform Act are referred to as the Ten Deadly Sins.

service function should be maintained, directed particularly to those who are not adequately served by the large for-profit private sector. Standards for private practitioners should be set and maintained so that Gresham's law does not prevail, particularly for those that serve the EITC community and also for those who peddle outrageously bad tax products to the wealthy. Policing shabby practitioners is more effective than searching out taxpayers who have received shabby advice.

As to the allocation of revenue agent resources among the many taxpayer segments, I would begin at the top. The largest corporations in this country should be audited regularly (not necessarily annually), and individuals with the highest income should be audited at a much higher rate than those with low income. There should be some audit presence, however, in each category. The current National Research Program, today's successor to TCMP, should improve audit selection and, subject to maintaining some presence in each category, those with higher scores should be audited ahead of those with lower scores. The IRS must develop better and more effective ways of dealing with noncompliance through the use of pass-through entities such as partnerships and limited liability companies.

The IRS should have a stronger voice on Capitol Hill; the law is so complex now as to be almost unadministrable, and using the Internal Revenue Code as the means to deliver all sorts of specific grants intended for the economic or social good should somehow be brought to a halt and reversed. Also, tax laws should not be used to punish taxpayers for real or perceived bad deeds unrelated to tax compliance.

In the chapter's fifth suggestion for improvement, the following statement is made:

"While Congress and the Treasury Department should consult with the IRS on the administrability of proposed changes to the Internal Revenue Code, IRS responsibility cannot be dodged when they fail to do so. It is one thing to be ignored; it is another to provide so little information that being ignored is easy."

The thinly veiled criticism is that it is the IRS's fault for not speaking up about administrability issues. This brings to mind section 4021 of the 1998 IRS Restructuring and Reform Act: "It is the sense of Congress that the Internal Revenue Service should provide the Congress with an independent view of tax administration, and that during the legislative process, the tax writing committees of Congress should hear from frontline technical experts at the Internal Revenue Service with respect to the administrability of pending amendments to the Internal Revenue Code of 1986."

Unless I am missing something, I do not think that the IRS is reluctant to speak to Congress; I think that the Treasury (and probably the Office of Management and Budget) is reluctant to let the IRS speak. This was certainly true in my day. Let us not blame the IRS for the Treasury squashing its efforts to talk to Congress, not that such talk would deter a Congress and an administration eager to spend through the Internal Revenue Code.

COMMENT BY
James W. Wetzler

Plumley and Steuerle correctly argue that we should not think of tax enforcement and taxpayer service as separate activities of a tax administration agency, each of which has its own objective. Rather, tax administration should be a unified program whose resources are allocated among its functions based on analysis of how each contributes to the program's overall objective. The authors examine what should be the objective of the Internal Revenue Service. They present data that reflect the priorities that have prevailed in the past twenty years—generally declining enforcement efforts relative to the large and possibly growing tax compliance gap, occasional injections of resources for short-lived revenue initiatives, declining productivity of the enforcement effort, and the recent substantial shift of resources away from enforcement toward taxpayer service. They make some helpful specific suggestions about how the IRS can improve the quantitative analysis of its activities. While they do not make this assertion, clearly the implication of the chapter is that the history of the enforcement effort over the past twenty years would have been different had priorities been chosen on the basis of rigorous quantitative analysis instead of through the political process.

The Plumley-Steuerle Objective Function for the IRS

Plumley and Steuerle believe that an objective of the IRS should be to promote fairness. Specifically it should use its available resources to strive to minimize an "objective function" equal to the weighted sum of (1) underpayments of tax, (2) overpayments of tax, and (3) the costs incurred by taxpayers in complying with the tax law. The relative weighting of these three elements should reflect the value society places on fair tax administration—on having taxpayers pay the amount of tax that the law says they owe. Resources should be allocated to each of the IRS's functions such that the marginal dollar spent on each function leads to an equal reduction in the weighted sum. Audit selection should reflect this principle as well. Were this concept to be implemented, political debate over the IRS's priorities could be narrowed to the rather dry topic of the appropriate weights to be used in the weighted sum; everything else would be delegated to technical experts, who would analyze the extent to which the individual functions and strategies contribute to minimizing the weighted sum.

As Plumley and Steuerle point out, one problem with this approach is that it gives no guidance on how large the IRS's budget should be. Because the IRS appears to have little control over the size of its budget, and Congress has shown little disposition in recent years to set the IRS budget on the basis of cost-benefit analysis, this may not be too serious a problem in practice. However, the issue of how much government should spend on tax administration is an important one, and it would be helpful to have an analytical model that helps resolve it, such as that provided in Joel Slemrod's chapter in this volume. It would also be helpful to have better data on the key parameters of the model, such as the indirect or spillover effect of the IRS's audit and debt collection activities on voluntary compliance with the tax law.

One potentially controversial issue in specifying the IRS's objective function is the relative weight to be assigned to corrections of overpayments and underpayments.[1] Plumley and Steuerle believe that citizens place a high value on fairness and will support expenditures on activities intended to correct tax overpayments. This contrasts with the usual justification for the tax administration agency's budget that, because the agency generates revenue, it should not have to compete for funds with other programs.

Overpayments and underpayments are not symmetrical errors. Collection of tax revenue involves a deadweight efficiency loss, because taxpayers modify their behavior in response to the tax. Refunding an overpayment does not recoup whatever deadweight loss arose from the taxpayer's behavior under the mistaken belief that he or she owed the tax. Yet, when revenue must be raised in the future from another source to make up for the overpayers' refunds, the deadweight loss is incurred a second time. Conversely raising revenue by correcting erroneous tax underpayments enables taxes to be reduced in the future on compliant taxpayers, reducing the deadweight loss associated with their behavior while not incurring any deadweight loss with respect to the noncompliant taxpayer. Hence correcting a one-dollar tax underpayment should be more valuable than correcting a one-dollar tax overpayment by an amount equal to twice the deadweight loss from raising an additional one dollar of revenue. Moreover, as a practical matter, the amount of injustice arising from erroneous tax overpay-

1. To a certain extent, correction of overpayments can be justified as a means to the end of reducing underpayments. For example, if a tax administration agency fails promptly to refund overpayments requested by taxpayers, tax compliance can be expected to fall, because taxpayers will perceive the system to be unfair and because they are motivated to take care that they are never in an overpaid status. The issue here is the extent to which correction of overpayments should be valued in its own right.

ments is limited by the fact that the private sector can and does correct them when the private costs of doing so are less than the amount of the overpayment (although the overpayer must incur those costs).

While much of the tax administrator's prefiling activity, such as disseminating accurate information about the tax laws or developing user-friendly tax forms and filing methods, works neutrally to reduce both mistaken overpayments and underpayments, one wonders whether a tax administration agency would ever devote a substantial portion of its budget specifically to postfiling activities to identify and correct tax overpayments. Surely it would run the risk of the legislature's redirecting those funds to what are perceived to be more urgent government priorities.

Recent History and Its Lessons

Plumley and Steuerle present data on the quantity and productivity of various types of IRS enforcement activity, which characterize the past two decades as a period of generally declining commitment to tax enforcement. However, enforcement activity by the IRS is not the only way to increase tax compliance; it is also possible to do so by imposing greater compliance burdens on taxpayers, which lessen the amount of work the IRS must do to achieve a given level of tax compliance.

Thus there are two principal inputs to the tax administration program—the resources provided to the tax administration agency and the compliance burdens imposed on taxpayers.[2] A government's commitment of resources to tax administration should be measured with respect to both inputs, as should the productivity of the tax administration effort.

The Tax Equity and Fiscal Responsibility Act of 1982 (TEFRA) initiated a period in which policymakers became willing to impose greater burdens on taxpayers in order to harvest the revenues from improved tax compliance. Faced with the need to restore fiscal stability after what they perceived as the excessive 1981 tax cuts, Senate Finance Committee Chairman Robert Dole and the other drafters of TEFRA reviewed numerous potential ways to raise revenue and concluded that improved tax compliance was a relatively attractive option.[3] Hence TEFRA imposed various additional reporting, penalty, and withholding burdens on taxpayers.[4] These tax compliance measures imposed significant burdens

2. There is some evidence that the compliance costs incurred by taxpayers are an order of magnitude larger than the IRS budget. See, for example, Slemrod and Blumenthal (1992).

3. The author served as chief economist of the Joint Committee on Taxation during the drafting of TEFRA.

4. The most controversial of these, withholding on interest and dividends, was repealed in 1983.

on taxpayers but were largely successful, at least temporarily, in dealing with such long-standing tax compliance problems as syndicated tax shelters, under-reporting of interest, dividends, and capital gains, and even underreporting of tip income.

Because the political support for stronger tax enforcement was driven to a certain degree by the exigencies of budget accounting, it was somewhat vulnerable to budgetary gamesmanship. As a result, the provision of additional inputs for the tax administration program consisted largely of additional burdens placed on taxpayers, not additional outlays for the IRS, because budget scorekeeping enabled policymakers to score revenue gained from legislation that imposed additional burdens on taxpayers toward their deficit-reduction targets but generally not revenue gained from additional funds appropriated to the IRS.

Thus the period 1982–1994 should properly be characterized as an era of strong bipartisan support for stronger tax enforcement, which found expression in a greater willingness to impose burdens on taxpayers.

The 1994 elections produced a Republican majority in both houses of Congress, which began to ask the IRS to shift its priorities away from revenue-raising and toward reducing inputs to the tax administration program. The IRS's mismanagement of its systems modernization project had left it open to legitimate criticism; however, the virulence of the attacks on the IRS came as a surprise to many observers, especially in light of the fact that efforts to strengthen tax administration by imposing greater burdens on taxpayers over the previous dozen years had had substantial bipartisan support and, indeed, had been initiated in 1982 by the man who was to become the Republican presidential candidate in 1996, Senator Dole.

The demand that the IRS change priorities was implicit in a steady drumbeat of criticism of the department from members of Congress about the excessive burdens the IRS was placing on taxpayers, including highly publicized hearings about specific (generally poorly substantiated) cases of abuse. It found legislative expression in the provisions of the IRS Restructuring and Reform Act of 1998, which not only added new taxpayer rights provisions that, unlike previous such bills, could be expected to have significant revenue consequences but also imposed significant penalties on IRS employees who violated various rules and procedures. Plumley and Steuerle document the decline in both resources devoted to enforcement activity and their productivity after 1995.

However, the new priorities do not appear to have been sustainable for very long. The decline in enforcement has not gone unnoticed by taxpayers. The same elected officials who were criticizing the IRS for paying insufficient attention to the burdens that tax enforcement activity was imposing on taxpayers are now demanding that it crack down on use of foreign trusts, what is perceived as overly aggressive tax planning, tax protester activity, and other forms of tax evasion. Congress may give the IRS new tools with which to deal with these concerns. If history is a guide, the congressional response will impose greater burdens on taxpayers rather than more funds for the IRS budget.

Lesson for the Future

The lesson of this brief recent history of tax enforcement is that the political leadership needs to establish a balanced, analytically based set of priorities for the IRS instead of constantly shifting those priorities in response to political, ideological, or budgetary needs. Fighting about priorities is not going to improve the Internal Revenue Service. What will improve it is more sustained focus on the politically unglamorous task of productivity improvement, which over a twenty-year period stands a much better chance of improving the agency's performance than does continuing to fight over priorities. Dedication to productivity improvement, which has the potential to produce both more revenue and lower burdens on taxpayers, would be a sea change in how the tax administration program is run, for there appears to have been little, if any, productivity improvement in recent years.

Commissioner Charles Rossotti's recent report to the IRS Oversight Board appears to embrace precisely this agenda.[5] He lays out what he believes is needed to improve both the enforcement effort and service to taxpayers, which together would require an increase in the IRS's budget of approximately 22 percent. He then recommends that additional appropriations be spent on a 2 percent increase in staffing and modernization for a 3 percent annual increase in productivity over five years. This is an ambitious agenda, but history suggests that it does appear to be the best strategy for sustaining improvements in IRS performance.

References

Dubin, Jeffrey, Michael Graetz, and Louis Wilde. 1990. "The Effect of Audit Rates on the Federal Individual Income Tax, 1977–1986." *National Tax Journal* 43 (4): 395–409.

Internal Revenue Service. 1984. *Commissioner's and Chief Counsel's 1984 Annual Report.* Publication 55.

———. 1996. *Federal Tax Compliance Research: Individual Income Tax Estimates for 1985, 1988, and 1992.* Publication 1415 (rev. 4-96).

———. 1998. *1998 IRS Databook.* Publication 55b.

National Quality Research Center. 1998. "American Customer Satisfaction Index (ACSI) Methodology Report." University of Michigan Business School (March).

5. Rossotti (2002).

Plumley, Alan H. 1996. "The Determinants of Individual Income Tax Compliance: Esti-
    mating the Impacts of Tax Policy, Enforcement, and IRS Responsiveness." IRS Publi-
    cation 1916 (rev. 11-96).
Rossotti, Charles O. 2002. "Report to the IRS Oversight Board. Assessment of the IRS
    and the Tax System." Internal Revenue Service. September.
Slemrod, Joel. 2002. "Tax Systems." *NBER Reporter* (Summer): 8–13.
Slemrod, Joel B., and Marsha Blumenthal. 1992. "The Compliance Cost of the U.S. Indi-
    vidual Income Tax System: A Second Look after Tax Reform." *National Tax Journal* 45
    (2): 185–202.
Steuerle, C. Eugene. 1986. *Who Should Pay for Collecting Taxes? Financing the IRS.* Wash-
    ington: American Enterprise Institute for Public Policy Research.

11

JEFFREY OWENS
STUART HAMILTON

Experience and Innovations
in Other Countries

G LOBALIZATION, THE INCREASED complexity of modern business structures, their financing, and the nature of their transactions are bringing a
host of new challenges for international and domestic taxation systems. We
remain optimisic that out of these challenges will emerge more robust, cost-
effective, and efficient tax systems and administrations, but it will not be a pain-
free transition, and some hard questions have to be answered.

There is no one right answer on how best to fund government infrastructure
and services, nor on how best to administer the tax system. While all Organization for Economic Cooperation and Development (OECD) countries operate
conceptually similar tax systems, they differ considerably in the relative size of
the government sector and in the specifics of the tax system's policy, thresholds,
rates, and administrative practices.

While there is significant diversity in OECD tax systems, there are also many
similarities. OECD members generally collect the bulk of their revenues from
the payment of individual income tax and associated social security contributions and from value-added or sales taxes. Other taxes and duties, such as those
on property, make up a much smaller cut of the tax pie. For those interested in
the detail, appendix 11A provides an overview of the tax levels and structures in
OECD countries.

One key point to make is that, whatever a government's approach is to tax
rates and the tax base, having the best tax policy and laws in the world will not
help if the tax administration is underfunded, incompetent, corrupt, or overzealous. In the OECD this is generally not the situation, though we return to the
issue of funding later.

In most countries in the OECD we suggest that the issue is not so much the behavior of the tax administration as what it is they have to administer. In looking at the root causes of problems in tax administration, what needs to be considered is what is being administered: the tax law and how it is interpreted. And problems caused by the law cannot be considered until one reflects on the efficacy and practicality of the tax policy that the law is meant to implement. The entire system, all of its players, their behaviors, and drivers of those behaviors need to be considered in an objective, holistic, and systemic manner if countries are going to tackle successfully their crises in tax administration. For it is not just a crisis of taxation complexity in the United States; all countries, OECD members or not, face a similar set of problems and have the same desire to simplify their tax systems.

Some Observations on Tax Simplification Strategies

Good data on tax system comparability, particularly regarding tax administration, are unfortunately lacking, so the bulk of this chapter is constructed around observations and experiences with a range of OECD member-country tax systems.

The issue of tax system complexity is not new nor is it confined to the United States. U.S. Treasury Secretary Paul O'Neill noted in February 2002: "Our tax code is an abomination. . . . It strangles our prosperity . . . and it is a drag on our ability to create jobs in this nation."[1] "It's as though we've hired 110,000 well-meaning, highly educated people and we've said to them: 'You've got to climb up this vertical steel wall . . . and we're going to grease the wall to make it impossible for you to do,' and then we make fun of these people because they can't climb up the wall."[2]

Over 200 years before that, the first secretary of the treasury, Alexander Hamilton, noted that: "Tax laws have in vain been multiplied; new methods to enforce the collection have in vain been tried; the public expectation has been uniformly disappointed."[3] This has continued to be true in all OECD member countries. For example, the United Kingdom's Tax Law Review Committee noted in 1996 that much of that country's tax legislation is impenetrable and incomprehensible, and even tax experts cannot understand parts of it.

Why is this and can anything realistically be done to address it? Looking at what has been tried in the past in OECD member countries yields some observations but no quick fixes. For example, much has been made, in the United

1. www.ustreas.gov/press/releases/po1033.htm.
2. http://abcnews.go.com/sections/2020/2020/GMAB 020412 taxes.html.
3. www.taxhistory.org/FederalistPapers/federalist12.html.

Figure 11-1. *Growth in Number of Words in the Internal Revenue Code,*
1955–2000

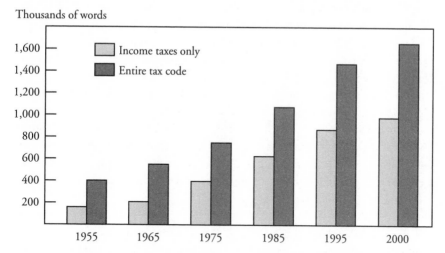

Thousands of words

Source: U.S. Tax Foundation, www.taxfoundation.org/compliancetestimony.html.

States and other countries, of the growth of the number of pages of tax legislation, a phenomenon common to many countries, as a measure of this growing
complexity. A U.S. Tax Foundation graph illustrates the growth in the U.S. tax
code (see figure 11-1).

A recent New Zealand review of business compliance costs noted: "Prima
facie, tax compliance costs will increase over time unless the rate of removal of
tax rules and regulations at least equals the rate of introduction of new rules and
regulations. Even then, the act of changing from one set of policy initiatives to
another will in itself create temporary increases in compliance costs."[4] Not
rocket science, but it is right. Some would say that this growth in size and complexity is a natural outcome of a complex, evolving world interacting over time
with the demands placed on our democratic systems of government and the
responses to those demands.

Coming from a consensus-based organization where thirty member countries
have to reach agreement on each word used in our documents, we have a degree
of sympathy for the plight of politicians trying to garner support for a policy in
the community and then in Congress. We have seen firsthand how a seemingly
simple principle can become a larger work of tortured and twisted text. That said,
it is clear that a degree of complexity in tax law is necessary if it is to be relevant

4. New Zealand Ministerial Panel on Compliance Costs, Final Report (July 2001) (www.
businesscompliance.govt.nz/reports/final/final-11.html).

to modern business structures and transactions. The U.S. Joint Committee on Internal Revenue Taxation summed it up concisely when it said, back in 1927, that: "It must be recognized that, while a degree of simplification is possible, a simple income tax for complex business is not."[5]

The world today is hardly like the world when income and consumption taxes were first introduced to replace customs and excise duties as the main source of government revenue. Just as a Boeing 747 is more complex than the Wright brothers' flyer, things have moved on. Modern financial innovations and globalization, the rise of multinational organizations, the formation of trading blocs such as the North American Free Trade Association and the European Union, and the development of new communication technologies that enable corporations to exploit the integration of national economies, all make the world of today inherently more complex than that of the past. The law largely reflects this.

There is also, no doubt, a large degree of clutter and duplication in the law, reflecting the incremental, some would say Band-Aid, approach to lawmaking that all governments by necessity use. Legal structures that seemed appropriate to legislators years ago do not reflect modern best practice in law design. Clearly stated objectives, plain English drafting, checklists, and consistent definitions of key terms all feature in modern law design, and they can make things simpler— to a limited extent. Tinkering with details can only get you so far. Evolution has to occasionally give way to revolution—a complete rewrite—but it also brings the chance to rethink tax concepts and approaches. You cannot bolt a 747 jet engine onto the Wright flyer and expect it to work well. Periodically governments need to completely rework their tax legislation if it is going to perform effectively in today's world.

Observation: Just Simplifying Tax Law Does Not Work

A number of countries—Australia, Canada, New Zealand, and the United Kingdom, for example—have already been down the path of extensive legislative simplification. What they found is that without simplifying the underlying tax policy you cannot really simplify the law. And if the law cannot be made simple, then it is inevitably going to be difficult to understand and administer.

For example, New Zealand's law, while simplified into plain English, still generates essentially the same administrative and compliance burden for taxpayers as it did before it was simplified. Here is what a review of the extensive New Zealand simplification efforts said:

5. www.taxfoundation.org/compliancetestimony.html.

From 1989 to 2001, eleven tax simplification/compliance cost reduction policy documents have been published. Eight of these have been released in the last five years. Despite their relative frequency, and their effort to simplify various taxes and processes, the initiatives have had little impact on the volume of tax regulation, its complexity, and the compliance loading on business taxpayers. . . . Businesses considered taxation their most significant business compliance cost. . . . Individuals expressed their anger, frustration, confusion, and alienation about their attempts to meet their tax commitments. . . . There was a great deal of support for the basic tax system itself, but very high levels of frustration in the way it was implemented. Business people told us that the complexity of the law made compliance difficult and very time consuming.[6]

Similar results emerge in Australia, where a major simplification effort has been under way for some years. They devoted significant drafting resources to their Tax Law Improvement Project, rewriting their tax act into what they thought was plain English. When they did a readability test on Australia's simpler Tax Act, which by political necessity preserved existing tax policy, they found that, while things had improved a bit, the level of readability still fell well below the benchmark considered acceptable for the general public. Indeed the majority of the new act still required a university-level education to understand it, and the length of the tax code had increased. Eleven lines of one key section became five paragraphs of plain English legislation.

No reduction in the length of the tax code nor in the complexity of complying with it is going to emerge from such a process. It seems clear that complex policy results in complex law and consequential difficulties in complying. Much of the complexity in tax laws globally appears to relate to policies designed to provide tax breaks while at the same time trying to limit those breaks or preempt tax avoidance activity. Complexity results from the desire of governments to ensure that tax law considers the detailed circumstances of every individual, putting fairness and equality ahead of efficiency and administrative feasibility. Complexity also reflects the difficulties that governments face in targeting anti-abuse provisions to taxpayers at risk.

It seems as if we are back in the cold war, engaging in a policy of escalation and mutually assured destruction, or, in this case, mutually assured tax complexity and compliance costs. While avoidance behaviors should rightly be seen as a key driver of tax complexity, perhaps legislative complexity is the wrong answer to the problem.

---

6. See www.businesscompliance.govt.nz/reports/final/final-11.html.

Observation: Policy Simplification Needs a Stronger Voice

The competitive pressures generated by globalization have led to a trend toward base-broadening simplification in many countries and reductions in tax rates, particularly on mobile capital income. The OECD has encouraged this trend, and Europe has led the way in cutting the top corporate and personal income tax rates—admittedly from a relatively high base. Appendix 11A provides more details on these trends.

Many of these efforts, while reducing headline tax rates, seem to have amplified seemingly simple economic distinctions between the nature of the income, the type of entity earning it, and the nature of the transaction, as governments try to shore up their revenue base. Each of these distinctions provides a point of complexity that builds over time. As taxpayers try to tailor their activities into categories that reduce tax, the government counters.

For example, the Nordic countries, and to a lesser extent Austria, Belgium, and most recently Italy, all adopted differing forms of dual income tax systems. In these systems all capital income, including corporate profits, is taxed at a lower, uniform, proportional headline rate, reducing the debt-equity distinction. Less geographically mobile labor income is taxed at higher, generally progressive rates, for vertical equity reasons. These dual income tax systems are similar in effect to the U.S. Treasury's 1992 comprehensive business income tax proposal.

The difference in tax rates between labor and capital encourages a blurring of the concept; wage and salary earners become subcontractors overnight. Anti-avoidance legislation based on master-servant concepts (an approach that appears to encourage avoidance opportunities) has been introduced or strengthened, increasing the complexity of the system.

Italy has tried one of the more innovative and conceptually simple dual income taxes. Rather than following the path of complexity, they essentially deem a rate of return (7 percent in the years 1997–2000) on the capital invested that is taxed at the concessional corporate rate. They do not try for a false level of equity; near enough is good enough in this case. They have accepted that you cannot have "designer" regimes that try to produce exactly the right results for all taxpayers—a path that the United States and most other countries have taken. It is rough but workable justice.

On the consumption tax front, only New Zealand stands out as having a relatively simple system. In Australia, as in Canada, Mexico, and Europe, the political left (who had the numbers in parliament) insisted upon an exemption from VAT for basic food because, they argued, the tax was regressive. And it is, if taken on its own. Studies in several countries indicate poor people spend more of their income on food than rich people do. The fact that rich people spend twice as much on basic food as the poor seems to have escaped them. That the poor spend more on taxed takeout food than the rich also escaped them. So, once again, complexity was introduced in the name of vertical equity, when carefully targeted, low-income welfare payments may well have achieved a much better overall equity result, with lower administrative and compliance costs.

Think of the difficulties a small, mixed business has keeping track of what is taxed and what is not in these systems, compared to a system where everything is taxed at the same low rate. The calculation of tax could be a simple matter of a percentage of receipts less expenditure for a period. Instead what is required is detailed record-keeping and checking by the business and the tax administration. A hot roast chicken is taxed, while a cold roast chicken is not. Does anyone expect tax administrators and business owners to have thermometers on hand when they do their tax calculations? We are exaggerating here a bit to make the point that some perfectly legitimate distinctions made for policy reasons create uncertainty, extra compliance burdens, and opportunities for abuse.

Among OECD members, only the United States does not operate a VAT now. It is something that the U.S. government may have to confront, particularly in light of falling revenues from sales taxes, the desire to reduce revenues from income taxes, and the pressure to increase spending on pensions, health, infrastructure, and homeland defense.

Many of the attempts to introduce greater vertical equity into the tax system appear to us to be evaluated in isolation, without considering that tax revenues are used to finance public expenditures, which in turn have major distributional effects. A different picture emerges when a more holistic systems view is taken. Figure 11-2 comes from the New Zealand 2001 Tax Review Final Report. We do not have comparative figures for the United States, but it would be surprising if there were much difference in the overall trends. Note that there is a significant income redistribution from the upper four income deciles to the lower four deciles. Note also that, at least in New Zealand but probably also in most OECD countries, this is mainly accomplished via government spending rather than through the effect of progressive tax rates. The second column is tax per decile if New Zealand adopted a 25 percent flat income tax. The result is not a large difference in equity outcomes for a large reduction in tax system complexity.

Serious tax simplification proposals should consider using other means, such as direct payments or nonwastable tax credits, to achieve desired welfare equity and market correction goals—for example, income-based payments to the poor to correct for regressive elements—and industry payments for market corrections. Indeed any progressive rate system can be appropriately matched by a flat rate tax coupled with a payment system. And payment systems are generally more transparent and more closely monitored than tax expenditure systems.

Figure 11-2. *Health, Education, and Welfare and Average Tax per Household,*
New Zealand, 2001

NZ $ per household

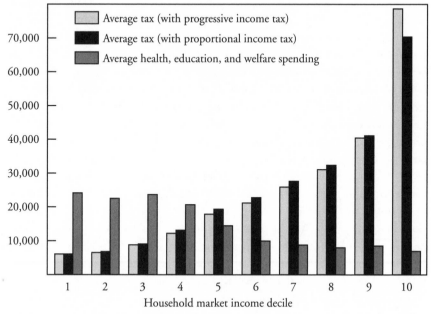

Source: New Zealand Tax Review Final Report, 2001 (www.treasury.govt.nz/taxreview2001/
finalreport/download.html).

Tax administrations in a growing number of countries are being asked to
administer other government functions via the tax system, such as welfare credits,
child support payments, pension administration, excise rebates, and the like.
Some administrations—Australia, Canada, and the United Kingdom, for example—are enthusiastically embracing this expansion in their role. They see it as an
acceptance by governments of the effectiveness of the tax administration. In most
OECD countries, tax administrations are arguably one of the most effective and
least corrupt parts of government. They have highly skilled staff spread throughout the country. They have information on the income of most households. All
these features make them attractive as agencies to deliver income-related expenditure programs. Also, where benefits can be set off against taxes, governments
need only make a net payment to citizens or receive a net payment from them.
This reinforces the link between taxes and benefits and can simplify the relationship between government and citizens.

In Canada this initiative is considered so important that in 1999 the tax
department was assigned agency status, giving it greater freedom to pursue new

business opportunities with provinces and territories to reduce overlap and duplication of tax administration.

Other tax administrations (for example, the Netherlands and Japan) have, for the moment, resisted this trend, arguing that the skills of the staff required to administer spending programs are different from those required to administer taxes. They also consider that such responsibility increases the complexity of the tasks facing tax administrations (at a time when resources are being cut) and that issues of confidentiality arise.

As politicians in OECD countries appeal to increasingly older voters, it seems unlikely that they will cut into expenditure programs that target these groups. Governments will continue to rely heavily on the income tax and social security systems to pick up the tab for these programs and will be forced to increase tax rates, widen the tax base, or move yet further up the complexity spiral to reduce avoidance activities, in an attempt to gain revenue. One can guess which way the politicians will move, in the absence of a push against further complexity. Simplicity needs a constituency with a stronger voice.

Observation: The Complexity of Policy and Law May Need To Be Reduced

Large groups of taxpayers find even simplified tax measures hard to understand and comply with. They always will. They tend to be the most numerous of the taxpaying groups—wage and salary earners, pensioners and retirees, and small businesses. For these people, most of whom are not lawyers or accountants (something we are eternally grateful for), any dealing with the government, particularly over financial matters, is a daunting and worrisome event. They are people who tend not to keep double-entry accounts of their income and expenditure, people for whom record keeping is a difficult and time-consuming task, undertaken periodically at best and with a great deal of frustration, people who keep their receipts in a shoebox, if they retain them at all. Yet, without records, how can taxpayers be expected to file accurate returns? Can we ever make the tax system simple enough so these people can file their own returns easily and correctly? We think not.

Many administrations have provided extensive assistance or encouraged the use of tax intermediaries for these groups. There is often a trade-off between the costs borne by the tax administration (visible) and those compliance costs borne by the taxpayer (generally hidden). A pragmatic balance is needed, while recognizing that such costs are a key, and often ignored, part of the economic deadweight waste of the tax system.

While direct administrative and compliance costs can be measured, many elements are more difficult to put a number on, such as the costs of avoidance.

In 1997 Schneider estimated the average 1994 OECD tax gap to be about 15 percent of GDP.[7] It has not changed much since then.

Tax gap figures have to be used with extreme caution around politicians, as they tend to get used as a yardstick to measure the tax administration rather than considered merely as one indicator of the health of the entire tax system. They are also used to fend off policy or tax rate changes by encouraging complex antiavoidance legislation, which affects all for the sake of catching the few. But the reality is that full compliance cannot be achieved by legislation or auditing; it is unattainable.

So, if the whole system cannot be made simpler to comply with and administer, what can be done? The strategy that a number of countries are adopting is to hide the complexity from those who do not need to know the details or who are poorly placed to deal with them. Just as you do not need to know the intricacies of a 747 to fly in it, you do not need to know how the tax system works to use it—if you trust someone else to operate it for you.

For taxpayers with regular income from well-defined domestic sources (wages, pensions, welfare benefits, dividends, interest, and the like) withholding and information reporting systems can allow the government to precomplete the taxpayer's entire return. Thirty-six countries now use this system, as we understand, and more are considering it. It makes administrative sense. Most returns from nonbusiness taxpayers do not result in large amounts of additional tax, but they can take just as much time and resources to process. Prefiling can be quite popular with taxpayers too, even if paying taxes never will be.

In Denmark, for example, the tax system reached the stage where Danish residents (not the tax administration) pressured nonresident financial institutions in Sweden to supply the Danish tax administration with details of dividends and interest so that the taxpayers do not have to file a form. Similarly farmers pressured the national farm cooperative to supply information so that large parts of their tax forms were precompleted. The tax administration precompletes the tax form and indicates the amount payable or the refund due. If the person has no other information or corrections, they just do not respond. And rather than require a taxpayer who owes tax to send in a payment, the tax administration adjusts the main withholding source, so the debt is paid off over the next year. No wonder it is popular. But it has taken the Danes fifteen years to get to this stage.

Prefiling is not a quick fix. The Internal Revenue Service Restructuring and Reform Act of 1998 requires the secretary of the treasury to implement a return-free system for appropriate individuals by 2007. It will be interesting to see if all the pieces—the information flows and the withholding arrangements—can be put in place by that time.

---

7. Schneider (1997). Empirical results show the size of the shadow economy of western European countries over time.

The "big brother" issues that were expected have not arisen. Taxpayers can see and correct any information filed about their income. The government is in effect putting all its cards on the table, rather than playing a game of "gotcha" when a taxpayer omits some interest income from an account. It is a better use of the information that is already routinely collected and matched from third-party income sources.

Such measures do not work for business income, however, and countries have tackled the administration issues for this group in differing ways.

Observation:
Small Business Needs Special Consideration

How should the tax affairs of small businesses be dealt with—people who cannot hire a bevy of tax accountants or lawyers to ensure that they get things right? These are people who generally are so caught up in running their businesses, often until late each night, that they have little time for the seemingly costly bureaucratic processes required to comply with tax obligations.

You have to make the system a lot simpler for such people if you expect them to be able to comply easily. Australia has implemented an optional simplified tax system for small businesses—those with a turnover of under a million dollars. It allows for cash rather than accrual accounting, it has simplified depreciation with broad, immediate write-off provisions, and it has simplified stock trading rules. Around 85 percent of all manufacturers qualify for the simplified tax system, although some reports are that complexity savings are not viewed by small businesses as very significant.

France has gone further. Their so-called microbusinesses, essentially sole proprietors, are presumed to have earned a taxable profit on their annual sales, with a threshold of 70 percent of sales (that is, 30 percent is profit) for the trading companies and 50 percent for other companies. All the small business has to track is sales. It cannot get much simpler than that.

Businesses in France with profits below 115,000 euros can also get a fixed deduction of 20 percent applied to their profits, if they affiliate with a management support center *(centre de gestion agréé)* or a similar institution. These institutions have been set up by providers of financial, accounting, and fiscal services, or by professional and trade organizations that provide fiscal and accounting support to associated companies. To get the deduction, the business must meet special requirements with regard to their accounting systems, auditing, and submitting of tax returns. The books and records of the associated companies must be kept by or under the supervision of a public accountant, and all the records of the affiliated company must be audited and certified by a public accountant. So someone else is doing the flying. In France, it seems, if you cannot make it simple, you can at least make it less costly, while at the same time getting better compliance. Not surprisingly most businesses in France belong to these institutions.

On the international side, e-commerce has opened the door for many small and medium-size businesses to trade across borders for the first time. Such businesses are poorly placed to be able to comply with tax jurisdictions that differ significantly from their own. As this international trade by small and medium businesses grows, we believe there will be an increased convergence and greater consistency and simplification across tax jurisdictions. Before we look at enforcing compliance, we have to enable it.

This is already occurring to some extent within trade blocs such as the European Union. We suspect that new and simpler ways of looking at international tax policy issues will come from it. Why should tax forms and transaction documentation requirements differ so radically between tax jurisdictions? Is there a standard, and how can it be tailored so that the greatest burden falls on the highest-risk taxpayers rather than on those at low risk? What is the role of the tax administrator in all of this?

The OECD is facilitating meetings between tax administrations and is working with business groups to try to derive a more consistent set of tax requirements among countries. This work on TaxXML and the provision of taxpayer services via electronic channels is only in its embryonic stages, but it is hoped that it will reduce the burdens placed on businesses dealing with multiple jurisdictions. A lot has been done, but there is a lot more to do, particularly in the realm of small business taxation.

Observation: New Compliance Approaches Are Needed

The OECD recently began facilitating meetings of tax administrators so they could exchange ideas and best practices on small business compliance, on taxpayer services, and more generally on how to manage a tax administration. What is emerging?

A number of OECD tax administrations are putting in place highly skilled teams to focus on ensuring that large, tax-driven arrangements (aggressive tax planning) that lack economic substance are regularly challenged and placed before the courts. Penalty systems are being reviewed to ensure that they scale appropriately, do not penalize honest mistakes, but do treat recidivists with progressive harshness. Do we need a three-strikes-and-you're-out approach for tax systems? What message would jailing more tax offenders send?

It is becoming clear that punishing the past is not always the most effective way to promote future compliance. Moreover, while taxpayers tend to grossly overestimate their risk of being audited, as system complexity drives taxpayers to intermediaries, who are more aware of the true relative risks, this deterrent effect appears to be losing its potency.

Some countries are looking at reducing reporting requirements for low-risk taxpayers and increasing them, in some cases augmented by withholding arrangements, for high-risk taxpayers or groups of taxpayers. Other administrations are working together with the relevant industry associations to derive a common viewpoint on good compliance and are producing reporting measures that are easier to comply with.

Perhaps a combination of these approaches is needed, whereby an industry with compliance problems is clearly warned to get its house in order and is able to assist in the design of strategies to do so or face the prospect of targeted documentation and withholding arrangements. What if the three worst-complying segments of society had such measures introduced for a five-year period? Would there be industry pressure to get compliance rates up? We have to make the connection between rights and responsibilities—the social compact between society, the citizen, and government—much more obvious.

A number of tax administrations have sought to effect what they call leverage approaches to compliance, to get more compliance bang for their buck. The United Kingdom has been sending letters to taxpayers who appear to present a risk, advising them that their return may be selected for audit next year. Sure enough, for this group, fewer deductions are claimed and more income is returned. Interestingly, when certainty was introduced, that is, "you will be audited next year," the results were less effective.

There is also a group for whom additional compliance tools appear to be needed. Unscrupulous tax intermediaries use their knowledge of the system and relationships with clients to peddle tax schemes that are inappropriate to the economic reality of the clients' situations. Often, if these schemes fail, the client bears the penalty, and the intermediary moves on to the next scheme, the next client, the next victim. Unfortunately industry self-regulation has not been effective in establishing the social compact needed for such a position of trust within the tax system. A number of countries have now decided to pursue the promoters of these schemes. Tax administrations need a deterrent that works against such repeat scheme promoters.

Australia, Canada, and New Zealand have introduced promoter penalties for those who aid and abet systemic tax fraud by their clients. The evidence is that those tax administrations that are consistently firm but fair in tackling tax avoidance, and whose courts decide on the basis of economic substance rather than apparent legal form, end up with a higher level of overall compliance.[8] This enables tax rates to be lower than they otherwise would be, which is of benefit to all.

8. See, for example, Hanousek and Palda (2003).

Observation: A New Compact Is Needed

One segment of the population that is a focus for public opinion is high-wealth individuals. If this group is seen by the general community to be not abiding by the spirit of the tax laws, then the community's confidence in the entire system is undermined. If Leona Helmsley's attitude toward taxation ("We don't pay taxes. Only the little people pay taxes.") became the norm, voluntary compliance would disappear. We cannot expect a wage or salary earner, a pensioner, or a small-business owner to believe in the system when some of the wealthiest in society pay less in percentage than they do. In some countries a few of the wealthiest have used schemes, complex structures, tax havens, political connections, and the like to achieve a total tax wipeout; some have even become eligible for low-income assistance.

This may be just good tax planning. But the danger is that tax can become just another cost minimization target, in which the use of any scheme is justified, even when it moves over the line from aggressive tax planning to evasion. The ability of a tax administration to address such systemic noncompliance should be a matter of priority in all countries, but it is difficult. It is not just a matter for the tax administration; it is a matter for all of society.

Achieving a tax result that, through a blatantly artificial avoidance sham, does not accord with the economic substance of the situation should never be a matter of pride. It is a matter of shame for those in the accountancy and legal professions who facilitate such unethical behavior. The seeds of the Enron and WorldCom scandals are planted by a society that condones such behaviors. What message does it send when a person who commits a few thousand dollars of welfare fraud goes to jail, while the perpetrators of a hundred-million-dollar tax scheme end up with a relatively small fine? Major tax avoidance and evasion should be considered in the same league as other forms of fraud. Is it any wonder that we end up with antiavoidance measures that impose complexity on legitimate transactions when courts and society allow, or even condone, the tit-for-tat tax arms race? High levels of noncompliance, besides leading to an arms race in tax avoidance legislation, also lead to increased corruption of the tax system and tax officials. And this has significant costs for business and society, typically two to three times that of the tax forgone.

A new approach, a new compact is needed, one that would appear to flow from President Bush's statement in September 2002: "It is time to reaffirm the basic principles and rules that make capitalism work: truthful books and honest people and well-enforced laws against fraud and corruption. All investment is an act of faith, and faith is earned by integrity. In the long run, there is no capitalism without conscience; there is no wealth without character."[9]

9. www.cnn.com/2002/ALLPOLITICS/07/09/bush.transcript.

Observation: Tax Administrations Are Underfunded

In many countries regular "efficiency dividends" have been carved out of tax administration resources. No doubt early on these produced a more streamlined, focused, and efficient tax administration. In some cases, such measures have now probably cut through to the bone and tax administrations are underfunded for the tasks they are being asked to do.

A tax commissioner faced with pressure to implement tax reforms and to advise and assist honest taxpayers to comply with increasingly complex laws generally has only one pool of talent to turn to: compliance staff. If the phones are not answered, letters are not responded to, or refunds are not processed, you can be sure there will be complaints to the commissioner and politicians. But if fewer audits are done, who complains, who notices, especially when better targeting of cases can keep the revenue stream constant in the short run?

Independent reviews have established that the tax administrations of Australia, Canada, Mexico, and Sweden have become underfunded by about 10 percent. Other administrations, such as the IRS, may be in the same boat. Most OECD tax administrations operate at a staff-to-population ratio of about 1 to 840. The IRS figures are, if our information is right, roughly 1 to 2,900. While undoubtedly the IRS is one of the most efficient tax administrations in the world, it is not likely three times as efficient!

Many countries pay their tax administrators at rates below those obtainable externally for the same skill set. Because an effective and efficient tax administration needs to maintain at least a core of talented staff, some flexibility in salary arrangements may be necessary. In times of significant tax reform, the poaching of staff by external firms can be a prime way of buying expertise without paying for the training, although this may be a good long-term investment for government. If salary arrangements deviate too much from the market norm, after taking into account the working conditions trade-off, then it seems likely that an administration will inevitably have lower-skilled people than are called for or that corruption will become an influence.

Another impact on underfunded tax administrations is that they tend to clamp down on recruitment to cut costs—a policy that has long-term ramifications for maintaining a balanced, skilled work force into the future. Some administrations are looking at a skills-and-experience crisis in the next few years, as a major portion of their experienced personnel retire.

The shift toward service-oriented tax administration is entirely appropriate. But in some countries the emphasis on services has led to a significant shift of resources out of compliance activities. (The IRS's auditing staff has shrunk by 29 percent since 1995.) This has reduced the risk of being audited and has also downgraded the audit function: If you want a high-flying career in a service-oriented tax administration, you increasingly go into the service rather than the audit area.

Summary

The frequently-asked-questions page of the U.S. Treasury website quotes Oliver Wendell Holmes, former justice of the Supreme Court: "Taxes are what we pay for a civilized society." The United States pays a lower price than most OECD members; its tax-to-GDP burden is significantly lower than the average. It also pays a lower administrative price to collect these taxes than the OECD average. So, some may ask, is there a crisis with the U.S. system? Based on what we have seen in the United States relative to other OECD members, we would say there is no crisis but lots of room for improvement.

What might be done, based on lessons learned from other countries? Drawing together the threads of our observations in reverse order, we would suggest the following:

—The funding arrangements for the IRS need to be closely considered, given the task it is being asked to do. To paraphrase Oliver Wendell Holmes, tax administration salaries are what we pay to collect taxes in a civilized society. In particular the long-term costs of underfunding compliance efforts need to be reflected upon.

—Politicians, business, and the broader community need to understand and accept what they are paying for through their tax system and embrace the payment of taxes as part of good citizenship, even as they debate the aims, ways, and means. The value of compliance should be explicitly recognized, and those that seek to undermine the system need to be called to account.

—Following on from the point above, new penalties and sanctions that truly affect the propensity for tax avoidance and the promotion of tax avoidance activities may be needed to achieve better compliance at individual, corporate, and industry levels. These need to be self-reinforcing and scaled so that the value of "trying on" the system is lessened.

—The tax system needs to better consider the needs of small businesses and not try for difficult-to-achieve levels of accuracy. Cash accounting and measures that tax turnover may need to be considered as workable proxies for the income taxation of microbusinesses.

—Reporting and withholding systems on regular forms of income should aim to reach the stage where the tax administration can essentially complete the tax returns of those not in receipt of business income.

—To enable the above, measures designed to achieve tax equity need to be reconsidered, in the light of a holistic view of wealth and income redistribution. When coupled with additional compliance resources and more effective penalties and sanctions, some of the more complex antiavoidance measures might be removed.

—If policy simplification follows from the point above, then it might be worthwhile investing the resources necessary to modernize U.S. tax codes.

Politicians and legislative designers would need to ensure that, where possible, concepts and definitions are coordinated across tax types and that the same value is used at national and subnational levels.

For example, property definitions and values should be consistent for property taxes, wealth taxes, capital gains taxes, value-added taxes on property, inheritance taxes, and the like. Transaction information and record-keeping requirements should be consistent where possible, so that one set of books suits all. Taxpayers' interactions with government need to be brought together in a way that makes sense to the business model of the taxpayer, so that the number of interactions, duplicate information transfers, and net financial flows are minimized to the extent possible.

Appendix 11A

This appendix addresses a number of complex issues that face tax reformers in OECD countries as they attempt to devise, implement, and administer tax systems appropriate for today's (and tomorrow's) global economy. The environment in which modern business is conducted, especially the business of multinational enterprises, has been referred to as "integrating" or, perhaps more prosaically, "small." This environment constrains the work of tax reformers by significantly limiting the range of policy options open to them for innovative reform, by triggering domestic responses from "tax shocks" occurring elsewhere in the world, and by challenging the skills and efforts of tax administrators everywhere.

The taxation of the income and consumption of individuals and households is also becoming more difficult. Highly paid professionals are increasingly geographically mobile. Middle-income groups have discovered the joys of tax havens, particularly by using credit cards. Consumers are increasingly finding that they can bypass consumption taxes by using the Internet. This appendix examines these problems and possible domestic and international responses to them and presents internationally comparable data on tax systems and trends within the OECD area.

Tax system reform has achieved unprecedented prominence in public debate in recent decades. The past three decades have seen major tax reviews, conducted in public, resulting in voluminous reports: the Carter Committee in Canada (1967), the Asprey Committee in Australia (1974), the Treasury I and Treasury II documents in the United States (1984, 1985), the Meade Committee in the United Kingdom (1978), the McCaw Task Force in New Zealand (1982), the Irish Commission on Taxation (1982–1985), the Draft White Paper in Australia (1985), the White Paper on Tax Reform in Canada (1987), the Australian ANTS (A New Tax System) I and II (1998–2000), the 2000 Ralph Review of Business Taxation in Australia, and many more recent proposals in the Nordic countries and North America. Many countries in Latin America and the Asian Pacific have also undertaken fundamental restructuring of their tax systems, with some (Chile and Singapore) pioneering new approaches to taxation.

The responses to these reviews have been turbulent and wide-reaching, and their outcomes are only now being thoroughly assimilated by taxpayers, their advisors, and tax administrators throughout the world. The extent of their commonality, and the fact that so many changes happened uniformly yet not as the result of a concerted or coordinated plan, foreshadows the kind and degree of interconnection among modern economies that is one of the themes underlying the work of the OECD.

We believe the most profound of the recent developments in tax reform was the dramatic and widespread reduction in marginal income tax rates in the 1990s, reflecting a reduction of the number of tax brackets, increased exemptions, and adjusted thresholds. At the time, these tax reductions were both praised and condemned. Most criticism concentrated on the implicit shift in the tax burden that some feared would accompany the change, reducing the level of tax on the wealthy when marginal rates were uniformly reduced. Others praised rate reductions for reducing tax-induced economic distortions of savings, investment, and work patterns; for counteracting the deleterious effects of high inflation rates in systems; and for reducing the incentives for tax evasion and unproductive investments in tax shelters and consequently the pressures on tax administrators.

The unfortunate coincidence of these reductions with the worldwide recession of the late 1990s presented difficulties for many governments needing to find additional sources of revenue. The typical initial response of many governments was to broaden the base of the income tax by including more elements as income and eliminating tax expenditures. The most common targets for increasing levels of revenue through base-broadening were employee fringe benefits, social benefits, and capital gains for individuals. Deductibility of mortgage interest was also limited in many countries. For corporations, incentives and concessions were commonly removed, apparently in tacit agreement with the general observation of a recent OECD study that the benefits of incentives are rarely found to outweigh their direct and indirect costs.[1] Similar rationalization of incentives occurred in Finland, Portugal, Spain, the United States, Austria, and a number of other countries (Indonesia and Chile being the most notable). Foreign-source income was also targeted, but perhaps for different reasons.

Governments and others seek to ensure that reforms improve the ease of tax administration. Any new tax base must be observable and verifiable, since the

---

1. OECD (2001b).

most important property of any tax is that it can be collected. New technologies and new financial practices have reduced both observability and verifiability.

Trends in Taxation

The following sections describe trends in three areas of taxation in OECD countries: the ratio of taxes to GDP, the distribution of tax revenue among major taxes, and the fiscal arrangements between the central and subcentral levels of government.

The Tax Burden

The measurement of tax burdens is subject to controversy.[2] The most commonly used gauge, the ratio of taxes to GDP, is only a rough indicator, for a variety of reasons:

—Institutional setups differ across countries in ways that significantly affect the reported tax-to-GDP ratio without having much impact on the burdens imposed by taxation. For example, there are differences across countries, and over time, in the taxation of transfer income, the size of tax payments by the public sector itself, and the mix of subsidies and tax expenditures (targeted exemptions, allowances, and credits).

—Some taxes may have a stronger impact on economic behavior—that is, act more as a burden—than others, and it is therefore useful to examine the breakdown of tax revenues by tax base. Different forms of taxation may also interact to result in pronounced differences in the marginal effective tax rates faced by particular groups, thus heavily affecting their economic choices. Such marginal tax rates have been calculated by the OECD and used to assess tax systems.

—The tax burden needs to be assessed in a wider context, including the burden stemming from regulation that mandates the private sector to provide social protection or public goods and services in the government's place.

Even so, bearing these caveats in mind, the ratio of tax revenues to GDP is useful as a scaling factor: To the extent that tax systems matter for economic efficiency, their costs are likely to rise as economic decisionmakers' exposure to taxation increases.

The evolution of tax revenue as a percentage of GDP in OECD countries since 1965 is reported in table 11A-1.

The stylized facts are the following:

2. See, for example, OECD (2000).

Table 11A-1. *Tax Revenue as Percent of GDP, OECD Countries, 1965–2001*

Country	1965	1970	1975	1980	1985	1990	1995	2000	2001[a]
Australia	21.9	22.5	26.6	27.4	29.1	29.3	29.7	31.5	n.a.
Austria	33.9	34.6	37.4	39.8	41.9	40.4	41.6	43.7	45.7
Belgium	31.1	34.6	40.1	42.4	45.6	43.2	44.6	45.6	45.3
Canada	25.6	30.8	31.9	30.7	32.6	35.9	35.6	35.8	35.2
Czech Republic	...	...	...	...	...	...	40.1	39.4	39.0
Denmark	29.9	39.2	40.0	39.8	47.4	47.1	49.4	48.8	49.0
Finland	30.4	31.9	36.8	36.2	40.1	44.8	45.0	46.9	46.3
France	34.5	34.1	35.9	40.6	43.8	43.0	44.0	45.3	45.4
Germany[b]	31.6	32.3	35.3	37.5	37.2	35.7	38.2	37.9	36.4
Greece	20.0	22.4	21.8	24.2	28.6	29.3	31.7	37.8	40.8
Hungary	...	...	...	...	...	...	42.4	39.1	38.6
Iceland	26.2	26.9	29.4	29.1	28.3	31.2	31.5	37.3	34.8
Ireland	24.9	28.8	29.1	31.4	35.0	33.5	32.7	31.1	29.2
Italy	25.5	26.1	26.1	30.4	34.4	38.9	41.2	42.0	41.8
Japan	18.3	20.0	21.2	25.1	27.2	30.1	27.7	27.1	n.a.
Korea	...	...	15.3	17.7	16.9	19.1	20.5	26.1	27.5
Luxembourg	27.7	24.9	37.3	40.2	44.8	40.8	42.0	41.7	42.4
Mexico	...	...	...	16.2	17.0	17.3	16.6	18.5	18.3
Netherlands	32.8	35.8	41.6	43.6	42.6	43.0	41.9	41.4	39.9
New Zealand	24.7	26.8	30.4	32.4	32.9	37.6	37.5	35.1	34.8
Norway	29.6	34.5	39.3	42.7	43.3	41.8	41.5	40.3	44.9
Poland	...	...	...	...	...	...	39.6	34.1	n.a.
Portugal	15.8	19.4	20.8	24.1	26.6	29.2	32.5	34.5	n.a.
Slovak Republic	...	...	...	...	...	...	...	35.8	33.1
Spain	14.7	16.3	18.8	23.1	27.8	33.2	32.8	35.2	35.2
Sweden	35.0	38.7	42.3	47.5	48.5	53.6	47.6	54.2	53.2
Switzerland	19.6	22.5	27.9	28.9	30.2	30.6	33.1	35.7	34.5
Turkey	10.6	12.5	16.0	17.9	15.4	20.0	22.6	33.4	35.8
United Kingdom	30.4	37.0	35.3	35.2	37.7	36.8	34.8	37.4	37.4
United States	24.7	27.7	26.9	27.0	26.1	26.7	27.6	29.6	n.a.
Total OECD Unweighted average	25.8	28.3	30.5	32.1	33.9	35.1	36.1	37.4	n.a.
European Union (15) Unweighted average	27.9	30.4	33.2	36.0	38.8	39.5	40.0	41.6	n.a.

Source: OECD, *Revenue Statistics, 1965–2001* (Paris, 2002).

a. Provisional estimates.

b. Unified Germany beginning 1991.

—There has been a persistent and largely unbroken upward trend in the ratio of tax to GDP since 1965 across most of the OECD area, though recent developments suggest the trend may be ending.

—A few countries have consistently resisted this long-term trend. Only in the Netherlands are tax ratios currently below their 1975 level, and in only three other countries—Mexico, the United Kingdom, and the United States—have tax receipts developed broadly in line with GDP over a long period.

—A few more countries, including Ireland, Japan, and Luxembourg, have succeeded in reducing the tax ratio from peak levels in 1985 or 1990, but not by large amounts. Recent data available for transition countries (former Communist countries moving into market economies) suggest that these countries are record-ing falling tax revenues relative to GDP as well, although this may in part reflect erosion of their tax bases while they are grappling with the transition process.

—Tax ratios in the European Union, averaging more than 40 percent of GDP, generally exceed those elsewhere. Outside Europe, only Australia, Canada, and New Zealand have tax ratios above 30 percent of GDP.

Declining tax ratios are currently reported more widely across countries. This largely reflects public expenditure trends,[3] although fiscal consolidation efforts during the 1990s have implied that the success a number of countries have had in reducing expenditure ratios has not yet been reflected in tax ratios that are actually falling. Moreover a favorable cyclical position has buoyed the tax take as a percentage of GDP, notwithstanding tax cuts implemented in many countries.

The forces shaping these developments in recent years have been diverse:

—Greece, Portugal, and Switzerland show increases in their tax burdens that are well above the OECD average increase. These countries all have tax ratios below the OECD average and could be seen as in a process of convergence within Europe. One immediate reason for the increase in Switzerland has been an increase in public expenditure on health. For Greece and Portugal, it has been a matter of developing social policy systems and infrastructure more in line with these prevailing elsewhere in the European Union and, in recent years, the need to curb deficits to meet the criteria for joining the European Monetary Union (EMU). As for the future, the funding of its second-pillar pension scheme means that Switzerland is less exposed to the pressures of an aging pop-ulation on public expenditure and taxation.

—Iceland and Spain experienced tax burden growth that was close to the OECD average, although Poland, like other transition countries, has reduced its burden in the past few years.[4] The data for Korea and Spain suggest that they will face substantial pressure to increase the tax burden over the next few

---

3. Heady and Van den Noord (2001).
4. For Poland, this is based on data contained in the *OECD Economic Survey.*

years,[5] but no similar expectation of increase is shown for the other countries in this group.

—The Czech Republic, Japan, and New Zealand have reduced their tax burdens since 1990, but for different reasons and from varying starting positions. Japan's tax reduction occurred in several steps from 1994 onward, mostly in response to cyclical developments. In contrast the reductions in the tax burden in New Zealand have been more consistent and reflect a definite policy choice. In this case the choice made was to reduce the role of the state in the economy, as reflected in sharp declines in the public expenditure share in GDP. The Czech Republic has not achieved such a trend decline in the expenditure ratio, and budget deficits have probably reached unsustainable levels.

—The Mexican tax burden is not only the lowest in the OECD but also less than half of the OECD unweighted average. It is also noticeable that there has been little increase in the tax-to-GDP ratio over the past decades.

—The United States has the fourth lowest tax burden in the OECD, although over the past thirty years the tax-to-GDP ratio has increased by 2 percentage points. This low tax burden in part reflects the way in which the United States chose to finance education, retirement, and health by the private sector, whereas in most other OECD countries these are primarily financed by the public sector.

The Structure of Taxation

The distribution of tax revenue among major taxes for OECD countries in 2000 is reported in table 11A-2.[6] Figure 11A-1 provides a graphic comparison of tax structures of the OECD and the three largest OECD economies.

The OECD average shows that the vast bulk of tax revenue—over 90 percent—comes from three main sources: income taxes, taxes on goods and services, and social security contributions (other payroll taxes are zero or small in most countries). However, countries vary considerably in the relative importance of these three main revenue sources. Notably Australia and New Zealand do not collect social security contributions but do collect payroll taxes.

---

5. This is mainly because of growing social security entitlements, associated with aging, but in Korea the prospect of reunification with North Korea also poses significant fiscal challenges.

6. A cautious interpretation of the numbers in this table is called for. The split between personal and corporate income tax can be seriously misleading, for two reasons. First, many OECD countries have some form of integration between corporate and personal income taxes, so that a portion of corporate taxes is refunded to the shareholders as a reduction in personal income tax. This is reflected in the statistics as a reduction in the revenue from personal income taxes, but it could just as well be regarded as a reduction in corporate tax revenue. Second, OECD countries vary in the extent to which businesses are incorporated. For example, German firms are much less likely to be incorporated than firms in the United States. This means that Germany reports a much lower share of tax revenue coming from corporate income tax, even though the taxes on business are higher.

Table 11A-2. *Distribution of Tax Revenue, OECD Countries, 2000*[a]

Percent

Country	Personal income[b]	Corporate income[b]	Social Security and other payroll	Property	Goods and services	
					Total	General consumption only
Australia	36.7	20.6	6.2	8.9	27.5	12.3
Austria	22.1	4.7	34.2	1.3	28.4	19.0
Belgium	31.0	8.1	30.9	3.3	25.4	16.3
Canada	36.8	11.1	16.4	9.7	24.4	14.4
Czech Republic	12.7	9.8	43.8	1.3	32.0	18.9
Denmark	52.6	4.9	4.6	3.3	32.5	19.6
Finland	30.8	11.8	25.6	2.5	29.1	18.0
France	18.0	7.0	36.1	6.8	25.8	16.9
Germany	25.3	4.8	39.0	2.3	28.1	18.4
Greece	13.5	11.6	30.1	5.1	36.1	22.7
Hungary	18.6	5.7	29.3	1.7	40.5	26.1
Iceland	34.4	3.3	7.8	7.1	45.0	29.4
Ireland	30.8	12.1	13.6	5.6	37.2	21.5
Italy	25.7	7.5	28.5	4.3	28.4	15.8
Japan	20.6	13.5	36.5	10.6	18.9	8.9
Korea	14.6	14.1	16.7	12.4	38.3	17.0
Luxembourg	18.3	17.7	25.6	10.6	27.3	14.3
Mexico	27.3[c]	...	17.5	1.4	53.1	18.7
Netherlands	14.9	10.1	38.9	5.4	29.0	17.3
New Zealand	42.8	11.7	0.9	5.4	34.5	24.7
Norway	25.6	15.2	22.5	2.4	34.4	19.7
Poland	23.2	6.9	29.4	3.3	36.6	22.2
Portugal	17.5	12.2	25.7	3.2	39.9	24.2
Slovak Republic	10.0	8.3	41.2	1.6	35.9	22.3
Spain	18.7	8.6	35.1	6.4	29.8	17.6
Sweden	35.6	7.5	28.1	3.4	20.7	13.4
Switzerland	30.6	7.9	33.6	8.1	19.7	11.5
Turkey	21.5	7.0	16.9	3.1	40.7	23.3
United Kingdom	29.2	9.8	16.4	11.9	32.3	18.4
United States	42.4	8.5	23.3	10.1	15.7	7.5
OECD Unweighted average	26.0	9.7	24.8	5.4	31.6	18.3
European Union Unweighted average	25.6	9.2	27.5	5.0	30.0	18.2

Source: OECD, *Revenue Statistics, 1965–2001* (Paris, 2002).

a. Rows do not add to 100 because some minor taxes are omitted and general consumption taxes (mainly VAT) are a subcategory of taxes on goods and services.

b. The breakdown of income tax into personal and corporate tax is not comparable across countries.

c. Combines personal and corporate income tax.

Figure 11A-1. *Tax Revenue Distributions, OECD and Largest OECD Economies, 2000*[a]

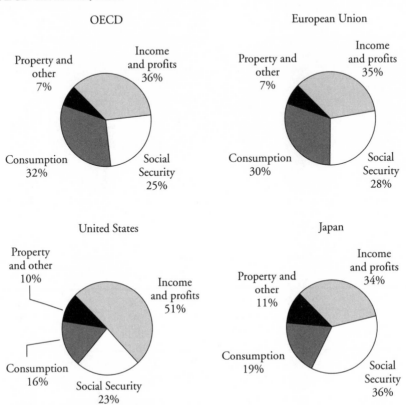

Source: OECD, *Revenue Statistics, 1965–2001* (Paris, 2002).

a. Income tax and profits includes taxes on personal and corporate income. Unweighted averages for zones.

There are also substantial differences across countries in the share of taxes on property, which are generally lower in continental Europe than elsewhere. Overall the European Union relies slightly more on consumption taxes and social security contributions and less on personal income tax than the OECD average.

In contrast the United States collects a larger share in personal income tax and property tax but a smaller one in consumption taxes and social security. Japan is similar to the United States in its low share of consumption taxes but collects much less in personal income tax, offsetting this with higher levels of corporate tax and social security contributions.

As tax-to-GDP ratios have risen, the largest part of the increases has taken the form of higher social security contributions, reflecting the expansion of social in-

Figure 11A-2. *Tax Revenue Distributions, OECD and Largest OECD Economies, 1965–2000*

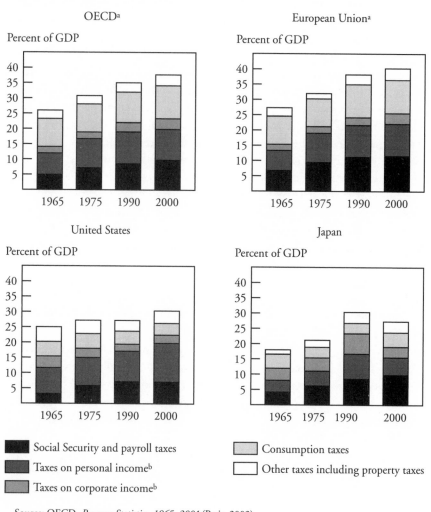

Source: OECD, *Revenue Statistics, 1965–2001* (Paris, 2002).
a. Unweighted averages.
b. The breakdown of income tax into personal and corporate tax is not comparable across countries.

surance systems substantially financed by such contributions. (See figure 11A-2.) Higher personal income taxes have also played a significant role, although most of the rise in these had taken place by 1975. Corporate income and wealth, possibly more constrained by the potential mobility of their bases than social security, and personal income taxes have risen more modestly, as have taxes on goods and services.

The Central-Local Allocation of Revenue-Raising Powers

Countries differ in prevailing fiscal arrangements between the central and sub-central levels of government.[7] Where federal constitutions as distinct from unitary constitutions apply, substantial fiscal autonomy exists at the intermediate level.

In most countries the tax revenues allocated to subcentral levels of government are insufficient to meet their expenditure commitments, and the balance is made up by borrowing or grants from the central government. An important exception occurs in Spain, where the Basque country and the Navarra region have a special arrangement in which they collect most of the taxes and remit a payment to the central government for the services that it provides.

A major factor in determining the gap between subcentral revenues and expenditures is the share of subcentral taxes in total tax revenues. The combined share of subcentral governments in total tax revenues in 1998 showed a wide variation, from 1 percent in Greece and 2 percent in Ireland to 45 percent in Canada. However, it is not only the share of tax revenue received by the subcentral levels of government that matters. The benefits of fiscal autonomy for subcentral governments depend on their ability to match local public provision to local needs and preferences. This in turn requires them to have a degree of discretion or control in adjusting their local tax revenue to the costs of the local public provision.

A recent study analyzed information on fiscal autonomy from a selection of OECD countries.[8] It found that, in most countries, the bulk of revenue comes from taxes where the base or rate of the tax is controlled by the subcentral governments (SCGs). Table 11A-3 updates and extends this information. In several other countries, a large part of revenue comes from shared taxes over which SCGs have some control. However, among the survey countries, the Czech Republic, Mexico, Norway, and Poland have systems where a substantial proportion of SCG tax revenue comes from sources over which SCGs have no formal control.

The Structure of Value-Added Tax in OECD Economies

At the core of the recent tax reform proposals made by many governments is the reform of the value-added tax, which is intended to broaden the tax base and thereby contribute to a significant increase in government revenues. There are

---

7. The economic analysis of these fiscal arrangements is generally referred to as the theory of fiscal federalism, even though it applies to both unitary and federal countries. Two classic works are Oates (1972) and Bird (1986). See also OECD (1999b).

8. OECD (1999b).

still many differences among OECD national VAT systems, with the continuing application of reduced rates, exemptions, and numerous special arrangements to meet particular policy demands. Much of this complexity stands in contradiction to the ethos of VAT, which was conceived as a simple tax to administer and collect. Differences remain even among the member states of the European Union, whose VAT laws share the same legislative roots, in the form of the EU's sixth VAT directive. However, increasing consideration is being given in most OECD countries to minimizing the tax compliance cost and promoting administrative simplification.

Table 11A-4 shows the rates of VAT from 1994 to January 1, 2000. Since 1998 Switzerland and Turkey have increased their standard rates by 1 percent and 2 percent respectively, though in the case of Switzerland the 3.5 percent reduced rates have been increased by 0.3 percent and 0.5 percent. The table also illustrates the broad spread of current standard rates of VAT, from 5 percent in Japan to 25 percent in Denmark, Hungary, and Sweden. The evolution of the average standard rate for OECD shows a global stabilization since 1998.

Personal Income Tax and Social Security Contributions

As noted above, the reform of personal income taxes and social security contributions has figured prominently in the tax reform debate. The general tendency has been for governments to substantially cut the top marginal rates of personal income taxes, reduce the number of income tax brackets, and at the same time eliminate tax relief directed at specific segments of the taxpaying population. Table 11A-5 shows the progressitivity of rates of income tax that apply to wage earners who are single and without children in 2000. It also shows the employee social security contributions for the same group.

Corporate Tax Rates

Table 11A-6 shows the basic combined central and subcentral statutory corporate income tax rates in the OECD in 2000. In the case of the United States, the statutory rate is relatively high by OECD standards, although it should be emphasized that these are scheduled, not effective, tax rates and therefore may not accurately reflect the marginal rate based on a new investment.

Table 11A-3. *Subcentral Government (SCG) and Central Government (CG) Taxing Authority Revenue, Selected OECD and Other Countries*

Percent

Country (year) and taxing level	SCG tax as percent of total tax	Set by SCG			Revenue sharing, SCG and CG					Total
		Tax rate and tax base	Tax rate only	Tax base only	Split set by SCG	Split changed only if SCG agrees	Split set by CG legislation	Split set by CG budget	CG sets both tax rate and tax base	
Bulgaria (2000) Local	10.0	—	—	—	—	—	39.0	61.0	—	100.0
Czech Republic (1999)										
Local	11.1	2.7	5.6	—	—	—	91.7	—	—	100.0
Estonia (1999) Local	16.2	—	9.2	—	—	—	90.8	—	—	100.0
Hungary (1999) Local	10.4	49.2	—	—	—	—	—	50.8	—	100.0
Latvia (1999) Local	17.1	—	—	—	—	—	—	—	100.0	100.0
Lithuania (1999)										
Local	22.0	—	—	—	—	—	—	—	100.0	100.0
Poland (1999) Local	8.3	—	41.9	0.6	—	—	57.6	—	—	100.0
Romania (2000) Local	10.5	—	6.0	0.6	—	—	—	75.0	18.4	100.0
Slovak Republic (2000)										
Local	4.0	7.0	28.2	—	—	—	—	64.8	—	100.0
Slovenia (2000)										
Local	7.9	16.7	0.6	0.4	—	—	82.3	—	21.8	100.0
Mean	11.8	7.6	9.2	0.2	0.0	0.0	36.1	25.2	21.8	100.0

Belgium (1995)									
Local	6.0	13.0	84.0	—	—	2.0	1.0	—	100.0
Community	13.0	—	3.0	—	97.0	—	—	—	100.0
Regional	10.0	8.0	92.0	—	—	—	—	—	100.0
Denmark (1995)									
Municipality	22.0	—	96.0	—	—	4.0	—	—	100.0
County	9.0	—	93.0	—	—	—	—	7.0	100.0
Netherlands (1995)									
Municipality	1.0	—	100.0	—	—	—	—	—	100.0
Polder board	1.0	—	100.0	—	—	—	—	—	100.0
Spain (1995)									
Local	9.0	33.0	51.0	—	16.0	—	—	—	100.0
Regional	5.0	15.0	7.0	—	78.0	—	—	—	100.0
Sweden (1995)									
Municipality	22.0	4.0	96.0	—	—	—	—	—	100.0
County	11.0	—	100.0	—	—	—	—	—	100.0
United Kingdom (1995) Local	4.0	—	100.0	—	—	—	—	—	100.0
Mean (by tier)	9.4	6.1	76.8	0.0	15.9	0.5	0.1	0.6	100.0

Source: Ministry of Interior and Health, *Decentralization: Trends, Perspectives, and Issues at the Threshold of EU Enlargement* (Copenhagen, 2003).

Table 11A-4. *VAT Rates, OECD Countries, 1994–2000*

		Standard rate			
Country	Reduced rate	2000	1998	1996	1994
Australia	...	10.0[a]	...	...	...
Austria	10.0/12.0	20.0[b]	20.0	20.0	20.0
Belgium	0/6.0/12.0	21.0	21.0	21.0	20.5
Canada	0.0	7.0/15.0[c]	7.0/15.0	7.0	7.0
Czech Republic	5.0	22.0	22.0	...	...
Denmark	...	25.0	25.0	25.0	25.0
Finland	8.0/17.0	22.0	22.0	22.0	22.0
France	2.2/5.5	20.6[d]	20.6	20.6	18.6
Germany	7.0	16.0	16.0	15.0	15.0
Greece	4.0/8.0[e]	18.0	18.0	18.0	18.0
Hungary	0/12.0	25.0	25.0	...	...
Iceland	14.0	24.5	24.5	24.5	24.5
Ireland	0/3.3/10/ 12.5	21.0[f]	21.0	21.0	21.0
Italy	4.0/10.0	20.0	20.0	19.0	19.0
Japan	...	5.0	5.0	3.0	3.0
Korea		10.0	10.0	...	...
Luxembourg	3.0/6.0/ 12.0	15.0	15.0	15.0	15.0
Mexico	0/10.0	15.0	15.0	15.0	10.0
Netherlands	6.0	17.5[g]	17.5	17.5	17.5
New Zealand	...	12.5[h]	12.5	12.5	12.5
Norway	0.0	23.0	23.0	23.0	22.0

(continued)

Table 11A-4. *VAT Rates, OECD Countries, 1994–2000 (Continued)*

Country	Reduced rate	Standard rate			
		2000	1998	1996	1994
Poland	7.0	22.0	22.0	22.0	22.0
Portugal	5.0/12.0	17.0[i]	17.0	17.0	16.0
Spain	4.0/7.0	16.0	16.0	16.0	15.0
Sweden	0/6.0/12.0	25.0	25.0	25.0	25.0
Switzerland	2.3/3.5	7.5[j]	6.5	6.5	6.5
Turkey	1.0/8.0[k]	17.0	15.0	15.0	15.0
United Kingdom	0.0/5.0	17.5[l]	17.5	17.5	17.5
Unweighted average	...	17.7	17.7	17.2	17.1

Source: National delegates, position as of January 1, 2000. OECD, *Consumption Tax Trends* (Paris, 2001), p. 16.

a. July 1, 2000.

b. 16 percent applies in the Austrian tax enclaves Mittelberg and Jungholz.

c. A 15 percent harmonized sales tax (HST) applied in provinces that harmonized their provincial retail sales tax with the federal GST (the 15 percent HST is composed of a provincial component of 8 percent and a federal component of 7 percent).

d. 19.6 percent as of April 1, 2000.

e. Tax rates reduced by 30 percent in some remote areas.

f. 20 percent as of January 1, 2001.

g. 19 percent as of January 1, 2001.

h. For long-term stay in a commercial dwelling, GST at standard rate was levied on 60 percent of the value of the supply.

i. In the autonomous regions of Madeira and the Azores, rates were, respectively 4 percent, 8 percent, and 12 percent.

j. 2.4 percent/3.6 percent/7.6 percent as of January 1, 2001.

k. There are also higher rates of 23/40 percent.

l. Applied to a reduced value on imports of certain works of art, antiques, and collectors' items, resulting in an effective rate of 5 percent.

Table 11A-5. *Income Tax Progressivity for Single Workers,*
OECD Countries, 2000[a]

Country	Low-wage progressivity[b]			High-wage progressivity[c]		
	Income tax	Employee contributions	Total[d]	Income tax	Employee contributions	Total[d]
Australia	5.6	0.0	5.6	5.4	0.0	5.4
Austria	7.0	0.0	8.7	3.9	0.0	5.0
Belgium	9.6	1.0	14.3	5.4	0.1	7.3
Canada	5.6	0.2	6.5	4.5	−1.1	2.0
Czech Republic	2.2	0.0	2.6	1.8	0.0	2.1
Denmark	6.9	−1.5	5.6	7.1	−0.6	7.5
Finland	8.2	0.1	9.2	5.4	0.0	6.1
France	5.3	0.0	16.6	2.8	−0.5	2.4
Germany	8.2	0.0	11.1	6.2	−1.2	5.5
Greece	2.2	0.0	2.7	3.2	0.0	3.8
Hungary	5.1	0.0	4.2	6.4	0.0	7.0
Iceland	9.4	−0.1	9.3	4.1	0.0	4.0
Ireland	4.8	5.4	15.1	7.9	0.1	8.7
Italy	5.7	0.0	6.4	3.6	0.0	4.1
Japan	1.1	0.0	1.3	1.8	0.0	2.1
Korea	1.5	0.0	1.6	2.7	0.0	2.9
Luxembourg	6.7	0.0	7.9	6.0	0.0	7.3
Mexico	6.8	0.4	6.5	3.9	0.3	4.2
Netherlands	3.0	3.1	8.2	9.4	−6.9	−0.7
New Zealand	1.0	0.0	1.0	3.5	0.0	3.5
Norway	4.2	0.0	4.7	5.5	0.0	6.2
Poland	1.5	0.0	2.0	0.6	0.0	0.8
Portugal	4.2	0.0	4.7	3.8	0.0	4.4
Slovak Republic	1.8	0.0	2.1	2.3	0.0	2.7
Spain	7.0	0.0	7.6	3.0	0.0	3.3
Sweden	2.9	0.0	3.3	5.9	−0.8	5.2
Switzerland	3.1	0.0	3.6	2.8	0.0	3.3
Turkey	1.8	0.0	2.2	2.0	−2.8	−4.1
United Kingdom	3.7	1.2	6.9	1.5	0.0	2.2
United States	2.4	0.0	2.7	4.1	0.0	4.5

Source: OECD, *Taxing Wages, 2000–2001* (Paris, 2002).

a. Higher numbers indicate higher progressivity; negative numbers point to regressive taxes.

b. Based on worker earning 67 percent of average production worker's wage.

c. Based on worker earning 167 percent of average production worker's wage.

d. Includes effect of employer contributions and so are not simply the sum of the income tax and employee contributions.

Table 11A-6. *Top Corporate Income Tax Rates, OECD Countries, 2000*

Country	Corporate tax rate
Australia	34.0
Austria	34.0
Belgium	40.2
Canada	44.6
Czech Republic	31.0
Denmark	32.0
Finland	29.0
France	36.7
Germany	52.0
Greece	40.0
Hungary	18.0
Iceland	30.0
Ireland	24.0
Italy	41.3
Japan	42.0
Korea	30.8
Luxembourg	37.5
Mexico	35.0
Netherlands	35.0
New Zealand	33.0
Norway	28.0
Poland	30.0
Portugal	35.2
Spain	35.0
Sweden	28.0
Switzerland	25.5
Turkey	33.0
United Kingdom	30.0
United States[a]	45.8

Source: OECD tax database.

a. Basic federal corporate income tax ratio was 35 percent, but was 29.2 percent when adjusted to take into account the deductibility of the tax levied at the subcentral level. The combined ratio is 45.8 percent.

COMMENT BY
Victoria Perry

Jeffrey Owens and Stuart Hamilton make a number of important points regarding the causes of, and possible solutions to, the "crisis" in tax administration. As I am in agreement with almost all these points, let me merely emphasize and elaborate upon some of them, from the perspective of one who is dealing with the problems of tax administration largely in non-OECD countries. The chapter distinguishes between problems and solutions arising in the two realms of policy and administration, and I will do the same.

Policy: Impact and Responses

Chapter 11 points to several causes of difficulty for the effective administration of tax laws, arising from changes in the external environment as well as from the complexity of the tax laws themselves. The authors mention the impact of globalization—specifically global economic integration, including innovation in financial instruments, multinational enterprises, and the rise of e-commerce. And they note, importantly and correctly, that it is complex economies and policies—not only, or even mostly, poorly constructed legal systems—that give rise to the tax rules that bedevil tax administrators, businesses, and citizens. Of course recognizing these facts makes it clear that the administrative problems caused by complexity are difficult to solve. Modern economies and businesses are complex, and legislated tax policies, while sometimes misguided, are not infrequently valid responses to this fact. Appropriate and accurate measurement of tax bases, particularly when the base is capital income, and equitable application of these underlying policies, becomes a daunting task in this environment.

The authors mention the so-called Nordic model as one policy response to the problem of imposing taxes in a world of mobile capital. There are other even more striking examples of world trends in tax structure, which are in some sense a response not only to the globalization problem but to the challenge posed by weak tax administrations, particularly outside the OECD countries. The rise of the VAT occurred in part because it is theoretically harder to measure income than consumption, and countries at lower levels of economic development tend to rely more heavily on the easily administered indirect taxes and less on income taxes—especially the personal income tax on capital and self-employment income—than do industrialized countries.

The spread of VAT to the least developed countries over the past fifteen years is in great part attributable to another aspect of globalization—the long-run revenue implications of trade reform and pressure on trade tax revenues from deepening trade liberalization.[1] VAT represents an attempt to replace this revenue with a stable indirect tax that (unlike the previous cascading and distortionary domestic turnover taxes) could be applied at high enough rates to generate the necessary revenues. It is notable in this context that, in many developing countries, 60 percent or more of gross VAT revenues are still collected by the customs administration on imports.

Administrative Trends

These various legislative trends have arisen, in part at least, in response to problems of tax administration and implementation where capacity is weak. And there are other approaches that could be said to bridge the line between policy and administration—for example, chapter 11 cites the Italian practice of imputing a rate of return to capital in the income of corporations. More generally, of course, the world has whole systems of more or less complicated "presumptive" taxes applied to small or moderate-sized taxpayers in various countries. These are designed again to avoid the need to measure income, in particular, or even value added, and normally rely either upon a measurement of gross turnover or a proxy for business size, such as floor area, number of seats, or the like. Such taxes have a long, if not always illustrious, history.

But, as the authors state succinctly, countries cannot legislate their way to compliance, a fact that is unfortunately not always grasped, or at least not always acknowledged, by legislators and ministers. There are no quick fixes or real replacements for the hard work of tax administration—implementing effective systems to identify taxpayers, register them, collect taxes, audit appropriately selected taxpayers, track delinquent filers and payers, and enforce collections. This remains true regardless of the underlying structural organization of the revenue authorities or the sophistication of their information technology systems.

That said, trends in the development of revenue administrations, and of the technical assistance advice given to them, are certainly visible, and I will discuss a few of these:

Successful tax administration modernization in all countries has followed a broadly similar path, though the elements applicable at any particular time in a particular country vary, depending upon the starting point. For countries with administrations at low levels of development (in contrast, say, to most OECD countries), the elements of such a package would generally need to include: first, the development of a strategic management capacity; second, the adoption of a functional organizational structure (generally replacing a tax-based structure, and

1. See Ebrill and others (2001).

preceding the more recent stage adopted in various industrial countries of a tax-payer-segment-based structure); third, adoption of self-assessment; fourth, implementation of a large taxpayer unit; fifth, implementation of a modern information technology system associated with a single, high-integrity, taxpayer identification number for each taxpayer; and sixth, as noted above, and of critical importance, bringing the basic tax administration functions up to a satisfactory level of function. Though these stages and factors must be present whether the country is developed, less developed, or in economic transition, the modernization aims may differ in the short term. For example, in industrial countries, the point of making changes in administration may be to increase efficiency and reduce costs to the government or to taxpayers. In a country at a lower level of development, the main point would likely be to increase revenue, though it is important that governments not rely on administrative enhancements alone to raise revenues in the short term.

More specifically, four evolving elements of administrative structures and approaches have been recent factors in developing and transition countries: first, as noted earlier, the spread of the value-added tax—with the accompanying need for self-assessment and problems of audit and refunds of excess credits—to countries at quite low levels of economic development; second, the development and spread of so-called large taxpayer units, designed to provide full management of a small percentage of the biggest taxpayers in a country; third, the currently spreading impulse toward unified revenue authorities—single, often quite autonomous organizations that cover domestic tax administration, customs administration, and sometimes social security collections; and fourth, less noticeable but still significant, the increasingly widespread contemplation for purely administrative reasons of final withholding as a way of collecting taxes on wage income or interest earned by individuals in a partial return toward the schedular income tax.

The Fiscal Affairs Department of the International Monetary Fund has recently studied in some depth the first two of these items—the spread of VAT and the development of large taxpayer units (the latter being a sort of initial subset of a taxpayer-segment-based organizational structure).[2] The VAT study evolved partly from an attempt to answer quickly the apparently straightforward question, Is VAT too complex for use in less-developed countries? Two years and 200 pages later, we decisively concluded, "not generally." More seriously, the benefits of this tax do appear to outweigh the difficulties, some of which were more apparent than real.

For example, the study concludes that, while the VAT may seem complicated in structure, in fact the structures of the indirect taxes that it replaced in Africa were themselves not only complex but much more likely to allow eco-

2. Ebrill and others (2001); IMF (2002).

nomic distortion. That this complexity was not widely perceived ex ante may be attributed to the fact that, when VATs were introduced, there was typically a major push to strengthen the tax administration in order to make the tax work, which made clear that proper tax administration—of any tax—was not possible under the previously existing circumstances. However, the study did highlight certain other factors. The VAT requires functioning self-assessment to work effectively, something that was not fully appreciated prior to introducing the tax in all developing country cases. And, even more important, the study formalized what had become increasingly apparent anecdotally—that the credit-refund mechanism of the VAT is its Achilles' heel, under conditions of weak tax administration. The temptations and opportunities posed by a system that requires government to write checks to taxpayers on a regular basis have not yet been addressed effectively, in transition countries especially.

The concept of a large taxpayer unit (LTU) has been recommended largely for the purpose of strengthening revenue performance by increasing control over the relatively few taxpayers responsible for more than half of a country's tax revenues and to improve their compliance over the short and medium term. In addition, in many countries, such LTUs have been pilots for the tax administration to test reforms that have later been extended to the rest of the taxpayer base. These reforms include self-assessment, single taxpayer master files, unique taxpayer identification numbers, functional organizational structure (at first within the LTU itself), electronic filing, and new computer systems. This is similar to arrangements adopted in developed countries, such as Australia, France, the Netherlands, New Zealand, the United Kingdom, and the United States, to reorganize operations around segments of the taxpayer population, especially by size, because such segments may require different strategies for managing them and also pose differing levels and types of risks.

However, there are risks associated with the move toward LTUs in developing countries, as well as potential benefits. The recent study highlights some of these risks—ignoring medium-size enterprises, in particular; failing to provide specific types of controls for large taxpayers, through partial or imperfect implementation of the concept; assigning too many taxpayers to the LTU, thereby undermining its purpose and effectiveness; allowing corruption to creep into the LTU (where the most money, of course, is available), through improper supervision; difficulty retaining high-quality staff who can handle the complex affairs of the largest businesses. Despite these factors, though, proper implementation of an LTU can provide significant benefits in the medium and even the short term.

The third element, unified revenue authority, is a phenomenon that bears further study. For the present, one can say with certainty that simply merging previously independent agencies or organizations under one umbrella is not in itself sufficient to achieve administrative gains. The opposite can often prove true—major reorganizations, without improvements in underlying problems in the basic functionality of the tax administration(s), can frequently distract attention and resources from these more fundamental issues. On the other hand, the adoption of a new agency or organization can permit, for example, improved compensation for tax administration personnel, who are frequently undercompensated relative to their other opportunities and to the responsibilities and temptations to which they are subjected, and who must abide by civil service rules in most cases. A new or reorganized agency can also unify revenue collection functions that may be duplicated (and poorly) among various parts of the government.

Owens and Hamilton's comments point out the damage of careless remarks from political and policy leaders, remarks that may seem to denigrate the efforts, and even the integrity, of civil servants. It is undeniable that corruption by both administrators and taxpayers remains a critical issue for many countries, and it must, as a first step, be publicly recognized, if confidence in the tax system is to be built. However, most officials are, as the authors note, working diligently and for little compensation to implement as best they can the methods chosen by their countries' citizens for financing their governments. They should be supported in these efforts. It is singularly unhelpful to undermine the will of taxpayers to comply with the legitimately enacted tax laws of their countries by denigrating those persons charged with implementing them.

COMMENT BY
Joop N. van Lunteren

The Chinese language has two characters, *wei* and *ji,* which together mean "crisis." Separately *wei* means "danger" and *ji* means "opportunity." Together the characters form the concept of a critical turning point: a moment of decisions to be taken, choices to be made, to escape from danger.

I have worked in the Netherlands' Tax and Customs Administration for thirty years, starting as a tax inspector in 1970 and ending as its chairman from 1993 into 2000. During those years I was told at least seven times that there was a crisis in tax administration. I must admit that I even told my political superiors so a number of times. During those years I was also told that tax fraud was growing progressively worse and tax shelters increasingly damaging. If all this had been true, we would long ago have reached the end of taxation.

Both this experience and the Chinese concept of crisis make me look optimistically to the subject of this book. Certainly in the Netherlands, and as far as I can see in most other countries in Europe, the present situation in taxation is not perceived as critical. That does not mean that tax administration has become a soft job. In general I wholeheartedly agree with the excellent and comprehensive overview of the problems in tax administration that Jeffrey Owens and Stuart Hamilton present in their chapter. We should, however, put those problems into perspective without dramatizing them. That will make it easier to recruit others to help tax administrators solve those problems.

Policy and Legislation

Few tax administrators and academics would disagree with the stand that Owens and Hamilton take against complex tax policy, complex tax laws, and the resulting complexity, ineffectiveness, and inefficiencies in tax administration. However, our ministers in general are not tax administrators or academics by origin, and they will judge the tax system by other standards. Simplicity— though of course lip service will be paid—is not necessarily, not even probably, one of them.

Ministers in EU member states can hardly distinguish themselves in the financial field by anything other than tax policy. National monetary policy no longer exists, and budgets are constricted within the euro rules. At least in the Netherlands, over the past ten years it was politically a lot easier to create a tax expenditure than a direct payment toward individuals or industry. Hence came new allowances for using the bicycle to go to work, for research and development in industry, for hiring long-term unemployed, for training employees, for investing in "green" projects, not only in the Netherlands but also in countries thousands of miles to the east; hence came our "Aunt Agatha" allowance for investing in small start-up businesses and the strong plea the Netherlands made in the EU for a low VAT rate for certain craftsmen, such as barbers and cobblers.

All of these programs worked, in the sense that the minister who proposed them became one of our most popular politicians; a number of the programs even worked in the sense that the desired results were obtained. Those spending programs—because that is what they are—did not simplify our tax system, but quite understandably the minister did not mind. I have found it more productive to argue that the allowances should fit into the tax law in a logical way than to holler "thief" every time ministers try to use taxation for other than purely budgetary purposes.

Complexity does not stand on itself. It is a function of the level of government interference and of public services that we want. High levels of government activity and public service generate high tax rates, and high tax rates create complexity. The call of tax people for simplicity will not break through that logic.

In addition, complexity hurts more in some taxes than in others. The VAT, where we impose a high administrative burden on many small businesses, should be kept simple. The same goes for withholding taxes, which billions of people are confronted with. They should be able to understand their pay slips. Corporate taxation in an international context will always be complex, and I do not think that can or will ever be repaired. Furthermore large corporate taxpayers can cope with complexity.

What has helped us in the Netherlands in tackling complexity is that the Tax and Customs Administration is not an agency, nor is it in any other way distanced from the political responsibility of the minister, so administration is as close to the minister as policy is. Also two separate directors-general are responsible for policy and legislation and for administration, which means that administration has its own voice at the highest level. In situations where those two are combined, abstract policy tends to win over down-to-earth administration in the long run.

We institutionalized testing new legislation for workability and enforceability, supported by artificial intelligence that tests for consistency while translating law into computerized systems. We also, in cooperation with industry, developed standardized models for simulating and calculating the administrative burden of existing and new legislation. All this helps, but it will in the end not make tax policy or tax law simple.

So, while subscribing to Owens and Hamilton's call for simple tax policy and tax law, I put simplicity into perspective, both as the reality and from lack of hope that anyone, including politicians, can bring it about. It would be wonderful if it happened, but tax administrators had better not wait for it and should trust themselves to move forward.

Administration and Innovation

The Netherlands Tax and Customs Administration has approximately 30,000 full-time employees (24,000 in tax and 6,000 in customs). It spends around 30 percent of its budget on information technology (IT), which is not far from the level of banks and insurance companies. It has been relatively fortunate in obtaining funding from subsequent cabinets, for a number of reasons.

First, we did not jump on the bandwagon of distancing tax administrations from the political arena, which has been fashionable for the past twenty years. Our reasoning was that more distance would make it easier for ministers to see us as silly, inefficient bureaucrats from a different world, whose budgets should be radically downsized. We were helped by public opinion that considers taxation to be so important that it does not accept a situation where nobody is politically responsible for both policy and individual cases.[1] In many countries this is exactly the reason to put the administration at a distance.

Second, we were able to demonstrate a marginal return on income of around 90 percent in counteracting fraud, and we shifted thousands of clerical jobs to

---

1. Of course, ministers do not interfere in individual cases.

taxpayer service and audit functions. In the same twenty years the tax consultancy community grew tenfold.

Third, we restructured the tax administration radically in a market-oriented way, not waiting for public or political dissatisfaction. The administration is now widely considered to be service-minded, effective, and efficient, resulting in new tasks and sufficient funding. We are reluctant to accept new tasks that are not consistent with core competencies for taxation or customs.

Fourth, we did not outsource the core of our IT operations, thus retaining the capacity to innovate our processes.

All of this could sound self-satisfied, even conceited. Let me therefore say that the main dilemmas for tax administration that Owens and Hamilton picture are still relevant, even in the Netherlands. The balance between service and other compliance activities, for instance, is a continuous source of differing opinions. At present about 30 percent of individual income tax returns are desk-audited, and on average a business is field-audited once every six to seven years. Higher management generally puts much faith in a service orientation, while street-level officers tend to be more skeptical.

Outsourcing of IT is unavoidable, but how far to go is difficult to decide.

Ministers of finance know that funding should be adequate but, since tax administration is often part of their organization, they are increasingly vulnerable in the cabinet if they exclude it from general efficiency dividends operations.

Wealthy individuals who should set an example do not always do so. They are more mobile than the general population and often are better supported in disguising taxable income as nontaxable yields. This has led to a change in the Netherlands' income tax (which does not tax capital gains outside business) toward a system where investment income is fixed at 4 percent of assets, which are then taxed at a flat 30 percent. This was accepted in late 1999, and it remains to be seen how long it will survive the present stock exchange climate.

Large businesses, which—the VAT, withholding tax, and social premiums included—account for close to 70 percent of revenue, are handled in large business units, but still, in an open economy like the Netherlands, transfer pricing and similar issues can create huge problems.[2]

Identity and Innovation in Tax Administration

The underlying dilemmas that were so comprehensively sketched by Owens and Hamilton will stay with us for many years to come. We should be aware of two dominating trends.

2. This reorganization took effect on January 1, 2003, when the large business units were integrated in district offices.

The tax administration of the future will be less and less an organization of clerical workers and more and more a group of professionals. This will mean that it can no longer be managed as the machine-bureaucracy it once was. Top management's main responsibility will be to install a sense of identity and purpose in the organization, a common sense of what it is to be a tax administrator, to motivate professionals. Only then will we be successful.

As in private business, the ability to innovate is the single most important factor to improve the results of the organization. We need to set aside adequate capacity for that purpose, manage it as our number-one priority, and not leave it to outside consultants. Because IT is an important enabler of innovation, the extent and method of outsourcing will be affected.

If tax administrators are aware of these trends and take the initiative to improve their organizations, it is hoped that they will earn the respect of politicians, who will then be more sensitive to the call for funds and simplification.

References

Bird, R. M. 1986. "Federal Finance in Comparative Perspective." Toronto: Canadian Tax Foundation.

Ebrill, L., and others. 2001. *The Modern VAT.* Washington: International Monetary Fund.

Hanousek, Jan, and Filip Palda. 2002. "Why People Evade Taxes in the Czech and Slovak Republics: A Tale of Twins" (http://ideas.repec.org/p/wpa/wuwppe/0205003.html).

Heady, Christopher, and Paul Van den Noord. 2001. "Tax and the Economy: A Comparative Assessment of OECD Countries." Tax Policy Studies 6. Paris: Organization for Economic Cooperation and Development.

International Monetary Fund. 2002. "Improving Large Taxpayers' Compliance: A Review of Country Experience." Occasional Paper 215. Washington.

Oates, W. E. 1972. *Fiscal Federalism.* Harcourt Brace Jovanovich.

Organization for Economic Cooperation and Development. 1999a. "Implementing the OECD Jobs Strategy: Assessing Performance and Policy." Paris.

———. 1999b. "Taxing Powers of State and Local Government." Tax Policy Studies 1. Paris.

———. 2000. "Tax Burdens: Alternative Measures." Tax Policy Studies 2. Paris.

———. 2001a. "Corporate Tax Incentives for Foreign Direct Investment." Paris.

———. 2001b. "Tax and the Economy: A Comparative Assessment of OECD Countries." Paris.

Schneider, Friedrich. 1997. "Empirical Results for the Size of the Shadow Economy of Western European Countries over Time." Working Paper 9710. Institut für Volkswirtschaftslehre, Linz University.

Contributors

Henry J. Aaron
Brookings Institution

Donald C. Alexander
Akin, Gump, Strauss, Hauer, and Feld

Joseph Bankman
Stanford Law School

Marsha Blumenthal
University of St. Thomas

Leonard E. Burman
Urban Institute

Charles Christian
Arizona State University

Frank Cowell
London School of Economics

William G. Gale
Brookings Institution

William M. Gentry
Columbia University

David Glickman
Baker and McKenzie

Gerald H. Goldberg
California Franchise Tax Board

Austan Goolsbee
University of Chicago

Stuart Hamilton
Organization for Economic Cooperation and Development

Morton A. Harris
Hatcher, Stubbs, Land, Hollis and Rothschild

James R. Hines Jr.
University of Michigan

Peggy A. Hite
Indiana University Business School

Janet Holtzblatt
Department of the Treasury

David Cay Johnston
New York Times

Mark J. Mazur
Internal Revenue Service

Janet McCubbin
Department of the Treasury

Nina Olson
Internal Revenue Service

Jeffrey Owens
*Organization for Economic
   Cooperation and Development*

Gerald W. Padwe
American Institute of CPAs

Victoria Perry
International Monetary Fund

Alan H. Plumley
Internal Revenue Service

Jeffrey Rohaly
Urban Institute

Deborah H. Schenk
New York University School of Law

John T. Scholz
Florida State University

Douglas A. Shackelford
University of North Carolina

Stephen E. Shay
Ropes and Gray

Joel Slemrod
University of Michigan

C. Eugene Steuerle
Urban Institute

David R.Tillinghast
Baker and McKenzie

Joop N. van Lunteren
*Tax and Customs Administration
   (The Netherlands)*

David Weisbach
University of Chicago Law School

James W. Wetzler
Deloitte and Touche

Index